Prentice Hall

WRITING and GRAMMAR

Communication in Action

Platinum Level

Extra Grammar and Writing Exercises

Prentice
Hall

Upper Saddle River, New Jersey
Glenview, Illinois
Needham, Massachusetts

ISBN 0-13-052668-1

2 3 4 5 6 7 8 9 10 OPM 07 06 05

Prentice
Hall

Contents

Introduction   v

The Elements of Writing   1

Answer Key for Elements of Writing   49

Problem Solver   77

Answer Key for Problem Solver   93

Grammar, Usage, and Mechanics   103

Answer Key for Grammar, Usage, and Mechanics   251

Vocabulary Practice for Standardized Tests   333

Answer Key for Vocabulary Practice   383

Introduction

Extra Grammar and Writing Exercises provides your students with ample practice in a broad range of topics. To engage students of different ability levels, each worksheet covers a topic by providing two or three exercise banks, arranged in order of difficulty. This arrangement allows you to select exercises appropriate to your studentsí needs.

Here is a summary of the contents of each section:

- **The Elements of Writing** provides extra practice in paragraph development and sentence structure; unity, coherence, and transitions in writing; sentence problems, such as fragments and run-on sentences; recognition of various parts of a sentence; word choice; tone and mood; voice; and figurative language.

- **Problem Solver** focuses on the errors that students most commonly make: run-on sentences, sentence fragments, subject-verb agreement, verb forms, pronoun problems, problems with modifiers, and missing commas.

- **Grammar, Usage, and Mechanics** provides extensive practice in all major grammar, usage, and mechanics topics, arranged in alphabetical order from Abbreviations to Voice.

- **Vocabulary for Standardized Tests** helps students build vocabulary while giving them practice in a variety of test formats.

Elements of Writing

Paragraph Structure

Parts of a Paragraph: Topic Sentences

EXERCISE A: Write whether or not each of the following sentences would be *effective* or *not effective* as the topic sentence for a paragraph. If the sentence would not be effective, explain why not.

> **Example:** In sign language, the symbol for the letter A looks like a fist.
> **Answer:** not effective; the sentence states a particular fact and does not introduce a topic that can be expanded or explored in a paragraph.

1. Sign language is one method of communication used by people who are deaf and hearing-impaired.
2. Sign language uses signs.
3. American Sign Language used gestures to represent ideas.
4. Laurent Clerc, a deaf teacher, helped to establish the first American school for the deaf in 1817.
5. Laurent Clerc was deaf in 1817.

EXERCISE B: Write a topic sentence to begin each paragraph below.

> **Example:** You don't need to spend a lot of money to find rocks and minerals. You can collect them from woods, beaches, and even junkyards. There are probably a great many interesting rocks right in your own backyard.
> **Answer:** Rock collecting is a fascinating and inexpensive hobby.

1. I set up a bird feeder in my backyard to attract a variety of birds. A pair of binoculars by the window helps me locate my favorites. The blue jays are pretty, but I am always happiest to see the catbird.
2. Point a strong telescope at the moon, and you will be able to see the intricate forms of lunar seas. Point it at Saturn and you will see the shadowy outlines of the rings. In fact, just about anywhere you look, you will find something wondrous and beautiful in the night sky.
3. When you take a long hike through the woods, your cardiovascular system is energized. A good, tough hike can be just as beneficial as a workout in a gym or jogging around a track. It can be a lot more interesting, too.
4. Some people like to collect things, such as stamps, coins, or old toys. Other people like to make things, such as sweaters, boxes, or models. Some hobbies are more athletic—rock climbing or rollerblading, for example. It can take time to find the one or two hobbies that you like best.

Developing a Paragraph with Facts or Statistics

EXERCISE A: Write whether the information provided in each sentence is primarily a *fact* or a *statistic*.

> **Example:** Skunks belong to the weasel family, *Mustelidae*.
> **Answer:** Fact

1. A skunk is a small furry animal with black and white markings.
2. There are three types of skunks: striped, hog-nosed, and spotted.
3. A skunk grows from 33 to 46 centimeters long, not counting its tail.
4. It may have a mass of 1.4 to 4.5 kilograms.
5. Skunks spray a foul-smelling liquid when they are in danger.

EXERCISE B: Rewrite the sentences, adding facts or statistics to make the sentences stronger. You may have to do research about the animals.

> **Example:** Mountain lions are found in several parts of the United States.
> **Answer:** Mountain lions are found from California to New Mexico, with smaller numbers in the Appalachian Mountains and in uninhabited parts of Florida.

1. Mountain lions have several different names.
2. This member of the cat family is a large animal.
3. An adult mountain lion may be gray or yellow.
4. Mountain lions are extremely agile.
5. During summer, these cats hunt over a large territory.

EXERCISE C: Use the facts below and others you may discover through research, to write a paragraph about English novelist Ian Fleming.

> **Example:** Ian Fleming wrote the famous James Bond novels.
> **Answer:** Ian Fleming (1908-1964) was an English novelist who created the famous James Bond spy novels.

1. Fleming worked for British Naval Intelligence during World War II.
2. The James Bond character spied for British Intelligence.
3. The plots concern Bond's efforts to overcome an evil adversary.
4. Bond is always aided by a woman who actually works for the enemy.
5. He uses technological gadgets in his work as a spy.

Developing a Paragraph with Sensory Details

EXERCISE A: Rewrite each sentence by adding sensory details.

> **Example:** Ralph entered his house after the fire.
> **Answer:** Ralph gingerly stepped among the charred rubble that he once called home.

1. Everything smelled like smoke.
2. The fireplace stood bare and blackened.
3. The kitchen was stripped of all but the appliances.
4. Clyde found it hard to enter his bedroom.
5. His computer lay in a lump on the floor.

EXERCISE B: Answer the following questions by writing a sentence that uses sensory details to describe the event.

> **Example:** What was it like driving at night on a dark road for the first time?
> **Answer:** As the muscles in the back of my neck tensed and my hands clamped onto the steering wheel with a tight grip, I ached to see a street sign or some vaguely familiar sight.

1. How did it feel to be awakened by the earthquake?
2. What did you do when you realized that your dog had escaped through the gate that you failed to close securely?
3. What will you serve when it's your turn to have the club meeting at your house?
4. How would you feel if you had been selected for a leading role in the school play?

EXERCISE C: Write a sentence describing each of the following, using sensory details.

> **Example:** a bike race, coming up to the final lap
> **Answer:** Dennis leaned forward, forcing his aching legs to turn those reluctant wheels—faster, faster.

1. your chance to make the only goal in the soccer game
2. winning two tickets to see your favorite pop star or group
3. reading a novel that you just can't put down
4. being out in a rowboat during a storm

Developing a Paragraph with Reasons

EXERCISE A: For each fact given, write the letter of the statement that supports it better.

Example: Rainforests act like sponges, soaking up moisture from the rain and releasing it again through the leaves. a. Rainforests are a beautiful region of the world. b. When rainforests disappear, the land becomes very dry.
Answer: b

1. The tropical rain forests are essential to maintaining biodiversity.
    a. The number of species in rain forests exceeds that in other areas.
    b. If the rain forests are cleared, many species will become extinct.
2. Rain forests are not the only place where habitats are destroyed.
    a. The Homestead Act of 1862 led settlers to clear land for farming.
    b. Americans cut 500 million acres of virgin forest in one hundred years.
3. It is not necessary that all reserves be closed to human beings.
    a. Rational multiple use of forest reserves is being pioneered today.
    b. People destroy the natural resources.
4. How small a workable rain forest can be is being defined in Brazil.
    a. Many areas of rain forest are being destroyed every day.
    b. Test areas range from 10,000 to 100,000,000 square meters.

EXERCISE B: For each topic given, write a supporting statement.

Example: Smoking is harmful to your health.
Answer: Smoking has been linked to heart disease, emphysema, and cancer.

1. Nicotine can cause addiction.
2. Athletes are not allowed to smoke when in training.
3. The life of a smoker may be eight years shorter than that of a nonsmoker.
4. Smoking has become less acceptable in business and social circles.

EXERCISE C: For each statement, write one possible reason in support of it.

Example: Budget cutbacks will eliminate activities, such as the clubs.
Answer: The Drama Club has given me an opportunity to find myself.

1. The library will be closed after school.
2. Classes will be larger next year.
3. Intramural sports will be retained.
4. The school board is considering shortening the school year.

Parts of a Paragraph: Concluding Sentences

EXERCISE A: The paragraph below lacks a concluding sentence. Read the paragraph. Write whether or not each of the sentences that follow it are *effective* or *not effective* as a concluding statement. If the sentence is not effective, explain why.

Skyscrapers would never have been possible without one important invention: the elevator. Although they were first developed early in the nineteenth century, it wasn't until Elisha Otis invented the safety elevator that elevators became popular. Otis's elevator included a device that prevented the elevator from falling even if the support rope broke.

Example: Otis was born in Yonkers, New York.
Answer: not effective; the sentence states another detail rather than concluding the paragraph.

1. Otis's invention helped pave the way for passenger elevators, which contributed to the urban boom of the Industrial Revolution.
2. There are more that two million elevators in buildings throughout the world.
3. Elevators are the most important invention of the nineteenth century.
4. With this added safety measure, skyscapers became possible and the modern city was born.

EXERCISE B: Write an effective concluding statement for each paragraph.

Example: Mathematicians can find patterns everywhere they look. Seeds in pine cones follow one pattern, the spiral of a snail's shell follows another.
Answer: Close inspection can reveal geometric patterns throughout the natural world.

1. Snowflakes have the shape of water crystals. They are beautifully symmetric and unique. Each one is an individual work of art.
2. My favorite season is the spring. I love to see the new growth after a long, hard winter. Nothing makes me happier than the sight of crocuses peaking up through a patch of snow.
3. I love to sleep near the ocean. The sound of waves crashing against the shore lulls me to sleep. The smell of saltwater reminds me of sunshine and happy dreams.
4. Yesterday, Ms. Riva heard the ocean for the first time. She grew up far, far away from the shore. For years, she saved money for a trip to California. As soon as she stepped onto the sand, she ran to the water's edge. Her ears were ringing with the sound of the waves.

Recognizing Effective Paragraphs

EXERCISE A: Rewrite each paragraph to improve its unity, coherence, and transitional expressions.

Example: Do some preparing before you take a test. You might need to take notes. You could quiz yourself. It helps to put your notes in order of importance.

Answer: Before you take a test, prepare yourself. First, take notes in order of importance. Then quiz yourself on the material.

1. When I filled out my job application, I made sure to look at all the blanks. It was a job in Burger-B-Ware. I could make about $4.50 an hour, so I was meticulous.
2. Lots of people are helping us decorate for the prom. The theme is "Moonlight." I can't wait for the dance. We're hanging silver moons everywhere. We're hanging stars, too.
3. Paul promised to dig up a dead tree and plant a new one. I guess my parents asked him to do it because he has a nice garden. Instead, he painted the dead tree green. That was a practical joke.
4. I built a doghouse from a barrel. I knocked one end off the barrel. I rolled the barrel next to the porch. I filled it with straw. I had a fine doghouse.
5. In April, the cherry blossoms bloom in Washington, D.C. We are going on a class trip to visit the Library of Congress. That's not till May, though. We will look through some of the archives.

EXERCISE B: For each of the following topics, write a paragraph that demonstrates unity, coherence, and the use of good transitional expressions.

Example: dental hygiene

Answer: For good dental hygiene, my dentist suggests three things. First, brush two or three times a day. Second, floss. Third, get regular checkups. Following these steps may save your teeth.

1. The Worst Game of the Season
2. An Unusual Fear I Have
3. How Studying Efficiently Can Make a Difference
4. My Favorite Magazine

Unity, Coherence, Transitions

Unity

EXERCISE A: Rewrite the paragraph, deleting the four details that do not support the main idea.

The importance of paleontology, the study of fossils, cannot be underestimated. Many people confuse paleontology and archaeology. Fossils, the preserved remains of plants and animals, are found in layers of rocks. The study of fossils aids paleontologists in learning what kinds of life have existed in Earth's past. Paleogeographers also study fossils, but with an eye to drawing maps of the world in its earliest stages. Fossil study has also enabled paleontologists to propose a history of life that begins more than 3 billion years ago with the oldest-known fossils of one-celled plants. Many paleontologists believe the human race to be a fairly recent "addition" in this long timeline. Ongoing fossil discoveries and studies add to and refine their theories. Paleontologists study fossils to determine the age of the rocks in which the fossils are preserved, as well as whether those rocks were formed on land or under the ocean. Studying fossils provides clues in finding oil deposits. Such deposits are often found in rocks that contain certain fossils. Oil companies are always delighted with such finds, and many employ their own paleontologists.

EXERCISE B: Rewrite the paragraph. Delete the two nonsupportive details; add two details that support the main idea. You may use phrases, clauses, or complete sentences.

Redecorating the family room was a great idea! Tony pictured the "new look" in his mind as he lugged the sofa cushions into the hall. New colors, more shelves, and a rearrangement would definitely produce a "high tech" effect to replace the current dilapidated decor. Home decorating can be quite a challenge, but it can also be especially rewarding. Back and forth he went. He was beginning to puff; luckily, the TV was on a wheeled stand.

Tony began emptying the shelves around the fireplace. "I don't believe all this junk," he muttered. Painting shelves can be the toughest part of redecorating. Behind and under the game and puzzle boxes that lined the shelves were lots of other small things that he couldn't identify. He dumped them all into the wastebasket he had found under the sofa. "There's enough stuff there to make a sculpture," he noted, "and it is all 'found' stuff, just like those sculptures at the museum." Tony grinned. "I wonder if the museum would display my sculptures when I get them done."

Coherence Through Time Order

EXERCISE A: Rewrite the sentences so that they present the correct order of events in automobile history.

1. Henry Ford produces his first Model-T, which sports many features invented in the previous twenty years.
2. During the next two decades, Ford sells more than 15 million Model-Ts, and the U.S. becomes known as a "nation on wheels."
3. Benz and Daimler produce the first successful cars, using the newly-invented internal combustion engine.
4. In the 1880s, the internal combustion engine is invented.
5. In the two decades following the first successful cars, improvements in the automobile happen rapidly: front-wheel drive, nine-horsepower engine, electric starters, four-wheel drive and brakes, all-steel bodies, mufflers.

EXERCISE B: Rewrite this summary of the events in Sir Walter Scott's classic poem "Lochinvar" so that it follows a more logical order.

Though members of her clan search the borders for the couple, they never find the two. Young Scottish nobleman Lochinvar learns that fair Ellen, the lady of his choice, is about to wed another man at her home, Netherby Hall. They reach the door, where Lochinvar's stallion stands waiting. The handsome knight drinks a toast to Ellen; then he takes her hand and leads her in a dance around the hall. Setting out immediately, he arrives at the Hall, only to have Ellen's father refuse him entrance. Lochinvar assures Ellen's father that he has come only to drink the health of the couple and to dance with the bride. With a word to the lovely Ellen, Lochinvar quickly swings her to the saddle, leaps onto the horse behind her, and carries her away.

EXERCISE C: Use coherence through time order to write a paragraph about one of the topics below.
- planning a barbecue, dinner, or picnic
- instructions to a younger child for tying shoes
- a scene from a favorite TV sitcom
- the plot of a short story or TV episode

Coherence Through Spatial Order

EXERCISE A: To each sentence below, add a second sentence that expresses the spatial relationship designated in parentheses.

> **Example:** A huge, ornate crystal chandelier hung from the ceiling. (under)
> **Answer:** Our concert seats were directly beneath the mammoth light.

1. Our safari guide motioned for us to stand completely still. (ahead)
2. The perfect blue diamond glittered and glinted in the light. (beneath)
3. The Ferris wheel groaned, then slowed to a stop. (below)
4. The most fascinating piece of furniture was a tall, glass-front cabinet. (inside)
5. Pairs of dancers, garbed in dazzling Mardi Gras costumes, twirled in the streets. (among)
6. The legend says that on nights when the moon shines redly, the ghostly trio still rides. (above)
7. She sat enthroned on a heavy, intricately carved chair of mountain cedar. (beside)
8. The audience quieted as the lights dimmed and strains of music began. (in front)
9. Dignified and proud in their caps and gowns, the graduates entered the auditorium. (side)
10. The pilot checked her gauges and then began her descent. (below)

EXERCISE B: Rewrite the paragraph, making it coherent through spatial order. Add sentences where indicated in parentheses.

Craig closed the door behind him and stood on the front steps of his old brownstone apartment house. The block party was in full swing. A wonderful assortment of aromas filled his nostrils; genial laughter and talk filled his ears. ( ) He could see neighbors. ( ) Proudly displayed ( ) were platters heaped high with favorite appetizers or sweets from many parts of the world. At each end of the block were orange "Detour" signs, advising motorists that the street was closed for the afternoon. The teenagers ( ) were dancing to a boom box blaring on the ground. Children ran around and among the adults, playing tag, using stationary adults as bases or "safe" zones. ( ) Mr. Pappino led his cronies in wavering renditions of ragtime hits. The scene overflowed with welcome and neighborliness.

Coherence Through Order of Importance

EXERCISE A: Write the following details in order of importance, beginning with the least important and proceeding to the most important.

1. *Titanic* was called "unsinkable"
2. 1,522 people drowned
3. Owned by the White Star ocean liner company
4. Struck an iceberg on April 14, 1912, and sank
5. Sailed on its maiden voyage in April 1912

EXERCISE B: Write the following sentences in paragraph form. Organize them in order of importance, beginning with the least important information.

1. Thirty-five African nations have wild elephants.
2. Half the elephants were killed by poachers and ivory-hunters.
3. Amazingly, six African nations want the ban on the ivory trade lifted.
4. All nations with elephants want to protect them.
5. Kenya values an elephant at $14,375 per year for its value for tourism.
6. In 1989, the African elephant was listed as an endangered species.
7. Ivory from an elephants tusks, on the other hand, is worth only $1,000.
8. By 1989, only about 600,000 elephants remained.
9. Since 1990, the ivory trade has been declared illegal in Africa.
10. In 1979, there were an estimated 1.6 million elephants in all of Africa.

EXERCISE C: Use the facts below to write a paragraph about William Faulkner. Organize the information in order of importance.

1. Financial success never caught up with his literary success.
2. Many novels take place in Yoknapatawpha County, a fictitious county in Mississippi.
3. One of America's greatest writers.
4. First earned a literary reputation with *The Sound and the Fury* in 1929.
5. Through much of his career, in fact, he worked in Hollywood as a scriptwriter in order to pay his bills.
6. Won a Pulitzer Prize for *A Fable* in 1954
7. Born in 1897 in Oxford, Mississippi.
8. Other well-known works include *A Light in August* and *Absalom! Absalom!*
9. Best works are about the South, from its early settlement to more recent times.
10. Won the Nobel Prize for Literature in 1949.

Coherence Through Order of Familiarity

EXERCISE A: The sentences below explain how sound works by comparing the process to the effect of a rock thrown in a pond. Write the sentences in paragraph form. Organize the sentences by order of familiarity, beginning with the most familiar.

1. The pebble hits and sends out ripples in an expanding circle.
2. In space there is no air.
3. Sound works the same as ripples on a pond.
4. Consequently, there can be no sound in space.
5. If you strike a drum, ripples in the air expand outward from the drum.
6. Throw a pebble in a still pond.
7. The ripples in the air are "heard" by the ear as sound.
8. If there is no water in the pond, there can be no ripples.
9. Similarly, if there is no air, there can be no sound.
10. Sound is a kind of vibration.

EXERCISE B: Combine the information given in the two sets of sentences that follow into a paragraph that explains how a compact disc records and plays music. Use Morse code as a familiar analogy to help explain the less familiar CD technology. You may add transitional sentences and change the wording to produce a well-written paragraph.

Morse code
• Morse code is a way of communicating by using a series of dots and dashes.
• Each combination of dots and dashes represents a letter.
• Complex messages can be communicated by spelling out each word, letter by letter, in dots and dashes.
• SOS, for example, is *dot-dot-dot, dash-dash-dash, dot-dot-dot.*

CD technology
• The surface of a CD is covered with microscopic pits and flat spots.
• Music is recorded and communicated in these pits and flat spots.
• A CD player scans the rotating disc with a laser beam.
• The laser beam reflects differently off the various pits and flat spots.
• The reflection bounces off a light-sensitive device that converts the light to electrical current.
• The CD player electronically decodes the message carried by the electrical current, amplifies it, and directs it through loudspeakers as music.

Coherence Through Comparison and Contrast

EXERCISE A: Complete each sentence. Then write whether it expresses a *comparison* or a *contrast*.

> **Example:** Jamie and Kristin are both very athletic, but they are interested in different sports. Jamie enjoys _____ while Kristin prefers _____.
> **Answer:** tennis / softball (contrast)

1. A lion and a Siamese cat both belong to the feline family, but they differ in that lions _____ and Siamese cats _____.
2. The two candidates for Student Council disagree on many issues, but both favor _____ and _____.
3. Not all high schools have the same focus. Our school, for example, emphasizes _____; neighboring schools tend to focus on _____.
4. My neighbors both love gardening; but while one grows _____, the other grows _____.
5. Although Elaine and Julia are constantly arguing, both _____, and neither _____.

EXERCISE B: Read the following notes on a pair of tenth-graders named Marcus and James. Then write a brief paragraph that compares and contrasts the two boys. You may choose to organize your paragraph (1) by giving all the comparisons and then all the contrasts (or vice-versa), (2) by presenting a point-by-point comparison, or (3) by using a combination of methods (1) and (2). However you choose to develop your topic, be sure to begin your paragraph with an appropriate topic sentence.

> **Example:** (1) Mark, who is the eldest of three brothers, loves to swim. James, on the other hand, is an only child. His favorite sport is basketball.

> **Example:** (2) While Mark shares a room with his two younger brothers, James, an only child, has a room all to himself. Unlike Mark, an excellent swimmer, James is happiest when he is on the basketball court.

> **MARK:** 17 years old; brown hair and brown eyes; not interested in team sports; gets good grades in math and English; has steady girlfriend named Daphne

> **JAMES:** 16 years old; brown hair and hazel eyes; plays center on basketball team; gets good grades in math and science; dates only occasionally

Coherence Through Cause and Effect

EXERCISE A: For each event given below, write a possible cause. Then write a possible effect.

  Example: The fire went out.
  Answer: There was not enough fuel. The hikers became chilly.

  1. The tent fell down.
  2. An owl hooted somewhere far away.
  3. We heard a crunching sound.
  4. Michael woke up abruptly.
  5. We smelled coffee and bacon.
  6. The pines sighed softly.
  7. Our dog began to bark.
  8. Lightning struck the far mountain.
  9. We packed our knapsacks quickly.
10. The moon was no longer visible.

EXERCISE B: Use each event described as the topic sentence of an original paragraph. For a sentence labeled *cause,* make your detail sentences present the *effects* of the event. For a sentence labeled *effect,* make your detail sentences give the *causes* of the event.

  Example: Many trees were cut down in the forest. (effect)
  Answer: Many trees were cut down in the forest. Some were needed for fuel. Others were cut to be used as timber for building the compound and fort. Still others were hollowed out and used to make canoes.

  1. People at school saw my name in the paper. (cause)
  2. The dog we picked was the runt of the litter. (cause)
  3. Jasper had always wanted to be an astronaut. (cause)
  4. Mom was unusually irritated this morning (cause)
  5. I simply did not want to practice today. (cause)
  6. We arrived home exhausted by our trip. (effect)
  7. The Green family finally bought a new house (effect)
  8. I had an experience that taught me a lesson. (effect)
  9. My grandparents refuse to eat in restaurants. (effect)
10. The ocean is now my favorite vacation spot. (effect)

Coherence Through Transitional Expressions

EXERCISE A: Write the transitional words and phrases used in each paragraph.

> **Example:** We planned an Arbor Day gala. First we purchased dozens of saplings. We then advertised the event in the newspaper. On Arbor Day, people planted trees with us.
>
> **Answer:** First, then, On Arbor Day

1. Before you dig, decide where you want the hole to be. Dig and then fill the space partway with peat moss. After that, balance the tree while your friend covers the roots with dirt. Finally, pat down the dirt and water the tree.
2. Not long after you plant your tree, it should begin to leaf. In the meantime, continue to water it. Keep this up even after leaves appear. At this point, the tree has proved to be healthy. Eventually you will be able to let it live on rainwater alone.

EXERCISE B: Rewrite each paragraph, adding transitional expressions to achieve coherence.

> **Example:** My picnic was a great success. I prepared sandwiches, cole slaw, and potato salad. I packed a basket with drinks, plates, and napkins. Everyone admired my work.
>
> **Answer:** My picnic was a great success. In the morning I prepared sandwiches and potato salad. Before I left, I packed a basket with lemonade, plates, and napkins. That afternoon, everyone admired my work.

1. Every Thanksgiving, our whole family gets together. My uncle and aunt arrive with my cousins. The children play touch football. Uncle Burt cooks the turkey. Mom makes a dozen side dishes. Great-Aunt Lucille bakes pies.
2. Cherissa prepared a long time for her oral report. She wrote the main points on note cards. She numbered the cards in order and underlined vital ideas in red. She practiced her report in front of the mirror. Her presentation was flawless.

Sentences

Recognizing Subjects and Predicates

EXERCISE A: Make two columns as shown. Then write each complete subject in the first column and each complete predicate in the second column. Underline each simple subject and simple predicate.

> **Example:** My cousin Meredith enjoys diving and sailing.
> **Answer:** Complete Subject   Complete Predicate
>   My cousin <u>Meredith</u>   <u>enjoys</u> diving

1. Our new car should arrive next week.
2. The clerks in the shoe department receive a commission.
3. Ginnie and Megan won the three-legged race.
4. The audience waited for the curtain to rise.
5. Dad needs a dental appointment soon.
6. The heat spell left the lawn dry and brown.
7. We bought refreshments during the intermission.
8. The bus to Phoenix departs at 10:15.
9. The ice on the pond is thick enough for skating.
10. Mom, Dad, Eric, and I agree.

EXERCISE B: Write ten sentences by adding a complete predicate to each complete subject. Draw a line between the complete subject and the complete predicate.

> **Example:** the man in the blue jacket
> **Answer:** The man in the blue jacket | is a friend of my father's.

1. None of the boys in our class
2. One of the best times in my memory
3. Most of my friends
4. The book on the top shelf
5. Grandparents
6. James and Alice
7. Some shows on television
8. Their neighbor
9. My brother-in-law
10. The hungry cat

EXERCISE C: Create a complete subject and a complete predicate from each simple subject and simple predicate below. Write a sentence using each complete subject and complete predicate.

> **Example:** branches swayed
> **Answer:** The *branches* of the old maple tree *swayed* in the breeze.

1. woman   sat
2. radio   blasted
3. train   arrived
4. guests   brought
5. cars   parked
6. teacher   announced
7. grandparents   came
8. artist   created
9. man   hopes
10. pianist   played

Special Positions of Subjects and Predicates

EXERCISE A: Write the simple subject and simple predicate in each sentence (Some of the subjects may be understood.)

> **Example:** Please wash the dishes before starting your homework.
> **Answer:** (You) wash

1. After school, meet me at the playground.
2. After lunch came a delicious dessert.
3. There is a storm warning in effect for this area.
4. Across the road strolled a family of geese.
5. Maria, please give me your new telephone number.

EXERCISE B: Write each sentence, replacing the parentheses with a subject or verb as indicated. Leave parentheses around subjects that are understood.

> **Example:** Jerry, (subject) (verb) the book on the shelf, please.
> **Answer:** Jerry, (you) put the book on the shelf, please.

1. Along the highway (verb) the (subject).
2. On the street (subject) (verb).
3. In the corner (verb) his (subject).
4. Here (verb) (subject) again.
5. The soccer (subject) (verb) down the field.
6. George, my (subject) (verb) yesterday.
7. Into the water (verb) a (subject).
8. When in doubt, (subject) (verb) with caution.
9. There (verb) the (subject)!
10. After school, (subject) (verb) in the park.

EXERCISE C: Use each verb in a sentence that gives an order or direction. Write the understood subject in parentheses.

> **Example:** remember
> **Answer:** Next time we meet, (you) remember to bring your textbook.

1. call
2. tell
3. give
4. turn
5. pass
6. order
7. stop
8. speak
9. take
10. put

Recognizing Effective Sentences

EXERCISE A: Rewrite each fragment or ineffective sentence so that it is clear and concise, conveys a comlete thought, and is phrased so as to emphasize its main idea. If the sentence is effective as written, write *Effective*.

Example: Spanning some 300 years between the Middle Ages and modern times, it began in Italy around the year 1300, and it was called the Renaissance.

Answer: The Renaissance, which began in Italy around the year 1300, spanned some 300 years between the Middle Ages and modern times.

1. The people of the Renaissance tried to model their lives on the classical civilizations of ancient Greece and Rome, and *renaissance* is the French word for "rebirth."
2. Artists and writers in Europe thrived during the Renaissance because a powerful middle class arose at that time and offered financial support to artists and writers throughout Europe.
3. Also, sculptors and architects.
4. Germany became the leading printer of scholarly books after Johannes Gutenberg introduced movable type to Europe in the mid-1400's.
5. The War of the Roses ended in 1485, after which the Renaissance reached England at the end of that war.

EXERCISE B: Rewrite the paragraph so that each sentence is clear and concise, conveys a complete thought, and is phrased so as to emphasize its main idea.

Example: I read a terrific fantasy novel, and I read it last week.
Answer: Last week I read a terrific fantasy novel.

Alexandra, the girl whom this book is about, is the protagonist. Alexandra is lost in the woods, and so is Sasha, who is her cat. Eldorf offers to help them find their way home, and he's this mysterious stranger they meet. The story reaches a surprising conclusion; but first Alexandra, Sasha, and Eldorf, the mysterious stranger whom they meet in the woods, have many thrilling adventures together. This novel that I am speaking of is highly recommended by me to anyone who enjoyes an exciting fantasy story, which I, for one, certainly do.

Sentence Problems

Sentence Fragments

EXERCISE A: Expand each fragment so that it becomes part of a complete sentence.

> **Example:** Startled by Amelia's reaction.
> **Answer:** All of us were startled by Amelia's reaction.

1. Traveled a long way without water.
2. If it snows sometime this week.
3. An original poem, a model of the setting, or a dramatic reading.
4. Whoever does not understand the assignment.
5. A lonely beach, cold in the winter wind.
6. Flying from Connecticut to New Mexico.
7. A dirty, shivering, obviously abandoned kitten.
8. Can expect delivery tomorrow?
9. Flattered by all the attention he was getting.
10. While we were on vacation!

EXERCISE B: Identify each item as a *phrase* fragment, a *clause* fragment, or a *series* fragment. Then use each in a complete sentence.

> **Example:** Concerned about the look of the sky.
> **Answer:** phrase; Concerned about the look of the sky, the sailors turned back.

1. Challenged by the coach of the other team.
2. Because time was running so short.
3. Lonely, inexperienced, and in charge.
4. Whether or not he can sell his old bicycle.
5. To find oneself in such a predicament.

EXERCISE C: Correct the five sentence fragments in the paragraph by joining them to the other sentence or by adding words.

> **Example:** The dramatic size of dinosaurs. Capitivates one's imagination.
> **Answer:** The dramatic size of dinosaurs capitivates one's imagination.

Although dinosaur bones have been weathering out of rocks for a very long time. The name *dinosaur* was first coined by Sir Richard Owen, a British anatomist. In 1841. Very large, land-living creatures. With pillar-like legs tucked beneath the body. The position of the legs was unusual. Totally unlike any other fossil reptiles.

Run-on Sentences

EXERCISE A: Correct the first two run-ons with a coordinating conjunction. Correct the remaining run-ons in the manner specified.

> **Example:** (simple sentence) Xavier finished his report, then he left.
> **Answer:** Xavier finished his report <u>and then</u> left.

1. Mom made me take my umbrella, it was raining outside.
2. The book was in Mona's locker, she couldn't find it.
3. (semicolon) The lake is beautiful at night, it has an eerie peace.
4. (semicolon) The Athletics Club banquet had been a success, everyone was satisfied.
5. (end mark) Have you heard the news Vicki is moving to Seattle.
6. (end mark) Do you know what I think, I think it's too expensive.
7. (simple sentence) Clark visited us last weekend, so did the rest of his family.
8. (simple sentence) I noticed the long, ragged rip, then I fixed it promptly.
9. (complex sentence) Ira wants a job, he needs money for his dilapidated car.
10. (complex sentence) The cat's away, the mice do play.

EXERCISE B: Rewrite the items, correcting run-on sentences in a variety of ways. If an item needs no changes, write *Correct.*

> **Example:** I'm not fond of peas, I also don't care for lima beans.
> **Answer:** I'm not fond of peas <u>or of</u> lima beans.

1. We each had to memorize a poem, I chose "The Chambered Nautilus."
2. Every Hawaiian feast includes poi, poi is crushed, cooked taro root.
3. Elizabeth I ruled England wisely she was the daughter of Henry VIII.
4. I asked my grandmother, she had faced that problem in her youth.
5. Castles have a romantic image, they were actually cold and damp.
6. The birds were agitated about something, so were the bears.
7. The old house had real charm, moreover, the landscaping was picturesque.
8. I bought two new albums, one by each of my favorite performers.
9. Regina couldn't do the new work, she'd never mastered the basics.
10. Leonard pitched a no-hitter, he achieved some local stardom.

Stringy Sentences

EXERCISE A: Rewrite the stringy sentences. In each case, change the conjuction to show a better relationship between ideas.

> **Example:** Sir Francis Drake's famous voyage around the world began on December 13, 1577, and he and 160 men sailed from England.
>
> **Answer:** Sir Francis Drake's famous voyage around the world began on December 13, 1577, <u>when</u> he and 160 men sailed from England.

1. Ferdinand Magellan had made an earlier trip, from 1519 to 1522, and he had discovered a passage from the Atlantic Ocean to the Pacific Ocean.
2. Magellan was a Portuguese sailor, and he had convinced Charles I of Spain to support his voyage of circumnavigation of the earth.
3. Conflict between the Portuguese and Spanish sailors was an ongoing problem, and the journey was fraught with great difficulty.
4. A mutiny broke out and threatened the success of the journey and Magellan and loyal members of the crew were able to resume control.
5. Magellan took part in a battle between rival groups in the Philippines, and he was killed before he could complete his famous voyage.

EXERCISE B: Rewrite each item so that it is no longer a stringy sentence.

> **Example:** The Polynesians were the first people to live in Hawaii and they sailed there in canoes from other islands in the Pacific.
>
> **Answer:** The Polynesians were the first people to live in Hawaii<u>; they</u> sailed there in canoes from other islands in the Pacific.

1. Many hundreds of languages are spoken in the Pacific Islands, and Melanesia has the greatest number.
2. English is used in many of the Pacific Islands, and it is the official language of Hawaii, Fiji, New Zealand, Tonga, and Western Samoa.
3. In some of the islands, the people speak Japanese, and they learned this language during the Japanese occupation from 1920 to 1945.
4. The first settlers in the Pacific Islands probably came from Asia thousands of years ago, and they arrived on rafts and dugouts.
5. The people in the islands differ from one another in appearance, and scientists have determined that they belong to different races.

Choppy Sentences

EXERCISE A: Revise the choppy sentences by combining related sentences.

> **Example:** The telephone is an invention. It is useful. It allows people to communicate quickly.
>
> **Answer:** The telephone is a useful invention, *for it* allows people to communicate quickly.

1. Alexander Graham Bell was an American scientist. He was also an educator. He invented the telephone.
2. Bell once was a young man. He studied how vowels are produced. He wanted to help the deaf to speak.
3. Bell did not have the time or the skill to make the necessary parts for his experiments. He went to an electrical shop. There, he asked Thomas Watson to help him.
4. One day, Watson was working on the wires in the next room. Bell at the other end of the line heard the wires being plucked.
5. The next day the instrument transmitted the sound of Bell's voice. The telephone was born.

EXERCISE B: Vary sentence length and structure to make the paragraph less choppy and more interesting.

> **Example:** The Morse code once was used to send messages by wire. Samuel Morse developed this system of dots, dashes, and spaces.
>
> **Answer:** Samuel Morse developed the Morse code, a system of dots, dashes, and spaces that once was used to send messages by wire.

1. Samuel Morse is remembered. He was the person who made the first successful telegraph. He began his career as an artist.
2. He painted the portrait *Marquis de Lafayette.* It is hanging in New York's City Hall. Morse wanted to do more than paint portraits.
3. He became a teacher of painting at the University of the City of New York. He taught sculpting there, too. His spare time and money went to working on the telegraph.
4. The first public demonstration of the telegraph was a failure. A ship's anchor caught onto the wire. That action brought the wire to the surface.
5. On May 24, 1844, Morse tapped out a famous message. It reached Baltimore from Washington, D.C. the message was, "What hath God wrought!"

Wordy Sentences

EXERCISE A: Rewrite the sentences. In each case, drop unnecessary, wordy expressions or replace them with something shorter.

> **Example:** What I want to know is what an aardvark is anyway.
> **Answer:** I want to know what an aardvark is.

1. I decided to do research on aardvarks because of the fact that all I know about aardvarks is the unusual way their name is spelled.
2. In spite of the fact that two a's do not occur in succession in English, the spelling is not at all unusual in the Dutch language.
3. The reason why the Dutch settlers in Africa called the animal aardvark was that the name means "earth pig" in Dutch.
4. The fact that the aardvark lives in the ground and has a snout probably earned the animal its name.
5. Aardvarks, which are ant and termite eaters, have a long, sticky tongue with which they catch these insects.

EXERCISE B: Rewrite the sentences. Delete words that do not add meaning; reduce explanations to as few words as possible.

> **Example:** Identifying rocks and giving them names may seem difficult or even impossible to figure out in the beginning when you first start rock collecting.
> **Answer:** Identifying rocks may seem difficult in the beginning.

1. You may want to do what a lot of beginning collectors do, which is to buy a reference collection so you can compare unknown specimens with known specimens.
2. Minerals have characteristics, such as chemical composition and color of a streak it makes, that will help you to identify them.
3. To find out the chemical composition, or what the rock is made of, you can do any number of chemical tests that will give you an idea of the mineral elements that make up the rock's contents.
4. To find out what the streak color is, which is also important, you can rub a mineral across a hard, rough surface such as porcelain that hasn't been glazed and observe the color of the powder that is obtained.
5. Knowing where a rock was found and how it looks may also help you to identify a rock, so you will know what kind of rock it happens to be.

Empty Sentences

EXERCISE A: Rewrite the sentences. Correct empty sentences by eliminating repetition.

Example: A Native American, Sequoyah was a Cherokee who developed a system of writing in the Cherokee language.

Answer: Sequoyah was a Cherokee who developed a system of writing in his native language.

1. Sequoyah's greatest and principal aim was to set down on paper and record for posterity in a permanent form the ancient traditions of his people.
2. The Cherokees began to use Sequoyah's system of writing to publish books, newspapers, and anything else in print.
3. Thousands of Cherokees decided to learn to read and write Cherokee.
4. After a time, Sequoyah also gained recognition and became well known for his efforts to improve the lives as well as the general welfare of Native Americans.
5. Sequoyah was honored and esteemed for his contributions to Native American culture by having the giant sequoia trees named after him and likewise Sequoia National Park.

EXERCISE B: Correct empty sentences by replacing vague ideas with meaningful supporting details. You may want to use reference books to aid you.

Example: Thomas Jefferson is best known for his role in the early history of the United States.

Answer: Thomas Jefferson is best known as the author of the Declaration of Independence and as the third President of the United States.

1. Jefferson was a leading architect of his time, having to his credit the design of important public buildings.
2. He also had a great deal to do with the present monetary system of the United States.
3. Thomas Jefferson showed his interest in Native Americans by preparing books related to them.
4. Many people do not realize that Jefferson also has a number of inventions to his credit.
5. Politicians today like to quote Jefferson for his view about government.

Lack of Parallel Structure I

EXERCISE A: Write whether each sentence is *parallel* or *not parallel*. If it is not parallel, write the word or phrase that needs rephrasing.

> **Example:** Being in the school band is exciting, fun, and teaches you a lot.
> **Answer:** not parallel; teaches you a lot

1. Ms. McDowell asks us to take care of our music, to study it at home, and we should practice when we can.
2. The trombonists are competing against the people who play trumpets.
3. Whichever group pays more attention at rehearsals, has the better attendance record, and logs more practice time will get movie passes.
4. If we win, should our film be a romance, adventurous, or a mystery?
5. Our band is so good that an appearance on TV, competing in the regional "play-offs," and touring in the spring are all possible.

EXERCISE B: Rewrite each sentence, correcting the faulty parallelism.

> **Example:** The photography was much better than how the music sounded.
> **Answer:** The photography was much better than the music.

1. To me, water skiing is far more enjoyable than to ski downhill.
2. Preparing a household budget is important; to stick to it is more important.
3. This liberal arts school has small classes, many clubs, and the faculty are nice.
4. What to wear to the junior prom was one question; paying for it was another; where to wear it afterward was another still.
5. I took this job in the laboratory because of the good pay and it has convenient hours.
6. Raising rabbits can take a lot more work than to keep a cat.
7. Sonya enjoys getting presents; she likes to give them even more.
8. Spain is well known for its lace, the friendliness of its people, and it has dramatic dances, such as the flamenco.
9. Marnie Jacobs is liked by her friends and by the people who are related to her for her intelligence, creativity, and being fair.
10. Ten-year-old Troy brushed his teeth, washing his face, and he came downstairs.

Lack of Parallel Structure II

EXERCISE A: Rewrite each sentence that is not parallel in structure. If a sentence is parallel, write *Correct.*

> **Example:** My hobbies are my rock collection, to bicycle, and reading.
> **Answer:** My hobbies are <u>collecting rocks, riding my bicycle</u>, and reading.

1. J. Jacob Jett, who is my favorite playwright, novelist, and he writes poetry, came to town last week.
2. He would give a reading, answering questions, and sign books.
3. Notices were printed in the paper and announced on the radio.
4. I spoke enthusiastically but with some degree of nervousness about Jett's visit.
5. When the day arrived, I raced down the street, around the corner, and I entered the bookstore.
6. Jett soon arrived, took off his coat, and he waved to the crowd.
7. To hear him read from his latest work was a thrill; asking him a question—and getting an informative answer—was an honor.
8. People stood in line for his autograph, take a picture, or just to say hello.
9. Talking to Mr. Jett was better than to read about him any day!
10. His greeting made me glad that I had come, eager to read his newest book, and with a greater interest in becoming a writer myself.

EXERCISE B: Combine each pair of sentences. Make sure that the new sentence is parallel in structure.

> **Example:** Sara Baker was a doctor and public health worker. She pioneered child health procedures, too.
> **Answer:** Sara Baker was a doctor, <u>a public health worker, and a child health pioneer</u>.

1. In Poughkeepsie, New York, Baker was born and raised. She also went to school there.
2. People that she was related to tried to discourage Baker from a career in medicine. Other doctors and even her mother did the same.
3. She earned her degree before working in a Boston clinic. Then she became a medical inspector in New York City.
4. To lower the infant death rate, Baker taught women how to feed children properly. She gave instruction about baths and clothing.
5. The promotion of preventative medicine was important to her. Advancing health education was one of her goals, as was organizing support for children's charities.

Confusing Shifts of Verb Tenses and Pronouns in Sentences

EXERCISE A: Write the confusing shifts in verb tense and pronouns; then write a word that would make the sentence correct.

> **Example:** Paul didn't hear the coach when he tells him to run to third base.
> **Answer:**   tells, told

1. The coach was booed by some parents when Paul is thrown out.
2. The coach ignored his response.
3. The umpire was also taunted by the parents when they called one of the boys out.
4. After one angry father yelled about the call, he threw a paper cup at the umpire.
5. The official told the parents that the game would be stopped if he didn't begin to behave.

EXERCISE B: The following passage contains twenty confusing shifts in verb tenses and use of pronouns. Rewrite the passage, correcting each error.

One day I, Rita Lee, decide to visit one of my neighbors, Mrs. Aurelia Jackson. Mrs. Jackson is a seventy-year-old woman who lives in a house that looks like something from a fairy tale. Mrs. Jackson greeted me at the door with a warm smile. She was wearing a cotton dress, a white sweater, and walking shoes. She eagerly showed me into the kitchen. Mrs. Jackson looked forward to my visits because she knew that I was interested in hearing her stories.

Mrs. Jackson was a first-grade teacher for thirty years and loved them. She liked to reminisce about her students, one of who was Rita Lee. Today she told a story about the time you cut the hair of one of my friends. She laughed and laughed. She brings out my first-grade class picture and told stories about the rest of the children, too.

Mrs. Jackson liked to reminisce about the past, but she also had many activities that keep her busy in the present. She volunteered at the library three mornings a week. She also tutored several children once a week after school. When I told her I was majoring in education, she seems pleased. I just hope that when I am seventy years old, I am as full of life and warmth as Mrs. Jackson.

Sentence Combining

Sentence Combining with Coordinating Conjunctions

EXERCISE A: Write the coordinating conjunction that would be appropriate for combining each pair of sentences. (For a few items, more than one answer is possible.)

> **Example:** Some early fish developed bony skeletons. Sharks developed a lighter skeleton made of cartilage.
> **Answer:** but (or yet)

1. The blue shark is among the ocean's great travelers. A shark tagged off Long Island may later turn up near Colombia.
2. A blue shark may weigh 400 pounds. A mako shark could weigh twice as much.
3. A shark maneuvers with exceptional grace. Its grace turns into violent thrashing during feeding.
4. Smaller fish in shark-infested waters must be careful. A 12-foot blue shark is an awesome predator.
5. The blue shark is not especially aggresive toward humans. Unprovoked attacks seldom occur.

EXERCISE B: Combine each set of sentences by using appropriate coordinating conjunctions. Underline all the coordinating conjunctions in your new sentences. Make any necessary changes in wording.

> **Example:** There are more than 16,000 known species of fish. A brief survey can examine only a few important species.
> **Answer:** There are more than 16,000 known species of fish, <u>so</u> a brief survey can examine only a few important species.

1. Some early fish migrated to coastal swamps. They migrated to lagoons. The water there was warmer than in the deep.
2. The warmer water contained less dissolved oxygen. A fish in these waters had to lift its head above water. It took in gulps of air.
3. The air went into a pouch surrounded by blood vessels. The pouch helped the fish maintain the proper level of oxygen.
4. Soon the fish dispensed with the dangerous process of coming to the surface. Many predators were waiting for them there.
5. Some fish adapted by filling the pouch with air from their own blood. The pouch made the fish float in the water.

Sentence Combining with Compound Subjects and Predicates

EXERCISE A: Add each idea in parentheses to the preceding sentence. Write the new sentence and label the new element as a *compound subject* or a *compound predicate*. (In one case, the new sentence will have both.)

> **Example:** Making notes at each step, Amanda continued the experiment. (her partner)
> **Answer:** Making notes at each step, <u>Amanda</u> and her <u>partner</u> continued the experiment. (compound subject)

1. Barry peered through the microscope. (checked the lab manual)
2. Then he said, "Amanda, you have something unusual here." (I)
3. "We should show it to Paul and Carrie Ann." (call Mr. Payne over)
4. Paul looked through the microscope. (Carrie Ann, Mr. Payne, promptly turned pale)

EXERCISE B: Combine each set of sentences, using a compound subject, a compound predicate, or both. Use any coordinating or correlative conjunctions that make sense. Label the compound elements in the new sentences.

> **Example:** The emerald is a precious gem. The ruby is a precious gem, as well.
> **Answer:** Both emeralds and rubies are precious gems. (compound subject)

1. Gem cutters can take a rough gemstone. They cut it. Then they polish it.
2. Minerals that are used in jewelry are called gems. Some other materials are also gems.
3. Amber is not a mineral. Coral is not a mineral, either.
4. Coral comes from the ocean. Amber is a product of ancient trees. Jet also was produced by ancient trees.
5. Among minerals, gems come in a variety of spectacular colors. Furthermore, they vary in hardness.
6. Sapphires are minerals that come in many colors. On the other hand, topazes are like that, too.
7. The diamond is the hardest mineral; it can scratch any other mineral. It cannot itself be scratched.
8. An opal's background color helps to determine its value. The color of its flashes is another factor.
9. Opal triplets result when opals are sliced thinly. Then they are glued together with a clear cement. Finally, they are covered with a glass top.
10. Jade is green. Emeralds are green. The two gems look quite different from each other.

Sentence Combining with Subordinating Conjunctions

EXERCISE A: Combine the sets of sentences, using appropriate subordinating conjunctions. (In many cases, more than one answer is possible.)

> **Example:** You think of the city of Galveston. You're remembering a Spanish nobleman and friend to the American Revolution.
>
> **Answer:** <u>When</u> you think of the city of Galveston, you're remembering a Spanish nobleman and friend to the American Revolution.

1. Spain was officially neutral in 1776. Bernardo de Galvez supported the Patriots.
2. Galvez was governor of Louisiana. He was in a unique position to help.
3. Arms were shipped from New Orleans. Fighters in the West would be supplied with weapons.
4. Spain officially sided with the Americans in 1779. Galvez moved against British troops in the South.
5. He captured forts and isolated soldiers. He weakened Britain's power.

EXERCISE B: Rewrite the excerpts from the letter. Combine ten pairs of sentences, using appropriate subordinating conjunctions.

> **Example:** I've wanted to write to you. Schoolwork has kept me too busy.
>
> **Answer:** <u>Although</u> I've wanted to write to you, schoolwork has kept me too busy.

I haven't mentioned English class before now. Let me tell you something aobut it. Class was letting out about three weeks ago. My teacher then assigned us "Dancer," a story by Vickie Sears. I did not read it until Sunday. I tend to procrastinate. Was I sorry to have waited! It was great!

"Dancer" applies Native American beliefs to modern problems. It tells the story of young Clarissa. Clarissa is only five. Nevertheless, she is living at her fourth foster home. However, her life changes. She watches Molly Graybull, a champion dancer. She starts dancing. Perhaps her life depended upon it. At the end of this powerful story, another dance is held. A more confident Clarrisa joins Molly in the circle.

I'll find a sequel to "Dancer." I'll read it right away!

Sentence Variety

Types of Sentence Structure

EXERCISE A: Label the structure of each sentence as *simple, compound, complex,* or *compound-complex.*

> **Example:** Leave peacefully, or I'll call the police.
> **Answer:** compound

1. South American rainforests provide much of the world's oxygen.
2. If I win, a new bridge will be built, for I keep my promises.
3. Sue, Diana, and Leah are the girls who will run the relay.
4. It's only been an hour; it's much too early to tell yet.
5. You can either turn down the heat, or we can all sit here and sweat.
6. Saris are robes that Indian women wear; obis are Japanese sashes.
7. I could not remember what the third major cause of the war was.
8. Isaac Asimov, a science-fiction writer, taught biochemistry.
9. Reading that book—a long difficult one—made Trisha feel proud.
10. Don't try to memorize the material; instead, try to understand it.

EXERCISE B: Expand each combination of simple subject and simple predicate to write a sentence of the type indicated in parentheses. Create a variety of declarative, interrogative, imperative, and exclamatory sentences.

> **Example:** we found (complex)
> **Answer:** We found a fossil when we were digging in the garden.

1. they planted (simple)
2. girl found (compound)
3. cleaning is (complex)
4. I saw (compound-complex)
5. Trisha is feeling (simple)
6. (you) stop (simple)
7. moths flew (complex)
8. Wayne knew (compound-complex)
9. Tom has studied (simple)
10. dogs barked (compound)
11. cows ambled (complex)
12. governor won (compound-complex)
13. boys rode (simple)
14. you realize (compound)
15. Helen ran (complex)
16. game began (compound-complex)
17. Luis was (simple)
18. (you) work (compound)
19. team practiced (complex)
20. Jesse plays (compound-complex)

Varying Sentence Structure

EXERCISE A: Use each subject and verb below to write a sentence of the type indicated in parentheses.

> **Example:** I finish (complex, interrogative)
> **Answer:** After I finish the test, will you meet me at the library?

1. Robert lost (simple, declarative)
2. Alice can teach (complex, interrogative)
3. violinist played (compound, declarative)
4. I am (simple, exclamatory)
5. Mrs. Stevenson went (complex, declarative)
6. girls will eat (compound, interrogative)
7. baby did sneeze (simple interrogative)
8. they do believe (compound, interrogative)
9. Marlene studied (compound-complex, declarative)
10. he thinks (compound-complex, exclamatory)

EXERCISE B: Rewrite the excerpt from a letter below. Change sentence structure and sentence type as needed to add variety, clarity, and interest. Try to have ten sentences in your finished excerpt.

> **Example:** We're having a wonderful time. We would like to stay longer. We wonder how everyone back home is.
> **Answer:** We're having a wonderful time and would like to stay longer. How is everyone back home?

It was great to see Pete and Marcia again after all these years. It was also great to see their kids. Sara is ten years old. It was hard to believe. She wants to be an actress. She joined the Drama Club at school. She's a good dancer. Her singing leaves something to be desired. Jerry is in junior high school. He is on the basketball team. He plays center. He looks just like Pete. He is already taller than his mother. Jerry has a girlfriend. Sara likes to tease him about her. The girlfriend's name is Jenny. I don't know if you remember Pete's friend Ellen. She's married now. She and her husband live right down the street. We all had dinner together. We had a terrific time.

Varying Sentence Length

EXERCISE A: Lengthen each choppy sentence by adding material as suggested in parentheses.

> **Example:** I hate winter. (Add a quotation)
> **Answer:** I hate winter, that so-called "season that tests one's mettle."

1. This winter was difficult. (Add a reason.)
2. December was bad. (Add a statistic.)
3. January was worse. (Add a descriptive detail.)
4. We welcomed spring. (Add a quotation.)
5. Now we feel better. (Add a reason.)

EXERCISE B: Rewrite each sentence twice, lengthening it by adding descriptive details, quotations, facts and statistics, or reasons.

> **Example:** I am starting an exercise program.
> **Answer:** At 5 foot 4 and 150 pounds, I am starting an exercise program. I am starting an exercise program because I believe that "an ounce of prevention is worth a pound of cure."

1. Bicycling is good for you.
2. Many people prefer jogging.
3. Dancers may be the best athletes.
4. My brother lifts weights.
5. Good health is important.

EXERCISE C: Rewrite the paragraph to lengthen choppy sentences by adding descriptive details, quotations, facts and statistics, or reasons.

> **Example:** Chocolate Labradors are rare.
> **Answer:** Chocolate Labradors, a mix of yellow and black, are rare.

Jon plans to buy a puppy. He wants a chocolate Labrador retriever. A breeder has promised him a female pup. He will name her Koko. He will train her.

Varying Sentence Beginnings

EXERCISE A: Vary each sentence beginning below by making changes as suggested in parentheses.

> **Example:** I asked her to visit. (Add an infinitive phrase.)
> **Answer:** To be friendly, I asked her to visit.

1. I made a nice dinner. (Add an adverb.)
2. I roasted a chicken. (Add a prepositional phrase.)
3. I tossed a mixed salad. (Add a subordinate clause.)
4. I invited her to sit down. (Add a participle.)
5. I served the food proudly. (Move a modifier.)

EXERCISE B: Rewrite each sentence twice, varying its beginning (1) by adding modifiers, phrases, or clauses or (2) by changing the order of words in the sentences.

> **Example:** Trees provide shade.
> **Answer:** In sunny, hot weather, trees provide shade. Luckily, trees provide shade.

1. Trees are homes to birds and animals.
2. Trees make the oxygen we breathe.
3. Fire spreads quickly through a forest.
4. Fire is a danger for both flora and fauna.
5. Fire may be caused by foolish campers.

EXERCISE C: Rewrite the paragraph to vary sentence beginnings by adding modifiers, phrases, or clauses, or by changing the order of words in the sentence.

> **Example:** I enjoy Uncle Miguel's visits.
> **Answer:** <u>Invariably,</u> I enjoy Uncle Miguel's visits.

I love seeing Uncle Miguel. I enjoy hearing about his travels. I look forward to his postcards and letters. I approve of his career with the Wildlife Fund. I hope to travel with him someday.

Word Choice

Using Connotation and Denotation

EXERCISE A: Rewrite the following sentences by changing the underlined words to create a different emotional effect.

>   **Example:** They had gathered to achieve a <u>meeting</u> of minds.
>   **Answer:**   They managed to achieve a <u>collision</u> of minds.

1. Jeff wanted to <u>discuss</u> the choice of play for the spring festival.
2. He hoped to <u>generate</u> interest among the other members of the club.
3. "We're fortunate in having Curtis as the <u>legendary</u> Sherlock Holmes."
4. Jeff liked to <u>tease</u> Curtis whenever he had the chance.
5. The drama coach <u>invited</u> Jeff to <u>lay his ideas</u> before the faculty.

EXERCISE B: Write related sentences for each set of synonyms. One sentence should demonstrate a positive emotional charge; the other, a negative emotional charge.

>   **Example:** announced, divulged
>   **Answer:**   The speaker <u>announced</u> the names of the winners.
>   The speaker <u>divulged</u> the names of those who had been eliminated.

1. artificial, counterfeit
2. mannerism, peculiarity
3. sweetly, cloyingly
4. strikingly, gaudy
5. facsimile, forgery

EXERCISE C: Study the paragraph and decide the kind of impression it is meant to convey. Then rewrite the paragraph, choosing the words in parentheses that strengthen that impression.

>   Deirdre is a (zealous, fanatical) conservationist. Her exhibit shows (odd, grotesque) photographs of the disappearing rainforests. She wanted viewers to see (shocking, amazing) scenes of what is happening in these areas. The crowd's (reaction, backlash) against her was expected. Deirdre (reasoned, contended) that people never respond well to a worthwhile cause.

Choosing Specific, Concrete Words

EXERCISE A: Write more interesting sentences by changing nonspecific words and adding more details.

> **Example:** The house was old.
> **Answer:** The dilapidated, ancient house stood empty and silent, guarding its hidden past.

1. There were no trees around the house.
2. At night the house looked like the typical haunted house in stories.
3. The house was filled with unusual patterns of light and shadow.
4. The broken windows allowed wind to blow noisily through the rooms.
5. No one would want to visit that old house at night.

EXERCISE B: Rewrite each sentence, improving it by adding vivid, descriptive words.

> **Example:** An estuary is part of a river that is covered by seawater when the tides come in.
> **Answer:** An estuary is the finicky mouth of a river that bathes in seawater brought in by tides.

1. When the tide goes out, the estuary fills with fresh water.
2. When the tide comes in, salt water displaces the fresh water.
3. Animals in the estuary are adapted to change.
4. The waters of the estuary contain nutritious food.

EXERCISE C: Using specific, concrete words, write a sentence that gives a clear, exact description of each topic.

> **Example:** the space shuttle at launching
> **Answer:** The giant space shuttle belched fiery gases that lifted it into the air.

1. a soccer game
2. old tennis shoes
3. a mountain stream
4. first snowfall

Varieties of English

Formal and Informal English

EXERCISE A: Label the language of each sentence as *formal* or *informal*. Write the three examples of slang in parentheses.

> **Example:** That band's music is awesome!
> **Answer:** informal (awesome)

1. This is a wonderful afternoon for an outdoor concert.
2. Let's get moving, guys, or we'll be late.
3. Just be cool, Mike; we've got lots of time.
4. The amphitheater will not be open for the audience until three o'clock.
5. You know what? I forgot the tickets.
6. What a lousy thing to happen right now.
7. Don't make a big deal of it.

EXERCISE B: Rewrite the sentences, replacing the words in parentheses with more formal words.

> **Example:** Alberto's brother has a (neat) car.
> **Answer:** Alberto's brother has a <u>stylish</u> car.

1. Did you hear that Maya (aced) her driving test?
2. Are you (kidding)?
3. She was a (wreck) beforehand, but everything was (cool) during the test.
4. I'm glad she didn't (blow) it; she'd have been (tough) to get along with.
5. She's going to want to use her sister's (wheels).
6. It (beats) me. Maybe her sister won't mind if she (splits) the gas.
7. I'll (catch) you later.

EXERCISE C: Rewrite these informal sentences, putting them into more formal English.

> **Example:** Getting to the basketball game was a real hassle.
> **Answer:** Getting to the basketball game was <u>very difficult</u>.

1. The basketball conference title is up for grabs this year.
2. We don't have a prayer of beating the Tigers.
3. Who says? We've got a great center.
4. Yeah, but look at the size of their guards.
5. Who cares? Ours are a lot quicker.

Regionalisms and Dialect

EXERCISE A: Match each example of dialect or regionalism with its more formal or familiar meaning.

    Example: this here   a. this   b. here
    Answer: a

1. ornery   a. oaf
2. klutz   b. you
3. y'all   c. far
4. a ways   d. cranky
5. hightail   e. move quickly

EXERCISE B: Rewrite each sentence, replacing dialect and regionalisms with more formal or standard language. Use a dictionary if you need one.

    Example: I ain't been there in a coon's age.
    Answer: I haven't been there in a long time.

1. Down them vittles, and let's make tracks.
2. He be working most every day.
3. We cooked up a mess of beans in the spider.
4. It's too hot to schlep to the city today.
5. Let's mosey on down to the library.

EXERCISE C: Rewrite the dialogue, replacing the use of dialect and regionalisms with more formal or standard language.

    Example: Get a move on!
    Answer: Hurry up!

Hank: Hunker down in them bushes, Dan. That varmint's sure to come a-runnin' back 'round.
Dan: I hear him hootin' and a-hollerin' back yonder.
Hank: Set a spell. I'll head him off.
Dan: I swan he's just funnin' with us.
Hank: Ain't that the truth! He smart as a whip.
Dan: Got me dog tired, that's for sure.
Hank: Y'all was born tired!

Clichés, Jargon, and Euphemisms

EXERCISE A: Identify each of the twenty expressions in parentheses as a *cliché, jargon,* or a *euphemism.* Then rewrite the expression to make it clear and fresh.

> **Example:** Getting a hit off this (fireballer) is (easier said than done).
> **Answer:** jargon, hard-throwing pitcher; cliché, easier than winning a spot on the Olympic team

1. That pitcher is (firing) some real (heat) today.
2. I'd be (perspiring) (to beat the band) if I was facing him.
3. The hitter is (cool as a cucumber), though.
4. He was at the park (bright and early) for betting practice.
5. He just (swung through) that (hard one).
6. He's too (bad-tempered)—and way too (stout)—to play in the major leagues.
7. Before he (passed away), they said that about another baseball player; then he'd hit another (long one).
8. Look at that (line drive) that he hit to the (hot corner)!
9. (As luck would have it), the third baseman (picked it off).
10. The shortstop touched the (bag) and threw it to first for a (double play).
11. That's the (last straw); I'm not staying to the (bitter end).

EXERCISE B: Revise the following passage, replacing the ten expressions containing *clichés, jargon,* or a *euphemism* with fresh, vivid language.

> **Example:** Quick as a wink, the driver turned on his blinker.
> **Answer:** In an instant, the driver turned on the directional signal.

"I won't detain you because you forgot to buckle up," the police officer said. "However, if I catch you again in this four-by-four truck, and you're not wearing your seat belt, I'll give you a ticket."

"That's clear as crystal, Officer," the portly gentleman replied, knowing he'd made a narrow escape. "From now on, I'm sticking to the straight and narrow," he said with a slick smile.

A half-hour later, the same driver had a fender-bender when the car in front stopped suddenly due to a traffic bottleneck. The driver wasn't injured, but his truck was damaged and had a blowout. Curiously enough, his truck, which was a stick shift, wouldn't move.

As he waited for assistance, he had ample opportunity to think about the events. He was not exactly an Einstein, but it dawned on him that the officer's timely advice might have prevented him from having an unpleasant physiologic experience in this mishap with the other car. He thanked his lucky stars.

Foreign Words and Phrases in English

EXERCISE A: Match each foreign-language word, phrase, or expression in the left-hand column with its definition in the right-hand column. Use a dictionary if necessary.

___ 1. *faux pas*	a. rest in peace
___ 2. *in situ*	b. a bungling loser
___ 3. *requiescat in pace*	c. it's well understood
___ 4. *verboten*	d. in an undertone
___ 5. *modus vivendi*	e. a social blunder
___ 6. *schlemiel*	f. by that fact itself
___ 7. *ipso facto*	g. the exact word
___ 8. *sotto voce*	h. way of living
___ 9. *mot juste*	i. forbidden
___ 10. *bien entendu*	j. in position

EXERCISE B: Rewrite the sentences, replacing each word or phrase in parentheses with one of the foreign-language words or phrases listed below. You may have to make some additional changes. Use a dictionary if necessary.

Example: Balloons, confetti, ribbons, gifts, a cake—it's (too much)!
Answer: Balloons, confetti, ribbons, gifts, a cake—it's *de trop*!

carte blanche	coup de grace	ad hoc	panache
raison d'etre	ad nauseam	persona grata	de trop
vade mecum	schlep	fait accompli	

1. Ambassador Rios is straightforward, fair, and polite; she's (an acceptable person) everywhere.
2. You don't have to (leave) that package home; we can deliver it.
3. The purchase is a (deed that's already been done).
4. Jaymes does everything with (flair and confidence).
5. Li Chang has (full authority) to decide how to spend the money.
6. The two sisters quarreled (to the point that it was disgusting).
7. The last serve was overpowering, a fitting (finishing stroke) to the match.
8. While exploring Yellowstone National Park, the trail guide was Aimee's (reference, which was always within reach).
9. Speaking out against injustice was the senator's (reason for living).
10. The council set up a (special purpose) committee to investigate ways to finance the expansion.

Tone and Mood

Choosing an Appropriate Tone

EXERCISE A: For each purpose listed, write the letter of any sentence that has the appropriate tone. You may write more than one letter for each purpose, and more than one purpose may fit each letter.

Example: to correspond with a sister or brother at camp
Answer: a, d

1. to gossip with a pal
2. to request something from a favorite author
3. to seek information from a municipal office
4. to order merchandise
5. to reply to a cousin

a. It was a cool idea.
b. Your help would be greatly appreciated.
c. Enclosed please find a self-addressed, stamped envelope.
d. Hope to see you soon!

EXERCISE B: Rewrite each sentence to give it a more formal tone.

Example: That would be neat!
Answer: That would be wonderful.

1. I just love Disney World to pieces!
2. It would be cool to see it again.
3. Don't you get a kick out of Fantasy World?
4. Central Florida . . . well, it's okay, I guess.
5. Of course, the climate is kind of sticky.

EXERCISE C: Rewrite the paragraph below twice, choosing an appropriate tone for each purpose listed.

Canoeing is fun, and it's great for your arms and back. Of course, it does take some coordination. Once you figure out a good paddling technique, though, it's a snap. There's nothing like being out on the lake on a hot day.
1. to inform a group of Cub Scouts
2. to persuade nervous tourists to try something new

Creating Mood (Atmosphere) in Writing

EXERCISE A: Rewrite the sentence below five times. Make it express each mood by completing the sentence with words that establish that mood.

    Example: The judge was _____ and _____. (humorous)
    Answer: The judge was <u>addlepated</u> and <u>incompetent</u>. The convict _____ out of his cell,
            _____ at the _____ around him.

1. menacing
2. cheerful
3. hostile
4. matter-of-fact
5. grisly

EXERCISE B: Rewrite each sentence. Give the dark ones a sunnier mood and the lighthearted ones a darker mood.

    Example: Clara laughed happily and shouted, "Hello."
    Answer: Clara sighed deeply and murmured, "Hello."

1. With her rheumy eyes, the crone glared at Clara.
2. Clara skipped down the hillside, scattering the sheep.
3. Outside the cozy cottage, a breeze began to blow.
4. Clara knelt silently beside the woman's footstool.
5. With a venomous yowl, the inky feline scratched Clara.

EXERCISE C: Add words to the paragraph below and rewrite it twice. The first time, give the paragraph a grim mood. The second time, give it a cheery mood.

    Example: I called _____ to the _____ boy.
    Answer: I called <u>piteously</u> to the <u>fiendish</u> boy.
             I called <u>merrily</u> to the <u>attractive</u> boy.

     As I left the _____ park, I noticed a _____ child standing by the wall and _____. A _____ went through me as I heard her _____ voice. I tried to catch her eye, but she _____ away _____. What a _____ incident! It reminded me of my _____ in the _____.

Voice and Style

Developing a Personal Voice

EXERCISE A: Match each sentence below with the most likely speaker named. Then rewrite the statement in your own voice.

> **Example:** If I make a mistake, just give me a break.
> **Answer:** rap star

rap star   grandmother   preacher   lawyer   child

1. Be the best you know how to be.
2. Try to be good.
3. Do your best; I'll do the rest.
4. Act in the best interests of those around you.
5. Give of yourself freely.

EXERCISE B: Rewrite each sentence as you yourself might say it.

> **Example:** I am pleased to introduce Horatio Lemarque.
> **Answer:** I'd like you to meet Horatio Lemarque.

1. Horatio is in possession of an unusual quality.
2. He, I venture to say, is unique among persons I know.
3. Horatio possesses a five-octave singing range.
4. He has more than a passing familiarity with the greatest of the operatic tradition.
5. His tenor tones are stunning and richly reminiscent of those of the great Caruso.

EXERCISE C: Think of two stories you know. They might be movie plots, fairy tales, or folktales. Write a brief summary of each one, using your own personal voice.

> **Example:** "Beauty and the Beast"
> **Answer:** Beauty was gorgeous, but the Beast was homely. This did not stop them from getting together, though. Beauty had a big heart; through her own kind eyes, she was able to see the goodness in the Beast and to love him for himself.

Choosing an Appropriate Style

EXERCISE A: Read each sentence. Label its style *ornate, succinct,* or *sarcastic.*

> **Example:** O, how splendid are the views of hill and dale from my Oregon estate!
> **Answer:** ornate

1. Oregon's a place where the men are men and the women wish they'd move to Montana.
2. I first moved here to attend college in Eugene.
3. The pine-scented breezes, the air fresh as a newborn day—these are the things that hold me here forever.

EXERCISE B: Rewrite each sentence, giving it the style named in parentheses.

> **Example:** It was nice to meet your father. (impersonal)
> **Answer:** Meeting one's friends' parents is always a pleasant experience.

1. Your father is quite interesting. (flippant)
2. He seems to be intelligent. (sincere)
3. Is he really a college professor? (pompous)
4. It might be interesting to sit in on a lecture. (personal)

EXERCISE C: Write a paragraph on any two of the topics below, using the style named in parentheses. For each finished paragraph, name an appropriate audience.

> **Example:** barbecuing (flowery)
> **Answer:** What could be more enjoyable than eating outdoors? The odor of the grill; the tang of the sauce; the wonderful, childlike feel of eating with one's hands—all combine to preserve barbecuing as our great American pastime. (for the readership of a family magazine)

1. barbecuing (direct)
2. world peace (earnest)
3. fashion (flippant)
4. college (personal)
5. college (impersonal)

Figurative Language

Simile

EXERCISE A: Write the simile contained in each sentence. Then identify what is being compared.

> **Example:** Markie's hands were cold as ice.
> **Answer:** cold as ice; hands—ice

1. Upon seeing my report card, my father exploded like a volcano.
2. The normally boisterous child grew quiet as a mouse.
3. The dancer moved about the stage with catlike grace.
4. Drew, stop chewing like a cow!
5. This new skin cream will make your skin as smooth as silk.
6. Josh turned as red as a tomato with embarrassment.
7. April lit up the room like a burst of sunshine.
8. Like ribbons of color, the fireworks lit the sky.
9. Jesse was so nervous that she ate like a bird.
10. The infant's cry sounded as shrill as a whistle.
11. In the morning, my sister is as grumpy as a bear.
12. The raindrops moved like dancers across the windshield.
13. Mrs. Scott turned white as a ghost when she saw a police car in front of her home.
14. The baseball moved like a bullet toward the batter.
15. My grandmother looked at her birthday present with childlike glee.
16. I had to use foxlike cunning to keep Martha from learning about her surprise party.
17. Exercise has caused Meg to become as thin as a rail!
18. My father's hair is starting to turn as white as snow.
19. This stale bread is as hard as a rock!
20. Paul's eyes are as blue as the ocean.

EXERCISE B: Write a sentence that contains a simile to describe each idea.

> **Example:** bright stars twinkling in a dark sky
> **Answer:** Hundreds of stars flickered like distant candle flames in the night sky.

1. a child riding on a swing squealing with delight
2. a runner sprinting along a track
3. ocean waves pounding the shore
4. power suddenly going out in your house
5. sweetness of a piece of fruit
6. heat radiating from a burning fire
7. how you feel upon reading a special letter
8. a car abruptly stalling on a busy highway
9. the sound of wind howling through the trees
10. how you feel now that you have finished this assignment

Metaphor

EXERCISE A: Write the metaphor in each sentence; then write a new sentence with the same metaphor.

Example: The raucous, macaw screams sent attendants scurrying to the patient's aid.
Answer: raucous, macaw screams; The antiquated machine cut out new tools, letting out <u>raucous, macaw screams</u> whenever it turned on or off.

1. The woodpecker's telegraphic Morse Code told Sandy to rise and shine.
2. Ice daggers hanging from the ceiling met ice spears rising from the floor of the cave.
3. The mound of spaghetti was covered by a tomato sauce lava flow.
4. The sonic boom of the coach's voice sent the team out on the court.

EXERCISE B: Write a sentence for each metaphor.

Example: the cough and sputter of a Model-T Ford
Answer: John D. Weatherbee launched his day with the cough and sputter of a Model-T Ford.

1. a bloodhound on the hunt
2. every bit the condor chick
3. the lighthouse beacon
4. shimmering pools of mystery and intrigue
5. two rubber bands

EXERCISE C: For each idea, write a sentence that contains an appropriate metaphor.

Example: the calls of a food vendor at the baseball park
Answer: The annoying crow calls of the vendor did not deter the hungry spectators from reaching for their wallets.

1. a flock of flying geese
2. an all-out attack in a football game
3. a man jumping onto the roof
4. enthusiasm for and dedication to work
5. a woman's bright smile

Personification

EXERCISE A: For each sentence below, identify the object or idea that is being endowed with human qualities.

Example: As he pulled in, his brakes squealed in protest.
Answer: brakes

1. Victory taunted the racecar driver.
2. As the flag fell, vehicles leapt forward anxiously.
3. Just ahead of Damien, the turn reared its ferocious head.
4. As he rounded the curve, the wall rose to meet him.
5. Luck by his side, he avoided a mishap.

EXERCISE B: Complete each personification by naming an object or idea that could have the human qualities given.

Example: Let's get out of this raging _____.
Answer: storm

1. _____ tapped me gently on the shoulder.
2. The song of the _____ lulled us to sleep.
3. _____ led me swiftly to the door.
4. The _____ seemed to glare at me.
5. _____ kept me company.
6. O _____! What a hard taskmaster you can be!
7. The _____ is not my friend.
8. He refuses to listen to the rantings of _____.
9. The _____ rose to greet me.
10. When I get too high and mighty, _____ scolds me.

EXERCISE C: Endow each of the following objects or ideas with human qualities. Personify each in a sentence.

Example: wind
Answer: The <u>wind</u> blew angrily as we exited the building.

1. train
2. greed
3. ice
4. envy
5. silence
6. flowers
7. highway
8. love
9. clock
10. joy

Symbol

EXERCISE A: Match each symbol in the left-hand column with its traditional interpretation. Write the letter of the correct match.

Example: flag   a. patriotism
Answer: a

___ 1. golden crown	a. death	
___ 2. bare branches	b. royalty	
___ 3. cornucopia	c. life; knowledge	
___ 4. tower	d. plenty	
___ 5. light	e. strength	
___ 6. river	f. sophistication	
___ 7. heart	g. time	
___ 8. Paris	h. love	
___ 9. robin	i. submission	
___ 10. sheep	j. spring	

EXERCISE B: Identify and interpret the symbol in each sentence below. Then use the same symbol in an original sentence.

Example: The weary travelers had nearly lost hope when the clouds finally lifted.
Answer: clouds—despair When the king died, the sky was black with clouds.

1. Jake will never give up his quest for the pot of gold.
2. Susan's the rotten apple in the barrel—she spoils every meeting she attends.
3. Like the mighty oak that spreads its branches over the valley, the castle stood, unaffected by time.
4. When Marnie and I broke up, Mom reminded me, "There are plenty of fish in the sea."
5. Violet is as delicate and lovely as her name suggests; her sister, however, is the perfect Rose—thorns and all.
6. We gasped as the black cat darted across our path.
7. The old spiritual tells of meeting the ferryboat captain after a life of pain.
8. They cast aside their spears and signed a treaty.
9. Many of us have a cross to bear; his seems heavier than most.
10. Did the leprechaun in the story find a pot of gold at the end of the rainbow?

Hyperbole

EXERCISE A: Rewrite each sentence so that it expresses the same basic idea without using hyperbole.

> **Example:** I laughed so hard I split my sides.
> **Answer:** I laughed so hard my sides ached.

1. Nam waited an eternity for Kenny.
2. I'm angry enough to chew nails!
3. Waves high as mountains crashed against the rocks.
4. He has a brain the size of a walnut.
5. If I study one more minute, my head is going to explode!
6. She was climbing the walls in anticipation of his arrival.
7. His heart broke into a million pieces when he read her letter.
8. When the jury announced its verdict, World War III broke out in the courtroom.
9. The assassin stood there gloating, evil oozing from every pore.
10. The thought of meeting his old enemy again made his blood boil.

EXERCISE B: Complete each sentence with an appropriate hyperbole.

> **Example:** When she smiles, _____.
> **Answer:** When she smiles, <u>the whole room lights up</u>.

1. Seeing my old friend again, _____.
2. Duane was so fast, _____.
3. Anita's so wise, _____.
4. I was so tired, _____.
5. That suggestion was so brilliant that _____.

EXERCISE C: Rewrite each sentence, adding hyperbole to make it more interesting.

> **Example:** It was cold at the bus stop.
> **Answer:** My hands turned to ice as I waited for the bus.

1. My feet hurt.
2. It's raining hard.
3. He felt frightened.
4. The room was crowded.
5. I'm hungry!
6. The friends argued.
7. We waited a long time.
8. I feel energetic.
9. It was a hard test.
10. This room is a mess!

Answer Key

Elements of Writing

Paragraph Structure

Parts of a Paragraph: Topic Sentences, EXERCISE A
1. effective
2. not effective; the sentence is too vague; it would not focus a paragraph on a specific idea.
3. effective
4. effective
5. not effective; the sentence is too vague and does not introduce a topic that can be extended in a paragraph.

Parts of a Paragraph: Topic Sentences, EXERCISE B
Answers will vary; possible answers are given.
1. I have become a veteran bird-watcher over the past few years.
2. A telescope can open your eyes to the wonders of the night sky.
3. Hiking can be a good form of exercise.
4. There are as many different hobbies as there are kinds of people.

Developing a Paragraph with Facts or Statistics, EXERCISE A
1. Fact
2. Fact
3. Statistic
4. Statistic
5. Fact

Developing a Paragraph with Facts or Statistics, EXERCISE B
Answers will vary; possible answers are given.
1. Over the years the mountain lion has been called several different names: *cougar* by the early settlers, *puma* by the Quechuans of South America, *panther* by settlers in the Eastern states, and *catamount* from "cat of the mountain."
2. This member of the cat family may grow to 1.5 meters long and weigh 103 kilograms.
3. An adult mountain lion may be either grayish or tawny-colored, with white fur on the throat, belly, and insides of its legs.
4. Mountain lions are extremely agile and often leap five meters abovethe ground.
5. During summer these cats may hunt over a large territory that extends to more than 300 square kilometers.

Developing a Paragraph with Facts or Statistics, EXERCISE C
Answers will vary; possible answers are given.
1. Ian Fleming, the English novelist, created the immensely popular James Bond series of novels.
2. Fleming drew upon his experience as assistant to the director of British Intelligence during World War II in developing his master-spy protagonist.
3. Each novel finds Bond in pursuit of an evil but wily adversary, whose only goal is the destruction of Western democracy.
4. Likewise, all the Bond novels have a romantic subplot in which a woman, usually in the employ of the villain, comes to Bond's aid.
5. Secondary to the plot but adding excitement to the scenes are the spectacular technological gadgets used by Bond in overcoming his adversary.

Developing a Paragraph with Sensory Details, EXERCISE A

Answers will vary; possible answers are given.

1. The irritating, smoky smell filled his nostrils as one more reminder of last night's insatiable flames.
2. The fireplace, once so comforting with its warm flickering embers, stood scorched and ghostly; only the blackend and bent grate, stark among the debris, remained.
3. The kitchen had traded its welcoming appeal and preserved only a huddled array of smoke-smudged, useless appliances.
4. Clyde hesitated at the door of his bedroom, wondering how his sleek new computer had fared.
5. Alas! His computer lay on the floor, reduced to a wrinkled glob of melted vinyl.

Developing a Paragraph with Sensory Details, EXERCISE B

Answers will vary; possible answers are given.

1. The relentless trembling quickly shook me to my senses, but I was completely powerless until the quaking giant settled down.
2. I froze, unable to move a finger, although inwardly I cringed at the thought that Scout might be lost because of my carelessness.
3. I will serve a piping hot pizza with sizzling pepperoni, buttery mushrooms, and plenty of mozzarella cheese toasted brown on top.
4. I'd probably faint right on the spot, ruining forever my chances of ever becoming a great star.

Developing a Paragraph with Sensory Details, EXERCISE C

Answers will vary; possible answers are given.

1. I lined up for the kick, my body tensed to knock the ball deftly out of the reach of the cagey goalkeeper.
2. Jan's hands shook with excitement as she opened the bright yellow envelope containing two tickets to see "The Grim," her favorite rock group.
3. His fingers quickly turning page after page of the novel, Randy was unable to stop reading until the plot had been resolved.
4. The boat rocked uncontrollably until a wave lifted it out of the water, turning it upside down, and leaving its passengers struggling to hang onto its sides.

Developing a Paragraph with Reasons, EXERCISE A

1. a
2. b
3. a
4. b

Developing a Paragraph with Reasons, EXERCISE B

Answers will vary; possible answers are given.

1. Some smokers who want to quit the habit find that they are unable to do so.
2. Smoking causes a shortness of breath and keeps an athlete from performing up to par.
3. Insurance companies charge more for a smoker's policy than for a nonsmoker's.
4. Many offices ban smoking; public places also limit the areas where people may smoke.

Developing a Paragraph with Reasons, EXERCISE C

Answers will vary; possible answers are given.

1. I will find it very difficult to complete assignments that require research if the library is closed after school.
2. Larger classes will cause a lot of tensions in the classroom.
3. I'm glad that the intramural program will be retained, since it offers an opportunity for more students to participate in sports.
4. I wouldn't mind a shorter school year because I could get a better job.

Parts of a Paragraph: Concluding Sentences, EXERCISE A

1. effective
2. not effective; the sentence states an unrelated detail.
3. not effective; the conclusion is not supported by the paragraph.
4. effective

Parts of a Paragraph: Concluding Sentences, EXERCISE B

Answers will vary; possible answers are given.

1. It seems almost sad that the beauty of snowflakes can't be preserved.
2. The optimist in me loves to see new life emerge from the cold, hard ground.
3. Ocean dreams are always the most memorable.
4. She listened carefully, totally absorbed in the noisy new sound.

Recognizing Effective Paragraphs, EXERCISE A

Answers will vary; possible answers are given.

1. I applied for a job at Burger-B-Ware. Since the job pays $4.50 an hour, I really hoped to get it. Therefore, I was meticulous as I filled out the application, and I made sure to complete every blank.
2. Lots of people are helping us decorate for the prom. Since the theme is "Moonlight," we are hanging silver moons and stars everywhere. I can't wait for the dance.
3. Paul played a practical joke on my parents. Because he has such a nice garden of his own, they asked him to dig up a dead tree and plant a new one. Instead, he painted the dead tree green.
4. I built a doghouse from a barrel. First, I knocked one end off the barrel. Next, I rolled the barrel next to the porch. Once I had filled the barrel with straw, I had a fine doghouse.
5. This May, we are going on a class trip to Washington, D.C. We plan to visit the Library of Congress. While there, we will look through some of the old archives.

Recognizing Effective Paragraphs, EXERCISE B

Paragraphs will vary.

Unity, Coherence, Transitions

Unity, EXERCISE A
Sentences to be deleted are underlined.

The importance of paleontology, the study of fossils, cannot be underestimated. <u>Many people confuse paleontology and archaeology.</u> Fossils, the preserved remains of plants and animals, are found in layers of rocks. The study of fossils aids paleontologists in learning what kinds of life have existed in Earth's past. <u>Paleogeographers also study fossils, but with an eye to drawing maps of the world in its earliest stages.</u> Fossil study has also enabled paleontologists to propose a history of life that begins more than 3 billion years ago with the oldest-known fossils of one-celled plants. <u>Many paleontologists believe the human race to be a fairly recent "addition" in this long timeline.</u> Ongoing fossil discoveries and studies add to and refine their theories. Paleontologists study fossils to determine the age of the rocks in which the fossils are preserved, as well as whether those rocks were formed on land or under the ocean. Studying fossils provides clues in finding oil deposits. Such deposits are often found in rocks that contain certain fossils. <u>Oil companies are always delighted with such finds, and many employ their own paleontologists.</u>

Unity, EXERCISE B
The sentences to be deleted are given.

Home decorating can be quite a challenge, but it can also be rewarding.
Painting shelves is the toughest part of redecorating.

Added details will vary; possible details are given. Additions are underlined.

Redecorating the family room was a great idea! Tony pictured the "new look" in his mind as he lugged the sofa cushions into the hall. New colors, more shelves, and a rearrangement would definitely produce a "high tech" effect to replace the current dilapidated decor. Back and forth he went <u>first pushing the sofa out, then the heavy recliner and then the coffee and end tables.</u> By then, he was beginning to puff; luckily, the TV was on a wheeled stand.

Tony began emptying the shelves around the fireplace. "I don't believe all this junk," he muttered. Behind and under the game and puzzle boxes that lined the shelves were <u>odd puzzle pieces, dusty game markers, old pencils, marbles, a half-chewed pink eraser—"Spaniel must have had quite a stomach after chewing on this!" he thought—and</u> lots of other small things that he couldn't identify. He dumped them all into the wastebasket he had found under the sofa. "There's enough stuff there to make a sculpture," he noted, "and it is all 'found' stuff, just like those sculptures at the museum." Tony grinned. "I wonder if the museum would display my sculptures when I get them done."

Coherence Through Time Order, EXERCISE A
The correct order is 4, 3, 5, 1, 2.

Coherence Through Time Order, EXERCISE B
Young Scottish nobleman Lochinvar learns that fair Ellen, the lady of his choice, is about to wed another man at her home, Netherby Hall. Setting out immediately, he arrives at the Hall, only to have Ellen's father refuse him entrance. Lochinvar assures Ellen's father that he has come only to drink the health of the couple and to dance with the bride. The handsome knight drinks a toast to Ellen; then he takes her hand and leads her in a dance around the hall. They reach the door, where Lochinvar's stallion stands waiting. With a word to the lovely Ellen, Lochinvar quickly swings her to the saddle, leaps onto the horse behind her, and carries her away. Though members of her clan search the borders for the couple, they never find the two.

Coherence Through Time Order, EXERCISE C

Paragraphs will vary; a possible paragraph, for the first topic, is given.

To plan a successful barbeque, begin by sending invitations or phoning guests. Once you know the number of people who will be coming, select your menu, making it easy to prepare. From your menu, develop a shopping list; then go shopping a day or two before the barbecue. On the day of the barbecue, set up tables and chairs, or spread blankets in the yard. Make hamburger patties and put them in the refrigerator until it is time for barbecuing. After you designate one table for the food, put out dishes, utensils, napkins, and glasses, in buffet style at one end of the table. About an hour before guests arrive, set out condiments and finger foods, such as potato chips and dips. Light coals about fifteen minutes before the guests are expected. Set out the rest of the food on the table; keep it covered until everyone is ready to eat.

Coherence Through Spatial Order, EXERCISE A

Sentences will vary; possible sentences are given, as is the original sentence that each new sentence follows.

1. Our safari guide motioned for us to stand completely still. Charging straight at us was an angry rhino, its head lowered, its horn fully visible.
2. The diamond glittered, perfect and white, under the light. The black velvet on which the jewel rested made its white perfection even more conspicuous.
3. The Ferris wheel groaned, then slowed to a stop. Swinging high on top, Ahmed watched small people enter miniature tents or pause at tiny concessions.
4. The most fascinating piece of furniture was a tall, glass-front cabinet. Squeezed together, covering every inch of the glass shelves inside, were chess pieces of every kind and size.
5. Pairs of dancers, garbed in dazzling Mardi Gras costumes, twirled in the streets. Masked merrymakers in bizarre costumes wove in and out among the swirling couples.
6. The legend says that on nights when the moon shines redly, the ghostly trio still rides. Through the clouds, you can see the riders on their wild mustangs, pounding across the sky.
7. She sat enthroned on a heavy, intricately carved chair of mountain cedar. At her side, on its haunches, with its long tail neatly tucked around its paws, sat an immense, gleaming black cat.
8. The audience quieted as the lights dimmed and strains of music began. From the depths of the stage suddenly rose a platform that held the band and singer.
9. Dignified and proud in their caps and gowns, the graduates entered the auditorium. Families and friends on both sides of the aisle stood to take pictures or applaud the graduates they knew.
10. The pilot checked her gauges and then began her descent. She could clearly see the designated runway stretching out below her, lit by rows of blue lights on either side.

Coherence Through Spatial Order, EXERCISE B

Answers will vary; possible answers are given.

Craig closed the door behind him and stood on the front steps of his old brownstone apartment house. The block party was in full swing. A wonderful assortment of aromas filled his nostrils; genial laughter and talk filled his ears. At the bottom of the steps, to one side, several neighborhood musicians tried to play in harmony and in time. Along both sides of the street he could see neighbors behind makeshift tables of sawhorses and planks. Proudly displayed on the planks were platters heaped high with favorite appetizers or sweets from many parts of the world. At each end of the block were orange "Detour" signs, advising motorists that the street was closed for the afternoon. The teenagers had established their turf in front of the barriers, and were dancing to a boom box blaring on the ground. Children ran around and among the adults, playing tag, using stationary adults as bases or "safe" zones. At the corner, Mr. Pappino led his cronies in wavering renditions of ragtime hits. The scene overflowed with welcome and neighborliness.

Coherence Through Order of Importance, EXERCISE A
The most logical order is 3, 1, 5, 4, 2.

Coherence Through Order of Importance, EXERCISE B
Answers vary somewhat; a possible order is given. Numbers in parentheses indicate original order.

(1) Thirty-five African nations have wild elephants. (10) In 1979, there were an estimated 1.6 million elephants in all of Africa. (8) By 1989, only about 600,000 elephants remained. (2) Half the elephants were killed by poachers and ivory-hunters. (4) All nations with elephants want to protect them. (5) Kenya values an elephant at $14,375 per year for its value for tourism. (7) Ivory from an elephant's tusks, on the other hand, is worth only $1,000. (6) In 1989, the African elephant was listed as an endangered species. (9) Since 1990, the ivory trade has been declared illegal in Africa. (3) Amazingly, six African nations want the ban on the ivory trade lifted.

Coherence Through Order of Importance, EXERCISE C
Paragraphs will vary; a possible paragraph is given. Numbers in parentheses indicate original order of notes.

(7) William Faulkner was born in 1897 in Oxford, Mississippi. (3) He was one of America's greatest writers. (4) He first earned a literary reputation with *The Sound and the Fury* in 1929. (8) Other well-known works include *A Light in August* and *Absalom! Absalom!* (9) His best works are about the South, from its early settlement to more recent times. (2) Many of the novels take place in Yoknapatawpha County, a fictitious county in Mississippi. (6) He won a Pulitzer Prize for *A Fable* in 1954. (10) He won the Nobel Prize for Literature in 1949. (1) His financial success never caught up with his literary success, however. (5) Throughout much of his career, in fact, he worked in Hollywood as a scriptwriter in order to pay his bills.

Coherence Through Order of Familiarity, EXERCISE A
Answers may vary somewhat; a possible order is given. Numbers in parentheses indicate original order.

(10) Sound is a kind of vibration. (6) Throw a pebble in a still pond. (1) The pebble hits and sends out ripples in an expanding circle. (3) Sound works the same as ripples on a pond. (5) If you strike a drum, ripples in the air expand outward from the drum. (7) The ripples in the air are "heard" by the ear as sound. (8) If there is no water in the pond, there can be no ripples. (9) Similarly, if there is no air, there can be no sound. (2) In space there is no air. (4) Consequently, there can be no sound in space.

Coherence Through Order of Familiarity, EXERCISE B
Paragraphs will vary; a possible paragraph is given.

Morse code and compact discs are two ways of communicating. Morse code uses a series of dots and dashes to communicate messages. Each combination of dots and dashes represents a letter. By spelling out words, letter by letter, in dots and dashes, complex messages can be sent and received. *SOS*, for example, is *dot-dot-dot, dash-dash-dash, dot-dot-dot*. A compact disc communicates music in a similar way. The surface of a CD is covered with microscopic pits and flat spots. Music is recorded and communicated in these pits and flat spots. A CD player scans the rotating disc with a laser beam, which reflects differently off the various pits and flat spots. The reflected beam bounces off a light-sensitive device that converts the light to an electrical current. The CD player then electronically decodes the message carried by the electrical current, amplifies it, and directs it through loudspeakers as music.

Coherence Through Comparison and Contrast, EXERCISE A

Answers will vary; possible answers are given.
1. are large and usually live in the wild / are small and are generally kept as a pet (contrast)
2. more teams / better food in the cafeteria (comparison)
3. math and science / language arts (contrast)
4. flowers / vegetables (contrast)
5. love to read / plays a musical instrument (comparison)

Coherence Through Comparison and Contrast, EXERCISE B

Paragraphs will vary; a possible paragraph is given.

Mark and James are alike in some ways and different in others. At 17, Mark is a year older than James. Both boys have brown hair, but Mark's eyes are brown and James's are hazel. Unlike James, who plays center on the basketball team, Mark shows little interest in team sports. Both boys excel at math, but Mark also does well in English while James is more interested in science. While James seldom goes out on dates, Mark spends as much time as he can with his steady girlfriend, Daphne.

Coherence Through Cause and Effect, EXERCISE A

Answers will vary; possible answers are given.
1. The tent pegs were loose. Grant was trapped inside.
2. Something disturbed the wildlife. The sound gave me a start.
3. Raccoons got into the trash. Harvey jumped to his feet.
4. I cried out. He hit his head on the tent pole.
5. Adrian rose early to cook. We woke with a smile.
6. A gentle breeze blew. We felt content.
7. A coyote howled. Bret told him to hush.
8. A storm came up quickly. We could see sparks.
9. We decided to leave at once. We forgot many items.
10. Clouds covered the sky. We could not even see the path.

Coherence Through Cause and Effect, EXERCISE B

Answers will vary; possible answers are given.
1. People at school saw my name in the paper. Mindy called me to tell me about it. Strangers whispered behind my back. In addition, Mr. Slack called on me twice.
2. The dog we picked was the runt of the litter. Because of this, she needed extra care. She was sickly at first and had to visit the vet often.
3. Jasper had always wanted to be an astronaut. He studied astronomy and physics. As soon as he was old enough, he applied for a job with NASA.
4. Mom was unusually irritated this morning. She snapped at me to take out the trash. Even the cat hid when he saw her coming.
5. I simply did not want to practice today. Instead, I put a dummy on the piano bench. Then I put on a tape and went outside to play ball.
6. We arrived home exhausted by our trip. The car had broken down twice. If that weren't bad enough, the map was wrong. Detroit was 75 miles further than we had thought.
7. The Green family finally bought a new house. Their old house teetered dangerously on a cliff edge. Constant threat of mudslides made their decision for them.
8. I had an experience that taught me a lesson. I turned on the oven but forgot to light it. When I remembered, I just held up a match. I could have set fire to my head!
9. My grandparents refuse to eat in restaurants. They insist that the food is better and cheaper at home. Grandpa hates to put on a jacket and tie. Grandma dislikes waiters.
10. The ocean is now my favorite vacation spot. We went to the beach for the first time last year. I had the best time of my life.

Coherence Through Transitional Expressions, EXERCISE A
1. Before/then/After that/while/Finally
2. Not long after/In the meantime/even after/At this point/Eventually

Coherence Through Transitional Expressions, EXERCISE B
Answers will vary; possible answers are given.
1. <u>Every Thanksgiving</u>, our whole family gets together. <u>In the morning</u>, my uncle and aunt arrive with my cousins. <u>While</u> the children play touch football, Uncle Burt cooks the turkey. <u>During the course of the day</u>, Mom makes a dozen side dishes. <u>Meanwhile</u>, Great-Aunt Lucille bakes pies.
2. Cherissa prepared a long time for her oral report. <u>First</u> she wrote the main points on note cards. She <u>next</u> numbered the cards in order and <u>then</u> underlined vital ideas in red. <u>All week</u>, she practiced her report in front of the mirror. <u>When the day arrived</u>, her presentation was flawless.

Sentences

Recognizing Subjects and Predicates, EXERCISE A
1. Our new <u>car</u> | <u>should arrive</u> next week.
2. The <u>clerks</u> | in the shoe department | <u>receive</u> a commission.
3. <u>Ginnie</u> and <u>Megan</u> | <u>won</u> the three-legged race.
4. The <u>audience</u> | <u>waited</u> for the curtain to rise.
5. <u>Dad</u> | <u>needs</u> a dental appointment soon.
6. The heat <u>spell</u> | <u>left</u> the lawn dry and brown.
7. <u>We</u> | <u>bought</u> refreshments during the intermission.
8. The <u>bus</u> to Phoenix | <u>departs</u> at 10:15.
9. The <u>ice</u> on the pond | <u>is</u> thick enough for skating.
10. <u>Mom</u>, <u>Dad</u>, <u>Eric</u>, and <u>I</u> | <u>agree</u>.

Recognizing Subjects and Predicates, EXERCISE B
Answers will vary; possible answers are given.
1. None of the boys in our class | will be going to the dance.
2. One of the best times in my memory | was our trip to the circus.
3. Most of my friends | like to play basketball.
4. The book on the top shelf | was about geology.
5. Grandparents | love to visit their grandchildren.
6. James and Alice | met in fifth grade.
7. Some shows on television | are very funny.
8. Their neighbor | grew up in a big city.
9. My brother-in-law | plays the oboe.
10. The hungry cat | rummaged through the garbage.

Recognizing Subjects and Predicates, EXERCISE C
Answers will vary; possible answers are given.
 1. The elderly woman sat on the park bench.
 2. The car radio blasted through the open window.
 3. Our train arrived right on time.
 4. The guests brought presents to the party.
 5. Three cars were parked behind the house.
 6. Our favorite teacher announced the date of the exam.
 7. Their grandparents came for a long visit.
 8. The famous artist created a beautiful sculpture.
 9. That man hopes to live forever.
10. The pianist at the concert played for two hours.

Recognizing Subjects and Predicates, EXERCISE A
Answers will vary; possible answers are given.
 1. (You) meet
 2. dessert came
 3. warning is
 4. family strolled
 5. (you) give

Recognizing Subjects and Predicates, EXERCISE B
Answers will vary; possible answers are given.
 1. Along the highway <u>grew</u> the <u>wildflowers</u>.
 2. On the street <u>music</u> <u>played</u>.
 3. In the corner <u>sat</u> his <u>brother</u>.
 4. Here <u>comes</u> <u>Diane</u> again.
 5. The soccer <u>players</u> <u>raced</u> down the field.
 6. George, my <u>goldfish</u> <u>died</u> yesterday.
 7. Into the water <u>plunged</u> a <u>seagull</u>.
 8. When in doubt, <u>beginners</u> <u>should proceed</u> with caution.
 9. There <u>goes</u> the <u>winner</u>!
10. After school, <u>children</u> <u>play</u> in the park.

Recognizing Subjects and Predicates, EXERCISE C
Answers will vary; possible answers are given.
 1. For information about the play, (you) call Mrs. Washington.
 2. (You) Tell me the big news—please!
 3. (You) Give me a quarter for a phone call.
 4. After about three minutes, (you) turn over the chicken.
 5. Hey, Pete—(you) pass me the ball!
 6. (You) Order the vegetarian pizza.
 7. Before the meeting, (you) please stop by my office.
 8. (You) Speak more slowly, Yoko!
 9. (You) Take me with you to the mall.
10. Zack, (you) put the box on this table.

Recognizing Effective Sentences, EXERCISE A
Answers will vary; possible answers are given.
1. The people of the Renaissance, which is the French word for "rebirth," tried to model their lives on the classical civilizations of ancient Greece and Rome.
2. Artists and writers throughout Europe thrived during the Renaissance because a powerful middle class arose and offered them financial support.
3. Sculptors and architects also thrived during the Renaissance.
4. Correct
5. The Renaissance reached England after the War of the Roses ended in 1485.

Recognizing Effective Sentences, EXERCISE B
Answers will vary; possible answers are given.
    The protagonist of the book is a girl named Alexandra. Alexandra and her cat, Sasha, are lost in the woods. They meet Eldorf, a mysterious stranger, who offers to help them find their way home. Alexandra, Sasha, and Eldorf have many thrilling adventures together before the story reaches its surprising conclusion. I highly recommend this novel to anyone who appreciates an exciting fantasy story the way I do.

Sentence Problems

Sentence Fragments, EXERCISE A
Answers will vary; possible answers are given.
1. <u>The explorers</u> traveled a long way without water.
2. If it snows sometime this week, <u>we'll go skiing</u>.
3. <u>We each have to do</u> an original poem, a model of the setting, or a dramatic reading.
4. Whoever does not understand the assignment <u>should stay after school</u>.
5. <u>We walked along</u> a lonely beach, cold in the winter wind.
6. Flying from Connecticut to New Mexico, <u>we stopped in Chicago</u>.
7. <u>Lisa found</u> a dirty, shivering, obviously abandoned kitten.
8. Can <u>we</u> expect delivery tomorrow?
9. Flattered by all the attention he was getting, <u>Jerome grinned warmly</u>.
10. <u>What a good time we had</u> while we were on vacation!

Sentence Fragments, EXERCISE B
Answers will vary; possible answers are given.
1. phrase; Challenged by the coach of the other team, <u>we accepted a rematch</u>.
2. clause; Because time was running so short, <u>we had to speed up our efforts</u>.
3. series; Lonely, inexperienced, and in charge, <u>Marcia regretted volunteering</u>.
4. clause; Whether or not he can sell his old bicycle, <u>Ron is buying a new one</u>.
5. phrase; To find oneself in such a predicament <u>is not a bit amusing</u>.

Sentence Fragments, EXERCISE C
Answers will vary; possible answers are given.
    Although dinosaur bones have been weathering out of rocks for a very long time, the name *dinosaur* was first coined by Sir Richard Owen, a British anatomist, in 1841. Dinosaurs were very large, land-living creatures, with pillar-like legs tucked beneath the body. The position of the legs was unusual, totally unlike any other fossil reptiles.

Run-on Sentences, EXERCISE A
Some answers may vary; possible answers are given.
1. Mom made me take my umbrella, <u>for</u> it was raining outside.
2. The book was in Mona's locker, <u>but</u> she couldn't find it.
3. The lake is beautiful at night<u>;</u> it has an eerie peace.
4. The Athletics Club banquet had been a success<u>;</u> everyone was satisfied.
5. Have you heard the news<u>?</u> Vicki is moving to Seattle.
6. Do you know what I think<u>?</u> I think it's too expensive.
7. Clark <u>and his family</u> visited us last weekend.
8. I noticed the long, ragged rip, <u>and fixed</u> it promptly.
9. Ira wants a job <u>because</u> he needs money for his dilapidated car.
10. <u>Once</u> the cat's away, the mice do play.

Run-on Sentences, EXERCISE B
Some answers may vary; possible answers are given.
1. We each had to memorize a poem<u>;</u> I chose "The Chambered Nautilus."
2. Every Hawaiian feast includes poi, <u>which is</u> crushed, cooked taro root.
3. Elizabeth I<u>, the daughter of Henry VIII,</u> ruled England wisely.
4. I asked my grandmother, <u>who</u> had faced that problem in her youth.
5. <u>Although</u> castles have a romantic image, they were actually cold and damp.
6. The birds <u>and the bears</u> were agitated about something.
7. The old house had real charm<u>;</u> moreover, the landscaping was picturesque.
8. Correct
9. Regina couldn't do the new work <u>because</u> she'd never mastered the basics.
10. <u>When</u> Leonard pitched a no-hitter, he achieved some local stardom.

Stringy Sentences, EXERCISE A
Answers may vary slightly; possible answers are given.
1. Ferdinand Magellan had made an earlier trip, from 1519 to 1522, <u>when</u> he had discovered a passage from the Atlantic Ocean to the Pacific Ocean.
2. <u>Although</u> Magellan was a Portuguese sailor, he had convinced Charles I of Spain to support his voyage of circumnavigation of the earth.
3. <u>Because</u> conflict between the Portuguese and Spanish sailors was an ongoing problem, the journey was fraught with great difficulty.
4. A mutiny broke out and threatened the success of the journey <u>until</u> Magellan and loyal members of the crew were able to resume control.
5. <u>When</u> Magellan took part in a battle between rival groups in the Philippines, he was killed before he could complete his famous voyage.

Stringy Sentences, EXERCISE B
Answers may vary slightly; possible answers are given.
1. Many hundreds of languages are spoken in the Pacific <u>Islands; Melanesia</u> has the greatest number.
2. English is used in many of the Pacific <u>Islands. In fact, it</u> is the official language of Hawaii, Fiji, New Zealand, Tonga, and Western Samoa.
3. In some of the islands, the people speak <u>Japanese. They</u> learned this language during the Japanese occupation from 1920 to 1945.
4. The first settlers in the Pacific Islands probably came from Asia thousands of years <u>ago, arriving</u> on rafts and dugouts.
5. The people in the islands differ from one another in <u>appearance; therefore, scientists</u> have determined that they belong to different races.

Choppy Sentences, EXERCISE A

Answers may vary slightly; possible answers are given.

1. Alexander Graham <u>Bell, an American scientist and educator, invented</u> the telephone.
2. <u>As a young man, Bell</u> studied how vowels are <u>produced because he</u> wanted to help the deaf to speak.
3. <u>Since Bell</u> did not have the time or the skill to make the necessary parts for his <u>experiments, he</u> went to an electrical <u>shop to ask Thomas</u> Watson to help him.
4. One <u>day, while Watson</u> was working on the wires in the next <u>room, Bell, at</u> the other end of the <u>line, heard</u> the wires being plucked.
5. The next <u>day, when</u> the instrument transmitted the sound of Bell's <u>voice, the</u> telephone was born.

Choppy Sentences, EXERCISE B

Answers may vary slightly; possible answers are given.

1. <u>Although Samuel</u> Morse is <u>remembered as the</u> person who made the first successful <u>telegraph, he</u> began his career as an artist.
2. <u>Even though his</u> portrait *Marquis de <u>Lafayette is</u>* hanging in New York's City Hall, Morse wanted to do more than paint portraits.
3. <u>When he</u> became a teacher of painting and sculpting at the University of the City of New <u>York, his</u> spare time and money went to working on the telegraph.
4. The first public demonstration of the telegraph was a <u>failure, for a</u> ship's anchor caught onto the <u>wire and brought it</u> to the surface.
5. On May 24, 1844, Morse tapped out a famous <u>message, "What hath God wrought!" that reached</u> Baltimore from Washington, D.C.

Wordy Sentences, EXERCISE A

Answers may vary; possible answers are given.

1. I decided to do research on aardvarks because all I know about these animals is the unusual spelling of their name.
2. Although two *a*'s do not occur in succession in English, the spelling is not at all unusual in the Dutch language.
3. The Dutch settlers called the animal *aardvark,* because the name means "earth pig" in Dutch.
4. The aardvark probably earned its name because it lives in the ground and has a snout.
5. Aardvarks have a long, sticky tongue with which they catch ants and termites.

Wordy Sentences, EXERCISE B

Answers may vary; possible answers are given.

1. Like many beginning collectors, you may want to buy a reference collection to help you compare unknown specimens and known specimens.
2. Minerals have identifiable characteristics, such as chemical composition and streak color.
3. To determine the chemical composition of the rocks, you can do any number of chemical tests.
4. To find out the streak color, you can rub a mineral across a hard, rough surface, such as unglazed porcelain, and observe the color of the powder obtained.
5. Knowing where a rock was found and how it looks may also help you to identify it.

Empty Sentences, EXERCISE A
Answers will vary; possible answers are given.
1. Sequoyah's principal aim was to record in a permanent form the ancient traditions of his people.
2. The Cherokees began to use Sequoyah's system of writing to publish books and newspapers.
3. Thousands of Cherokees learned to read and write their own language.
4. Sequoyah later gained recognition for his efforts to improve the lives of Native Americans.
5. Sequoyah was honored for his contributions to Native American culture when the giant sequoia trees and Sequoia National Park were named after him.

Empty Sentences, EXERCISE B
Answers will vary; possible answers are given.
1. Jefferson was a leading architect of his time, having to his credit the design of the Virginia Capitol, the University of Virginia, and Monticello.
2. He also had a great deal to do with the present monetary system of the United States, for he developed the decimal system of coinage based on dollars and cents.
3. Thomas Jefferson showed his interest in Native Americans by preparing written vocabularies of Native American languages.
4. Many people do not realize that Jefferson also has a number of inventions to his credit, such as a decoding system, a lap desk, and an improved plow.
5. Politicians today like to quote Jefferson for his belief that there should be as little government as possible.

Lack of Parallel Structure I, EXERCISE A
1. not parallel; we should practice when we can
2. not parallel; the people who play trumpets
3. parallel
4. not parallel; adventurous
5. not parallel; an appearance on TV

Lack of Parallel Structure I, EXERCISE B
Answers will vary slightly; possible answers are given.
1. To me, water skiing is far more enjoyable than <u>downhill skiing</u>.
2. <u>To prepare</u> a household budget is important; to stick to it is more important.
3. This liberal arts school has small classes, many clubs, and <u>a nice faculty</u>.
4. What to wear to the junior prom was one question; <u>how to pay</u> for it was another; where to wear it afterward was another still.
5. I took this job in the laboratory because of the good pay and <u>the convenient hours</u>.
6. Raising rabbits can take a lot more work than <u>keeping a cat</u>.
7. Sonya enjoys getting presents; she likes <u>giving them</u> even more.
8. Spain is well known for its lace, <u>its friendly people</u>, and <u>its dramatic dances</u>, such as the flamenco.
9. Marnie Jacobs is liked by her friends and by <u>her relatives</u> for her intelligence, creativity, and <u>fairness</u>.
10. Ten-year-old Troy brushed his teeth, <u>washed his face, and came</u> downstairs.

Lack of Parallel Structure II, EXERCISE A
Answers will vary slightly; possible answers are given.
1. J. Jacob Jett, who is my favorite playwright, novelist, and <u>poet</u>, came to town last week.
2. He would give a reading, <u>answer</u> questions, and sign books.
3. Correct
4. I spoke enthusiastically but <u>somewhat nervously</u> about Jett's visit.
5. When the day arrived, I raced down the street, around the corner, and <u>into the bookstore</u>.
6. Jett soon arrived, took off his coat, and <u>waved</u> to the crowd.
7. <u>Hearing</u> him read from his latest work was a thrill; asking him a question—and getting an informative answer—was an honor.
8. People stood in line <u>to get</u> his autograph, take a picture, or just <u>say</u> hello.
9. Talking to Mr. Jett was better than <u>reading</u> about him any day!
10. His greeting made me glad that I had come, eager to read his newest book, and <u>more interested</u> in becoming a writer myself.

Lack of Parallel Structure II, EXERCISE B
Answers will vary slightly; possible answers are given.
1. In Poughkeepsie, New York, Baker was born<u>, raised, and educated</u>.
2. <u>Relatives, other doctors, and even her mother</u> tried to discourage Baker from a career in medicine.
3. She earned her degree<u>, worked</u> in a Boston clinic<u>, and then</u> became a medical inspector in New York City.
4. To lower the infant death rate, Baker taught women how to feed<u>, bathe, and clothe children</u> properly.
5. <u>Promoting</u> preventative medicine<u>, advancing</u> health education<u>, and organizing</u> support for children's charities <u>were important to her</u>.

Confusing Shifts of Verb Tenses and Pronouns in Sentences, EXERCISE A
1. is, was
2. his, their
3. they, he (or she)
4. yelled, had yelled
5. he, they

Confusing Shifts of Verb Tenses and Pronouns in Sentences, EXERCISE B
Answers may vary slightly; possible answers are given.

One day I, Rita Lee, decide to visit one of my neighbors, Mrs. Aurelia Jackson. Mrs. Jackson is a seventy-year-old woman who lives in a house that looks like something from a fairy tale. Mrs. Jackson <u>greets</u> me at the door with a warm smile. She <u>is</u> wearing a cotton dress, a white sweater, and walking shoes. She eagerly <u>shows</u> me into the kitchen. Mrs. Jackson <u>looks</u> forward to my visits because she <u>knows</u> that I <u>am</u> interested in hearing her stories.

Mrs. Jackson was a first-grade teacher for thirty years and loved <u>it</u>. She <u>likes</u> to reminisce about her students, one of <u>whom</u> was Rita Lee. Today she <u>tells</u> a story about the time <u>I</u> cut the hair of one of my friends. She <u>laughs</u> and <u>laughs</u>. She brings out my first-grade class picture and <u>tells</u> stories about the rest of the children, too.

Mrs. Jackson <u>likes</u> to reminisce about the past, but she also <u>has</u> many activities that keep her busy in the present. She <u>volunteers</u> at the library three mornings a week. She also <u>tutors</u> several children once a week after school. When I <u>tell</u> her I <u>am</u> majoring in education, she seems pleased. I just hope that when I am seventy years old, I am as full of life and warmth as Mrs. Jackson.

Sentence Combining

Sentence Combining with Coordinating Conjunctions, EXERCISE A
Some answers may vary; possible answers are given.
1. and
2. but
3. yet
4. for
5. so

Sentence Combining with Coordinating Conjunctions, EXERCISE B
Answers may vary slightly; possible answers are given.
1. Some early fish migrated to coastal swamps <u>and</u> lagoons, <u>but</u> the water there was warmer than in the deep.
2. The warmer water contained less dissolved oxygen, <u>so</u> a fish in these waters had to lift its head above the water <u>and</u> take in gulps of air.
3. The air went into a pouch surrounded by blood vessels, <u>and</u> the pouch helped the fish maintain the proper level of oxygen.
4. Soon the fish dispensed with the dangerous process of coming to the surface, <u>for</u> many predators were waiting for them there.
5. Some fish adapted by filling the pouch with air from their own blood, <u>and</u> the pouch made the fish float in water.

Sentence Combining with Subjects and Predicates, EXERCISE A
Answers may vary slightly; possible answers are given.
1. Barry <u>peered</u> through the microscope and <u>checked</u> the lab manual. (compound predicate)
2. Then he said, "Amanda, <u>you</u> and <u>I</u> have something unusual here." (compound subject)
3. "We <u>should show</u> it to Paul and Carrie Ann or <u>call</u> Mr. Payne over." (compound predicate)
4. <u>Paul, Carrie Ann</u>, and <u>Mr. Payne looked</u> through the microscope and promptly <u>turned</u> pale. (compound subject, compound predicate)

Sentence Combining with Subjects and Predicates, EXERCISE B
Answers may vary slightly; possible answers are given.
1. Gem cutters can take a rough gemstone, cut it, and then polish it. (compound predicate)
2. Minerals and some other materials that are used in jewelry are called gems. (compound subject)
3. Neither amber nor coral is a mineral. (compound subject)
4. Coral comes from the ocean, but amber and jet are products of ancient trees. (compound subject)
5. Among minerals, gems not only come in a variety of spectacular colors but also vary in hardness. (compound predicate)
6. Sapphires or topazes are minerals that come in many colors. (compound subject)
7. The diamond is the hardest mineral; it can scratch any other mineral yet cannot itself be scratched. (compound predicate)
8. Both an opal's background color and the color of its flashes help to determine its value. (compound subject)
9. Opal triplets result when opals are sliced thinly, glued together with a clear cement, and finally covered with a glass top. (compound predicate)
10. Jade and emeralds are green but look quite different from each other. (compound subject, compound predicate)

Sentence Combining with Subordinating Conjunctions, EXERCISE A

Answers may vary slightly; possible answers are given.

1. <u>Although</u> Spain was officially neutral in 1776, Bernardo de Galvez supported the Patriots.
2. <u>Because</u> Galvez was governor of Louisiana, he was in a unique position to help.
3. Arms were shippped from New Orleans <u>so that</u> fighters in the West would be supplied with weapons.
4. <u>After</u> Spain officially sided with the Americans in 1779, Galvez moved against British troops in the South.
5. <u>Wherever</u> he captured forts and isolated soldiers, he weakened Britain's power.

Sentence Combining with Subordinating Conjunctions, EXERCISE B

Some answers may vary slightly; possible answers are given.

    <u>If</u> I haven't mentioned English class before now, let me tell you something about it. <u>As</u> class was letting out about three weeks ago, my teacher assigned us "Dancer," a story by Vickie Sears. <u>Since</u> I tend to procrastinate, I did not read it until Sunday. Was I sorry to have waited, <u>because</u> it was great!

    <u>While</u> it tells the story of young Clarissa, "Dancer" applies Native American beliefs to modern problems. <u>Although</u> Clarissa is only five, she is living at her fourth foster home. However, her life changes <u>after</u> she watches Molly Graybull, a champion dancer. She starts dancing <u>as if</u> her life depended upon it. At the end of this powerful story, <u>when</u> another dance is held, a more confident Clarissa joins Molly in the circle.

    <u>If</u> I ever find a sequel to "Dancer," I'll read it right away!

Sentence Variety

Types of Sentence Structure, EXERCISE A

1. simple
2. compound-complex
3. complex
4. compound
5. compound
6. compound-complex
7. complex
8. simple
9. simple
10. compound

Types of Sentence Structure, EXERCISE B
Sentences will vary; possible sentences are given.
1. They planted a tree.
2. The girl found the cat, and the boy found the dog.
3. Cleaning, which I enjoy, is an important task.
4. I saw a girl whom I used to know; we now have become close friends.
5. Is Trisha feeling angry?
6. Stop bothering me.
7. Moths, which are not my favorite creatures, flew around the campfire.
8. Wayne knew that he needed to study, but he was too lazy to open his books.
9. Has Tom studied for the exam?
10. Dogs barked, and the wind howled.
11. Cows ambled through the field that the farmer had recently plowed.
12. The governor, who is my uncle, won the election, but his opponent demanded a recount.
13. How skillfully the boys rode!
14. You realize the need for an apology, but are you prepared to do it?
15. Helen ran to her mother, who was at their neighbor's house.
16. The game began at noon, but not everyone who planned to come arrived on time.
17. Luis was late.
18. Work at this job for an hour; then I'll relieve you.
19. The team practiced every day, which was difficult for some of the players.
20. When Jesse plays softball, his friends come to watch, and everyone shouts encouragement from the stands.

Varying Sentence Structure, EXERCISE A
Sentences will vary; possible sentences are given.
1. Robert lost his way.
2. Can Alice, who is an excellent athlete, teach Robin how to swim?
3. The violinist played beautifully, but the cellist was terrible.
4. How furious I am!
5. Mrs. Stevenson went inside the house that used to be ours.
6. Will the girls eat lunch now, or will they eat later?
7. Did the baby sneeze?
8. Do they still believe in Santa Claus, or has someone told them otherwise?
9. Marlene, who is a gifted student, studied all night; as a result, she fell asleep in the middle of the exam.
10. How angry it makes me to see how important he thinks he is!

Varying Sentence Structure, EXERCISE B
Answers will vary; possible answers are given.

How great it was to see Pete and Marcia and their kids again after all these years! Can you believe Sara is ten years old? Sara wants to be an actress, so she joined the Drama Club at school. She's a good dancer, too, although her singing leaves something to be desired. Jerry, who is in junior high school, plays center on the basketball team. He looks just like Pete, and he's already taller than his mother. Jerry has a girlfriend named Jenny, about whom Sara loves to tease him. Do you remember Pete's friend Ellen? She's married now; she and her husband live right down the street. What a terrific time we all had at dinner together!

Varying Sentence Length, EXERCISE A

Answers will vary; possible answers are given.
1. Because of its severe ice storms, this winter was difficult.
2. December, with its forty inches of snow, was bad.
3. January—a month of constant snow, sleet, rain, and hail—was worse.
4. We welcomed spring "at the close of a winter's day."
5. Now that we can see the grass, we feel better.

Varying Sentence Length, EXERCISE B

Answers will vary; possible answers are given.
1. Because it is aerobic, bicycling is good for you.
   Bicycling, which is enjoyed by people of all ages, is good for you.
2. Many people—perhaps twice as many—prefer jogging.
   Many people prefer jogging, which they do anywhere.
3. Because they must be strong and flexible, dancers may be the best athletes.
   Dancers, those "defiers of gravity," may be the best athletes.
4. My brother lifts weights of about 50 to 75 pounds.
   To strengthen his upper body, my brother lifts weights.
5. Good health, or "good estate of body," is important.
   Good health is important to good emotional well-being.

Varying Sentence Length, EXERCISE C

Answers will vary; possible answers are given.

To keep him company in the field, Jon plans to buy a puppy. He wants a chocolate Labrador retriever, a fairly unusual dog. A breeder in the village on Candor has promised him a female pup. He will name her Koko as a kind of play on the word *chocolate.* Keeping in mind that "the dog is the god of frolic," he will train her.

Varying Sentence Beginnings, EXERCISE A

Answers will vary; possible answers are given.
1. Yesterday I made a nice dinner.
2. During the afternoon, I roasted a chicken.
3. While I waited for my guest, I tossed a mixed salad.
4. Bowing, I invited her to sit down.
5. Proudly, I served the food.

Varying Sentence Beginnings, EXERCISE B

Answers will vary; possible answers are given.
1. Throughout the year, trees are homes to birds and animals.
   Grand and welcoming, trees are homes to birds and animals.
2. Most important, trees make the oxygen we breathe.
   As if that were not enough, trees make the oxygen we breathe.
3. Quickly, fire spreads through a forest.
   During the dry season, fire spreads quickly through a forest.
4. To be sure, fire is a danger for both flora and fauna.
   For both flora and fauna, fire is a danger.
5. Foolish campers may cause fire.
   As you may know, fire may be caused by foolish campers.

Varying Sentence Beginnings, EXERCISE C
Answers will vary; possible answers are given.

 <u>Without a doubt</u>, I love seeing Uncle Miguel. <u>To be honest</u>, I enjoy hearing about his travels. <u>Eagerly</u>, I look forward to his postcards and letters. <u>Since his career takes him all over the world</u>, I approve of his work with the Wildlife Fund. <u>Someday</u>, I hope to travel with him.

Word Choice

Using Connotation and Denotation, EXERCISE A
Answers will vary; possible answers are given.
1. Jeff wanted to <u>dispute</u> the choice of play for the spring festival.
2. He hoped to <u>incite</u> the members of the club against the selection.
3. "We're fortunate in having Curtis as the <u>farcical</u> Sherlock Holmes."
4. Jeff liked to <u>ridicule</u> Curtis whenever he had the chance.
5. The drama coach <u>summoned</u> Jeff to <u>defend his impertinences</u> before the faculty.

Using Connotation and Denotation, EXERCISE B
Answers will vary; possible answers are given.
1. The <u>artificial</u> flowers looked real. The <u>counterfeit</u> money looked real.
2. Dana recognized his friend's <u>mannerism</u> of raising his eyebrows to emphasize his words. Bobby Ray had the annoying <u>peculiarity</u> of raising his eyebrows whenever he spoke.
3. The voice on the phone was <u>sweetly</u> concerned. The voice on the phone was <u>cloyingly</u> sweet, just dripping with affectation.
4. Ann's choice of costume was <u>striking</u>. On the other hand, Dorinda's costume, was downright <u>gaudy</u>.
5. Here is a <u>facsimile</u> of the document. Here is a <u>forgery</u> of the document.

Using Connotation and Denotation, EXERCISE C
Answers may vary; a suggested answer is given.

 Deirdre is a <u>zealous</u> conservationist. Her exhibit shows <u>grotesque</u> photographs of the disappearing rainforests. She wanted viewers to see <u>shocking</u> scenes of what is happening in these areas. The crowd's <u>backlash</u> against her was expected. Deirdre <u>contended</u> that people never respond well to a worthwhile cause.

Using Connotation and Denotation, EXERCISE A
Answers will vary; possible answers are given.
1. The yard was barren, without the comfort of either trees or garden.
2. Moonlight trickling through the slate roof cast an eerie glow in the rooms beneath the eaves.
3. Shadowy kaleidoscopes danced throughout the rooms and hallways.
4. Wind through the shattered windows murmured, moaned, and sighed.
5. Not even a stalwart adventurer would dare to explore that ghostly relic after sunset.

Using Connotation and Denotation, EXERCISE B
Answers will vary; possible answers are given.
1. When the tide loses its grip, the estuary is once more bathed in fresh water.
2. Then, like clockwork, the tide regains its strength, allowing salty water to cover the river's mouth with brine.
3. Animals in the estuary respond to the rhythmic changes by numerous adaptations.
4. All day long, animals of the estuary are honored guests at a bountiful seafood banquet.

Using Connotation and Denotation, EXERCISE C

Answers will vary; possible answers are given.
1. Chasing that elusive soccer ball strengthened my sagging lungs and sharpened my tiring wits.
2. These old, battered tennis shoes have withstood many a skirmish, both on the court and off.
3. The gurgling mountain stream conjures up memories of my grandfather, hip-deep in boots with the scent of trout in his nostrils.
4. The gentle splatter of the first snowfall was soon a cascade of white velvet around me.

Varieties of English

Formal and Informal English, EXERCISE A
1. formal
2. informal
3. informal (be cool)
4. formal
5. informal
6. informal (lousy)
7. informal (make a big deal)

Formal and Informal English, EXERCISE B
Answers may vary; possible answers are given.
1. Did you hear that Maya <u>did extremely well</u> on her driving test?
2. Are you <u>making a joke</u>?
3. She was <u>worried and nervous</u> beforehand, but everything was <u>calm</u> during the test.
4. I'm glad she didn't <u>do poorly</u> on it; she'd have been <u>difficult</u> to get along with.
5. She's going to want to use her sister's <u>car</u>.
6. It <u>puzzles</u> me. Maybe her sister won't mind if she <u>shares</u> the gas.
7. I'll <u>talk with</u> you later.

Formal and Informal English, EXERCISE C
Answers will vary; possible answers are given.
1. Any team can win the basketball conference title this year.
2. We do not have a change of defeating the Tigers.
3. That is not true. We have an excellent center.
4. Yes, but consider the size of their guards.
5. Size is not that important. Our guards are much quicker.

Regionalisms and Dialect, EXERCISE A
1. d
2. a
3. b
4. c
5. e

Regionalisms and Dialect, EXERCISE B
Answers will vary; possible answers are given.
1. Eat that food, and let's go.
2. He has been working nearly every day.
3. We cooked a lot of beans in the frying pan.
4. It's too hot to go to the city today.
5. Let's take a leisurely walk to the library.

Regionalisms and Dialect, EXERCISE C
Answers may vary; suggested answers are given.
Hank: Crouch down in these bushes, Dan. That animal will certainly come running back around.
Dan: I hear him making noise behind us.
Hank: Sit for a while. I will redirect him.
Dan: I am sure that he is fooling us.
Hank: That's true. He is very smart.
Dan: He has certainly tired me out.
Hank: You were born tired!

Clichés, Jargon, and Euphemisms, EXERCISE A
Answers will vary; possible revisions are given.
1. jargon, throwing; jargon, very hard-thrown baseball
2. euphemism, sweating; cliche, like a hot dog on a grill
3. cliche, relaxed as a cat sunbathing on a windowsill
4. cliche, before the sun cleared the outfield wall
5. jargon, completely missed; jargon, hard-thrown baseball
6. euphemism, ornery; euphemism, fat
7. euphemism, died; jargon, fly ball that goes over the outfield fence
8. jargon, a hit ball that flies almost horizontal to the ground; jargon, third base
9. cliche, In spite of hitting the ball really well; jargon, caught it
10. jargon, base; jargon, two outs on one play
11. cliche, last poor play that I will watch; cliche, to watch the final play

Cliches, Jargon, and Euphemisms, EXERCISE B
Revisions will vary; possible revisions are given.
   "I won't <u>arrest</u> you because you forgot to <u>buckle your seat belt</u>," the police officer said. "However, if I catch you again in this truck <u>that has traction in all four wheels</u>, and you're not wearing your seat belt, I'll give you a ticket."
   "<u>There's no misunderstanding your warning</u>, Officer," the <u>stout man</u> replied, knowing he'd <u>narrowly avoided</u> getting a ticket. "From now on, I'm <u>obeying the law</u>," he said with a <u>beautiful smile</u>.
   A half-hour later, the same driver had a <u>minor traffic accident</u> when the car in front stopped suddenly due to a <u>narrowing of the traffic lanes, which forced the cars into fewer lanes</u>. The driver wasn't injured, but his truck was damaged and had a <u>punctured tire</u>. <u>Peculiarly</u>, his truck, which <u>had a standard transmission</u>, wouldn't move.
   As he waited for assistance, he had <u>time</u> to think about the events. He was <u>not smart</u>, but <u>he understood</u> that the officer's <u>well-timed warning</u> might have prevented him from having an <u>injury</u> in this <u>auto accident</u>. He <u>appreciated his good fortune</u>.

Foreign Words and Phrases in English, EXERCISE A
1. e
2. j
3. a
4. i
5. h
6. b
7. f
8. d
9. g
10. c

Foreign Words and Phrases in English, EXERCISE A
1. Ambassador Rios is straightforward, fair, and polite; she's a *persona grata* everywhere.
2. You don't have to *schlep* that package home; we can deliver it.
3. The purchase is a *fait accompli*.
4. Jaymes does everything with *panache*.
5. Li Chang has *carte blanche* to decide how to spend the money.
6. The two sisters quarreled *ad nauseam*.
7. The last serve was overpowering, a fitting *coup de grace* to the match.
8. While exploring Yellowstone National Park, the trail guide was Aimee's *vade mecum*.
9. Speaking out against injustice was the senator's *raison d'etre*.
10. The council set up an *ad hoc* committee to investigate ways to finance the expansion.

Tone and Mood

Choosing an Appropriate Tone, EXERCISE A
Answers may vary; possible answers are given.
1. a, d
2. b, c
3. b, c
4. b, c
5. a, d

Choosing an Appropriate Tone, EXERCISE B
Answers will vary; possible answers are given.
1. I think Disney World is marvelous.
2. It would be lovely to see it again.
3. Do you enjoy Fantasy World?
4. Central Florida has its good points.
5. However, the climate is hot and humid.

Choosing an Appropriate Tone, EXERCISE C
Answers will vary.
   Number 1 may be close to the orginal tone; number 2 should be more formal and more sophisticated.

Creating Mood (Atmosphere) in Writing, EXERCISE A
Answers will vary; possible answers are given.
1. The convict <u>shuffled</u> out of his cell, <u>brandishing a weapon</u> at the <u>armed guards</u> around him.
2. The convict <u>strolled</u> out of his cell, <u>waving</u> at the <u>reporters</u> around him.
3. The convict <u>blasted</u> out of his cell, <u>sneering</u> at the <u>photographers</u> around him.
4. The convict <u>walked</u> out of his cell, <u>staring</u> at the <u>people</u> around him.
5. The convict <u>crawled</u> out of his cell, <u>smirking</u> at the <u>bodies</u> around him.

Creating Mood (Atmosphere) in Writing, EXERCISE B
Answers will vary; possible answers are given.
1. With her glowing eyes, the elderly woman smiled at Clara.
2. Clara bolted down the hillside, terrifying the sheep.
3. Outside the cramped hut, a gale began to howl.
4. Clara cowered dumbly beside the crone's footstool.
5. With a soft purr, the black cat sidled up to Clara.

Creating Mood (Atmosphere) in Writing, EXERCISE C
Answers will vary; possible answers are given.

As I left the <u>frigid</u> park, I noticed a <u>tattered</u> child standing by the wall and <u>weeping</u>. A <u>chill</u> went through me as I heard her <u>heartbroken</u> voice. I tried to catch her eye, but she <u>turned</u> away <u>sobbing</u>. What a <u>disturbing</u> incident! It reminded me of my <u>years</u> in the <u>orphanage</u>.

As I left the <u>sunny</u> park, I noticed a <u>small</u> child standing by the wall and <u>singing</u>. A <u>thrill</u> went through me as I heard her <u>angelic</u> voice. I tried to catch her eye, but she <u>ran</u> away <u>laughing</u>. What a <u>delightful</u> incident! It reminded me of my <u>childhood</u> in the <u>country</u>.

Voice and Style

Developing a Personal Voice, Exercise A
Statements will vary; most likely matches are given.
1. grandmother
2. child
3. rap star
4. lawyer
5. preacher

Developing a Personal Voice, Exercise B
Answers will vary; possible answers are given.
1. Horatio is a one-of-a kind character.
2. I'd guess that he's the most unusual guy I know.
3. Horatio's voice can stretch across five octaves.
4. He knows all about opera.
5. His super tenor voice reminds people of Caruso's.

Developing a Personal Voice, EXERCISE C
Answers will vary.

Choosing an Appropriate Style, EXERCISE A
1. sarcastic
2. succinct
3. ornate

Choosing an Appropriate Style, EXERCISE B
Answers will vary; possible answers are given.
1. Your father is kind of fascinating, which is surprising, since he is related to you.
2. I think he must be very smart.
3. Can he truly be wasting his talents on a horde of undergraduates?
4. I'd love to sit in on a lecture.

Choosing an Appropriate Style, EXERCISE C
Paragraphs will vary; possible audiences are given.
1. a cookbook reader
2. a newspaper editor
3. a school newspaper audience
4. a relative
5. a guidance counselor

Figurative Language
Simile, EXERCISE A
1. like a volcano; father—volcano
2. quiet as a mouse; child—mouse
3. catlike grace; dancer—cat
4. like a cow; Drew—cow
5. as smooth as silk; skin—silk
6. as red as a tomato; Josh—tomato
7. like a burst of sunshine; April—sunshine
8. Like ribbons of color; fireworks—ribbons
9. like a bird; Jesse—bird
10. as shrill as a whistle; cry—whistle
11. as grumpy as a bear; sister—bear
12. like dancers; raindrops—dancers
13. white as a ghost; Mrs. Scott—ghost
14. like a bullet; baseball—bullet
15. childlike glee; grandmother—child
16. foxlike cunning; I—fox
17. as thin as a rail; Meg—rail
18. as white as snow; hair—snow
19. as hard as a rock; bread—rock
20. as blue as the ocean; eyes—ocean

Simile, EXERCISE B
Answers will vary; possible answers are given.
 1. Liam squealed <u>like a pig</u> as his swing flew into the sky.
 2. Jack accelerated <u>like a racecar</u> around the oval track.
 3. The waves pounded the shore <u>like a mallet</u>.
 4. Suddenly, the power went out and the room became <u>as black as pitch</u>.
 5. The ripe peach tasted <u>as sweet as honey</u>.
 6. Heat from the fire wrapped around me <u>like a blanket</u>.
 7. His tender words caused my emotions to flow <u>like a river</u>.
 8. The car stopped <u>as if having a heart attack</u> on the interstate.
 9. The wind howled, <u>phantomlike</u>, through the forest.
10. I feel <u>as proud as a peacock</u> that my work is correct!

Metaphor, EXERCISE A
Sentences will vary; possible answers are given.
 1. telegraphic Morse Code; The drum beat out, in <u>telegraphic Morse Code</u>, a rhythmic message for the eager dancers.
 2. Ice daggers, ice spears; <u>Ice daggers</u> and <u>ice spears</u> on the window frame protected our family from the raging storm.
 3. tomato lava flow; A <u>tomato sauce lava flow</u> tumbled down the sides of the pasta.
 4. The sonic boom; The <u>sonic boom</u> of the detonation marked the end of the landmark movie theater.

Metaphor, EXERCISE B
Answers will vary; possible answers are given.
 1. <u>A bloodhound on the hunt</u>, Inspector Reilly narrowed his search to three vacated buildings on the Lower East Side.
 2. Little Jimmy, <u>every bit the condor chick peeking out of a precipitous nest</u>, watched the happenings below through the upstairs railing.
 3. The tiny candle flickering in the window was <u>his lighthouse beacon</u>.
 4. Drusilla's dark eyes were <u>shimmering pools of mystery and intrigue</u>.
 5. His legs became <u>two rubber bands</u>, collapsing beneath him and leaving him helpless.

Metaphor, EXERCISE C
Answers will vary; possible answers are given.
 1. The sky was blackened with <u>a storm cloud of geese</u>.
 2. A <u>blitzkrieg response</u> followed the team's offensive play.
 3. <u>With the leap of a mountain lion</u>, the fugitive landed on the roof next door.
 4. <u>An industrious beaver</u>, Stella attacked the project.
 5. Her smile was <u>a burst of sunlight</u> that warmed his timid heart.

Personification, EXERCISE A
 1. Victory
 2. vehicles
 3. turn
 4. wall
 5. luck

Personification, EXERCISE B

Answers will vary; possible answers are given.

 1. Memory
 2. pines
 3. Anxiety
 4. plate
 5. Misery
 6. Love
 7. mirror
 8. guilt
 9. floor
10. conscience

Personification, EXERCISE C

Answers will vary; possible answers are given.

 1. <u>The train sighed mournfully</u> as it crossed the ravine.
 2. <u>Greed put its foot down</u> as I tried to seem gracious.
 3. <u>The ice</u> glittered, <u>laughing</u> at my fall.
 4. Seeing his good fortune, <u>envy pinched me hard</u>.
 5. <u>Silence enfolded</u> us in her dark cloak.
 6. <u>The flowers nodded gracefully</u> in the spring sunshine.
 7. <u>The highway stretched its arms</u> in both directions.
 8. <u>Love pierced her heart with his arrow</u>.
 9. <u>Grumpily, the clock reminded me</u> to hurry.
10. Unbeknownst to us, <u>our joy had not long to live</u>.

Symbol, EXERCISE A

 1. b
 2. a
 3. d
 4. e
 5. c
 6. g
 7. h
 8. f
 9. j
10. i

Symbol, EXERCISE B

Sentences will vary; possible sentences are given.

 1. pot of gold—financial success; Every business leader hopes to find that pot of gold.
 2. rotten apple—spoiler; There is a rotten apple in every family.
 3. mighty oak—age and strength; In our household, Grandpa is the mighty oak; the rest of us, mere acorns.
 4. fish in the sea—possibilities; When it comes to looking for a mate, remember that there are plenty of fish in the sea.
 5. rose—lovely but prickly; She is a beautiful but thorny rose.
 6. black cat—bad luck; A black cat seems to be perched on my shoulder.
 7. ferryboat captain—Death, personified; The ferryboat captain will lead us across to Jordan.
 8. spears—war; Break the spears and welcome peace.
 9. cross—burden; My guilt is a hard cross to bear.
10. rainbow—good fortune; The appearance of the rainbow after the storm seemed to say that our luck would change.

Hyperbole, EXERCISE A

Answers will vary; possible answers are given.
 1. Nam waited a long time for Kenny.
 2. I'm extremely angry.
 3. Very tall waves crashed against the rocks.
 4. He isn't very intelligent.
 5. If I study one more minute, I'm going to get a terrible headache.
 6. She could hardly sit still in anticipation of his arrival.
 7. He was very sad when he read her letter.
 8. When the jury announced its verdict, an argument broke out in the courtroom.
 9. The assassin stood there gloating, seeming to radiate evil.
10. The thought of meeting his old enemy again made him very angry.

Hyperbole, EXERCISE B

Answers will vary; possible answers are given.
 1. Seeing my old friend again, my heart popped out of my chest.
 2. Duane was so fast, we saw only a blur as he raced by.
 3. Anita's so wise, owls come to her for advice.
 4. I was so tired, I was asleep on my feet.
 5. That suggestion was so brilliant that it left a trail of light.

Hyperbole, EXERCISE C

Answers will vary; possible answers are given.
 1. My feet screamed for a bit of relief.
 2. A waterfall is thundering from the clouds.
 3. Hearing the chilling moan, his blood turned to ice.
 4. The room was a sardine can of well-wishers.
 5. I could eat about six pizzas right now.
 6. Pat and Dana went to war over plans for the camping trip.
 7. I don't want to say that we waited a long time—but by the time the doctor finally saw us, our clothes were out of fashion.
 8. I could lift the world on my shoulders this morning!
 9. That algebra test drained the last few brain cells from my head.
10. Did a bomb go off in this room, or what?

Problem Solver

Run-on Sentences

Run-on Sentences

EXERCISE A: Correct each run-on sentence. If a sentence needs no changes, write *Correct*.

> **Example:** Their favorite band was in town, they wanted to see the show.
> **Answer:**   Their favorite band was in town, and they wanted to see the show.

1. The show starts at eight o'clock we don't want to be late.
2. I have money for tickets, I just hope they're still available.
3. We can get to the theater by train or bus, my friend's father has offered to drive us.
4. Chuck, Linda, and Kerry all want to go but may not be able to afford tickets.
5. Almost everyone at school likes this band, some of my friends think that it is too loud.
6. Do you like soft rock, do you think hard rock is more interesting?
7. I liked their first album; the new CD is boring.
8. Go to the concert, but be home before midnight!
9. Everyone enjoyed the performance, we're very glad we were able to go.
10. That was a wonderful concert, did you like it as much as I did?

EXERCISE B: Rewrite the paragraph, correcting all run-on sentences.

> **Example:** We are studying ancient history I find the subject very interesting.
> **Answer:**   We are studying ancient history, and I find the subject very interesting.

Assyria was a powerful nation in Mesopotamia it was located in the northern part of present-day Iraq. The Assyrians were great conquerors they were famous for their superior weapons and military organization. To the south lay the ancient kingdom of Babylonia, the two kingdoms were constantly at war. Assyrian men wore tunics and sandals most men had long hair and beards. Nineveh, Assur, and Kalhu were the largest cities, most farmers lived in small villages, they grew barley and raised livestock. The buildings of Assyria were usually made of unbaked mud bricks, some of the foundations were made of stone, all the buildings had flat roofs. The early Assyrians decorated their buildings with wall paintings, later, they decorated palace walls with intricately carved slabs of stone. Assyria eventually came under the control of the Babylonians, the empire collapsed completely more than 2,500 years ago.

Sentence Fragments

Sentence Fragments That Require Subjects or Verbs

EXERCISE A: Label each item as a *sentence* or a *fragment*.

> **Example:** Can be yours for only pennies a day.
> **Answer:** fragment

1. Available in a wide assortment of sizes and colors.
2. Undoubtedly, the largest and most impressive item in our fall catalog.
3. Order now.
4. Cannot be used in combination with other coupons or special offers.
5. Cartons waiting to be shipped from the warehouse.

EXERCISE B: Rewrite each fragment to make it a complete sentence. If the item already is a complete sentence, write *Correct*.

> **Example:** The largest gorilla in the enclosure.
> **Answer:** fragment The largest gorilla in the enclosure <u>was named Wally</u>.

1. Leaped quickly from limb to limb.
2. Never had seen such odd animals before.
3. The people collecting the tickets.
4. A lengthy visit to the gift shop near the cafeteria.
5. A lion growled.
6. Feeding the seals at three o'clock every afternoon.
7. Two divers in orange scuba gear.
8. Visiting the zoo was a wonderful experience.
9. To see the reptile house?
10. Polar bears, larger than any bears they had ever seen before.

EXERCISE C: Rewrite the paragraph, changing all sentence fragments to complete sentences.

> **Example:** The Essex County Fair, which is the largest in the state.
> **Answer:** <u>We went to</u> the Essex County Fair, which is the largest in the state.

Could hardly wait to go to the fair! Carla, Jimmy, and all the children. Especially excited about seeing the animals. All kinds of baked goods and other wonderful things to eat. To go on all the rides. Slipped in the mud and dropped her cotton candy. Was helped by a tall man in a big straw hat and overalls. A booth that sold nothing but kites. Their mother, who is sometimes afraid of heights. Everyone in the family.

Subordinate Clauses as Sentence Fragments

EXERCISE A: Write *sentence* if the item is a complete sentence or *fragment* if the item is a subordinate clause.

>   **Example:** When you talk to the teacher.
>   **Answer:**   fragment

1. Although I didn't have an appointment.
2. Where the chess club meets every Thursday.
3. If you have a few minutes to spare.
4. Whoever comes will have a good time.
5. Because of the wonderful things he does.
6. Since you first moved to this town.
7. That would be all right.
8. When would you like to begin?
9. What role she might take in the performance?
10. Which he seemed to enjoy very much!

EXERCISE B: Write a complete sentence by expanding each subordinate-clause fragment. If an item is a complete sentence, write *sentence*.

>   **Example:** Until we got to knew them better.
>   **Answer:**   <u>We didn't like the new students</u> until we got to know them better.

1. Although none of us knew why.
2. Where they wanted to go.
3. Because he came from a small town.
4. How was your trip?
5. Wherever the class decides to go.

EXERCISE C: Rewrite the paragraph so that all sentences are complete and the paragraph makes sense. You may use more than one subordinate clause in a sentence.

>   **Example:** How artists get their ideas.
>   **Answer:**   <u>Our class has been discussing</u> how artists get their ideas.

Since we went to the art museum. Because our teacher loves art. Before our visit. When we toured the galleries. While we were in the museum. If a person feels sad. That I really enjoyed. As the main gallery closed. Although I still don't know that much about art. Whenever I think about our trip.

Other Kinds of Sentence Fragments

EXERCISE A: Label each item as a *sentence* or a *fragment*.

   Example: Swimming in the stream behind the wooden cottage.
   Answer: fragment

   1. Looking for his sneakers in the back of the closet.
   2. To find out if Alberto could go to the movies with him on Saturday.
   3. Under the bridge, in a secret hiding place.
   4. To leave early was an excellent idea.
   5. What a beautiful day!

EXERCISE B: Write a complete sentence by expanding each fragment. If an item is a complete sentence, write *Sentence*.

   Example: Realizing her error.
   Answer: Realizing her error, <u>Paige apologized</u>.

   1. Making other plans without even asking their parents.
   2. To consider other possibilities and investigate the alternatives.
   3. How delightful!
   4. To sing was her greatest pleasure.
   5. Beyond the river, where the wildflowers grow.
   6. Running just as fast as she could.
   7. Thinking about all the money that he could earn.
   8. The green jacket with his name stitched on the front in gold.
   9. Before entering, please knock.
  10. In the side drawer of his dresser, underneath the socks.

EXERCISE C: Rewrite the paragraph so that all sentences are complete and the paragraph makes sense. You may use more than one fragment in a sentence.

   Example: Having waited a long time.
   Answer: Having waited a long time<u>, he was glad they were finally going</u>.

   Looked forward to seeing his cousins. How eager! A tiny woman with a very big smile. Running out to greet them. To play with the other children. In the backyard. Eating a large supper in the dining room. Having helped clear the table. A fine instrument that had been in the family for generations. Waving good-by.

Subject-Verb Agreement

Subject-Verb Agreement: Compound Subjects

EXERCISE A: Choose the verb in parentheses that correctly completes each sentence.

> **Example:** Neither Lynn nor Laura (like, likes) to go fishing.
> **Answer:** likes

1. Rehearsals and meetings usually (lasts, last) for an hour.
2. Neither the expert nor the amateurs (climbs, climb) alone.
3. Two cards and a package (has, have) arrived for you.
4. Either a jacket or a sweater (is, are) heavy enough.
5. Corned beef and cabbage (is, are) today's special.

EXERCISE B: Combine each pair of sentences. Make sure that all verbs agree with their compound subjects.

> **Example:** Erin hopes to become an engineer. Edmund hopes to become an engineer.
> **Answer:**   <u>Erin and Edmund hope</u> to become engineers.

1. Math is an important subject for engineering. Physics is an important subject for engineering.
2. Foreign languages don't interest Erin. Geography doesn't interest Erin, either.
3. Is a knowledge of art useful to an engineer? Is a knowledge of history useful to an engineer?
4. This bridge was built by the Army Corps of Engineers. That canal was built by the Army Corps of Engineers.

EXERCISE C: Rewrite the paragraph, correcting any errors in subject-verb agreement.

Planning cargo loads and loading cargo ships requires a great deal of time and labor. Everything from bottles of perfume to television sets are placed into metal boxes called containers. Containers or bulk items, such as wheat, is stored in the ship's hold. Tankers and supertankers transports petroleum and other kinds of liquid cargo. Powdered detergents, wood chips, and fertilizer is piled in the hold of dry bulk carriers.

Subject-Verb Agreement: Special Subjects

EXERCISE A: Write the verb from the choice in parentheses that correctly completes each sentence.

> **Example:** A number of students in our school (ride, rides) the bus.
> **Answer:** ride

1. The number of riders (tends, tend) to increase in winter.
2. Sixty passengers a day (seem, seems) like a lot.
3. "Buses" (is, are) a poem we wrote about our bus.
4. News of the convenience of riding the bus (has, have) been spreading.
5. Behind the school (sits, sit) three buses right now.

EXERCISE B: Write the subject of each sentence. Then write the verb that agrees with it.

> **Example:** Politics (is, are) an interesting topic.
> **Answer:** Politics is

1. A number of my friends (have, has) worked in political campaigns.
2. Volunteers (plays, play) a role in politics.
3. The volunteers' contribution (is, are) hours of phone calls.
4. The number of small jobs (varies, vary) from campaign to campaign.
5. Each of the campaigns (is, are) different.
6. "Guide to Politics" (happen, happens) to be a useful book.
7. The number of people active in politics (seem, seems) to be decreasing.
8. The measles (has, have) some volunteers home in bed.
9. The people (needs, need) to be involved in their government.
10. Better candidates (is, are) the result of citizen action.

EXERCISE C: Rewrite the newspaper article, correcting any errors in subject-verb agreement.

"The Lucky Dreamers" are what the Oranges are being called for establishing a new high in runs scored in a single game. After a number of the Oranges was held hitless through seven innings, the team exploded in the eighth. Thirteen runs was scored before Williams ended the inning on a foul fly. The team hope to repeat its performance in tomorrow's game.

Subject-Verb Agreement: Other Agreement Issues

EXERCISE A: Write the verb that correctly completes each sentence.

> **Example:** A number of these clubs (receives, receive) newsletters.
> **Answer:** receives

1. The guests at the meeting (speaks, speak) to the members.
2. Many a speaker (has, have) spoken about community service.
3. Someone usually (act, acts) as the discussion leader.
4. Each of the club members (have, has) a chance to speak.
5. None of this year's guests (have, has) been boring!
6. There always (is, are) many interesting ideas shared.
7. Which of these topics (interests, interest) you the most?
8. Among my favorites (is, are) community history and ecology.
9. Community service, as well as health care and the environment, (have, has) become popular.
10. There (are, is) a list of ideas being planned for next year.

EXERCISE B: Write the subject of each sentence. Then write the verb that agrees with it.

> **Example:** The spot in the woods (was, were) a good place for a cabin.
> **Answer:** spot was

1. There (is, are) plenty of fresh water in the nearby creek.
2. The rich soil, together with the climate and growing season, (makes, make) farming profitable.
3. Many a settler (was, were) attracted by the offer of land.
4. None of the land (has, have) been given away yet.
5. The promise of plentiful crops (is, are) encouraging.

EXERCISE C: Rewrite the paragraph, correcting any errors in subject-verb agreement.

There is several remarkable things about this dog. The dog, unlike my two cats and the canary, recognize the sound of my voice. On most mornings, she bring me her leash when it's time for a walk. The sound of her howling and barking scare away burglars. My family like having her to guard the house.

Verb Forms

Verbs: Irregular Forms

EXERCISE A: Write the verb that correctly completes each sentence.

> **Example:** The wind (blowed, blew) down trees in our neighborhood.
> **Answer:**   blew

1. A large oak tree (fell, falled) across our driveway.
2. We (feeled, felt) it hit the ground.
3. The ground (shook, shaked) when the old oak came down.
4. We (seed, saw) other trees fall, too.
5. I never (knew, knowed) how big that tree was!
6. The top part of the tree (broke, breaked) in pieces.
7. Parts of that tree really (teared, tore) up my mom's garden.
8. We (payed, paid) some workers to saw the trunk into pieces.
9. They (leaved, left) us plenty of wood for our fireplace.
10. It was a shame that we (losed, lost) that old tree.

EXERCISE B: Rewrite each sentence, supplying the past or past participle of the verb given.

> **Example:** lend   Karen had _____ me a book of poems by Walt Whitman.
> **Answer:**   Karen had <u>lent</u> me a book of poems by Walt Whitman.

1. write   Whitman _____ about democracy and the United States.
2. grow   He _____ up in Brooklyn, New York, in the early part of the nineteenth century.
3. teach   He _____ school and worked as a journalist, too.
4. seek   Whitman _____ to reflect the mood of the growing nation.
5. weave   Whitman _____ some poems around Civil War themes.

EXERCISE C: Write two sentences for each verb—once for the past form, and once for the past participle.

> **Example:** wear
> **Answer:**   The kids <u>wore</u> their jackets on the playground.
>   I have <u>worn</u> these socks to shreds.

1. drive
2. give
3. speak
4. throw
5. sink

Verbs: Past and Past Participle Forms

EXERCISE A: Write the verb that correctly completes each sentence.

   Example: Have you (spoke, spoken) to Mr. Phelps about the assignment?
   Answer: spoken

1. Wayne has already (gave, given) me the information.
2. I (went, gone) back to Mr. Langston's office, but he had already (went, gone) out.
3. He had (leaved, left) tools, photos, and the map from Peter.
4. We finally found where the tools were (hid, hidden).

EXERCISE B: Write the correct past or past participle form of each verb in parentheses. Label each form correctly.

   Example: Michelle has (ride) in many bicycle races.
   Answer: ridden (past participle)

1. Last spring she (take) second place in an all-city race.
2. She has (wear) her lucky racing hat in every race.
3. She has never (fell) off her bike during a race.
4. Once, when her chain (break), she couldn't complete the race.
5. Another time, her front tire (blow) after the first mile.
6. In one race, Michelle (lead) from start to finish.
7. Through it all, Michelle never (lose) her enthusiasm for cycling.
8. We (see) her set the school cycling record last spring.
9. She really (fly) around that track!
10. Her racing skills have (bring) her fame to our school.

EXERCISE C: Write the past and the past participle of each verb. Then use each form in a sentence.

   Example: draw
   Answer: I <u>draw</u> a seascape for my art project.
            Everyone in my class <u>has drawn</u> something special and personal.

1. steal
2. freeze
3. fly
4. ride
5. burst

Verbs: Problems With Tenses

EXERCISE A: Write the verb that correctly completes each sentence.

    Example: During the night we (were watching, watched) for signs of bad weather.
    Answer: watched

  1. Since we (had begun, began) this vacation, we have had fun.
  2. We (had closed, have closed) the tent windows before the storm started.
  3. During the night the wind howled and the rain (beat, was beating) against the tent.
  4. After we (dried, had dried) our clothes, we started breakfast.
  5. We went for a hike after we (had finished, finished) eating.

EXERCISE B: Rewrite each sentence, using the correct tense of the verb in parentheses.

    Example: After we (decide) to bake the cookies, we went to the store.
    Answer: After we <u>had decided</u> to bake the cookies, we went to the store.

  1. Since we (chose) to make Chelsea's favorite, we (buy) chocolate chips.
  2. By the time we (return) home, we (tear) into those chips!
  3. While the cookies (bake), we (drink) milk
  4. We (sit) in Chelsea's kitchen and (wait) patiently.
  5. As soon as we (taste) those cookies, we agreed that they were the best that we ever (eat).

EXERCISE C: Complete each sentence. Be sure to use verb tenses correctly.

    Example: After we took our seats.
    Answer: After we took our seats, <u>the play began</u>.

  1. While we waited for the play to begin, _____.
  2. Before _____, the stage manager checked the lights.
  3. By the time the show started, _____.
  4. As the actress spoke, _____.
  5. After _____, we applauded loudly.

Pronoun Problems

Pronouns: Awkward or Indefinite Antecedents

EXERCISE A: Write the choice in parentheses that correctly completes each sentence.

> **Example:** None of the boys passed (their, his) driving test.
> **Answer:** his

1. After the test, (the examiners, they) tell you your score.
2. Each parent was invited to express (his, his or her) opinion.
3. (They, Experts) predict that the flu will be bad this winter.
4. From where I live, (you, one) can see the hospital.

EXERCISE B: Rewrite the sentences, corecting any errors in pronoun usage. If a sentence needs no changes, write *Correct.*

> **Example:** Remove the sandwich from the bag and throw it away.
> **Answer:** Remove the sandwich from the bag and throw <u>the bag</u> away.

1. The movie was amusing, but they could have made it shorter.
2. Neither of the women shared their view with the committee.
3. Remove the stamps from the envelopes and give them to me.
4. To train for the marathon, you must run every day.
5. All three of those boys have finished their assignments.
6. Her mother told Hillary the news as soon as she entered the room.
7. On the news it mentioned that unemployment rates are down.
8. Mother read to Mark until he fell asleep.
9. You must speak Spanish to be considered for that job.
10. When Ms. Gonzalez and Mr. Johnson arrive, ask them to come to my office.
11. At our assembly they lectured on fire safety.
12. In this book it suggests that the assassination was part of a conspiracy.
13. Please take the towel from the dryer and fold it.
14. In those days, you had to work hard in order to survive.
15. If anyone is unable to attend, he or she should bring a note from home.
16. Not a single one of us was willing to offer their support to the candidate.
17. Amanda told Janet that she had to leave by 10 P.M.
18. To prepare for the exam, one should study all three chapters in the textbook.
19. Before arriving at the polling place, you should have made your choices.
20. One of those girls can't find their ticket.

Pronouns: Other Pronoun Problems

EXERCISE A: Write the choice in parentheses that correctly completes each sentence.

> **Example:** I like the community center, but (I, you) don't always feel like going.
> **Answer:** I

1. When (you, they) enter the tunnel, drivers should turn on the car's headlights.
2. Roger likes New Year's Eve because (he, you) can stay up past midnight.
3. Please clean your room, (a task that, which) will take about an hour.
4. Alicia worked in the boutique and enjoyed (the job, it) very much.
5. When someone works hard, (they, he or she) should be rewarded for the effort.
6. If your girlfriend doesn't study, (you're, she's) not going to pass the test.
7. They didn't like the movie at first, but (you, they) started to enjoy it before too long.
8. His best friend was ill, (which, a fact that) troubled him deeply.
9. The webbed feet of a duck helps (it, them) to swim.
10. We liked the part of the play where (we, you) were allowed to talk back to the actors.

EXERCISE B: Rewrite the sentences, correcting any errors in pronoun agreement. If a sentence needs no changes, write *Correct*.

> **Example:** The typical student thinks that they get too much homework.
> **Answer:** The typical student thinks that <u>he or she</u> gets too much homework.

1. Chip likes gym class because you get to play basketball.
2. This book is full of long words, which makes it difficult to read.
3. One of my neighbors tripped and broke their ankle.
4. If a person wants to succeed, you have to be willing to work hard.
5. I like the kind of movie that leaves you smiling at the end.
6. Alice announced that she would not run for class president, which came as a big surprise.
7. We didn't like the new teacher at first, but you started to appreciate her after a while.
8. Even the tiniest holes in a pipe can cause it to leak.
9. The friends worked hard on their project, but the judges didn't choose them for first prize.
10. Your plan to get rich quick was unsuccessful, which I expected from the start.

Problems with Modifiers

Misplaced Modifiers

EXERCISE A: Write each misplaced modifier. If a sentence contains no misplaced modifiers, write *Correct.*

> **Example:** Dogs once were far more important to humans, regarded now merely as pets.
> **Answer:** regarded now merely as pets

1. Dogs were domesticated by humans descended from wolves and jackals.
2. Wild dogs, scavenging food, may have frequented the camps of hunters.
3. With the dogs' help, humans discovered that they could hunt more effectively.
4. As they became domesticated, dogs developed traits not shared with wild canines.
5. Dogs learned to bark, unlike wolves, to alert humans to danger.

EXERCISE B: Rewrite the sentences, correcting any misplaced modifiers.

> **Example:** The book was a masterpiece of boredom that we read.
> **Answer:** The book <u>that we read was a masterpiece of boredom</u>.

1. The girl disappeared into the crowd with the odd hairstyle.
2. Topped with cream sauce, the child eagerly ate the cake.
3. Moaning in pain from her twisted ankle, the nurse comforted Piper.
4. The boy dropped into the river swinging from a rope.
5. Confused by our complex schedule, I tried to help the student.
6. The squirrel sat unmoving on the branch, alerted by some noise.
7. The reasons can be clearly stated for this decision.
8. The actor stared blankly at the audience, paralyzed by stage fright.
9. The data should always be rechecked that confirm a theory.
10. Her arms piled high with books on the steps, Kiri tripped.

EXERCISE C: Rewrite the paragraph, correcting misplaced modifiers.

> **Example:** Leroi showed Helen the comic strip roaring with laughter.
> **Answer:** <u>Roaring with laughter</u>, Leroi showed Helen the comic strip.

Two New York newspapers introduced modern comic strips, competing for readers. Comics had been around for a long time, appearing as a single frame. The *New York Herald* began publishing a comic "strip" in 1894 to gain readers. An immediate hit, the *Herald* gained an advantage because of its comic strip. The competing *Morning Journal* responded with a comic supplement in 1896, trying to regain readers. Both newspapers discovered that readers enjoyed the "funnies" at the same time.

Dangling Modifiers

EXERCISE A: Write each dangling modifer. If a sentence contains no dangling modifiers, write *Correct.*

> **Example:** Circling the sun like a planet, scientists are studying the asteroid Eros.
> **Answer:** Circling the sun like a planet

1. Excited by the prospects, a space probe is heading to the asteroid Eros.
2. Having reached Eros, the craft will go into orbit around the asteroid.
3. The probe, called NEAR, will be in orbit for a year.
4. Orbiting fifteen miles above Eros, scientists will get a close look.
5. Slated for a 1996 launch, it will take NEAR three years to get to Eros.

EXERCISE B: Rewrite the sentences, correcting any dangling modifiers.

> **Example:** Recently purchased by investors, twenty houses would be built.
> **Answer:** <u>Twenty houses would be built on the land</u> recently purchased by investors.

1. Wandering through the old city, many sights were fascinating.
2. Questioned by experts, the truth came out.
3. With a great deal of patience, origami can be learned.
4. Fatigued by all the exercise, the comfortable chair felt wonderful.
5. Bundled up in heavy coats and scarves, the wind had no effect.
6. Wandering through the museum, every exhibit deserved attention.
7. Summoning her last reserve of strength, the final yards were run.
8. Surrounded by enemies on all sides, there seemed no hope of escape.
9. Crashing through the underbrush, the ducks screamed and took flight.
10. Believing in the accuracy of the report, the decision was made.

EXERCISE C: Rewrite the paragraph, correcting dangling modifiers.

> **Example:** Looking about, the Old West seemed to come alive.
> **Answer:** Looking about them, <u>Dawn and Jasmine could see the Old West come alive</u>.

   Walking down the deserted streets of the ghost town, the buildings invited Teresa and Carol to explore. As they walked through the buildings, a thick layer of dust covered everything. Looking about them, many objects lay where they had last been used. Even plates and silverware lay in place settings on the hotel tables, leaving everything as it was. Perhaps the townspeople had intended to come back, but for some reason, could not. Getting up from dinner, the town had simply closed down.

Problems with Possessives

Using Possessive Forms Correctly

EXERCISE A: Write the word in parentheses that correctly completes each sentence.

> **Example:** Is that the boy (who's, whose) sister is getting married?
> **Answer:** whose

1. I was looking at the pictures of (your, you're) cousin's wedding.
2. (John and Alan's, John's and Alan's) father took the photographs.
3. I saw your invitation, but I didn't see (their's, theirs).
4. Your dress is missing one of (its, it's) buttons.
5. Are we spending Sunday afternoon at the (Jones's, Joneses')?

EXERCISE B: Rewrite each sentence, correcting any errors in the use of the possessive form. If a sentence needs no changes, write *Correct*.

> **Example:** The brilliance of his' ideas surprised us.
> **Answer:** The brilliance of <u>his</u> ideas surprised us.

1. They're having a party at there house tomorrow night.
2. Are those books her's or are they yours?
3. Gus and Maria's reports are both due on Friday.
4. Edward and Lois's baby is adorable!
5. There's no way those sneakers could be their's!
6. It's time to take your dog to the vet for its shots.
7. We need to borrow their notes, for we seem to have misplaced our's.
8. Who's responsible for deciding who's drawings will be included?
9. Our class' project won first prize in their annual competition.
10. These three book's plots are very similar, but their themes are quite different.

EXERCISE C: Write ten sentences, using the possessive forms of the items below.

> **Example:** boss
> **Answer:** boss's They waited for the <u>boss's</u> instructions.

1. you
2. Charles
3. it
4. somebody
5. they
6. he
7. girl
8. brothers-in-law
9. mothers
10. who

Missing Commas

Missing Commas

EXERCISE A: Rewrite each sentence, adding any missing commas. If a sentence needs no commas, write *Correct*.

   Example: Tia took rolls of pennies nickels and dimes to the bank.
   Answer: Tia took rolls of pennies, nickels, and dimes to the bank.

1. We like butter maple syrup and powdered sugar on our pancakes.
2. We enjoyed a long relaxing vacation at the seaside resort.
3. Would you like some fresh green peppers from our garden?
4. Thomas Jefferson James Madison and James Monroe were all Virginians.
5. My sister a senior in college would like to get married buy a house and join a law firm.

EXERCISE B: Rewrite the paragraph, adding commas as needed.

   Example: They had fun hiking swimming and taking photographs.
   Answer: They had fun hiking, swimming, and taking photographs.

   My father my uncle and Steve my brother-in-law, went on a camping trip last week. Uncle Dan is a tall skinny man with bright red hair. His favorite activities are sailing fishing and playing golf. When the warm summer breezes start to blow he likes to stop whatever he's doing call up a couple of friends and set off on an adventure. My father is usually a quiet, stay-at-home person, but he occasionally joins Uncle Dan on his trips into the great outdoors. Steve—a young energetic teacher—is always eager to throw some clothes into his duffel bag load his camper and head for the woods. Next year, I hope to join them on their annual summer outing.

EXERCISE C: Write a sentence using each group of words below. Add commas where needed.

   Example: chickens rabbits and pigs
   Answer: They enjoyed feeding the chickens, the rabbits, and the pigs at the farm.

1. bluejays robins and sparrows
2. tall thin dark-haired
3. who will pick up a book and read whenever she can
4. boiling hot
5. cow chicken and stables

Answer Key

Problem Solver

Run-on Sentences

Run-on Sentences, EXERCISE A
Answers may vary; possible answers are given. Corrections are underlined.
1. The show starts at eight o'clock, and we don't want to be late.
2. I have money for tickets. I just hope they're still available.
3. We can get to the theater by train or bus, but my friend's father has offered to drive us.
4. Correct
5. Almost everyone at school likes this band, but some of my friends think that it is too loud.
6. Do you like soft rock, or do you think hard rock is more interesting?
7. Correct
8. Correct
9. Everyone enjoyed the performance; we're very glad we were able to go.
10. That was a wonderful concert. Did you like it as much as I did?

Run-on Sentences, EXERCISE B
Answers may vary; possible answers are given. Corrections are underlined.

Assyria was a powerful nation in Mesopotamia. It was located in the northern part of present-day Iraq. The Assyrians were great conquerors, and they were famous for their superior weapons and military organization. To the south lay the ancient kingdom of Babylonia; the two kingdoms were constantly at war. Assyrian men wore tunics and sandals, and most men had long hair and beards. Nineveh, Assur, and Kalhu were the largest cities, but most farmers lived in small villages; there, they grew barley and raised livestock. The buildings of Assyria were usually made of unbaked mud bricks, but some of the foundations were made of stone. All the buildings had flat roofs. The early Assyrians decorated their buildings with wall paintings. Later, they decorated palace walls with intricately carved slabs of stone. Assyria eventually came under the control of the Babylonians, and the empire collapsed completely more than 2,500 years ago.

Sentence Fragments

Sentence Fragments That Require Subjects or Verbs, EXERCISE A
1. fragment
2. fragment
3. sentence
4. fragment
5. fragment

Sentence Fragments That Require Subjects or Verbs, EXERCISE B
Answers will vary; possible answers are given.
1. <u>The tiny creatures</u> leaped quickly from limb to limb.
2. <u>The children</u> never had seen such odd animals before.
3. The people collecting the tickets <u>were very helpful</u>.
4. <u>They paid</u> a lengthy visit to the gift shop near the cafeteria.
5. Correct
6. Feeding the seals at three o'clock every afternoon <u>is a big responsibility</u>.
7. Two divers in orange scuba gear <u>jumped into the tank</u>.
8. Correct
9. <u>Did you have time</u> to see the reptile house?
10. Polar bears, larger than any bears they had ever seen before, <u>were the main attraction</u>.

Sentence Fragments That Require Subjects or Verbs, EXERCISE C
Answers will vary; possible answers are given.

  <u>The family</u> could hardly wait to go to the fair! Carla, Jimmy, and all the children <u>talked about nothing else for weeks</u>. <u>Jimmy felt</u> especially excited about seeing the animals. All kinds of baked goods and other wonderful things to eat <u>were available at the fairgrounds</u>. To go on all the rides <u>was the children's desire</u>. <u>Poor Carla</u> slipped in the mud and dropped her cotton candy. <u>She</u> was helped by a tall man in a big straw hat and overalls. <u>The children were delighted to find</u> a booth that sold nothing but kites. Their mother, who is sometimes afraid of heights, <u>even went on the Ferris wheel</u>. Everyone in the family <u>agreed to return next year for sure!</u>

Subordinate Clauses as Sentence Fragments, EXERCISE A
1. fragment
2. fragment
3. fragment
4. sentence
5. fragment
6. fragment
7. sentence
8. sentence
9. fragment
10. fragment

Subordinate Clauses as Sentence Fragments, EXERCISE B
Answers will vary; possible answers are given.
1. We were fascinated by her story, <u>although none of us knew why</u>.
2. I asked them <u>where they wanted to go</u>.
3. <u>Because he came from a small town</u>, he had never seen tall buildings before.
4. Complete Sentence
5. Our teacher agreed to take us <u>wherever the class decides to go</u>.

Subordinate Clauses as Sentence Fragments, EXERCISE C
Answers will vary; possible answers are given.

  Since we went to the art museum, <u>I have a better understanding of the creative process</u>. Because our teacher loves art, <u>he took us on the field trip</u>. Before our visit, <u>I never thought much about art</u>. When we toured the galleries, <u>I was amazed</u>. <u>I felt very happy</u> while we were in the museum. If a person feels sad, <u>looking at great art can help</u>. <u>I saw many things</u> that I really enjoyed. As the main gallery closed, <u>the guards suggested a return trip</u>. Although I still don't know that much about art, <u>I am interested in learning more</u>. Whenever I think about our trip, <u>I feel like going back again</u>.

Other Kinds of Sentence Fragments, EXERCISE A
1. fragment
2. fragment
3. fragment
4. sentence
5. fragment

Other Kinds of Sentence Fragments, EXERCISE B
Answers will vary; possible answers are given.
1. Making other plans without even asking their parents <u>was a bad idea</u>.
2. <u>They agreed</u> to consider other possibilities and investigate the alternatives.
3. How delightful <u>the weather is today</u>!
4. Sentence
5. <u>They journeyed</u> beyond the river, where the wildflowers grow.
6. Running just as fast as she could, <u>she felt her heart pounding in her chest</u>.
7. Thinking about all the money that he could earn <u>was exhilarating</u>.
8. <u>He lost</u> the green jacket with his name stitched on the front in gold.
9. Sentence
10. In the side drawer of his dresser, underneath the socks, <u>lay the key</u>.

Other Kinds of Sentence Fragments, EXERCISE C
Answers will vary; possible answers are given.

    <u>Luis looked</u> forward to seeing his cousins. How eager <u>he was to tell them about all the new friends he had made</u>! <u>His aunt</u> a tiny woman with a very big smile <u>came running to greet him</u>. <u>The little ones couldn't wait</u> to play with the other children in the backyard. Eating a large supper in the dining room, <u>everyone seemed to be talking at once</u>. Having helped clear the table, <u>Luis joined the others in the parlor. His uncle played his violin</u>, a fine instrument that had been in the family for generations. <u>Later</u>, waving good-by, <u>Luis and his family reluctantly headed home</u>.

Subject-Verb Agreement

Subject-Verb Agreement: Compound Subjects, EXERCISE A
1. last
2. climb
3. have
4. is
5. is

Subject-Verb Agreement: Compound Subjects, EXERCISE B
Answers will vary slightly; possible answers are given.
1. <u>Math and physics are</u> important subjects for engineering.
2. <u>Neither foreign languages nor geography interests</u> Erin.
3. <u>Is</u> a knowledge of <u>art or history useful</u> to an engineer?
4. <u>This bridge and that canal were built</u> by the Army Corps of Engineers.

Subject-Verb Agreement: Compound Subjects, EXERCISE C
    Planning cargo loads and loading cargo ships <u>require</u> a great deal of time and labor. Everything from bottles of perfume to television sets <u>is</u> placed into metal boxes called containers. Containers or bulk items, such as wheat, <u>are</u> stored in the ship's hold. Tankers and supertankers <u>transport</u> petroleum and other kinds of liquid cargo. Powdered detergents, wood chips, and fertilizer <u>are</u> piled in the hold of dry bulk carriers.

Subject-Verb Agreement: Special Subjects, EXERCISE A
1. tends
2. seems
3. is
4. has
5. sit

Subject-Verb Agreement: Special Subjects, EXERCISE B
1. number have
2. Volunteers play
3. contribution is
4. number varies
5. Each is
6. "Guide to Politics" happens
7. number seems
8. measles has
9. people need
10. candidates are

Subject-Verb Agreement: Special Subjects, EXERCISE C
"The Lucky Dreamers" <u>is</u> what the Oranges are being called for establishing a new high in runs scored in a single game. After a number of the Oranges <u>were</u> held hitless through seven innings, the team exploded in the eighth. Thirteen runs <u>were</u> scored before Williams ended the inning on a foul fly. The team <u>hopes</u> to repeat its performance in tomorrow's game.

Subject-Verb Agreement: Other Agreement Problems, EXERCISE A
1. speak
2. has
3. acts
4. has
5. have
6. are
7. interests
8. are
9. has
10. is

Subject-Verb Agreement: Other Agreement Problems, EXERCISE B
1. plenty is
2. soil makes
3. settler was
4. None has
5. promise is

Subject-Verb Agreement: Other Agreement Problems, EXERCISE C
There <u>are</u> several remarkable things about this dog. The dog, unlike my two cats and the canary, <u>recognizes</u> the sound of my voice. On most mornings, she <u>brings</u> me her leash when it's time for a walk. The sound of her howling and barking <u>scares</u> away burglars. My family <u>likes</u> having her to <u>guard the</u> house.

Verb Forms

Verbs: Irregular Forms, EXERCISE A

1. fell
2. felt
3. shook
4. saw
5. knew
6. broke
7. tore
8. paid
9. left
10. lost

Verbs: Irregular Forms, EXERCISE B

1. Whitman <u>wrote</u> about democracy and the United States.
2. He <u>grew</u> up in Brooklyn, New York, in the early part of the nineteenth century.
3. He <u>taught</u> school and worked as a journalist, too.
4. Whitman <u>sought</u> to reflect the mood of the growing nation.
5. Whitman <u>wove</u> some poems around Civil War themes.

Verbs: Irregular Forms, EXERCISE C

1. We <u>drove</u> all night long. / We had <u>driven</u> for two hours before the sun rose.
2. When I was cold, Mel <u>gave</u> me his sweater. / Have you <u>given</u> Annie her piano lesson?
3. The guest <u>spoke</u> on the topic of civil responsibility. / He has <u>spoken</u> for forty-five minutes already!
4. Jaime <u>threw</u> a wicked fast ball. / Haven't you <u>thrown</u> out that junk yet?
5. The ship <u>sank</u> rapidly in the storm. / After the boats had <u>sunk</u>, the Coast Guard held out little hope for survivors.

Verbs: Past and Past Participle Forms, EXERCISE A

1. given
2. went, gone
3. left
4. hidden

Verbs: Past and Past Participle Forms, EXERCISE B

1. took (past)
2. worn (past participle)
3. fallen (past participle)
4. broke (past)
5. blew (past)
6. led (past)
7. lost (past)
8. saw (past)
9. flew (past)
10. brought (past participle)

Verbs: Past and Past Participle Forms, EXERCISE C

Sentences will vary; possible sentences are given.

1. A shadowy figure <u>stole</u> into the room. / I'm innocent; I have <u>stolen</u> nothing!
2. The roads <u>froze</u> quickly after the snowstorm began. / The pan of water had <u>frozen</u> solid by the time Kelsey got home.
3. My dad <u>flew</u> to Charlotte for his uncle's funeral. / The small plane was <u>flown</u> by a novice pilot.
4. I jumped on my bike and <u>rode</u> over the Mariposa's house. / If you've <u>ridden</u> in Rachel's car, then you know what a bucket of bolts it is.
5. When the child squeezed the balloon too hard, it <u>burst</u>. / The groceries would have <u>burst</u> from the bag if I hadn't double-sacked them.

Verbs: Problems With Tenses, EXERCISE A

1. began
2. had closed
3. beat
4. had dried
5. had finished

Verbs: Problems With Tenses, EXERCISE B

1. Since we <u>had chosen</u> to make Chelsea's favorite, we bought chocolate chips.
2. By the time we <u>returned</u> home, we <u>had torn</u> into those chips!
3. While the cookies <u>baked</u>, we <u>drank</u> milk.
4. We <u>sat</u> in Chelsea's kitchen and <u>waited</u> patiently.
5. As soon as we <u>tasted</u> those cookies, we agreed that they were the best that we had ever <u>eaten</u>.

Verbs: Problems With Tenses, EXERCISE C

Answers will vary; possible answers are shown below.

1. While we waited for the play to begin, <u>we read the program</u>.
2. Before <u>the curtain went up</u>, the stage manager checked the lights.
3. By the time the show started, <u>I had finished my peanuts</u>.
4. As the actress spoke, <u>she looked directly at the audience</u>.
5. After <u>the performance had ended</u>, we applauded loudly.

Pronoun Problems

Pronouns: Awkward or Indefinite Antecedents, EXERCISE A

1. the examiners
2. his or her
3. Experts
4. one

Pronouns: Awkward or Indefinite Antecedents, EXERCISE B

Answers may vary slightly; possible answers are given.

1. The movie was amusing, but <u>the director</u> could have made it shorter.
2. Neither of the women shared <u>her</u> view with the committee.
3. Remove the stamps from the envelopes and give <u>the stamps</u> to me.
4. To train for the marathon, <u>a contestant</u> must run every day.
5. Correct
6. Her mother told Hillary the news as soon as <u>Hillary</u> entered the room.
7. On the news <u>the announcer</u> mentioned that unemployment rates are down.
8. Mother read to Mark until <u>Mark</u> fell asleep.
9. <u>An applicant</u> must speak Spanish to be considered for that job.
10. Correct
11. At our assembly <u>a speaker</u> lectured on fire safety.
12. <u>This book</u> suggests that the assassination was part of a conspiracy.
13. Please take the towel from the dryer; <u>then fold the towel</u>.
14. In those days, <u>people</u> had to work hard in order to survive.
15. Correct
16. Not a single one of us was willing to offer <u>his or her</u> support to the candidate.
17. Amanda told Janet, <u>"I have to leave by 10 P.M."</u>
18. Correct
19. Before arriving at the polling place, <u>one should have made one's choices</u>.
20. One of those girls can't find <u>her</u> ticket.

Pronouns: Other Pronoun Problems, EXERCISE A

1. they
2. he
3. a task that
4. the job
5. he or she
6. she's
7. they
8. a fact that
9. it
10. we

Pronouns: Other Pronoun Problems, EXERCISE B

Answers may vary slightly; possible answers are given.

1. Chip likes gym class because <u>he gets</u> to play basketball.
2. This book is full of long <u>words and is therefore</u> difficult to read.
3. One of my neighbors tripped and broke <u>his</u> (or <u>her</u>) ankle.
4. If a person wants to succeed, <u>he or she has</u> to be willing to work hard.
5. I like the kind of movie that leaves <u>me</u> smiling at the end.
6. Alice announced that she would not run for class president, <u>and that announcement</u> came as a big surprise.
7. We didn't like the new teacher at first, but <u>we</u> started to appreciate her after a while.
8. Correct
9. The friends worked hard on their proejct, but the judges didn't choose <u>it</u> for first prize.
10. Your plan to get rich quick was unsuccessful, <u>a result that</u> I expected from the start.

Problems with Modifiers

Misplaced Modifiers, EXERCISE A
1. descended from wolves and jackals
2. Correct
3. With the dogs' help
4. Correct
5. unlike wolves

Misplaced Modifiers, EXERCISE B
1. The girl <u>with the odd hairstyle</u> disappeared into the crowd.
2. The child eagerly ate the cake <u>topped with cream sauce</u>.
3. The nurse comforted Piper <u>moaning in pain from her twisted ankle</u>.
4. The boy <u>swinging from a rope</u> dropped into the river.
5. I tried to help the student <u>confused by our complex schedule</u>.
6. The squirrel <u>alerted by some noise</u>, sat unmoving on the branch.
7. The reasons <u>for this decision</u> can be clearly stated.
8. The actor, <u>paralyzed by stage fright,</u> stared blankly at the audience.
9. The data <u>that confirm a theory</u> should always be rechecked.
10. Her arms piled high with books, Kiri tripped <u>on the steps</u>.

Misplaced Modifiers, EXERCISE C
   <u>Competing for readers</u>, two New York newspapers introduced modern comic strips. <u>Appearing as a single frame</u>, comics had been around for a long time. The *New York Herald* began publishing a comic "strip" in 1894 to gain readers. The *Herald* gained an advantage because of its comic strip, <u>an immediate hit</u>. <u>Trying to regain readers</u>, the competing *Morning Journal* responded with a comic supplement in 1896. Both newspapers discovered <u>at the same time</u> that readers enjoyed the "funnies."

Dangling Modifiers, EXERCISE A
1. Excited by the prospects
2. Correct
3. Correct
4. Orbiting fifteen miles above Eros
5. Slated for a 1996 launch

Dangling Modifiers, EXERCISE B
Answers may vary.
1. Wandering through the old city, <u>we were fascinated by many sights</u>.
2. <u>Since they were questioned by experts</u>, the truth came out.
3. With a great deal of patience, <u>one can learn origami</u>.
4. Fatigued by all the exercise, <u>they found the comfortable chair wonderful</u>.
5. Bundled up in heavy coats and scarves, <u>we felt no effect of the wind</u>.
6. Wandering through the museum, <u>we thought that every exhibit deserved attention</u>.
7. Summoning her last reserve of strength, <u>Laverne ran the final yards</u>.
8. Surrounded by enemies on all sides, <u>we saw no hope of escape</u>.
9. <u>Hearing something crashing through the underbrush</u>, the ducks screamed and took flight.
10. Believing in the accuracy of the report, <u>we made our decision</u>.

Dangling Modifiers, EXERCISE C
Answers may vary; possible answers are given.

Walking down the deserted streets of the ghost town, <u>Teresa and Carol were eager to explore the buildings</u>. As they walked through the buildings, <u>they saw that a thick layer of dust covered everything</u>. Looking about them, <u>Teresa and Carol saw many objects lying where they had last been used</u>. Perhaps the townspeople had intended to come back, but for some reason, could not. Getting up from dinner, <u>they had simply closed down the town</u>.

Problems with Possessives

Using Possessive Forms Correctly, EXERCISE A
1. your
2. John and Alan's
3. theirs
4. its
5. Joneses'

Using Possessive Forms Correctly, EXERCISE B
1. They're having a party at <u>their</u> house tomorrow night.
2. Are those books <u>hers</u> or are they yours?
3. <u>Gus's and Maria's</u> reports are both due on Friday.
4. Correct
5. There's no way those sneakers could be <u>theirs</u>!
6. Correct
7. We need to borrow their notes, for we seem to have misplaced <u>ours</u>.
8. Who's responsible for deciding <u>whose</u> drawings will be included?
9. Our <u>class's</u> project won first prize in their annual competition.
10. These three <u>books'</u> plots are very similar, but their themes are quite different.

Using Possessive Forms Correctly, EXERCISE C

Sentences will vary; possible answers are given.

1. What time is <u>your</u> mother coming to pick you up?
2. Wasn't <u>Charles's</u> report fascinating?
3. The program had several guest stars in <u>its</u> cast.
4. I have some ideas, but I surely could use <u>somebody's</u> opinion.
5. These sweaters must be <u>theirs</u>.
6. I don't know <u>his</u> plans for the weekend, but I'll find out.
7. Does anyone know the new <u>girl's</u> name?
8. At my brother's wedding, my <u>brothers-in-law's</u> prank caused a lot of laughter.
9. Their <u>mothers'</u> pies were delicious.
10. <u>Whose</u> tape player did you borrow?

Missing Commas

Missing Commas, EXERCISE A

1. We like butter, maple syrup, and powdered sugar on our pancakes.
2. We enjoyed a long, relaxing vacation at the seaside resort.
3. Correct
4. Thomas Jefferson, James Madison, and James Monroe were all Virginians.
5. My sister, a senior in college, would like to get married, buy a house, and join a law firm.

Missing Commas, EXERCISE B

My father, my uncle, and Steve, my brother-in-law, went on a camping trip last week. Uncle Dan is a tall, skinny man with bright red hair. His favorite activities are sailing, fishing, and playing golf. When the warm summer breezes start to blow, he likes to stop whatever he's doing, call up a couple of friends, and set off on an adventure. My father is usually a quiet, stay-at-home person, but he occasionally joins Uncle Dan on his trips into the great outdoors. Steve—a young, energetic teacher—is always eager to throw some clothes into his duffel bag, load his camper, and head for the woods. Next year, I hope to join them on their annual summer outing.

Missing Commas, EXERCISE C

Sentences will vary; possible sentences are given.

1. Bluejays, robins, and sparrows filled the yard.
2. Who is that tall, thin, dark-haired stranger?
3. Kelly, who will pick up a book and read whenever she can, is working her way through the school library.
4. Add the spaghetti to the boiling hot water and cook until just tender.
5. My jobs on the farm included milking the cow, feeding the chickens, and cleaning out the stables.

Grammar, Usage, and Mechanics

Abbreviations

Abbreviating Names and Titles

EXERCISE A: Rewrite the following items, using the abbreviated form of the words in parentheses.

> **Example:** (Professor) Gordon (Gerard) Sikes
> **Answer:** Prof. Gordon G. Sikes

1. (North Atlantic Treaty Organization)
2. (Lieutenant) Angelo Pareti
3. (Superintendent) Mary Fuller
4. Meredith Helm, (Doctor of Dental Surgery)
5. Irwin Kroll, (Master of Science)
6. (Franklin Delano Roosevelt)
7. (Senator) Claudia Pappas
8. Rosalie Cooper, (Master of Business Administration)
9. (Federal Deposit Insurance Corporation)
10. (Governor) Miguel Fuentes

EXERCISE B: Write the abbreviation for each item in parentheses. If it is acceptable in formal writing, rewrite the sentence, using the abbreviation.

> **Example:** (General) Andrew Jackson later ran for public office.
> **Answer:** Gen.; Gen. Andrew Jackson later ran for public office.

1. My favorite program is on (Columbia Broadcasting System) at 7:00 P.M.
2. (Professor) Chang's history class meets in (Room) 184.
3. Bill applied for a job at Bentwood Manufacturing, (Incorporated).
4. (Attorney) Veronica Chávez works for the (Federal Bureau of Investigation).
5. You can see the art of Ana Ríos, (Master of Fine Arts), at the gallery.
6. Daniel Parker, (Junior), has opened his own accounting firm.
7. The (Reverend) Percy Maddux has an appointment to see (Sergeant Edward Ames).

EXERCISE C: Each sentence contains one or more underlined words that can be abbreviated. First write the abbreviated form. Then use the abbreviation in an original sentence.

> **Example:** <u>Madam</u> Capet works for the <u>Organization of American States</u>.
> **Answer:** Mme., OAS; Mme. Capet spoke before the OAS on behalf of abused children.

1. I dread my visit to Benjamin Parks, <u>Senior</u>, <u>Medical Doctor</u>.
2. <u>Attorney</u> Carl Baker is representing the <u>United Auto Workers</u>.
3. Piri Villanueva, Doctor of <u>Philosophy</u>, is lecturing at the conference.
4. The <u>Honorable</u> Helen Drake ruled on the case involving the <u>American Federation of Teachers</u>.
5. <u>Ambassador</u> Kyoko Mizumura spoke at <u>Voice of America</u> headquarters and then at the <u>United Nations</u>.

Other Types of Abbreviations

EXERCISE A: Rewrite each item below, substituting the tratitional abbreviation for the word in parentheses.

   Example: 3 (teaspoons) of honey
   Answer: 3 <u>tsp</u>. of honey

   1. (Monday,) June 11
   2. (Mount) Olive
   3. Boston, (Massachusetts)
   4. 8 (hours)
   5. 11:05 (in the morning)
   6. 1349 (North) Berry Rd.
   7. St. Charles (County)
   8. milk, eggs, salt, (et cetera)
   9. 100 (kilometers)
   10. 37 degrees (Celsius)
   11. 5 (liters) of milk
   12. Lansing, (Michigan)
   13. 6421 Lindell (Boulevard)
   14. 14 (grams)
   15. 10 (minutes) 40 (seconds)
   16. (Fort) Union
   17. (for example), books, pencils, chalk
   18. (September) 4, 1947
   19. 3.6 (centimeters)
   20. Logan (Brothers) Moving (Company)

EXERCISE B: Write the abbreviation for each item in parentheses. Rewrite any sentence in which the abbreviations can be used appropriately in formal writing.

   Example: Diogenes, the Greek philosopher, was born (about) 412 B.C.
   Answer: ca.; Diogenes, the Greek pholosopher, was born ca. 412 B.C.

   1. In (the year of our Lord) 1066, the Normans conquered England.
   2. Mark lives at 216 Lincoln (Avenue), Springfield, (Illinois).
   3. Add 2 (teaspoons) of salt and 3 (tablespoons) of butter.
   4. My grandfather lives in Franklin (County) in (Missouri).
   5. Which is larger: 1 (gallon) or 1 (liter)?
   6. Our flight arrives in Washington, (District of Columbia), at 9:00 (in the morning).
   7. Tanya Denton (and others) edited this book.
   8. How many (kilometers) is it from Los Angeles, (California) to Cheyenne, (Wyoming)?
   9. My car holds 14 (gallons) of gasoline and 4 (quarts) of oil.
   10. The aurora borealis—(that is) the northern lights—appeared at 11:30 (at night).
   11. These flint tools were made in the year 8000 (before Christ).

Addresses

Writing Addresses Correctly

EXERCISE A: Rewrite each item. Use commas, numerals, and abbreviations correctly.

Example: Sixty-five Day St.
Portland OR 97219

Answer: <u>65</u> Day St.
Portland, OR 97219

1. 186 Forest Dr. Camden AR 71701
2. 76 Nineteenth St. Suite Seven-A
3. One hundred two Mountain View Rd. Milwaukee WI 53202
4. They live in Laconia Township Belknap County.
5. Send the poster to me at Fifteen Adams St. Grand Forks ND 58201.

EXERCISE B: Rewrite each item. Use commas, numerals, and abbreviations correctly. Then rewrite the addresses as they would appear in a paragraph in the body of a letter.

Example: Twelve hundred Bryant Ct.
Tulsa OK 74101

Answers: <u>1200</u> Bryant Ct.
Tulsa, OK 74101
<u>1200</u> Bryant <u>Court</u>, Tulsa, <u>Oklahoma</u> 74101

1. 145 Twelfth St.
   Charleston SC 29401
2. 672 Mellon Ave.
   Bountiful UT 84010
3. Washburn
   Bayfield County WI
4. 12 Bay Blvd., Apartment Eight
   Providence RI 02904
5. Village of Madison
   Boone County WV

EXERCISE C: Use these letter parts in the addresses and the body of at least two business letters. Remember to use commas, numerals, and abbreviations correctly.

1. Ninety-five Cedar La.
2. Atchison KS 66002
3. Goshen IN 46526
4. Eighteen Alder St., Apartment Two
5. Pierre SD 57501

Positioning Adjectives Effectively

EXERCISE A: Rewrite each item, changing the position of the adjective. Your revision need not be a complete sentence.

> **Example:** The river was empty.
> **Answer:** the empty river

1. It was a misty morning.
2. Cool, damp fog had settled on the river.
3. The sun, yellow and weak, shone through the mist.
4. The river looked lovely and dreamlike.
5. Canoeists were chilly and quiet.
6. Canoeists grew nervous.
7. Noisy, white rapids thundered.
8. Vicious rocks protruded from the water.
9. The day seemed ominous.
10. The morning was no longer peaceful.

EXERCISE B: Rewrite each sentence, moving the adjective or adjectives in parentheses.

> **Example:** Madeleine L'Engle's *An Acceptable Time* is a (fantasy) book.
> **Answer:** Madeleine L'Engle's *An Acceptable Time* is <u>fantasy</u>.

1. Polly O'Keefe, is the (adventuresome, red-haired) main character.
2. Polly lives with her grandparents in a (large, rambling) home.
3. Polly finds a gate in time and passes through to a (strange, exotic) world.
4. She enters the (ancient and magical) era of the Celts.
5. It is the time of the Druids and their (mysterious, forgotten) lore.
6. Polly meets many (admirable) leaders of the People of the Wind.
7. Peace-loving Karralys is a healer and religious leader of his tribe.
8. Tav, (courageous and wise), is the chief of the warriors.
9. Polly has (dangerous) adventures in the land of the Celts.
10. Another tribe captures her, planning to sacrifice her to an (angry) god.

EXERCISE C: Rewrite the paragraph, changing the position of adjectives in five of the sentences.

> **Example:** John felt nervous but eager as he waited for the starting gun.
> **Answer:** John, nervous but eager, waited for the starting gun.

John had trained for months for this marathon, which was arduous. The gun fired, and a thousand hopeful and determined runners were off. A dozen more-experienced runners pulled ahead. John kept them in sight for the easy first ten miles. His goal was simply to finish. The test would be Heartbreak Hill, a two-mile-long hill that already-tired runners had to conquer at mile nineteen.

Identifying and Using Proper Adjectives

EXERCISE A: Write the proper adjectives in each sentence.

   Example: Southern bands still play the best blues.
   Answer: Southern

 1. Most of our music originated in European countries hundreds of years ago.
 2. Classical music, such as English symphonies, are examples.
 3. French and Italian opera became fashionable in the seventeenth century.
 4. Chamber music has a Germanic origin, but it soon spread throughout Europe.
 5. About 1900, African-American musicians developed jazz and the blues.
 6. In the 1960's, the "British Invasion" exploded onto the American scene.
 7. Later, some Australian and Dutch groups gained popularity.
 8. Today, Brazilian music is popular.
 9. West Indian music can be heard on the radio.
10. African rhythms have been incorporated into popular music.

EXERCISE B: Write sentences using the ten proper nouns as adjectives. Use a dictionary if necessary.

   Example: Shakespeare
   Answer: We have tickets for a production of a <u>Shakespearean</u> play.

 1. Elizabeth I
 2. Liverpool
 3. Rome
 4. India
 5. Victoria
 6. China
 7. Hindu
 8. Dickens
 9. Uganda
10. Shaw

Identifying and Using Demonstrative and Indefinite Adjectives

EXERCISE A: Write the demonstrative and indefinite adjectives in the sentences. Label each as demonstrative or indefinite.

Example: Neither bird-watcher has moved during this past hour.
Answer: Neither—indefinite; this—demonstrative

1. Are all those people here just to watch birds?
2. Each spring the preserve is filled with birds.
3. People wanting to see the first migrants crowd into this place.
4. Every watcher has a pair of binoculars swinging from his or her neck.
5. Don't any birds feel overwhelmed by all the attention?

EXERCISE B: Rewrite each sentence, supplying the adjectives designated in parentheses.

Example: (Indefinite) photographers prefer photographing landscapes.
Answer: <u>Some</u> photographers prefer photographing landscapes.

1. David Muench is one of (demonstrative) photographers who concentrate on landscapes.
2. (Demonstrative) photograph shows (indefinite) kinds of wildflowers.
3. (Indefinite) picture shows the rocky bluffs of (indefinite) mountains.
4. In (indefinite) photographs, Muench shows colorful subjects, such as (demonstrative) laurel, set in neutral surroundings, such as gray rocks.
5. Ansel Adams prefers (demonstrative) subjects, too, but (indefinite) photographs I've seen of his have been in black and white.
6. (Indefinite) photograph shows texture or the contrast of shadow and light.

EXERCISE C: Write whether a *demonstrative adjective* or an *indefininte adjective* belongs in each space. Then rewrite the sentence, supplying the missing word.

Example: _____ cartoon is not about just _____ tiger.
Answer: demonstrative, indefinite   That <u>cartoon</u> is not about just <u>any</u> tiger.

1. _____ people like _____ cartoon with Calvin and Hobbes.
2. Does _____ person think the idea behind _____ cartoon makes sense?
3. It happens _____ time a child plays with one of _____ stuffed animals.
4. _____ imaginary adventures, which _____ children have, are real to them.
5. _____ things are more real than _____ conversations with a teddy bear.

Comparing with Adjectives

EXERCISE A: Rewrite each phrase, replacing the underlined word with the form of comparison indicated in parentheses.

> **Example:** <u>hopeful</u> students (superlative)
> **Answer:** most hopeful students

1. <u>bad</u> health (comparative)
2. <u>distant</u> city (superlative)
3. <u>wide</u> truck (comparative)
4. <u>unusual</u> clothing (superlative)
5. <u>forgetful</u> son (comparative)
6. <u>good</u> news (superlative)
7. <u>far</u> star (superlative)
8. <u>remote</u> chance (comparative)
9. <u>bizarre</u> sense of humor (comparative)
10. <u>little</u> opportunity (comparative)
11. <u>early</u> class (superlative)
12. <u>funny</u> comedian (comparative)
13. <u>much</u> vegetables (comparative)
14. <u>fundamental</u> baseball (superlative)
15. <u>sought-after</u> actor (comparative)
16. <u>available</u> player (superlative)
17. <u>clever</u> performer (superlative)
18. <u>serious</u> discussion (comparative)
19. <u>predictable</u> behavior (superlative)
20. <u>awful</u> taste (superlative)

EXERCISE B: Write each sentence, filling in the blank with an adjective in the appropriate form of comparison.

> **Example:** The (bad) disaster in the universe is an exploding star.
> **Answer:** The <u>worst</u> disaster in the universe is an exploding star.

1. Was Albert Einstein or Isaac Newton the (brilliant) physicist?
2. Einstein developed the theory of relativity, one of the two or three (important) concepts ever developed in physics.
3. However, Newton developed the theory of gravity; was it (insightful)?
4. Both theories are used to explain black holes, which may be the (mysterious) of all celestial phenomena.
5. Black holes form when (large) stars than our sun burn out and collapse in on themselves.
6. (Small) stars do not have enough mass to form black holes.
7. Our sun has (little) mass than is required to form a black hole.
8. Black holes have the (strong) gravitational pull of any object in space, attracting all nearby matter and energy, including light.
9. No light escapes, so even our (good) telescopes cannot see them.
10. Some scientists say that black holes don't exist, but a (good) guess is that there are thousands in our galaxy alone.

Avoiding Double and Illogical Comparisons

EXERCISE A: Write the word in parentheses that correctly completes each sentence.

> **Example:** Of all the storytellers in our family, Ruth is the (best, better) one.
> **Answer:** best

1. Wanda seems (happier, happiest) than she was last week.
2. Was his essay as good as a professional (writer, writer's)?
3. Harold is (stronger, more stronger) than the other boys.
4. Today my wake-up call was (earlier, more earlier) than usual.
5. Did you assign me the (harder, hardest) of the three jobs?

EXERCISE B: Write the form of the word in parentheses that expresses a clear and balanced comparison.

> **Example:** Jeb likes to travel (much) than I do.
> **Answer:** more

1. Alison's opinion of this music is even (little) than mine.
2. Our school's music program is better than most (schools).
3. Charles appeared to be (eager) than George.
4. Which of these three volumes is (easy) to read?
5. The song of a robin is more familiar to me than a (bluebird).

EXERCISE C: Rewrite the sentences, correcting any errors in comparison. If a sentence needs no changes, write *Correct*.

> **Example:** Of the two candidates, Ms. Jenner is the most qualified.
> **Answer:** Of the two candidates, Ms. Jenner is the <u>more</u> qualified.

1. Do you think Ramona is more smarter than Lois?
2. Randy's car is in worst condition than Arthur.
3. The pitch of a piccolo is higher than a flute.
4. Which of those three stereo systems has the better sound?
5. If the ending were different, this novel would be more perfect.
6. Who has traveled the fartherest distance to be here?
7. Tom and Vicki's mural is much more colorful than Bob and Bess's.
8. This month's telephone bill is lower than last month.
9. John's visits are more oftener during the summer.
10. That diamond, the only one of its kind in the world, is a most unique gem.

Avoiding Incomplete Comparisons

EXERCISE A: If a comparison is incomplete, rewrite the sentence to correct it. If a sentence needs no changes, write *Complete*.

> **Example:** Elissa knows more about history than anyone I know.
> **Answer:** Elissa knows more about history than _anyone else_ I know.

1. Isaac has more foreign stamps than any member of our club.
2. Ursula knows more about gardening than anyone I know.
3. The Alps are larger than any other mountains in Europe.
4. Your apple pie is better than anyone's in this state, so it's sure to win first prize.
5. A diamond is harder than any natural substance.
6. Wendell gets better grades than any other student in our school; he makes the honor roll every time.
7. My sister Whitney is better at fixing bicycles than anyone I know.
8. No scientist in the twentieth century was as famous as Albert Einstein.
9. Are his pitches harder to hit than anyone's in the entire league?
10. Richard knows more about trivia than anyone else I know.

EXERCISE B: Complete each sentence with a logical comparison. Use the word *other* or *else* as part of the comparison.

> **Example:** Your report was better than _____.
> **Answer:** Your report was better than _any other report in the class_.

1. Lawrence's science project is better than _____.
2. They spent more time talking about their boyfriends than _____.
3. Carol's story was longer than _____; in fact, it almost put me to sleep!
4. Is she a better musician than _____?
5. Their house is bigger than _____.
6. The committee's new plan is better than _____.
7. The pizza at that restaurant is more delicious than _____.
8. Brad spends more time on the basketball court than _____.
9. Because Julio sings better than _____, he probably will get a leading role in the spring play.
10. Taller than _____, my dad can be spotted in any crowd.

Developing Your Style: Using Precise Adjectives

EXERCISE A: Rewrite each sentence, using vivid adjectives in place of the underlined words.

Example: Some of the <u>young</u> ballplayers played a <u>bad</u> game on opening day.
Answer: Some of the <u>inexperienced</u> ballplayers played a <u>disappointing</u> game on opening day.

1. Jacob Fields, a <u>nice</u> new baseball stadium, came with a <u>high</u> price tag.
2. The Cleveland Indians were <u>happy</u> when they finally moved into their <u>neat</u> stadium.
3. At their first home game, however, the ballplayers seemed somewhat <u>nervous</u> in their <u>strange</u> surroundings.
4. The <u>nice</u> weather brought out a <u>large</u> crowd on opening day.
5. I took my <u>new</u> seat and pulled out a pair of <u>good</u> binoculars.
6. The President threw out the first ball with <u>real</u> style on that <u>special</u> day.
7. Then the <u>nice</u> announcer called to the <u>emotional</u> crowd, "Play ball!"
8. We all gave a <u>loud</u> greeting to the first batter—and we went crazy when his bat connected with the ball with a <u>loud</u> CRACK!
9. The smell of hot peanuts and <u>tasty</u> lemonade added to the <u>good</u> atmosphere.
10. After the <u>good</u> game, we talked in the <u>busy</u> corridors, agreeing that the team was looking <u>good</u> and <u>fit</u>.

EXERCISE B: Complete each sentence by adding vivid adjectives. Write each new sentence.

Example: A _____ mass of snow that moves with a _____ motion down a mountainside is known as an avalanche.
Answer: A <u>sizeable</u> mass of snow that moves with a <u>swift</u> motion down a mountainside is known as an avalanche.

1. The _____ snowstorm dumped six inches of _____ snow in the city.
2. In the mountains, the already _____ slopes looked like _____ ice-cream cones.
3. In a snow avalanche, _____, huskies are used to rescue the survivors.
4. The sudden, _____ noise that signals an avalanche is both _____ and _____.
5. As tons of snow crash down the mountainside, the _____ weight serves as a truly _____ force.

Developing Your Style: Avoiding Overuse of Adjectives

EXERCISE A: Write the letter of the sentence that gives a clearer image by using a precise and vivid noun or verb.

> **Example:** a. The real-estate agent had an impressive effect on the buyer.
>
> b. The real-estate agent impressed the buyer.
>
> **Answer:** b

1. a. The real-estate agent was known for her reliable quality.
   b. The real-estate agent was known for her reliability.
2. a. Although often in competition with other real-estate agents, this agent managed to sell her quota of houses.
   b. Although often in a competitive-type situation with other real-estate agents, this agent managed to sell her quota of houses.

EXERCISE B: Rewrite each sentence, using the word or group of words in parentheses that is more vivid or precise.

> **Example:** Economics is the science of the production, distribution, and (consumption, a consumable use) of goods and services.
>
> **Answer:** Economics is the science of the production, distribution, and <u>consumption</u> of goods and services.

1. If a company or government doesn't (manage in economical ways, economize) on expenses, it will go into debt.
2. A company may (apply protective measures for, protect) its investments with strict spending policies.
3. Another firm may (educate, use educational methods on) its staff on how to cut costs.
4. Such a policy (promises, has a promising influence for) (successful times, success) in the future.

EXERCISE C: Rewrite each sentence, replacing the group of words in parentheses with a more vivid noun or verb.

> **Example:** The cordless mini-duster is a (convenient type of machine) for quick cleaning.
> **Answer:** The cordless mini-duster is a <u>convenience</u> for quick cleaning.

1. The upholsterer (changed the decorative style of) the chair with colorful fabric.
2. The old chair looked like new with this (improved repair).
3. This fabric hides all (imperfect-like conditions) in the chair.
4. The special fabric also (protects against) dirt and stains.

Grammar, Usage, Mechanics • Adjectives

Adverbs

Identifying and Using Adverbs That Modify Verbs

EXERCISE A: Write the adverb in each sentence. In parentheses after each adverb, write the verb that it modifies; then write another adverb that could substitute for that adverb.

> **Example:** Uncle Ed walked briskly through the park.
> **Answer:** briskly (walked); quickly

1. Our football team narrowly escaped with a victory.
2. Megan moved gracefully across the stage.
3. The car was completely covered with snow.
4. Greg arrived late for his biology class.
5. The road signs could never be seen through the fog.

EXERCISE B: Complete each sentence with an adverb that answers the question in parentheses. Then write the verb that the adverb modifies.

> **Example:** The students worked (in what manner?) in biology lab.
> **Answer:** carefully (worked)

1. All lab reports must be submitted (when?).
2. Val dictated (in what manner?) while Chi wrote (in what manner?).
3. Debbie looked (where?), but she found nothing.
4. The students arrived (when?) for the lab exam.
5. They cleaned the equipment (how?).

EXERCISE C: Complete the sentences with adverbs. Then write the verb that the adverb modifies.

> **Example:** The audience waited _____ for the concert to begin.
> **Answer:** restlessly (waited)

1. The stadium had _____ sold out _____.
2. Fans who did _____ have tickets waited _____.
3. Some people _____ clapped their hands.
4. Because the band arrived _____, even devoted fans grumbled _____.
5. _____ the lights in the stadium _____ dimmed.

Identifying and Using Adverbs That Modify Adjectives and Other Adverbs

EXERCISE A: Write each adverb in parentheses, the word it modifies, and the part of speech. Then write another adverb that could substitute for the adverb.

> **Example:** Eleanor Roosevelt was a (very) intelligent woman.
> **Answer:** very (intelligent - adjective); extremely

1. Eleanor Roosevelt worked (quite) diligently on her husband's behalf.
2. As First Lady, she traveled at a (nearly) exhausting pace.
3. She (almost) never turned away an opportunity for service.
4. Mrs. Roosevelt served her country (quite) capably.
5. Other First Ladies have served (most) admirably in this position.
6. Lady Bird Johnson campaigned (rather) enthusiastically for beautification of America's highways.
7. Barbara Bush was a (very) visible champion for the cause of literacy.
8. Edith Wilson—a (truly) amazing woman—proved herself (quite) able to carry on her husband's work after he had a stroke.
9. Hillary Rodham Clinton has been an (unusually) forceful speaker for health-care reform.

EXERCISE B: Write an answer to each question. In your answer, include an adverb that will modify an adjective or other adverb. Underline the adverb you added. Then write whether the adverb modifies an *adjective* or an *adverb*.

> **Example:** How quickly did the tickets disappear?
> **Answer:** The tickets disappeared <u>extremely</u> quickly. (adverb)

1. How excited did the people in line feel?
2. How polite were the fans after such a long wait?
3. How happily did the crowd react when the ticket booth opened?
4. How quickly did the line move?
5. How expensive were the tickets to the game?
6. How patient were fans at the end of the line?
7. How smoothly did the ticket sales go?
8. How thrilled was that girl when she got her tickets?
9. How busy are the ticket-sellers now?
10. How did the fans who lost out on tickets act?

Distinguishing Adverbs From Adjectives and Prepositions

EXERCISE A: Label each underlined word as an *adverb,* an *adjective,* or a *preposition.*

> **Example:** Dale left her bicycle <u>outside</u>, in the rain.
> **Answer:** adverb

1. The little dog, free at last, ran <u>beneath</u> the open gate.
2. Mom and Dad will be going <u>out</u> for the evening.
3. Leslie dived <u>from</u> the floating dock and into the water.
4. On the <u>off</u> chance that they hadn't heard, I retold my story to Glenda and Reba.
5. We sent your package <u>by</u> rail.
6. Randy tripped in the playground and fell (down).
7. Nancy came <u>down</u> the water slide headfirst, like a seal.
8. We took the <u>down</u> escalator.
9. Funny—I never noticed that STOP sign <u>before</u>.
10. Has Mr. Schultz appeared as a witness <u>before</u> the jury?

EXERCISE B: Complete each sentence with the part of speech in parentheses. The word you choose will be either an adverb or a preposition.

> **Example:** Don't run (preposition) the stairs!
> **Answer:** Don't run <u>down</u> the stairs!

1. The children were playing all (preposition) the house.
2. Somebody was hiding (preposition) the bed, making not a sound.
3. A few children had sneaked (adverb).
4. They were playing enthusiastically (preposition) the snow.
5. The nurse walked (preposition) the playroom.
6. She ran (adverb), intent on finding her missing charges.
7. The children hid (preposition) the tool shed, but the nurse spotted them.
8. The nurse yelled, "Come (adverb) right now!"
9. As the children ran, they fell (adverb) in the snow and got (preposition) a snowball fight.
10. Soon the children came (preposition) the house and sat (adverb) at the kitchen table for milk or fruit.

Comparing with Adverbs

EXERCISE A: Rewrite the sentences, using the correct form of each adverb in parentheses.

    Example: Brendan Walsh jumped (high—superlative) of all.
    Answer: Brendan Walsh jumped <u>highest</u> of all.

1. Brendan Walsh did (well—comparative) than any other player.
2. (Amazingly—superlative), he won three school championships in a row.
3. No one trained (hard-comparative) than Walsh.
4. His records will last (long-comparative) than many others.
5. Walsh will be remembered as one of the (great-superlative) high-school basketball players of all time.

EXERCISE B: Write the form of the adverb in parentheses that correctly completes each sentence. Then write whether the form of the adverb is *positive, comparative,* or *superlative.*

    Example: Today's practice went (better, best) than yesterday's.
    Answer: better, comparative

1. Annie jumped (most cleanly, cleanly) this morning.
2. She performed a double flip (more skillfully, most skillfully) of all the skaters.
3. Now she is spinning (less awkwardly, least awkwardly) than before.
4. On one move, she jumped (farther, farthest) than ever.
5. Of all the competitors, Annie skated (better, best).

EXERCISE C: Complete each sentence with an appropriate adverb in the correct form. Then write whether your choice is in the *positive, comparative,* or *superlative* form.

    Example: The doorbell rang.
    Answer: loudly, positive

1. Belinda ran for the door than I did.
2. Belinda whispered, "It's for me!"
3. She smiled than I'd ever seen her do before.
4. "Belinda's talking to her new boyfriend," I explained to Dad.
5. When Belinda came back inside, she sighed _____ than she ever had.

Apostrophes

Using Apostrophes in Possessives and Contractions

EXERCISE A: Rewrite the word or words in parentheses. If one word is given, write the correct possessive form. If two words are given, change them into a contraction.

> **Example:** Fred (will not) be attending the (band) spring concert.
> **Answer:** won't, band's

1. Did you pack the (children) lunch?
2. (Who is) going to bring the potato salad?
3. I liked (Phyllis) new coat.
4. They (will not) tell anybody what their decision will be.
5. The (jury has) listened to the (witness) testimony.

EXERCISE B: Rewrite each sentence to correct any errors in showing possession or in forming contractions. If a sentence needs no changes, write *Correct.*

> **Example:** You're explanation was not clear.
> **Answer:** <u>Your</u> explanation was not clear.

1. The barones's schedule was changed.
2. Please let us know if you've changed you're mind.
3. My sister and brother-in-law's house is in the neighborhood.
4. Considering the alternatives, their's would appear to be the best plan.
5. Will you or wont you be coming home for dinner?
6. The teachers meeting for all staff will be held at three o'clock.
7. Its getting late, and you won't want to miss the last bus.
8. These boy's book reports were handed in a week late.
9. We've been looking forward to spending the summer months at the beach.
10. I wouldn't say that they're project has achieved all it's objectives.

EXERCISE C: Write the possessive form of each noun or pronoun and a contraction for each pair of words. Then write a sentence using both words.

> **Example:** someone/has not
> **Answer:** someone's/hasn't   <u>Someone's</u> guardian <u>hasn't</u> signed the permission slip.

1. everybody/has not
2. Chris/he is
3. girls/have not
4. sister-in-law/would not
5. Joneses/they/have
6. mechanics/are not
7. treasurer/had not
8. guests/will not
9. boss/was not
10. children/will

Other Uses of Apostrophes

EXERCISE A: Rewrite each sentence, using apostrophes where needed to indicate plural forms or to show missing letters in the item in parentheses.

> **Example:** "(Yall) better git," he drawled.
> **Answer:** "Y'all better git," he drawled.

1. The (x) at the bottom of the letter stand for kisses.
2. William Shakespeare died in the early (1600).
3. "I reckon I'll be goin now," he said.
4. This contract contains an awful lot of (*whereas*).
5. Have our (*C.O.D.*) arrived from the Post Office?

EXERCISE B: Rewrite each sentence, making any necessary changes to show the correct plural form or to indicate any omitted letters.

> **Example:** My mother attended a reunion of the clas of 71.
> **Answer:** My mother attended a reunion of the class of '71.

1. I promised to arrive by seven oclock.
2. The children tried counting to 100 by 3s.
3. "I never was much good at writin," he muttered.
4. That veterinary school graduates more *D.V.M.*s every year than any other in the world.
5. How many *g*s are there in your name?
6. Boeing 747s are very large airplanes.
7. That child is old enough to learn her *ABC*s.
8. "Get em while they're hot!" called the cook.
9. My aunt was born in the late 1950s.
10. Those %s in the ad are called *percent signs*.

EXERCISE C: Write a sentence using the plural of each of the following numbers, symbols, letters, or words. Be sure to use apostrophes where they are needed.

> **Example:** *-ed*
> **Answer:** The *-ed's* in these examples usually indicate past participles.

1. *4*
2. *1800*
3. *$*
4. *if*
5. *;*
6. *and*
7. *?*
8. *+*
9. *m*
10. *&*

Appositives

Identifying and Punctuating Appositives

EXERCISE A: Write the appositive or appositive phrase in each sentence. Then write the noun or pronoun that each renames.

> **Example:** My brother Jack is an expert on the ski slopes.
> **Answer:** Jack (brother)

1. Their new car, a Ford, came equipped with all the options.
2. If Myra can't help you, my brother Sean can.
3. All of us were introduced to the new employee, an engineer.
4. The novelist William Faulkner wrote important literary works.
5. CPR—cardiopulmonary resuscitation—saves many lives.

EXERCISE B: Rewrite each sentence, underlining the appositive or appositive phrase and adding commas where needed.

> **Example:** I was scratched by the cat a high-strung Persian.
> **Answer:** I was scratched by the cat, a high-strung Persian.

1. Her destination Cincinnati seemed farther away than ever.
2. I don't know much about the songwriter Irving Berlin.
3. The new rug a rag rug woven in Kentucky made the room look great.
4. Our dog Rover truly lives up to his name.
5. The new teacher Mrs. Mansfield coaches softball.
6. Hercule Poirot a Belgian detective was created by Agatha Christie.
7. The poet begged assistance of Orpheus the Greek god of music.
8. Is the lamp that brass piece Victorian?
9. Their anniversary party a catered affair was a huge success.
10. The Olivers won a marvelous prize a weekend at a country inn.

EXERCISE C: Write ten sentences, using each item below as an appositive or appositive phrase. Be sure to use commas correctly.

> **Example:** a graduate of Harvard
> **Answer:** My mother, a graduate of Harvard, taught English at Cornell.

1. stamp collecting
2. Leslie
3. Wolfgang Amadeus Mozart
4. a collection of short stories
5. the smallest state
6. the captain of the team
7. "The Raven"
8. a comedy
9. a six-page listing of luscious foods
10. the fifth planet from the sun

Developing Your Style: Appositives

EXERCISE A: Combine each group of sentences to create a new sentence that uses at least one appositive or appositive phrase. Use commas where needed.

> **Example:** Jamal lives in Denver, Colorado. Jamal is my cousin.
> **Answer:** Jamal, my cousin, lives in Denver, Colorado

1. My sister explained the examination procedure to me. She is a doctor.
2. Our neighbors just bought a Chihuahua. A Chihuahua is a tiny dog.
3. The new teacher is named Mr. Roberts. He is a strict disciplinarian.
4. Mt. Everest is in Asia. It is the highest mountain in the world.
5. Please ask Mr. Trask about the change. He is the sophomore class advisor.
6. Albany is much smaller than New York City. The capital of New York is Albany.
7. This poem was written by Elizabeth Barrett Browning. The poem is a sonnet.
8. A dictator ruled Russia from 1922 to 1953. His name was Joseph Stalin.
9. Mars has two moons. They are called Deimos and Phobos. Mars is smaller than Earth.
10. Franklin Delano Roosevelt had three vice presidents. Roosevelt was the thirty-second President. His vice presidents were John Garner, Henry Wallace, and Harry Truman.

EXERCISE B: Complete each sentence with an appropriate appositive or appositive phrase. Be sure to use commas correctly.

> **Example:** Mr. Warner _____ enjoys reading mystery novels.
> **Answer:** Mr. Warner, _my next-door neighbor,_ enjoys reading mystery novels.

1. Our cat _____ won second prize in the cat show.
2. We gave Pedro and Carmen _____ a tour of the city.
3. Our favorite restaurant _____ is closed for renovations.
4. My sister _____ was elected class president.
5. Everyone agrees that Walter _____ is a very unusual pet.
6. The rescue squad arrived in time to save Chester _____.
7. Zebras _____ grazed on the grassy plain.
8. William Shakespeare _____ was born in 1564.
9. Africa _____ is a leading producer of gold, diamonds, and uranium.
10. Isn't the famous novelist _____ one of her favorites?

Using Brackets Correctly

EXERCISE A: Rewrite the sentences, adding brackets for any parenthetical items already within parentheses.

Example: He studies rabbits (lagomorphs as opposed to rodents).
Answer: He studies rabbits (lagomorphs [as opposed to rodents]).

1. With his mentor (Dr. Mary Li formerly of the University of Pennsylvania), Chet studies rabbits.
2. They recently published a paper in *Biology Today* (in the April issue volume VII).
3. According to Chet (who is only hard to believe a junior), rabbits make an ideal subject of study.
4. Chet (with his co-workers most of whom are seniors) will attend a symposium at Cold Spring Harbor.

EXERCISE B: Rewrite the sentences, adding parentheses and brackets where needed.

Example: I read a book by Karen Roth once a student of Freud's or so I understand.
Answer: I read a book by Karen Roth (once a student of Freud's [or so I understand]).

1. Did you read Roth's book on dreams similar to Freud's theories although much easier to understand?
2. Dreams which are interesting as long as they're your own are the subject of much speculation.
3. Roth has written often on dreams. See *Superego Monthly,* May 1993 volume XII.
4. Roth works with victims of insomnia. Sleep disorders especially psychologically based ones are her focus.

EXERCISE C: Expand each sentence by adding a parenthetical element within a parenthetical element. Be sure to use parentheses and brackets correctly.

Example: My garden is in bloom.
Answer: My garden (I use the term loosely [mostly it's weeds]) is in bloom.

1. I grow all my own vegetables.
2. Zucchini is easy to grow.
3. A fresh tomato is a work of art.
4. How do you keep the pests away?

Capitalization

Capitalizing Names and Titles of People

EXERCISE A: Write the names and titles of people in each sentence, adding capital letters where needed.

> **Example:** President woodrow wilson had been a college professor.
> **Answer:** Woodrow Wilson

1. amy mcDonnel is our national correspondent.
2. Have you ever seen morris, the finicky cat, in television commercials?
3. republicans and democrats hope to win seats in the senate.
4. helen keller graduated with honors from radcliffe college.
5. helen and her teacher, anne sullivan macy, raised money for the american foundation of the blind.
6. The first voyage of christopher columbus was financed by queen isabella and king ferdinand.
7. In our comparative religions course, we're studying christianity, hinduism, islam, and judaism, among others.
8. Some new americans, including koreans and pakistanis, are my classmates.
9. Excuse me professor; didn't you teach at roosevelt high school?
10. The study of scientists—such as galileo, copernicus, and the curies—is part of the science curriculum.

EXERCISE B: In each pair, capitalize the name or title and write it correctly. Use that proper noun in a sentence of your own.

> **Example:** robert / my brother-in-law
> **Answer:** <u>Robert</u> is my brother-in-law's name.

1. martin luther king, jr. / a doctor of philosophy
2. a judge / Judge Carlton
3. aunt sarah / my aunt
4. a lieutenant / colonel soto
5. a bank vice president / the vice president of the united states
6. dr. florence rosenberg / an internist
7. a baseball team / the atlanta braves
8. lana landry / a well-known actress
9. a legislator / senator john glenn
10. the reverend john michaels / his minister

Capitalizing Names of Places

EXERCISE A: Rewrite each sentence, adding the missing capital letters.

> **Example:** Mr. Bell sailed to australia on a luxury ship.
> **Answer:** Mr. Bell sailed to <u>Australia</u> on a luxury ship.

1. One of the world's largest cities is são paolo, brazil.
2. Many industries have left the northeast and moved south.
3. The second largest planet in the solar system is saturn.
4. The english channel separates england and france.
5. The sears tower, in chicago, is a very tall building.

EXERCISE B: Write the place names from the sentences, using correct capitalization. If a sentence needs no capitalization, write *Correct*.

> **Example:** Sue's family vacations in ocean city, maryland, each summer.
> **Answer:** Ocean City / Maryland

1. The northerly wind caused much damage in the last storm.
2. The zoo is located on riverside drive, near pine lake.
3. We took the ferry from cape cod to nantucket on our vacation.
4. When Kamal graduates from college, he'll cross the atlantic ocean and visit india, saudi arabia, and egypt.
5. Have you visited the empire state building, in new york city?

EXERCISE C: Rewrite each sentence, adding the missing capitals. Then write a new sentence, substituting a different proper noun for each place name given.

> **Example:** The capital of iowa is des moines.
> **Answers:** The capital of <u>Iowa</u> is <u>Des Moines</u>.
>
> > The capital of <u>Maryland</u> is <u>Annapolis</u>.

1. After studying the Civil War my class went to gettysburg, pennsylvania.
2. Can you spot the big dipper, the little dipper, and orion?
3. I am going to yellowstone national park this summer.
4. Someday I'd like to climb mt. rainier, or maybe go rafting down the colorado river.
5. I'd also love to see the rocky mountains.

Capitalizing Other Names

EXERCISE A: Write correctly the words in each sentence that need to be capitalized. If a sentence needs no capitalization, write *Correct.*

> **Example:** This year, passover will begin on a wednesday.
> **Answer:** Passover, Wednesday

1. We studied the magna carta in world history 101.
2. In late july or early august, I'll go to the tanglewood music festival.
3. The battle of new orleans occurred during the war of 1812.
4. My favorite time of year is autumn.
5. Since Cary wants to be a translator, he's taking both spanish and french this year.
6. Thanksgiving is the fourth thursday in november.
7. Our class took a photograph with Congressman Sands on the steps of the capitol.
8. The hero in "the most dangerous game" makes an escape.
9. Would you like to sail to Europe on the *queen mary*?
10. In the sophomore world civilization course, students study the bronze age and the industrial revolution.

EXERCISE B: Rewrite this part of a letter, adding capitals in the ten places where they are needed.

> **Example:** memorial day is a good time for me to write letters.
> **Answer:** Memorial Day is a good time for me to write letters.

During the first week of june, my history class will be taking a trip to Washington, D.C. We will be visiting the washington monument, the lincoln memorial, and arlington national cemetery. At the smithsonian institution, we'll see the *apollo* spacecraft and a replica of the Wright Brothers' plane *kitty hawk.* My english teacher, Mrs. Quinn, will be a chaperone on this trip. I knew she was my favorite teacher when I saw her driving a *firebird* and eating in burgers, that fast-food restaurant.

Capitalizing Proper Adjectives

EXERCISE A: Write the proper adjectives from the sentences, adding capitals as needed.

Example: How beautiful these french fashions are!
Answer: French

1. I usually start the day with colombian coffee and danish pastry.
2. A japanese violinist and a spanish guitarist played in the subway station.
3. Would you like some swiss cheese or american cheese on your sandwich?
4. This korean salad bar offers low-calorie italian dressing.
5. Did russian demonstrators protest the polish officials' decision?

EXERCISE B: Rewrite the sentences, adding any missing capitals.

Example: Caroline bought her father a swiss watch.
Answer: Caroline bought her father a <u>Swiss</u> watch.

1. Is this silk japanese, indian, or chinese?
2. My brother travels on various american airlines for his north american trips.
3. An english guide led the canadian and australian tourists in Guatemala.
4. Have you seen the new swedish stamps or the old roman coins?

EXERCISE C: Change each phrase with a proper noun into a proper adjective phrase, supplying capitals where needed. Then write a sentence with each proper adjective phrase.

Example: crown jewels from Kuwait
Answer: I saw the <u>Kuwaiti</u> crown jewels on display in the museum.

1. a scientist from Israel
2. citizens of Mexico
3. the cuisine of Italy
4. a resort in Cyprus
5. a symphony written in England
6. pounds used in Britain
7. a comedy written by Shakespeare
8. a committee in Congress
9. chocolates from Belgium
10. a person from San Francisco

Using Capitals to Mark Beginnings of Sentences and Direct Quotations

EXERCISE A: Rewrite the sentences, adding capitals where needed or making other changes in capitalization. If a sentence needs no capitalization, write *Correct*.

> **Example:** Alex complained, "this crossword puzzle is challenging."
> **Answer:**   Alex complained, "<u>T</u>his crossword puzzle is challenging."

1. "tomorrow we will try some new experiments," announced Phil.
2. "after dinner," asked my brother, "Will you help me with my homework?"
3. wonderful! how soon can you begin?
4. i know what will please her: she adores the classical guitar.
5. truman said, "if you can't stand the heat, stay out of the kitchen."
6. "i stopped to talk to Tom," Adele said, "and that's why I was late for school."
7. let's ride our bicycles. where?
8. "surprisingly," she remarked, "no one has noticed it."
9. listen carefully! I won't repeat these directions.
10. "the highest of distinctions is service to others."—King George VI
11. did you see Georgie yesterday? when?
12. oh, no! we missed the 9:00 train to Philadelphia!
13. "Remember," said Jeremy, "to call me tonight after dinner."
14. "i will win," he boasted. "this time i am ready."
15. "when you call me that, smile!"—Owen Wister
16. "When you see Bill," she said, "give him this note."
17. fred told us the news: a frog had escaped from the laboratory.
18. a slogan of the U.S. Air Force was "keep 'em flying."
19. Eleanora gathered the necessary items: paint, paper, and pens.
20. "liberty, like charity, must begin at home."—James Bryant Conant

EXERCISE B: Rewrite the paragraph, correcting any errors in capitalization.

   when we first moved to New York from Puerto Rico, I had difficulty adjusting to my new home. although my aunt and uncle were kind to me, I felt like a visitor on an alien planet. my uncle told me, "you belong in this country now. give yourself time; you'll fit in." it was strange to be living with so many people. after we got our own apartment, though, I felt more relaxed. "home, sweet home," I sang to myself, as I unpacked my special things. i began to make more friends and invite them to my house. now I can admit that I enjoy my life in the United States.

Using Capitals to Mark Other Beginnings

EXERCISE A: Rewrite each item, adding capitals where needed.

> **Example:** very truly yours,
> **Answer:** Very truly yours,

1. dear sir or madam:
2. in sympathy
3. "the music that can deepest reach,/and cure all ill, is cordial speech."
   —Ralph Waldo Emerson
4. dearest Adrienne,
5. sincerely yours,
6. dear superintendent miller:
7. "the world no longer let me love,/my hope and treasure lie above."
   —Anne Bradstreet
8. my best regards,
9. "he met a pilgrim shadow—/'shadow,' said he,/'where can it be—/this land of Eldorado?'"
   —Edgar Allan Poe
10. I. qualities needed for training a dog
    A. intelligence
    B. desire to please

EXERCISE B: Rewrite this letter, correcting any errors in capitalization.

dear alexandra,

I'm sending you a writer's magazine because you're interested in writing. Notice the article entitled "reading like a writer," by Dennis S. Anders. I think he gives good advice when he says to "read in order to understand how the writer has worked." I especially enjoy Shakespeare's comment: "words, words, mere words, no matter from the heart."

The magazine may give you some good ideas for your English report, following this sample outline:

I. american poets
   A. walt whitman
   B. langston hughes

Let me know what you think of the magazine!

with much love,

aunt lee

Clauses

Identifying and Using Main and Subordinate Clauses

EXERCISE A: In each sentence, draw one line under the main clause.

> **Example:** Whenever we visit Uncle Marco, we eat spaghetti.
> **Answer:** Whenever we visit Uncle Marco, <u>we eat spaghetti</u>.

1. I'll count the money if you'll drive me home afterward.
2. Glynis bought the coat, although it was really too expensive.
3. When Keith made honor roll, his father bought him the promised bike.
4. Your offer, which comes as a surprise, could make the difference.

EXERCISE B: Write a complex sentence by expanding each subordinate clause.

> **Example:** who has made an outstanding contribution in a certain field
> **Answer:** A Nobel Prize is awarded to an individual who has made an outstanding
> contribution in a certain field.

1. that I have always wanted to visit
2. because two volunteers reneged on their promise
3. which works to protect birds
4. since Florida is a semi-tropical state

EXERCISE C: Use each clause to write two sentences—one in which the clause is a main clause, and one in which the clause is a subordinate clause.

> **Example:** I'm a big fan of the Dallas Cowboys.
> **Answer:** <u>I'm a big fan of the Dallas Cowboys</u>, but I like the Miami Dolphins even better.
> (main clause)
>
> <u>Since I'm a big fan of the Dallas Cowboys</u>, I try to go to most of their home games.
> (subordinate clause)

1. Tina played a trumpet solo at the concert
2. Dave is a terrific softball player
3. you can find it easily
4. would you rather take a walk

Identifying and Using Adjective Clauses

EXERCISE A: Replace the adjective clause in each sentence with another that modifies the same word. Underline that word.

> **Example:** A television show that I like has been canceled.
> **Answer:** A television show <u>that features adventure stories</u> has been canceled.

1. Our wood stove, which also burns coal, has saved us a lot of money.
2. Yes, this is the place where I spent my happiest years.
3. Mrs. Nakamura is a teacher whom I greatly admire.
4. Bo, who spent last summer in Venezuela, has some wonderful stories.
5. Trigonometry is one class that I can't afford to miss.

EXERCISE B: Combine each pair of sentences to produce a complex sentence with an adjective clause.

> **Example:** Abraham Lincoln was the sixteenth President. He was called Honest Abe.
> **Answer:** Abraham Lincoln, <u>who was called Honest Abe,</u> was the sixteenth President.

1. Lincoln's family moved to Indiana in 1816. Indiana had no slavery.
2. In 1837 Lincoln was elected to the Illinois General Assembly. He was only twenty-five years of age.
3. Lincoln was elected to the U.S. House of Representatives in 1846. He was the candidate for the Whig Party.
4. Lincoln was elected President of the United States in 1860. Stephen A. Douglas defeated him in the 1858 Senate race.

EXERCISE C: Write a sentence by expanding each adjective clause.

> **Example:** where I was born
> **Answer:** On the corner of Western and Riverside, I saw the house <u>where I was born</u>.

1. which helped a great many people
2. who often spoke about her childhood
3. that my grandfather carved out of oak
4. whose lives have left such an impression on my own

Distinguishing Between Restrictive and Nonrestrictive Clauses

EXERCISE A: Write whether the underlined words are *restrictive, nonrestrictive,* or *not a clause.*

Example: The person who wrote this story was a Southerner.
Answer: restrictive

1. Eudora Welty, <u>whose stories are famous,</u> also wrote novels.
2. Her stories, <u>which are collected in this book,</u> are sometimes disturbing.
3. The book <u>that won the Pulitzer prize</u> was published in 1972.
4. Have you read <u>that particular novel?</u>
5. The character <u>whom I most enjoy</u> is in *Delta Wedding.*

EXERCISE B: Write the adjective clause from each sentence. Then identify it as *restrictive* or *nonrestrictive.*

Example: The girl whom I first asked was unable to attend.
Answer: whom I first asked (restrictive)

1. Our prom, which was attended by hundreds of students, was held on the the last weekend in May.
2. The decorations that our committee designed were great.
3. Students who came dateless had a terrific time anyway.
4. One chaperone whom I knew was Mr. Ky, my math teacher.
5. The Kys, whose graciousness was acknowledged, danced in a corner.

EXERCISE C: Use the word in parentheses to add an adjective clause to each sentence. Be sure to punctuate nonrestrictive clauses correctly.

Example: That sculptor created a monstrosity. (whose)
Answer: That sculptor, <u>whose work is infamous,</u> created a monstrosity.

1. The sculptor is Rodin. (whom)
2. His work is in stone. (which)
3. I worked with a hammer and chisel. (that)
4. My teacher, Mr. Dexter, assisted me. (who)
5. Dexter was commissioned to build a monument. (whose)

Identifying and Using Adverb Clauses

EXERCISE A: Write the word that is modified by each underlined adverb clause.

> **Example:** <u>Although the sun was warm</u>, the wind cut keenly.
> **Answer:** cut

1. <u>Wherever Skip strolls</u>, he observes wildlife.
2. <u>As soon as a bird flies by</u>, Skip identifies it.
3. He reacts to each new bird <u>as if it were a rare jewel</u>.
4. He seems enthusiastic <u>because he loves nature</u>.
5. He is more curious now <u>than he ever was</u>.

EXERCISE B: Write the adverb clause in each sentence. Underline the subordinating conjunction. In parentheses, write the word that the clause modifies.

> **Example:** Unless you say otherwise, we will proceed.
> **Answer:** <u>Unless</u> you say otherwise (will proceed)

1. Before Eisenhower was elected President, he served in the Army.
2. Please call me when you feel rested.
3. After we finished our breakfast, Myron read aloud.
4. Ana's singing voice is better than it was a year ago.
5. Dana jumped painfully, as if she had been burned.

EXERCISE C: Expand each sentence by adding an adverb clause that begins with the subordinating conjunction in parentheses. You may position the adverb clause before or after the main clause.

> **Example:** He wears his old trenchcoat. (wherever)
> **Answer:** He wears his old trenchcoat <u>wherever he goes</u>.

1. The detective answered the phone. (because)
2. He would take any case offered. (unless)
3. He swung into action. (as soon as)
4. In his bag he packed a spyglass. (so that)
5. He rarely made much money on his cases. (although)

Identifying and Using Noun Clauses

EXERCISE A: Write the noun clause in each sentence.

Example: Linda gives whatever she does her full attention.
Answer: whatever she does

1. Whomever the board picks will receive a scholarship.
2. How they select a winner is of no importance.
3. Biology is what Linda wishes to study.
4. Do you suppose that she will win?

EXERCISE B: Write each sentence and underline the noun clause(s). Then write how each underlined noun clause is used as *subject, predicate nominative, direct object, indirect object,* or *object of a preposition.*

Example: The Red Cross did what it could.
Answer: The Red Cross did <u>what it could</u> (direct object)

1. How the storm began makes an interesting story.
2. The news was that a hurricane was coming.
3. I don't remember who alerted the town.
4. I'm not sure about what occurred after that.
5. I told whoever was in charge that I would help.

EXERCISE C: Expand each sentence by adding a noun clause that uses the word in parentheses. (In some cases, you may need to add other words as well.)

Example: astronomy is a subject (that)
Answer: Astronomy is a subject <u>that fascinates me</u>.

1. will learn about the movements of the planets (whoever)
2. it seems clear to me (that)
3. most astronomers agree (whatever)
4. read this article on black holes (whomever)
5. the author can teach you (what)

Using Clauses Correctly

EXERCISE A: For each sentence, write *Correct* if the main clause contains the main idea. Write *faulty subordination* if the main idea is misplaced in the subordinate clause; then rewrite only the correct main clause.

> **Example:** After the charitable organization distributed the clothes and toys to the needy, the charitable organization received the donations.
> **Answer:** faulty subordination   the charitable organization distributed the clothes and toys to the needy

1. Unless they may get sicker, the hungry children receive food donations immediately.
2. Since these people need help, they are without food and shelter.
3. If people can help others less fortunate, everyone benefits.
4. When many homeless children fall behind in their education, they don't attend school.

EXERCISE B: Rewrite a sentence if it has faulty subordination, correcting the error. If a sentence does not contain this error, write *Correct*.

> **Example:** Because the room felt like a hot oven, the air conditioning broke down.
> **Answer:** Because the air conditioning broke down, the room felt like a hot oven.

1. Since most students will dress lightly tomorrow, the air conditioning won't be repaired for a couple of days.
2. If you wave a sheet of paper in front of your face, you can feel a slight breeze.
3. They were uncomfortable and irritable from the heat because the principal dismissed the students early.
4. Whenever the class moaned, the science teacher talked about the physical composition of snow.

EXERCISE C: Rewrite the sentences, correcting faulty subordination.

> **Example:** Although we were still cold, the fire was blazing.
> **Answer:** Although the fire was blazing, we were still cold.

1. Because we shouldn't pollute it, we breathe the air.
2. Cars burn fuel when they emit carbon dioxide into the atmosphere.
3. If temperatures begin to rise, there is too much carbon dioxide in the air.
4. When you help fight pollution, you use your bicycle instead of your car.

Colons

Using Colons Correctly

EXERCISE A: Rewrite the sentences. Add colons, or replace other punctuation with colons, where needed. If a sentence needs no changes, write *Correct*.

> **Example:** This label says, "Warning Not to be taken internally."
> **Answer:** This label says, "Warning: Not to be taken internally."

1. My watch must be running fast; it can't be 1000 already!
2. This route goes through Washington, Oregon, and northern California.
3. Caution The next five miles are under construction.
4. If I miss the 245 bus, I'll have to wait until 320 for the next one.
5. To begin this project, gather these materials two cups of flour, a bowl of water, and several newspapers.
6. The letter from Acme Manufacturing said, in part, "Dear Ms. Bryant, We were quite impressed with your letter of March 14."
7. Teaching kindergarten calls for several important traits, organizational skills, the ability to explain things well, and patience.
8. I'll need lettuce, carrots, green pepper, and tomatoes for this salad.
9. The announcement began as follows "To all sophomores Congratulations on a job well done!"
10. Attention, We will close at 730 P.M. to prepare for tomorrow's sale.

EXERCISE B: Rewrite this excerpt from a business letter. Add colons, or replace other punctuation with colons, in the ten places where they are needed.

Dear Mr. and Mrs. Harper

Thank you for your letter of November 18, in which you expressed concern about several important issues, health-care reform, rising taxes, and gun control. As your new representative, I am concerned about these issues, too. During my campaign, I set these goals to make the issues clear to the community, to know how people feel about them, and to act in the people's best interest. To begin fulfilling those goals, I have scheduled a series of "Explore the Issues" meetings. They will be held from 730 to 900 P.M. at Town Hall on the following dates, November 24, December 1, and December 8.There also will be a Saturday morning meeting— from 945 to 1115—on December 10. These meetings will be attended by a variety of community leaders Mayor Dunn, members of the City Council, law-enforcement officials, and local businesspeople.

Please note a list of scheduled topics is enclosed. I hope to meet you there.

Sincerely,

Jeremy Ortega

Commas

Using Commas with Coordinating Conjunctions

EXERCISE A: Use a coordinating conjunction to combine each pair of sentences. Add commas where needed.

 Example: Radio is a common mode of communication. Many people rely on it each day.
 Answer: Radio is a common mode of communication, and many people rely on it each day.

1. Radio waves travel great distances. They can pass through air and some solid objects.
2. The military depends upon rapid communications. Military planes and ships are equipped with radios.
3. Radio was once the leading form of entertainment. It has been surpassed by television.
4. Many people get their news from radio. They listen to its music.
5. There are about 10,000 radio stations in the United States. Americans own some 500 million radios.

EXERCISE B: Expand each clause so that it becomes a compound sentence. (You may position each clause anywhere so that it makes sense in the new sentence.) Add commas where needed.

 Example: Marcus wants a portable radio.
 Answer: Marcus wants a portable radio, but he can't decide on the model.

 1. "Baby boomers" enjoy listening to the radio.
 2. "Air wars" frequently take the form of contests and giveaways.
 3. Kareem never listens to "Top Ten" radio.
 4. Amber loves soccer and softball.
 5. Myra stays tuned to weather reports.
 6. I turn it on right after dinner.
 7. This station plays classical music until 8:00 P.M.
 8. A third is ready to go on the air.
 9. KHIP, the all-jazz station, seemed an unlikely choice for this market.
10. No one station can play all my favorite songs.

Using Commas with Subordinating Conjunctions

EXERCISE A: Combine each pair of sentences, using a subordinating conjunction. Add commas where needed.

> **Example:** Ronald Reagan entered politics. Earlier he had been an actor.
> **Answer:** <u>Before Ronald Reagan entered politics,</u> he had been an actor.

1. He graduated from college. "Dutch" Reagan got a job as a sports announcer.
2. He had impressed some Hollywod executives. He was later signed to a movie contract.
3. Reagan first served in public office in 1966. He was elected governor of California.
4. His campaign for the Presidency in 1976 was unsuccessful. He did attract great support from conservatives.
5. Reagan campaigned again in 1980. He gathered even more support and defeated Jimmy Carter, the incumbent.

EXERCISE B: Complete each sentence by adding a subordinate clause. Be sure to use commas correctly.

> **Example:** Politics really interests me.
> **Answer:** <u>Although I don't intend to run for office,</u> politics really interests me.

1. You should know about our political leadership.
2. Look for information about local politics.
3. Candidates can always use volunteers.
4. Political commentators offer valuable insights.
5. They may suggest the legislative effects of the news.
6. Voters are attracted by many personal qualities.
7. Some people obviously seem to take for granted their right to vote.
8. The polls are rarely busy.
9. What kind of campaign would you organize?
10. The choice of President may reflect the nation's mood.

Using Commas with Adjectives

EXERCISE A: Rewrite each sentence, adding commas where needed. If a sentence needs no commas, write *Correct*.

> **Example:** The tired happy teens climbed down from the ship.
> **Answer:** The tired, happy teens climbed down from the ship.

1. Their parents anxious yet relieved greeted them at the gate.
2. From the start, the rusted greasy ship had not seemed seaworthy.
3. Its sails had been ripped apart by fierce howling hurricane-like winds.
4. The ordeal both frightening and interminable ended with a daring rescue.
5. Two courageous sailors had rowed out to collect the youths in the dark storm.

EXERCISE B: Rewrite the paragraph, adding commas where they are needed.

> **Example:** The island was known for its lush hardy vegetation.
> **Answer:** The island was known for its lush, hardy vegetation.

Towering graceful palms ringed the island. The interior cool and shady offered a welcome relief from the hot humid afternoon. Banana trees fragrant and filled with ripe fruit bent under their heavy loads. Green snakelike vines hung suspended across the forest canopy. Even the surrounding coral reef supported various species of plants.

EXERCISE C: Rewrite the sentences, adding adjectives where directed. Be sure to use commas correctly.

> **Example:** The beach was full of (adjective) (adjective) tourists.
> **Answer:** The beach was full of <u>excited, carefree</u> tourists.

1. The (adjective) (adjective) hotel was located near the beach.
2. The manager (adjective) and (adjective) was standing in the lobby.
3. The new guest (adjective) but (adjective) spoke Spanish fluently.
4. His postcard home said, "Having a (adjective) (adjective) time. Wish you were here."
5. No one wanted to leave the (adjective) (adjective) vacation resort.

Using Commas with Introductory Words and Phrases

EXERCISE A: Write the introductory material in each sentence; follow it with a comma, and write the word following the comma.

> **Example:** With a determined expression she announced her plan.
> **Answer:** With a determined expression, she

1. Before the next major snowstorm I will buy a jeep.
2. Trimming the front hedges Dad accidentally slipped.
3. In spite of the cool temperature the walk was pleasant.
4. Actually I've just completed the story "The One-Egg Cake."
5. In the beginning of the story Gene has just returned to school.
6. Indeed he had made "a separate peace."
7. Instead of waiting until tomorrow let us begin at once.
8. As always Grandma listened patiently to all I had to say.
9. Rushing to catch the bus Donald twisted his ankle.
10. After four or five days the boys had become great friends.

EXERCISE B: Rewrite the sentences, adding commas where appropriate. If a sentence needs no comma, write *Correct.*

> **Example:** Without a doubt the Louisiana Purchase was an important event.
> **Answer:** Without a doubt, the Louisiana Purchase was an important event.

1. In a bold transaction the United States bought land from France.
2. From the Mississippi River to the Rocky Mountains this land spread.
3. Almost doubling the area of the country the land cost $15 million.
4. Finally word came that Spain had ceded the land to France.
5. Napoleon then sold the entire territory to the United States.

EXERCISE C: Rewrite the paragraph, adding commas where appropriate.

In 1725 Peter the Great of Russia sent Vitus Bering to explore the North Pacific. Oddly enough he wanted to know whether Asia was connected to North America by land. On his second expedition Bering sighted the Alaskan mainland. After proving that Asia and North America were not connected Bering returned to Russia. Establishing Russia's claim to Alaska a Russian fur trader began the first European settlement there in 1784.

Using Commas with Interrupters

EXERCISE A: Rewrite each sentence, adding commas where needed.

> **Example:** Bruce is in the first place an experienced driver.
> **Answer:** Bruce is, in the first place, an experienced driver.

1. The show was however an immediate success.
2. She became as you know a great star.
3. I will play Philip if you will accompany me.
4. Isabelle's essay not mine won an award.
5. Faye Doran the well-known actress hosted the program.

EXERCISE B: If a sentence contains an essential expression, write *Essential.* If a sentence contains a nonessential or parenthetical expression, rewrite the sentence, adding the necessary commas.

> **Example:** The President's wife although not well hosted many parties.
> **Answer:** The President's wife, although not well, hosted many parties.

(1) John Quincy Adams the sixth President of the United States was the son of a former President. (2) This as you can imagine was an unusual situation. (3) It had never occurred before and has not occurred since as the records show. (4) His father was John Adams the second President of the United States. (5) John Quincy Adams was an experienced diplomat as history attests before he took office. (6) The policies shaped by Adams when he was Secretary of State were major ones. (7) One policy that he helped shape is known as the Monroe Doctrine. (8) This doctrine which warned Europe against interfering in the Americas was quite important. (9) As President not as Secretary of State Adams had to deal with a hostile Congress. (10) Adams who was not re-elected became the only former President to serve in Congress.

EXERCISE C: Use the following words or phrases as nonessential material within sentences about a sport that you enjoy. Be sure to use commas correctly.

> **Example:** as you know
> **Answer:** Soccer, as you know, is an aerobic sport.

1. the goalkeeper
2. if they do their job well
3. for example
4. on the other hand
5. needless to say

Using Commas in Series

EXERCISE A: Rewrite the sentences, adding commas where needed. If a sentence needs no commas, write *Correct*.

> **Example:** I am taking my snowshoes skis and poles with me.
> **Answer:** I am taking my snowshoes, skis, and poles with me.

1. I can travel to school by car by private bus or by subway.
2. A French bakery a pizzeria a kosher delicatessen and a Korean restaurant are just a few of the dining spots in my neighborhood.
3. Do you want this picture near the sofa above the fireplace or opposite your desk?
4. We will be looking for energetic eager and cooperative trainees.
5. The author told us about her latest novel described its major characters read us a short selection and then answered questions.
6. How enthusiastically the boys and girls and their parents applauded!
7. We serve three kinds of sandwiches: bologna and cheese peanut butter and jelly and lettuce and tomato.
8. "Which explorer," Capt. Reynolds asked, "has traveled along the Amazon River climbed Mt. Everest and excavated ruins in Egypt?"
9. We listened graciously to her sincere and moving apology.
10. Among William Butler Yeats's best-known poems are "The Wild Swans at Coole" "Easter 1916" "Lapis Lazuli" and "Sailing to Byzantium."

EXERCISE B: For each question, write an answer that contains items in a series. Be sure to use commas correctly. (You may need to do some research to answer a few of the questions.)

> **Example:** What could we do today?
> **Answer:** Today we could go to the beach, visit a museum, or just relax at home.

1. What does Ken like for breakfast?
2. Where did Vanessa search for her dog?
3. Who has been chosen to serve on the Entertainment Committee?
4. Which countries does Jill hope to visit when she is older?
5. What are some of the federal holidays?
6. What is the weather like today?
7. What are some of the things for which Thomas Jefferson is remembered?
8. Which musical performers are your favorites?
9. How do you find out about your favorite performers?
10. If you had a recording contract, which songs would you want on your first CD?

Using Commas with Direct Quotations

EXERCISE A: Rewrite the sentences, adding commas where needed.

    Example: Linda murmured "It was hard to run on a sprained ankle."
    Answer: Linda murmured, "It was hard to run on a sprained ankle."

1. The coach said "You had to signal for a replacement."
2. "Wait on the sidelines for a stretcher" the referee directed.
3. Rita announced "That shouldn't have happened to our star player."
4. "I can't imagine a star player leaving the game" Linda sighed.
5. "Forget the melodramatics" Maria complained "and get on with the game!"

EXERCISE B: Rewrite the sentences, adding any missing punctuation.

    Example: There is no protection against slander wrote Molière.
    Answer: "There is no protection against slander," wrote Molière.

1. Andrew Jackson declared One man with courage makes a majority.
2. Neither current events nor history show that the majority rules, or ever did rule wrote Jefferson Davis.
3. What is history Napolean asked but a fable agreed upon?
4. Love is space and time measured by the heart penned Proust.
5. Better die once for all noted Aesop than live in continual terror.
6. Albert Einstein advised Let every man be respected as an individual.
7. I will back the masses said Gladstone over the classes.
8. Bertrand Russell wrote Men fear thought as they fear nothing else.
9. Whatever you cannot understand explained Goethe you cannot possess.
10. My country right or wrong is a thing no patriot would think of saying G. K. Chesterton affirmed.

EXERCISE C: Write five sentences, using each of the items below as a direct quotation. Be sure to use commas and quotation marks correctly.

    Example: Let's go to the store.
    Answer: Kay said, "Let's go to the store."

1. Why? What do we need?
2. We're out of milk, and I need tomatoes for our salad.
3. How I wish we'd grown our own tomatoes.
4. Do you wish we had our own cow, too?
5. Yes, if you would be the one to milk it.

Other Uses of Commas

EXERCISE A: Rewrite each item, adding commas where needed. If an item needs no commas, write *Correct.*

   Example: 14000 square feet
   Answer: 14,000 square feet

 1. Hanoi Vietnam
 2. Tuesday June 7 1994
 3. Act III scene ii
 4. Dear Mr. Markova
 5. Yours truly
 6. 1000000 pounds
 7. January 1880
 8. Volume 2 page 24
 9. last October 10
10. Akron Ohio

EXERCISE B: Rewrite the sentences, adding commas where needed.

   Example: On Friday November 25 we visited the museum.
   Answer: On Friday, November 25, we visited the museum.

 1. We had planned our trip to New York for Thanksgiving 1994.
 2. On November 21 1994 we were finally on our way.
 3. Marc read from *Tour Guide to NYC* Chapter 5 page 230.
 4. It said that in 1988 7000000 people lived here.
 5. We visited the Convention and Visitors Bureau 2 Columbus Circle New York New York.
 6. Sunday November 27 was a great day for us.
 7. We went to see *Ah Wilderness!* by Eugene O'Neill.
 8. During Act I scene i I recognized a friend.
 9. Kristy had come all the way from Lubbock Texas.
10. My postcard home said, "Dear Mom What a great place!"

EXERCISE C: Rewrite the letter, adding commas where needed.

   Example: Des Moines IA 50309
   Answer: Des Moines, IA 50309

                                                                    May 1 1995

Dear Uncle Leo

   Please come see my school play on Saturday May 20 at 7:00 P.M. I'm not the star, but I have a big scene in Act II scene ii that I know you will love. For a clue, look at your copy of *Favorite Plays for Children* page 235. The play will be given at Harold Dawes School Route 20. The auditorium seats 1500, so there should be no problem getting tickets.

                                                                    Your niece

                                                                    Dorrie

Using Comma Sense

EXERCISE A: Read each sentence, noting the placement of the comma. Then answer the question in parentheses.

> **Example:** After leaving the room, quietly Jon shut the door. (Did Jon leave the room quietly, or shut the door quietly?)
> **Answer:** Jon shut the door quietly.

1. As we filed out solemnly, he spoke to Mrs. Wicker. (Did we file out solemnly, or did he speak solemnly?)
2. As we filed out, solemnly he spoke to Mrs. Wicker. (Did we file out solemnly, or did he speak solemnly?)
3. Once we had dispersed into the room, a strange woman stumbled. (Did we disperse into the room, or did the woman stumble into the room?)
4. Once we had dispersed, into the room a strange woman stumbled. (Did we disperse into the room, or did the woman stumble into the room?)

EXERCISE B: Read each sentence. Then rewrite it by using commas to show the meaning suggested in parentheses.

> **Example:** Do you recall meeting my friend Sharon Martin? (Martin is the person being addressed.)
> **Answer:** Do you recall meeting my friend Sharon, Martin.

1. Sharon Martin studies the novels of Scott Paul. (Sharon is being addressed.)
2. Sharon Martin studies the novels of Scott Paul. (Paul is being addressed.)
3. After studying Scott for years in England I began to work on a book. (I began the book in England.)
4. After studying Scott for years in England I began to work on a book. (I studied Scott in England.)

EXERCISE C: Rewrite the paragraph, inserting the five commas where they are needed. Remember to use your "commas sense" in making decisions.

> **Example:** After purchasing the dog P. J. and I drove home.
> **Answer:** After purchasing the dog, P. J. and I drove home.

Intrigued by dog training P. J. talked to breeders. After studying books on several breeds he decided on an Irish setter. He talked to a breeder Ms. Jane Fried on a trip to Pennsylvania. Ms. Fried promised him the pick of the litter the best puppy in the batch.

Commonly Confused or Misused Words

Commonly Confused or Misused Words I

EXERCISE A: Write the word in parentheses that correctly completes each sentence.

> **Example:** The coach's speed had a great (effect, affect) on the team's performance.
> **Answer:** effect

1. The speaker (alluded, eluded) to a painting by Picasso.
2. After listening for half an hour, we decided that we knew that information (all ready, already).
3. Davis felt that he had played (bad, badly).
4. Can't you (except, accept) the fact that the ring is lost?
5. Is "free will" merely an (allusion, illusion)?
6. Once in (awhile, a while) a great thinker comes along to challenge traditional ideas.
7. Was there anyone (beside, besides) Janet who saw the accident?
8. Because of (averse, adverse) conditions, the game was postponed.
9. If you want my (advice, advise), Rikki, wear the red sweater.
10. Is it (alright, all right) if I take my dog to the park?

EXERCISE B: Rewrite the paragraph, correcting any words that have been confused or misused.

> **Example:** Against everyone's advise, Yoko entered the contest.
> **Answer:** Against everyone's <u>advice</u>, Yoko entered the contest.

Yoko loves to except every challenge. She has a few mistaken allusions about herself; thus, we were already for Yoko to fail. Between the three finalists, Yoko was certainly the most enthusiastic. In the end, I guess, she didn't do too bad.

EXERCISE C: Write five sentences, using each pair of words correctly.

> **Example:** lend/borrow
> **Answer:** If you <u>lend</u> me that book, I won't have to <u>borrow</u> it from the library.

1. accept/except
2. adapt/adopt
3. advise/advice
4. allusion/illusion
5. between/among

Commonly Confused or Misused Words II

EXERCISE A: Rewrite the sentences, using the correct words in parentheses.

> **Example:** Take a deep (breath, breathe); now (breath, breathe) slowly and calmly.
> **Answer:** Take a deep <u>breath</u>; now <u>breathe</u> slowly and calmly.

1. You (may, can) take notes if you wish so that you (may, can) review your "James Bond" assignment later.
2. The dictator's (capital, capitol) city is in a hot, dry (desert, dessert).
3. (Choose, Chose) (clothes, cloths) that are inconspicuous but cool.
4. Did you (choose, chose) a trench coat to (complement, compliment) that outfit?
5. Don't go to sleep; your (continual, continuous) vigilance is essential.
6. No government is (disinterested, uninterested) when it comes to intelligence gathering.
7. Be (discreet, discrete) when inquiring about (discreet, discrete) events.
8. (Bring, Take) a camera with you; (bring, take) back photographs.
9. The (council, counsel) is planning something; my (council, counsel) is to proceed cautiously.
10. With you on this assignment, I can (breath, breathe) more easily.
11. Our actions are a (capital, capitol) crime—so don't fail!
12. Our informant will (emigrate, immigrate) to Brazil when the mission is completed.
13. Keep me posted; I am not (disinterested, uninterested) in your progress.

EXERCISE B: Rewrite the sentences, correcting any errors in words that have been confused or misused.

> **Example:** The spy gives polite, discrete answers to the custom agent's questions.
> **Answers:** The spy gives polite, <u>discreet</u> answers to the custom agent's questions.

1. Welcome to our country. Are you emigrating or visiting?
2. Ah! I see from your passport that you are an imminent doctor.
3. Why did you chose to come to the desert on your vacation?
4. Did you bring a camera here to photograph our beautiful capital building?
5. I like your cloths, but you will not need a trench coat in the desert.
6. Can I have your permission to open your suitcase so that I can look inside?
7. Bring it here, please. Why do you breath so fast? Are you hiding something?
8. I complement you on your camera. What a long lens it has!
9. Did you choose to stay in the capital, or will you go further inland?
10. Take my counsel and try the desert in the hotel cafe; it's capital!

Commonly Confused or Misused Words III

EXERCISE A: Write the word in parentheses that fits each definition.

Example: (leave, left): to go away
Answer: leave

1. (learn, teach): to instruct or show how
2. (ingenious, ingenuous): naive or unsophisticated
3. (imply, infer): to understand a hint or suggestion
4. (formally, formerly): politely or according to customs and rules of behavior
5. (indigent, indigenous): native or local
6. (imply, infer): to hint or suggest
7. (formally, formerly): earlier or previously
8. (indigent, indigenous): poor
9. (ingenious, ingenuous): clever, brilliantly intelligent
10. (oral, aural): referring to speech

EXERCISE B: Rewrite the paragraph, correcting any confused or misused words.

Example: My friend learned me to play the guitar.
Answer: My friend <u>taught me</u> to play the guitar.

   In fewer than three weeks, I could play songs. I can play some popular songs good, but I am also learning how to make up my own songs, too. Now I literally play by ear. I don't mean to infer that I am any kind of musical genius; it's just that I enjoy music and I practice every chance that I get.

EXERCISE C: Define each word.

Example: imply
Answer: imply: to hint or suggest

1. indigent
2. formerly
3. ingenious
4. loose
5. oral

Commonly Confused or Misused Words IV

EXERCISE A: Rewrite the sentences, using the correct words in parentheses.

>   **Example:** We (passed, past) Canyonlands National Park that afternoon.
>   **Answer:** We <u>passed</u> Canyonlands National Park that afternoon.

1. The park (personal, personnel) told us how to (precede, proceed) to find Druid Arch, our (principal, pinciple) objective.
2. Rather (than, then) start immediately, we found a nice campground and (set, sit) up our new tent.
3. We decided to (raise, rise) early the next day and get started.
4. The (weather, whether) was hot, so we stopped often to (set, sit).
5. We didn't know (weather, whether) we were going in the right direction.
6. Many other people had (preceded, proceeded) us, leaving prints in sand.
7. We didn't know (whose, who's) fingerprints they were.
8. Druid Arch is a (real, really) arch; (your, you're) going to love it.
9. I couldn't (set, sit) down the camera; there were so many great views!
10. We returned to camp just as the sun began to (sit, set).
11. I got out some (stationary, stationery), wrote a letter to the park superintendent, and signed it "(Respectfully, Respectively) yours."

EXERCISE B: Rewrite the sentences, correcting any errors in words that have been confused or misused.

>   **Example:** Do not set too long in the desert heat; it will fry you're brain.
>   **Answer:** Do not <u>sit</u> too long in the desert heat; it will fry <u>your</u> brain.

1. The park is really managed by personal from the National Parks Department.
2. The responsibility is there's to protect the park's natural resources.
3. Irregardless of whether your traveling by car or on foot, Canyonlands National Park is as really breathtaking place to explore.
4. If you precede on your trip by foot, carry plenty of water.
5. In the passed, people who have hiked there have suffered from dehydration.
6. Rather then risk a tragedy, tell park personnel where you are hiking.
7. Whomever explores by car should also think about there safety.
8. Whether can change quickly; really violent thunderstorms may cause water to raise suddenly in the canyons, washing out roads.

Conjunctions

Identifying and Using Coordinating Conjunctions

EXERCISE A: Write a coordinating conjunction that can appropriately complete each of the sentences.

> **Example:** Both the stars and the planets are in motion, _____ some of them move quickly.
> **Answer:** and

1. We do not see the stars move, _____ they are so far away that they seem to be motionless.
2. Pluto _____ Jupiter are far from Earth, _____ a large telescope is needed to see them.
3. People wonder if Mars ever had any vegetation _____ if Earth is the only planet with plant life.
4. Saturn's rings are composed of billions of particles, _____ from great distances they appear to be solid masses.
5. Venus is similar in size to Earth, _____ its atmosphere is very different.

EXERCISE B: Combine each set of sentences by using coordinating conjunctions. (Some sentences require more than one coordinating conjunction.)

> **Example:** Marty brought his autoharp to the party. Travis brought his guitar.
> **Answer:** Marty brought his autoharp to the party, and Travis brought his guitar.

1. The airline will sell discount tickets. People need to make reservations early.
2. Nancy brought Molly a birthday gift. Kelly also brought one. Linda forgot hers.
3. Lucy lost her library card. She couldn't take out books and complete her assignment.
4. One hundred years ago, farmers used horses for power. Today they utilize tractors.
5. Cindy may baby-sit for us Saturday night. Matt may baby-sit for us Saturday night.
6. Each year the cost of cassette tapes and CD's increases. Teenagers are the largest group of music consumers.
7. Tony cannot take the job. Bob is not available.
8. At the campground, the family secured their food supply in locked coolers. They had spotted black bears in the area. Raccoons were also spotted.
9. Camping is so much fun. It's also an inexpensive way to spend a vacation.
10. Mountain climbing is similar to spending a few days in the woods. It's more expensive.

Identifying and Using Correlative Conjunctions

EXERCISE A: Complete the sentences with appropriate correlative conjunctions.

    Example: _____ sand _____ chemical foam can smother an oil fire.
    Answer: <u>Either</u> sand <u>or</u> chemical foam can smother an oil fire.

1. _____ Anita _____ Marti will be at the dance Friday because they both have to work.
2. _____ corn _____ beans are common ingredients in Southwest cuisine.
3. _____ Garth _____ Gloria will go fishing with us.
4. We don't know _____ to schedule the class picnic for May _____ to wait until June.
5. _____ Gary _____ Jan and Merle went to the game early to get good seats.

EXERCISE B: Combine each set of sentences by using correlative conjunctions. (Some sentences require two correlative conjunctions.)

    Example: Gale-force winds are expected before morning. There will be high tides as well.
    Answer: <u>Both</u> gale-force winds <u>and</u> high tides are expected before morning.

1. Andy's mother was not at the opening performance of his play. Andy's brother was not there, either.
2. Teresa loves Latin American music. Latin music is a favorite of Carlos's also.
3. Lasagna makes a good inexpensive meal. Spaghetti is another choice.
4. The teacher hasn't decided if she will test us on Thursday. She may have another review.
5. New homes will be built on the west side of town. A shopping mall also will be built there.
6. Bad weather will not stop Jody from going home for Thanksgiving. Illness will not stop her either, since Ray will be coming home. Sarah will also be coming. (2)
7. If Diana comes, the party is sure to be a success. If Ellen comes, the party is sure to be a success.
8. The twins will be arriving in Boston. Their parents will be arriving in Boston. Their arrivals may be tonight or tomorrow morning. (2)
9. A hurricane is predicted. Floods are expected.
10. One bad day at the office will not cause Duane to quit. A poor performance review will not cause Duane to quit.

Identifying and Using Subordinating and Conjunctive Adverbs

EXERCISE A: Write and label each conjunctive adverb and subordinating conjunction in the sentences.

>   **Example:** Roy forgot his watch; thus, he did not know the time.
>   **Answer:** thus—conjunctive adverb

1. Glen wants to buy a car; however, he doesn't have enough money.
2. While the team was not favored to win the game, they did win.
3. Joe is a waiter at a restaurant; in addition, he writes plays.
4. After the dike overflowed, many homes were flooded.
5. I do not need a large car; furthermore, I do not like vans, since I have difficulty parking them.

EXERCISE B: Combine each sentence—once by using a conjunctive adverb and once by using a subordinating conjunction.

>   **Example:** The rain was heavy. The baseball game was postponed.
>   **Answers:** The rain was heavy; <u>therefore</u>, the baseball game was postponed.
>
>   The baseball game was postponed <u>because</u> the rain was heavy.

1. That movie received bad reviews. Many people went to see it.
2. The bus was very slow. We were late for our dance lessons.
3. Tom was failing geometry. He needed a tutor.
4. Lionel is a gifted singer. He plays piano well.
5. Lisa arrived ten minutes late. She did not have her homework.
6. The Murrays waited three months for their new CD player. It was delivered to their apartment.
7. Terry's car is not dependable. It rarely starts on cold mornings.
8. Cats will drink water. They prefer milk.
9. The singer had many fans. Tickets for her concerts were hard to get.
10. Our car would not start. Dad called a towing service.

Distinguishing Between Conjunctions and Prepositions

EXERCISE A: Write each word in parentheses and label it as a *conjunction* or a *preposition*.

> **Example:** Karen went bowling (after) she finished her homework.
> **Answer:** after—conjunction

1. Allan has grown much taller (since) I last saw him.
2. Mom took me to a movie (after) work.
3. Bring your new CD, (as) you promised to do.
4. The children were dressed (as) circus animals for the play.
5. I can hardly wait (until) the circus comes around next year!
6. Sato has not written us (since) school started.
7. Billy started to run (before) he had control of the football.
8. Our science project is not due (until) Monday.
9. Loni has been out (since) noon; please call back (before) dinner.

EXERCISE B: Rewrite the sentences, using conjunctions and prepositions to complete them. Label each choice as a *conjunction* or a *preposition*.

> **Example:** Richard was nervous the math test.
> **Answer:** Richard was nervous <u>before</u> the math test. (preposition)

1. Candice accepted the trophy she was introduced as captain.
2. lunch, we will drive to the airport.
3. I've said, the typewriter will be in the repair shop on Friday.
4. Graciela begins college, she will visit Spain, a graduation present.
5. the soccer game, I will drive Victor home his mother is working late.
6. Joey has been sick Saturday and he'll have to stay in bed he sees the doctor on Wednesday.

EXERCISE C: Use each word in two sentences—once as a conjunction and once as a preposition.

> **Example:** before
> **Answer:** We'll have to cut the grass <u>before</u> the rain begins. (conjunction)
>
> John is supposed to be home before dark. (preposition)

1. until
2. since
3. after
4. before
5. as

Using Conjunctions Correctly

EXERCISE A: Write whether each sentence is *correct* or *incorrect* in its use of conjunctions.

> **Example:** Every year many Americans visit Canada, some even own vacation homes near Canada's lakes and rivers.
> **Answer:** incorrect

1. Canada can offer a variety of tourist attractions; the reason is because it is such a large country.
2. And a cruise up the St. Lawrence Seaway makes a pleasant vacation.
3. Travelers also can sail from Seattle to Victoria; then they can travel from Victoria to Vancouver.
4. Tourists can find their favorite products like they were shopping in Britain.
5. A popular resort is Banff and Lake Louise, this region is quite beautiful.

EXERCISE B: Rewrite each item, correcting any misuse of conjunctions.

> **Example:** And we can go to the zoo if it's a sunny day.
> **Answer:** We also can go to the zoo if it's a sunny day.

1. Josh was disappointed; the reason is because his team lost the game.
2. Dad bought some gas, Mom and I finished shopping.
3. Bobby is not only my cousin. But he is also my best friend.
4. Nicky looks like he is ready to fall asleep.
5. Carlos has little experience, he is a hard worker.
6. We could go to a movie. Or we could head for the roller rink.
7. Nina missed the dress rehearsal for the concert. The reason is because she had a stomach virus.
8. Ted still enjoys playing with trains. Yet he is almost twenty.
9. The clerk apologized, he had kept us waiting a long time.
10. The coach yelled at Lily like she had gone deaf.

Developing Your Style: Conjunctions

EXERCISE A: Choose the correct coordinating or subordinating conjunction from the choice in parentheses to combine the following sentences. Revise the sentences and underline the conjunctions. Add punctuation as needed.

> **Example:** Maya Angelou's most famous work remains *I Know Why the Caged Bird Sings*, it was published in 1970. (and, yet)
>
> **Answer:** Maya Angelou's most famous work is *I Know Why the Caged Bird Sings,* <u>yet</u> it was published in 1970.

1. A recent book by Maya Angelou tells of her African travels, this book also describes her search for a sense of belonging. (but, or)
2. Angelou has written, produced, and directed television productions and movies, she might voice her experiences as an African American. (yet, so that)
3. Maya Angelou received an award for a television documentary, she also had earned awards for her books. (before, for)
4. She hosted a thirty-part study course for public television, she wrote a television script for *I Know Why the Caged Bird Sings.* (because, and)
5. Angelou shares her personal story intimately in her books, she has greater room for details. (or, where)

EXERCISE B: Combine each set of sentences by using a subordinating and/or coordinating conjunction. (Some sentences require more than one conjunction.)

> **Example:** Gold has been sought for hundreds of years. Gold has been sought in many parts of the world.
>
> **Answer:** Gold has been sought for hundreds of years <u>and</u> in many parts of the world.

1. People have been looking for gold for centuries. People have not found much gold.
2. One property of gold that makes it valuable is its beautiful color. Another valuable property is its softness.
3. Pure gold can be worked into various shapes. Pure gold can be minted as coins.
4. Gold is used in jewelry. It is usually combined with other metals to make it harder. Adding other metals makes gold more durable.
5. Jewelers use the term *karat* to measure the purity of gold. A twenty- four-karat gold ring is one hundred percent gold.
6. Eighteen-karat gold is often used in jewelry. This type of gold is equal to eighteen parts of gold. Six parts of another metal is added to the gold.
7. Finding gold in a jewelry store is easy. Finding gold in its natural state is not. Gold is found far below the earth's surface in veins of ore.
8. In 1848 gold was struck in California. Hundreds of thousands of people flocked to the gold fields.
9 A little later, gold was found in the Yukon Territory. The gold rush was on!
10 The famous author Jack London went to the gold fields of the Yukon. He wrote about his thrilling adventures.

Contractions

Identifying and Forming Contractions

EXERCISE A: Write the contraction for each item.

> **Example:** they would
> **Answer:**   they'd

1. she is
2. who would
3. will not
4. where is
5. he will
6. they are
7. does not
8. should have
9. have not
10. she has not

EXERCISE B: Rewrite the paragraph. If a contraction is given, write the two words that it contains. If two words are given, write the contraction that they would form.

> **Example:** (Wouldn't) you like to go to the planetarium with me?
> **Answer:**   <u>Would not</u> you like to go to the planetarium with me?

(I'm) planning a trip to the Hayden Planetarium. (It is) located on 81st Street in New York City. I (can't) wait to see the seventy-five-foot dome that forms the setting for the sky shows. (There is) also a space theater that presents slides on twenty-two screens simultaneously. After I see each presentation, (I'll) look at the exhibits. (Won't) it be exciting to see a 14-ton meteorite? (Who would) want to miss it? Of course, (I'd) also like to see the library, where (they've) accumulated an impressive collection of books on astonomy. (I have) set aside an entire day for this excursion.

EXERCISE C: Write the contraction for each pair of words in parentheses. Then use the same contractions in a paragraph of your own.

> **Example:** (He will) tell us about Kansas.
> **Answer:**   He'll

(Randy is) in Kansas for the summer. (He is) learning about that state as he travels through it. Before he left he (did not) know much about Kansas. Now, (you would) be surprised how informative his letters are. He surprised me by writing that the land in Kansas (is not) all prairie.

Distinguishing Between Possessive Pronouns and Contractions

EXERCISE A: Write the word in parentheses that correctly completes each sentence.

> **Example:** (They're, Their) having a talent contest next week.
> **Answer:** They're

1. (Its, It's) open to everyone in the neighborhood.
2. (Your, You're) dad said that we could use this for a costume.
3. I wonder (who's, whose) able to play the piano.
4. (Your, You're) not planning on telling jokes, are you?
5. (Whose, Who's) idea was this in the first place?

EXERCISE B: Rewrite the sentence to correct any misuse of possessive pronouns or contractions. If a sentence needs no changes, write *Correct.*

> **Example:** This basket of apples is our's.
> **Answer:** This basket of apples is <u>ours</u>.

1. I opened the car door to look at its interior.
2. In my family, everybodys' favorite meal is Chicago-style pizza.
3. Whose the man in the gray suit, holding the portfolio?
4. Our race is finished, but they have not yet run their's.
5. This museum is known for it's collection of pre-Columbian art.
6. How eagerly we listened to you're stories!
7. There's a basket with that red bicycle.
8. Excuse me, Ma'am, is this your seat?
9. Have you seen they're design for the cover?
10. Our homeroom is along the west hall, as is theirs.

EXERCISE C: Rewrite each sentence, using an appropriate possessive pronoun or contraction as designated in parentheses.

> **Example:** (Possessive Pronoun) is a very friendly neighborhood.
> **Answer:** <u>Theirs</u> is a very friendly neighborhood.

1. Does (possessive pronoun) cabin face west?
2. (Contraction) building a highway around the lake.
3. Can you tell me (possessive pronoun) bike that is?
4. The truck made (possessive pronoun) way through the mountains.
5. (Contraction) in charge here?

Dashes

Using Dashes Correctly

EXERCISE A: Rewrite each sentence, adding dashes where appropriate.

Example: One place Rio de Janeiro is the right setting.
Answer: One place—Rio de Janeiro—is the right setting.

1. This fruit Have you ever seen one? grows in the tropics.
2. The story a fable that I always enjoy has an important moral.
3. Precious jewels for example, diamonds are appraised here.
4. Some cities Cleveland, Pittsburgh, Detroit have a distinctive flavor.
5. The ending was a real surprise but that's enough for now.
6. The woman an actress of great talent lives in Cincinnati.
7. The violinist Have you ever heard such a stunning performance? bowed before the enthusiastic audience.
8. Flour, honey, and raisins these are the basic ingredients.
9. Is the costume a traditional folk-dancing outfit valuable?
10. The inventor a pioneer in the development of video recording equipment was honored by her colleagues.

EXERCISE B: Use dashes to combine each pair of sentences.

Example: Tides follow regular patterns. Tides are the rise and fall of ocean water.
Answer: Tides—the rise and fall of ocean water—follow regular patterns.

1. Tides are beneficial in many ways. Have you ever observed them?
2. The moon's gravity creates two high tides each day. This part may be hard to understand.
3. During high tides, ocean boats enter or leave the harbor. Ocean boats might otherwise become stuck in the shallow waters.
4. High tide takes place on the opposite side of the earth. It is the moon's pulling of the solid earth through the ocean.
5. Spring tides are caused by the pull of the moon combined with the pull of the sun. Spring tides are extremely dramatic.

Dates

Writing Dates Correctly

EXERCISE A: Rewrite each item correctly.

Example: february 29 1970
Answer: February 29, 1970

1. the Seventeenth century
2. december 1 1917
3. friday
4. thanksgiving
5. fall and Winter
6. wednesday
7. march 1 1991
8. the Elizabethan age
9. saturday
10. memorial day

EXERCISE B: Rewrite each sentence, capitalizing and puncutating all dates correctly. If a sentence contains no errors, write *Correct.*

Example: She was born on august 2 1932.
Answer: She was born on August 2, 1932.

1. Eleanor was born in the Summer of 1932.
2. From that date until may 2 1948 she lived in Chicago.
3. She lived in Hollywood until labor day.
4. One sunday she was playing volleyball on the beach.
5. She broke her leg and returned to Chicago in the Fall.
6. Eleanor attended the University of Chicago from september 5 1948 until sometime in 1951.
7. On november 1 1952 she married a classmate.
8. During the 1950's, the young couple traveled across the country.
9. They settled in New York State in the latter half of the twentieth Century.
10. Eleanor retired on june 15 1995 from the social services job she had held since the 1970's.

EXERCISE C: Rewrite the letter excerpt, correcting any errors in capitalization or punctuation of dates.

july 3 1995

Dear Uri,

   I will be lecturing around the country from august 19 until Columbus day or halloween. I hope to be in your area on tuesday or wednesday of the week of september 18 1995. Would you like to attend my talk? The title is "The Victorian Era." Afterward, you might show me the Autumn colors in New Hampshire.

Sincerely,

Derek

Double Negatives

Avoiding Double Negatives

EXERCISE A: Choose the word in parentheses that makes each sentence negative without forming a double negative.

Example: Diana didn't mention (anything, nothing) before 7:00 P.M.
Answer: anything

1. They don't expect (anyone, no one) before 7:00 P.M.
2. The storekeeper seldom wants (nothing, anything) gaudy in the window.
3. We haven't (ever, never) performed before such a large audience.
4. The President refused to say (anything, nothing) about the budget.
5. William would allow hardly (no one, anyone) to ride his motorcycle.

EXERCISE B: If a sentence contains a double negative, correct it in two ways. If it needs no changes, write *Correct*.

Example: I never told Sid nothing about the plan.
Answer: I never told Sid anything about the plan.

or

I told Sid nothing about the plan.

1. Gene hadn't never seen such a colorful parade.
2. You shouldn't do nothing until next week.
3. Phillip wouldn't admit his mistake to nobody.
4. We weren't surprised by anything we saw.
5. Claire and I haven't made no decisions yet.
6. Can't Roberta find her notebook nowhere?
7. These reports don't mention nothing about it.
8. We won't place no one in a dangerous situation.
9. I've rarely observed any deer in this location.
10. Nancy hasn't never been to Los Angeles, so she can't hardly wait to go.

EXERCISE C: Each phrases contains a double negative. Correct the error; then expand each phrase into a sentence.

Example: haven't barely begun
Answer: They <u>have barely begun</u> to rebuild the hospital.

1. didn't hardly understand
2. never found no evidence
3. couldn't buy nothing
4. wasn't scarcely completed
5. won't bother nobody

Ellipses

Using Ellipsis Points Correctly

EXERCISE A: Study each item. If ellipses are used correctly, write *Correct*. If they are not, rewrite the sentence correctly.

> **Example:** Said Napoleon, "The greatest general. . . . makes the fewest mistakes."
> **Answer:** Said Napoleon, "The greatest general . . . makes the fewest mistakes."

1. I am interested in . . . well, I guess you might call it the "military-industrial complex."
2. A wag wrote, "If it moves, salute it. . . If you can't pick it up, paint it."
3. Jefferson insisted, "For a people who are free. . . . a well-organized . . . militia is their best security."
4. Washington states, "Discipline is the soul of an army. It. . . . procures . . . esteem to all."
5. Did you. . . . pardon my asking. . . did you read the writings of Sun Tze on strategy?

EXERCISE B: Add ellipses to the second sentence in each pair to indicate what was omitted from the original citation. If there is only one sentence, rewrite it, using ellipses to indicate pauses.

> **Example:** Willa Cather, I think, is an American original.
>
> Willa Cather is an American original.
> **Answer:** Willa Cather. . . is an American original.

1. Willa was born in the East but grew up in Nebraska. Willa grew up in Nebraska.
2. Cather wrote novels. Many were set in the Midwest. A few were set in the Southwest.
3. Her work well, she is one of my favorite authors.
4. Honestly, excuse me you should read *O Pioneers!*
5. Her main theme is the immigration to and settlement of the American Middle West. Her main theme is the settlement of the Middle West.

Exclamation Points

Using Exclamation Points Correctly

EXERCISE A: Rewrite each item, using exclamation points correctly.

> **Example:** That's terrific
> **Answer:** That's terrific!

1. What a pity
2. Watch out
3. Stop, Doreen
4. How beautiful you look
5. What an awesome movie
6. Just in time Whew
7. Ugh How disgusting
8. That was a close call
9. Ivy said, "This is my lucky day"
10. Did Ed say, "Let's get out of here"?

EXERCISE B: Rewrite each item, adding information to it and using at least one exclamation point correctly.

> **Example:** A beautiful sunset
> **Answer:**   What a beautiful sunset that is!

1. Quiet
2. Such colors
3. Watch how you walk
4. Move away from the railing
5. Mind your own business
6. Look at that
7. Wow
8. How spectacular that is
9. What a sight I must look
10. Shh

EXERCISE C: Write phrases and sentences as directed. Be sure to use exclamation points correctly.

> **Example:** (Exclamatory phrase)
> **Answer:**   What a sight!

1. (Interjection)
2. (Exclamatory sentence)
3. (Command)
4. (Interjection)
5. (Exclamatory phrase)
6. (Command)
7. (Interjection)
8. (Exclamatory sentence)
9. (Command)
10. (Exclamatory sentence)

Gender

Using Gender References Correctly

EXERCISE A: Write whether each underlined pronoun is *correct* or *incorrect* in its usage. If it is incorrect, write the correct form of the pronoun.

> **Example:** Everybody has <u>their</u> favorite music.
> **Answer:** incorrect; his or her

1. Janice or Simon likes rock and roll, but <u>he</u> also enjoys country music.
2. Brad and Mark like country music, but <u>they</u> hate rock-and-roll.
3. Country music has good rhythm, and <u>she</u> always tells a good story.
4. Brenda and Andrew like rock, but <u>he and she</u> absolutely love blues.
5. If either Ann or Bill wants to hear rap, <u>they</u> can borrow Carol's CD's.

EXERCISE B: Complete each sentence with the correct pronouns.

> **Example:** Would Mario or Jennifer get _____ driver's license first?
> **Answer:** Would Mario or Jennifer get <u>his or her</u> driver's license first?

1. Mario's mother lent him _____ car when he took _____ driving test.
2. Her car was very small, so it was easier for _____ to park _____.
3. Everyone worries when _____ is about to take the test if _____ tester will be Officer Mary Ott.
4. Officer Ott never smiles when _____ tests teenagers, who are nervous when _____ are tested.
5. Mark and Jennifer got _____ licenses; each claimed that _____ had scored higher.

EXERCISE C: Rewrite the sentences, correcting errors in gender reference.

> **Example:** Katherine Paterson wrote *Lyddie;* she's a historical novel.
> **Answer:** Katherine Paterson wrote *Lyddie;* <u>it's</u> a historical novel.

1. *Lyddie* is about Lyddie, a girl who has to earn your own way in the 1840's.
2. *Lyddie* begins when a bear gets into her family's home, and he tears the place apart.
3. Lyddie's father has left home, and all it has left the family is a poor farm.
4. Everyone in the family is trying their best to pay the farm's debts.
5. Taking the youngest children with them, Lyddie's mother moves to a city.
6. Lyddie and her brother stay on their farm, trying to pay off her debts.
7. Neither of them is happy when they are sent for by his or her mother.
8. Each wants to stay and do their part in saving the family home.
9. Lyddie goes to work in a mill; no employee is happy with their situation there.
10. Lyddie and many other employees are forced to leave his or her job.

Hyphens

Using Hyphens for Syllabification and Line Breaks

EXERCISE A: Decide whether each word can be hyphenated if it occurs at the end of a line. If it can be hyphenated, write the part of the word that would appear at the end of a line. If it cannot be hyphenated, write the complete word.

> **Example:** apartment
> **Answer:** apart-

1. trademark
2. billion
3. defense
4. fury
5. self-taught
6. even
7. bought
8. background
9. Finland
10. part-time

EXERCISE B: Read each sentence and decide if the divided and hyphenated word has been divided correctly. If so, write *Correct*. If not, write the correct form.

> **Example:** At the picnic, we ate chic-
> ken sandwiches.
> **Answer:** chick-en

1. Bernard wants to con-
   vince us he is right.
2. We have been spen-
   ding too much money.
3. I am left–hand-
   ed, and so is Mariana.
4. We do not know the i-
   dentity of the suspect.
5. Did you know that my brother-in-law is from Italy?

EXERCISE C: In the following sentences, a slash is used to represent the end of a line. If the word division at the end of the line is correct, write *Correct*. If not, rewrite the sentence to correct the error.

> **Example:** Tiffany was cons- / idering the offer.
> **Answer:** Tiffany was con- / sidering the offer.

1. Did your pa- / ckage arrive on time?
2. When he wink- / ed, I understood.
3. Our trip to Wash- / ington was postponed.
4. Children who mis- / behave will be punished.
5. Please don't be so sel / fish anymore.

Grammar, Usage, Mechanics • Hyphens **167**

Other Uses of Hyphens

EXERCISE A: Write the following, adding hyphens where needed.

    Example: thirty four
    Answer: thirty-four

1. so called friend
2. African American literature
3. self reliant
4. sister in law
5. mid February snowstorm
6. three quarters empty
7. step by step approach
8. three hour meeting
9. how to book
10. our ex governor

EXERCISE B: Rewrite the following, adding hyphens where needed.

    Example: The measure needs a two thirds vote.
    Answer: The measure needs a <u>two-thirds</u> vote.

1. The president elect will take office in January.
2. Are those three four year olds triplets?
3. My friend's parents went on a six day cruise of the Caribbean.
4. No technical jargon is used in these easy to understand directions.
5. His great grandparents are in very good health.

EXERCISE C: Rewrite each sentence, correcting all errors in hyphenation. If there are no errors in hyphenation, write *Correct.*

    Example: Our class was un-able to attend the concert.
    Answer: Our class was <u>unable</u> to attend the concert.

1. They left home early in the morning and arrived by midafternoon.
2. That nation was already semiindependent even before the revolution.
3. She took a parttime job teaching crafts at the after-school center.
4. Is it more economical to buy a new sofa or to recover the old one?
5. The union is demanding higher wages and a 35 hour week.
6. Our ex-mayor did not show much self control in the recent election campaign.
7. The fraction twenty three thirty sixths cannot be further reduced.
8. My brother refused to play with the other 12-year-olds at the picnic.
9. We usually meet on Mondays, but it's not a hard and fast rule.
10. Many businesses prospered in the post World War II economic boom.

Interjections

Identifying and Punctuating Interjections

EXERCISE A: Write the interjection or interjections in each item.

> **Example:** Whew! It's time for a rest.
> **Answer:** Whew

1. Hey! Nobody's paying any attention to me!
2. Oh, I didn't know you were serious.
3. I, uh, don't really know how to say this.
4. You'll really go out with me? Hurray!
5. Ouch! That bee just stung me!
6. You were invited to the governor's mansion? Wow!
7. Ah! What a marvelous feast this is!
8. Well, I guess I'd better be going now.
9. Ugh! That's disgusting!
10. No—I'll do no such thing!

EXERCISE B: Write each sentence, adding an interjection that shows the indicated emotion.

> **Example:** (surprise) I never expected you to remember my birthday!
> **Answer:** <u>Wow,</u> I never expected you to remember my birthday!

1. (delight) That was a wonderful performance.
2. (disgust) I can't believe that Elisa's eating snails!
3. (hesitation) Maybe it would be better if you resigned.
4. (distress) I think I flunked the exam.
5. (joy) How I wish that this night could last forever!
6. (exhaustion) These suitcases must weigh a ton!
7. (self-satisfaction) I learned how to set the VCR.
8. (pain) I think that I've sprained my ankle!
9. (impatience) You'll just have to try harder next time, won't you?
10. (frustration) You make me so angry sometimes!

EXERCISE C: Write a sentence with an interjection that conveys each of the following emotions.

> **Example:** joy
> **Answer:** <u>Hurray!</u> I was invited to Nancy's party!

1. surprise
2. doubt
3. reluctance
4. disappointment
5. disapproval
6. hesitation
7. contempt
8. enthusiasm
9. distress
10. triumph

Nouns

Noun-Forming Suffixes

EXERCISE A: The suffixes *-ance / -ence, -ant / -ent, -cy, -dom, -er / -or, -hood, -ion, -ism, -ist, -logy, -ment, -ness*, and *-ship* form nouns. Write the nouns in the sentences below that have been formed by one of these suffixes.

    Example: The occupant is an assistant to the senator.
    Answer: occupant, assistant, senator

1. Was it a coincidence that the lawyer also was a pianist?
2. The internist commented on her low blood pressure.
3. The director used her friendship with the community to help the neighborhood.
4. Robert's tendency of saying whatever was on his mind often got him into bad predicaments.
5. Democracy was a goal espoused by the Founding Fathers.

EXERCISE B: Use the suffixes *-ance / -ence, -ant / -ent, -cy, -dom, -er / -or, -hood, -ion, -ism, -ist, -logy, -ment, -ness*, and *-ship* to make new nouns from the words below. Then use each new noun in a sentence.

    Example: wise
    Answer: wisdom   The queen was known for her great <u>wisdom</u>.

1. abandon
2. partner
3. feminine
4. parent
5. contract
6. widow
7. prison
8. resident
9. guide
10. king

EXERCISE C: Write ten nouns using the suffixes *-ance / -ence, -ant / -ent, -cy, -dom, -er / -or, -hood, -ion, -ism, -ist, -logy, -ment, -ness*, and *-ship*. Then use each noun in a sentence. (Do not use any suffix more than once.)

    Example: *-ment*
    Answer: The <u>announcement</u> of the couple's <u>engagement</u> appeared in the newspaper.

Identifying and Using Common and Proper Nouns

EXERCISE A: Replace each common noun with a proper noun in the same category. Replace each proper noun with a common noun in the same category.

> **Example:** day
> **Answer:** Friday

1. Detroit Tigers
2. city
3. Emily Dickinson
4. Fourth of July
5. Africa
6. airport
7. ocean
8. Kentucky
9. Jupiter
10. relative

EXERCISE B: Rewrite the sentences, replacing one common noun or noun phrase in each sentence with a proper noun.

> **Example:** We visited a battlefield last summer.
> **Answer:** We visited Yorktown last summer.

1. Our teacher can speak another language.
2. I asked a relative if I could borrow the car.
3. Next month our class will travel to the capital.
4. That city is located on a river.
5. That play received a good review in the newspaper.

EXERCISE C: Rewrite the letter, substituting ten proper nouns for the words in parentheses.

> **Example:** Did you write to (a person)?
> **Answer:** Did you write to Aunt Celine?

(a month) 12, 1995

Dear (a person),

   I am writing you from (a state). (A person) and I are staying at the (a hotel). On (a day) we visited (a landmark). It reminded me of a scene in (a movie)—you know, something in which (a celebrity) might have been seen.

Love,

(a person)

Identifying and Using Collective Nouns

EXERCISE A: Write the collective noun from each sentence. Tell whether it is used with a *singular* or *plural* verb.

> **Example:** The class elects a president.
> **Answer:** class, singular

1. The group appoints a secretary and a treasurer.
2. Usually the pair work separately on issues of the day.
3. Our crowd recommends people for the offices.
4. We put together an assembly, which acts independently.
5. Occasionally, the committee prepare individual reports.

EXERCISE B: Write the collective noun from each sentence. If the sentence is correct, write *Correct*. If not, rewrite it so that nouns, verbs, and pronouns agree in number.

> **Example:** The faculty report on its decision.
> **Answer:** faculty, The <u>faculty reports</u> on <u>its</u> decision.

1. A committee is formed to recruit students.
2. The staff visit schools across the nation.
3. They watch each team as it play basketball.
4. The panel argue about their decision.
5. One family prefer Michigan to Wisconsin.
6. Another family disagrees about their desires.
7. Sometimes the public are concerned with the choice.
8. After all, the audience need to be entertained.
9. The crowd determine the revenue.
10. We hope that the group decides wisely.

EXERCISE C: Choose five collective nouns from the choices below. Use each in a sentence. Then write whether you treated the noun as *singular* or *plural*.

> **Example:** herd
> **Answer:** The <u>herd</u> roams down the mountain. (singular)

army	association	band
Congress	crew	jury
squad	Senate	trio

Identifying and Using Concrete and Abstract Nouns

EXERCISE A: Label each noun as *concrete* or *abstract*.

Example: honesty
Answer: abstract

1. school
2. peach
3. luck
4. tractor
5. mountain
6. harmony
7. antelope
8. friendship
9. singer
10. imagination

11. tulips
12. park
13. knowledge
14. health
15. computer
16. sheep
17. photography
18. Christianity
19. Indian Ocean
20. breath

EXERCISE B: Write all the nouns in each sentence, putting parentheses around each abstract noun.

Example: The future of the company did not look promising.
Answer: company (future)

1. Hilda received an important promotion.
2. Matthew has many happy memories of his childhood.
3. The mayor showed compassion for the homeless families.
4. Have economists predicted a mild recession?
5. The boxer demonstrated both cunning and agility.

EXERCISE C: Complete the speech by writing ten nouns as indicated in parentheses.

Example: He worked for (concrete) and for (abstract).
Answer: He worked for <u>money</u> and for <u>honor</u>.

We meet to honor a (concrete) who has shown us (abstract) and (abstract). His (concrete) should feel great (abstract) in his (abstract). This (concrete) has worked hard in the (concrete), demonstrating (abstract) and (abstract) in everything that he has done.

Spelling Plural Nouns Correctly

EXERCISE A: Write the plural form of each noun.

Example: dairy
Answer: dairies

1. nickel
2. witch
3. superhero
4. fox
5. moose
6. donkey
7. quality
8. calf
9. attorney-at-law
10. crisis

11. jury
12. branch
13. schoolbus
14. Friday
15. wisdom tooth
16. chef
17. contralto
18. ox
19. son-in-law
20. spoon

EXERCISE B: Rewrite each sentence, writing the plural form of each noun.

Example: I put the book on the shelf.
Answer: I put the <u>books</u> on the <u>shelves</u>.

1. The library opened as the clock struck.
2. Outside, along the walkway, the woman waited.
3. I balanced my box near my foot.
4. The door opened, and the First Lady entered.
5. My armful spilled across the counter.
6. The computer connected me to the encyclopedia.
7. Your analysis of the datum seemed correct.
8. Did your sister-in-law send you the table of contents?
9. I read the speech by the Revolutionary hero.
10. Then I checked out *The Life of Our Child.*

EXERCISE C: Rewrite the paragraph, correcting its misspellings.

Many familys met yesterday to discuss the recent increases in taxs. Our believes were represented by June and Jeb Ellery. The Elleries made speechs about the need for better utilitys. Even the childs listened to the discussions on their radioes. Sevral handsful of attorney-at-laws called for a vote.

Developing Your Style: Choosing Specific, Concrete Nouns

EXERCISE A: Rewrite each sentence, replacing each underlined noun or noun phrase with one that is more specific and concrete. Be sure to spell all nouns and noun phrases correctly.

> **Example:** When <u>the holiday</u> arrives, we always plan <u>an event</u>.
> **Answer:** When <u>Valentine's Day</u> arrives, we always plan <u>a party</u>.

1. Jamie sipped her <u>beverage</u> while Manuel spoke to <u>the girl</u>.
2. "Heart-shaped <u>decorations</u> are exactly what your <u>place</u> needs!"
3. Jamie's <u>parent</u> came in, carrying a <u>container</u> that Jamie's pet eyed with interest as well as with eagerness.
4. As they ate, Ryan talked about his <u>sentiment</u> at recognizing <u>a politician</u> at <u>a restaurant</u> last month.
5. As <u>the people</u> set out for the <u>building</u> on their <u>vehicles</u>, they looked forward to the next meeting.

EXERCISE B: Rewrite the paragraphs, using specific, concrete nouns and noun phrases.

> **Example:** In _____, _____ and I attended an incredible _____.
> **Answer:** In <u>August,</u> <u>Lee</u> and I attended an incredible <u>concert</u>.

We arrived at _____ early and went in at _____. Was that place ever crowded—just full of _____ and _____, _____ and _____! I looked at the _____ that were for sale; then I bought _____ and _____. _____ helped us find our _____ just as the lights dimmed.

A _____ swept the _____; every _____ looked toward the _____. Then _____ filled the stage with color, and _____ filled the air. _____ danced in the aisles when _____ began to play _____. The band performed for _____. During the last _____, _____ shot into the air, and the crowd went wild. What _____ fills our hearts when we remember that _____!

Numerals

Ways of Writing Cardinals and Ordinals

EXERCISE A: Rewrite each numeral as a word; then label it as *cardinal* or *ordinal*.

> **Example:** 175th
> **Answer:** one hundred seventy-fifth   ordinal

1. 91
2. 23rd
3. 440
4. 4,404
5. 287th
6. 612
7. 7,015th
8. 3,322nd
9. 50,005
10. 11,000,000

EXERCISE B: Rewrite the passage, changing numerals to number words where needed. If a numeral does not need to be changed, put it in parentheses.

Peat Moss would be in town for 2 shows only. 1 day before tickets went on sale at Blue Tiger Music, 3 of my friends and I thought about camping in from of the store—from about 10 o'clock or so—to make sure that we got good seats. Mr. Adams told me that tickets cost $32.00 each, plus a $4.00 service charge, that he could sell only 6 per customer—and that each customer's place in line would be determined by a lottery!

"You mean, we could be 1st in line but 50th at the cash register?" I gasped.

"You even could be 100th—this'll be a popular gig," he replied.

Sure of our strategy, we met the next morning and took the #10 bus to the mall. 35 people were already standing outside Blue Tiger Music! "Swell," Melanie complained. "I knew we should have been here by 8 o'clock!"

"It doesn't matter," I reminded her. "We have just as good a chance of being 1st as they do."

2 hours later, we were congratulating ourselves. The person 4 places ahead of Melanie was pulled in the lottery, giving her the 5th position for buying tickets. We were poorer—but we had 12th-row tickets to see Peat Moss!

Using Numerals Correctly

EXERCISE A: Rewrite each item, using numerals and number words correctly.

Example: the 1st day of the year two thousand one
Answer: the <u>first</u> day of the year <u>2001</u>

1. Apartment Nineteen-C
2. I have 3 rolls of quarters.
3. five twenty-five P.M.
4. Is this ninety-three Morningstar Circle?
5. B. Camels
    one. Dromedary
    two. Bactrian
6. about five hundred B.C.
7. Seventeen hundred Beach Drive
8. 6525 5th Avenue North
9. I've collected three hundred seventy aluminum cans.
10. For the party, we'll need ten pizzas, thirty cans of pop, and about 180 minutes of music.

EXERCISE B: Rewrite the business letter, using numerals and number words correctly.

> Two Hunded Ninety Griswold Street
> Waldo, OH 43356
> October three, nineteen ninety-four

Pampered Pets, Inc.
Fourteen Hundred Eleven Lane Avenue
Suite Twenty-A
Solana Beach, CA 92075

Dear Sir or Madam:

On September sixteen I placed a mail order with Pampered Pets, Inc. Here's what I ordered:

A. Accessories
    one. three dog collars
    two. a "fire hydrant" bandana

B. Health-care products
    1. a box of NutriTreats
    two. 2 bottles of Flea Free Dip

The order arrived only 9 days after I'd mailed it (about three-thirty P.M.). The collars, the bandana, and the shampoo were fine.

However, I have 1 complaint about the NutriTreats. According to the catalog, a box of NutriTreats is supposed to contain "one hundred fifty nutritious nibbles." The box I received contained not one hundred fifty, not one hundred forty-nine, but one hundred forty-six pieces! Pepper (my dog) and I would appreciate your sending those four missing NutriTreats. I've enclosed a self-addressed, stamped (twenty-nine¢) envelope for that purpose.

Thank you for your cooperation.

> Sincerely,
>
> Zane Wilkins

Parentheses

Using Parentheses Correctly

EXERCISE A: Rewrite each sentence, adding parentheses where needed.

Example: A four-thousand-dollar $4,000 scholarship enabled Gabrielle to continue her studies.
Answer: A four-thousand-dollar ($4,000) scholarship enabled Gabrielle to to continue her studies.

1. The dorm was draped with bougainvillea tropical vines with bright flowers.
2. Gabrielle What a good student she is! loves Keats.
3. John Keats 1795-1821 wrote "Lamia."
4. Gaby reads aloud to me. She does have a nice voice. Hearing the poetry helps me understand it.

EXERCISE B: Rewrite each sentence, adding parentheses correctly. If needed, add capitalization and punctuation.

Example: How warm the temperature is today 35 degrees C!
Answer: How warm the temperature is today (35 degrees C)!

1. He wore a lugubrious very mournful expression.
2. Sixty percent of the boys 25 joined the club.
3. Humphrey Bogart 1899-1957 won an Academy Award.
4. Few people liked the film the subtitles did not help.
5. Dwight raised his hand does he never give up the class tried to ignore him.

EXERCISE C: Add an item in parentheses to each sentence. Follow the instructions to know what kind of item to add.

Example: I am training my dog, and he is making excellent progress. (Identify the type of dog.)
Answer: I am training my dog (a German shepard), and he is making excellent progress.

1. The punishment was ostracism. (Define the word ostracism.)
2. Carla spent two weeks in Switzerland. (Add an exclamatory sentence that interrupts the sentence.)
3. The house rents for five hundred dollars a month. (Add the amount in numerals.)
4. Tennis is a tricky game. (Add a phrase that interrupts the sentence.)

Periods

Using Periods at the Ends of Sentences and Direct Quotations

EXERCISE A: Rewrite the sentences, adding periods where needed. If a sentence needs some other kind of end punctuation, write *Other*.

> **Example:** Stephanie had been dating Tony since December
> **Answer:**   Stephanie had been dating Tony since December.

1. In May, however, a friend introduced her to Jim
2. Although she still liked Tony, she started thinking a lot about Jim
3. Stephanie asked Patty, her best friend, "What should I do"
4. Patty said that she really didn't know
5. She asked, "Has Jim invited you out"
6. "Yes! He's asked me to go to a movie with him," Stephanie replied
7. Patty exclaimed, "Great"
8. "It would be great—if I knew what to do," Stephanie sighed
9. "Tell Tony that you want to date other guys," Patty advised
10. "After all, you're not married, you know"

EXERCISE B: Rewrite the paragraph, adding periods and changing capitalization where needed.

We had a wonderful time, but we should have planned our trip better the park opens at 10:00 but we didn't get there until 12:30 as we bought our tickets, the clerk said, "Take this map" by that time, we were starving we found a restaurant and ordered lunch meanwhile, we studied the map I explained, "This shows where all the attractions are and what time the various shows start" a show called "Symphony of the Sea" began at 1:30 at the White Whale and Dolphin Stadium unfortunately, the restaurant was crowded, and it took us a long time to be served, we missed the 1:30 show, so we decided to go and see the sharks being fed

EXERCISE C: Write five sentences that end in periods. Include at least one example of a declarative sentence, an imperative sentence, and a direct quotation. Write about one of these topics:

- a sporting event
- a garage sale
- reading at the library
- watching a movie

Other Uses of Periods

EXERCISE A: Rewrite each item, using periods to show initials, decimals, and to separate dollars and cents.

> **Example:** Edward Cameron Robles
> **Answer:** E. C. Robles

1. four point five miles
2. seven dollars and thirty-five cents
3. Patricia Ann Reyes
4. seven and eight-tenths liters
5. twenty-one dollars and eighty cents
6. eleven and three-tenths kilograms
7. John Elliot Kingsland
8. one hundred seventy dollars and fifty-two cents
9. ninety and four-hundredths meters
10. Hayley Katherine Brown

EXERCISE B: Rewrite this excerpt from a business letter, adding periods where needed.

> **Example:** The item cost four dollars and three cents.
> **Answer:** The item cost $4.03.

I am writing to complain about the service I have received from your company. On June 4, 1994, I ordered a tote bag from your catalog. I wanted to use it when I went swimming at the YMCA this summer. The bag cost five dollars and ninety-five cents. I sent a check for that amount and signed it SA Beecher.

I waited a month but heard nothing from your company. When I called, the salesperson said that since the bag weighed one point two pounds, I should have sent one dollar and four cents extra for postage. How was I supposed to know that? Please cancel my order and refund my money.

Sincerely yours,

S A Beecher

EXERCISE C: Write five sentences, on a topic of your own choice, that show the proper use of periods. Include at least one example of initials, of decimals, and of dollar amounts.

Phrases

Identifying and Using Types of Phrases

EXERCISE A: Identify each phrase in parentheses as an *adjective phrase, adverb phrase, verb phrase, participial phrase, gerund phrase, infinitive phrase,* or *appositive phrase.*

> **Example:** (Getting stopped for speeding) just may save your life.
> **Answer:** gerund phrase

1. Speedtraps are used (to keep people) from driving at unsafe speeds.
2. The first (of the speed traps) was set up in rural New England.
3. William McAdoo, (a New York City police chief), was an early victim.
4. He was stopped (for driving twelve miles per hour) in an eight mile per hour zone.
5. One deputy (using a stopwatch) timed the car from one marker to another.
6. He used a telephone (to call ahead) to a deputy, who stopped the speeder.
7. (Receiving a speeding ticket) didn't upset the police chief very much.
8. He saw the trap as a useful tool that he (could use) in New York.
9. He asked the New England constable (to set up a speed trap in New York).
10. Since then, the idea has spread (throughout the world.)

EXERCISE B: Write the phrases in each sentence and identify each as an *adjective phrase, adverb phrase, verb phrase, participial phrase, gerund phrase, infinitive phrase,* or *appositive phrase.* Then rewrite each sentence, replacing each phrase with another of the same type.

> **Example:** Throughout her life, Christina Rossetti seemed unable to find happiness.
> **Answers:** Throughout her life, adverb phrase; to find happiness, infinitive phrase
>
> <u>During her lifetime</u>, Christina Rossetti seemed unable <u>to be happy.</u>

1. Christina Rossetti is known best as a poet, but she also was a painter.
2. Lacking self-confidence, Rossetti didn't try to become a famous poet.
3. Having a melancholy nature also was a roadblock to her potential.
4. Rossetti, a voluminous poet, wrote some poems of poor and uneven quality.
5. At her best, however, she penned exquisitely beautiful poems.

EXERCISE C: Use the phrases to write a one-paragraph story.

- a strange, other-worldly creature (appositive phrase)
- looking about gleefully (gerund phrase)
- to get a camera (infinitive phrase)
- laughing hysterically (participial phrase)
- in the long grass (adverb phrase)
- eyeing the ground (participial phrase)
- to take pictures (infinitive phrase)
- will believe (verb phrase)
- on my summer vacation (adverb phrase)
- with green skin (adjective phrase)

Identifying Functions of Phrases

EXERCISE A: Label the function of each underlined phrase as that of a *noun*, an *adjective,* or an *adverb.*

> **Example:** <u>Exploding violently</u>, the volcano spewed ash and lava.
> **Answer:** adjective

1. Spread <u>across the earth's surface</u> are fifteen plates.
2. <u>Floating on a layer of partly molten rock</u>, the plates move about <u>on the earth's crust</u>.
3. Volcanoes often are found near the edge <u>of the plates</u>.
4. Volcanoes <u>located along the edge of the plates</u> periodically become active.
5. <u>Monitoring volcanoes continually</u> is one way in which scientists try <u>to predict an eruption</u>.
6. <u>Bordering the Pacific Ocean</u>, most <u>of the world's active volcanoes</u> form a ring.
7. The Ring of Fire, <u>this belt of active volcanoes</u>, includes Hawaii and the West Coast.

EXERCISE B: Write whether each underlined phrase functions as an *adjective,* an *adverb,* or a *noun.* Then write a new sentence, using the same phrase as indicated in parentheses.

> **Example:** The player driving for the basket is Jevon! (noun)
> **Answer:** adjective; <u>Driving for the basket</u> requires concentration and power.

1. <u>Keeping up with the opposing guard</u> was hard work for Jevon. (adjective)
2. <u>To gain an advantage</u>, Jevon pulled up and shot a three-pointer. (noun)
3. <u>Shooting a three-point basket</u> is one of the hardest shots. (adjective)
4. The player <u>at the free-throw line</u> was nervous. (adverb)
5. The player <u>shooting a free throw</u> was under great pressure. (noun)

EXERCISE C: Rewrite the paragraph, filling in an appropriate phrase at each parentheses as indicated.

> **Example:** (Adjective), Marie stepped (adverb).
> **Answer:** <u>Peering cautiously about her</u>, Marie stepped <u>through the doorway</u>.

(Adjective), Marie noticed something unusual about the sunlight. (Noun) gave her a feeling (adjective). She moved (adverb), but something held her (adverb). Something peculiar was happening. The sun, (adjective), didn't beat down (adverb). Shadows (adjective) were not as deep. Then she realized (adverb) that she was experiencing a solar eclipse! (Noun) was an exciting event!

Using Commas with Phrases

EXERCISE A: Write whether each sentence is *correct* or *incorrect* in its use of commas.

> **Example:** With sirens screaming the car screeched to a halt at the door.
> **Answer:** incorrect

1. The detective, Bart Lukas, arrived just in time.
2. Questioning Sam the butler he took precise notes.
3. To get at the truth Lukas administered a truth serum to the butler.
4. Sam, a balding, elderly man wearing a toupee, talked freely.
5. He told how the thieves, dressed all in black, had entered, by a window.
6. Speaking rapidly Sam identified them as two men and a woman, Shari.
7. "I knew her, from the hardware store in town," Sam explained.
8. Lukas, knowing that the serum would soon wear off, asked what they had taken.
9. "Only a picture, dating from the eighteenth century," Sam muttered.
10. "It was expensive, having been bought at an auction in Italy last year."

EXERCISE B: Rewrite each sentence, correcting any comma errors. If a sentence needs no changes, write *Correct.*

> **Example:** Antaeus a giant and highwayman was a mythic wrestler of ancient Greece.
> **Answer:** Antaeus, a giant and highwayman, was a mythic wrestler of ancient Greece.

1. Knowing that the loser died the strongest trembled having little hope of victory.
2. Looking for a fight, Heracles the greatest hero of all visited Antaeus.
3. Being a great fighter himself, Heracles was dismayed at the giant's strength.
4. By touching the earth Antaeus grew stronger laughing as Heracles tired.
5. Heracles discovering the secret lifted Antaeus into the air keeping him off the ground.

EXERCISE C: Rewrite the paragraph, correcting five errors in punctuating phrases.

Homer the most famous ancient Greek storyteller is more mythic than his stories. According to legend he was blind. To claim that he lived around 1000 B.C., is only a guess, though a reasonable one. The stories that Homer told are much older having been passed down orally by generations of storytellers. Homer's two best-known poems the *Iliad* and the *Odyssey* date from hundreds of years before Homer lived.

Using Phrases Correctly

EXERCISE A: Write whether each sentence is correct or incorrect in its use of phrases. If it is incorrect, revise the sentence to make the usage correct.

> **Example:** Speeding into space, messages are carried from Earth.
> **Answers:** incorrect; Speeding into space, Voyager carries messages from Earth.

1. Two U.S. *Voyager* spacecraft carry messages to outer space.
2. Designed to explore the planets, NASA prepared them to exit our system.
3. Carrying with them a gold-coated copper phonograph record.
4. The record to tell any alien life about Earth has audio and video messages.
5. On the record are 118 pictures of people, plants, animals, and so on.
6. To identify our location, our solar system and galaxy are described.
7. Considered a universal language, math equations communicate where we are.
8. Extraterrestrials will know exactly where we are finding the spacecraft.
9. The wisdom of sending the message depends on how friendly any aliens may be.
10. The message to any alien life forms from around the world also includes music.

EXERCISE B: Rewrite the paragraph, correcting its ten errors in phrase usage.

> **Example:** As a series of letters, the first English novel took form.
> **Answer:** The first English novel took form as a series of letters.

The English novel has a peculiar history, appearing in 1740. Its origin can be traced to a social gathering in Samuel Richardson's London home of young women. Serving as a sort of eighteenth-century *Dear Abby*, the young ladies received advice on personal matters. He often wrote letters to suitors on their behalf, going even further. Writing the letters frequently, they were successful. Perhaps writing an entire book of universal letters about specific problems. The book might be popular. Needing a good letter, the appropriate one could be chosen from the book, copied, and sent. Richardson wrote the book, and it was a hit. Richardson then wrote *Pamela*, the first English novel inspired by his success. It was written to and from a young woman, Pamela, as a series of letters. Pamela desperately needed advice, being aggressively pursued by a man.

Developing Your Style: Phrases

EXERCISE A: Rewrite the sentences in the left-hand column, completing each one with a phrase from the right-hand column, to create more interesting sentences.

> **Example:** ____, Iris thinks of ice-cold orange juice. Plodding up the arroyo
> **Answer:** Plodding up the arroyo, Iris thinks of ice-cold orange juice.

1. Iris had been walking for hours ____.
2. To get to that cold bottle ____ was all she could imagine.
3. ____, Iris had gone for a walk without carrying water.
4. She had become lost in the arroyo, ____.
5. Iris had followed the wrong side-canyon, ____.
6. Heat bounced ____ off the arroyo's walls.
7. She stumbled along, ____.
8. Finally, ____, she saw the trail.
9. ____, Iris climbed the bank of the arroyo.
10. Her car, ____, stood a few yards away.

a. Although knowing better
b. a dry, sandy dead-end
c. in the 100-degree heat
d. rounding a bend
e. of orange juice
f. shimmering in the heat
g. in palpable waves
h. In a stupor of exhaustion
i. tripping in the deep sand
j. wandering aimlessly

EXERCISE B: Rewrite the sentences, making them more interesting by adding phrases of the kind indicated in parentheses.

> **Example:** Charles Dickens, (noun phrase), wrote *Great Expectations*.
> **Answer:** Charles Dickens, a nineteenth-century novelist, wrote *Great Expectations*.

1. Lyle Medwick, (noun phrase), wants to become a novelist.
2. (Noun phrase) with the power of Dickens is his goal.
3. Like Dickens, he tries (noun phrase).
4. He creates characters (adjective phrase) from people in his neighborhood.
5. (Adjective phrase), his characters seem rather unrealistic.
6. Lyle writes (adverb phrase).
7. (Adjective phrase), Lyle's focuses on less serious subjects.
8. (Noun phrase) is very difficult for Lyle, who has trouble mixing serious themes and high comedy.
9. Lyle shares one other characteristic (adjective phrase).
10. He describes events (adverb phrase) that his stories become lengthy.

Possessives

Identifying and Forming Possessive Nouns and Pronouns

EXERCISE A: Write the correct possessive noun or possessive pronoun from the choice in parentheses.

> **Example:** The (White Houses', White House's) rooms have interesting histories.
> **Answer:** White House's

1. (It's, Its) Oval Office has been the work area of many Presidents.
2. This (office's, offices') furniture changes with each President.
3. Abigail (Adams, Adams') laundry was hung in the unfinished East Room.
4. The Kennedy (children's childrens') antics once enlivened the White House.
5. Do you ever wish that (someone elses', someone else's) room was (your's, yours)?

EXERCISE B: Rewrite each sentence, inserting apostrophes where needed. If a sentence needs no changes, write *Correct*.

> **Example:** The Clevelands wedding in 1886 brought romance to the White House.
> **Answer:** The <u>Clevelands'</u> wedding in 1886 brought romance to the White House.

1. Frances was beautiful—and Frans popularity won Grover Cleveland many votes.
2. The distress in Congress after President Wilsons stroke was understandable.
3. Afterward, the Presidents signature did not resemble those on earlier documents.
4. One of Mrs. Kennedys contributions was to change upholstery.
5. Landscaping requires a full-time gardeners attention.
6. During the Wilson administration, the sheeps grazing kept the lawn trimmed.
7. The Tafts lived in the White House in 1908; the Tafts cow was named Pauline.
8. Theirs was the last White House cow.
9. The Clintons cats name is Socks.
10. Caroline Kennedy said that the pony was hers.

EXERCISE C: Use the possessive form of the following nouns or pronouns to write five sentences.

> **Example:** visitors
> **Answer:** The guide overheard the <u>visitors'</u> remarks.

1. roses
2. President Hayes
3. diplomat
4. ours
5. its

Using Possessive Forms Correctly

EXERCISE A: Rewrite each sentence, using the correct possessive form in parentheses.

> **Example:** (Mel's and Kim's, Mel and Kim's) dream became a reality.
> **Answer:** <u>Mel and Kim's dream</u> became a reality.

1. The Spanish, (whose, who's) treasure ship sank in 1622, were stunned.
2. (It's, Its) name was the *Atocha.*
3. (It's, Its) said that in (it's, its) hold were forty-seven tons of gold and silver.
4. Mel Fisher and his sons Dirk and Kim wanted the gold to be (there's, theirs).
5. (Mel's and Dirk's, Mel and Dirk's) boats sailed in different directions.
6. Unfortunately, (Dirk and his wife's, Dirk's and his wife's) boat sank.
7. Lyon, a friend of (Fisher, Fisher's), helped research the ship's location.
8. (Fisher's and Lyon's, Fisher and Lyon's) research paid off.
9. Fisher located the (*Santa Margarita's* and the *Atocha's*, *Santa Margarita* and *Atocha's*) treasures.
10. (Who's, Whose) responsible for deciding (who's, whose) treasure it is?

EXERCISE B: Rewrite each sentence, using possessive nouns or possessive pronouns instead of the underlined words or phrases. Make any other changes that are needed.

> **Example:** The map <u>belonging to Kate and Jim</u> indicated the treasure's location.
> **Answer:** Kate and Jim's map indicated the treasure's location.

1. The shovels were <u>Juan's and Jill's.</u>
2. They lifted the box and found <u>the box's</u> contents heavy.
3. The dog <u>belonging to Jason and Erik</u> began to howl.
4. A brother <u>of whom</u> is calling?
5. A brother of <u>Jack</u> is calling.

EXERCISE C: Combine the information in each pair of sentences by using possessive nouns or pronouns.

> **Example:** Lewis and Clark had an interpreter. She was named Sacajawea.
> **Answer:** Lewis and Clark's interpreter was named Sacajawea.

1. Sacajawea and Charbonneau had a son. William Clark helped educate him.
2. The expedition used rafts. Clark owned a raft.
3. The Shoshones gave their information. The Mandans gave their information.
4. Marquette and Joliet had made an earlier expedition. It took place in 1673.
5. The death of whom is a mystery? He was found shot to death in an inn.

Developing Your Style: Streamlining Sentences with Possessive Forms

EXERCISE A: Rewrite each pair of sentences. Replace the underlined phrase in the first sentence with a possessive noun. Replace the underlined phrase in the second sentence with a possessive pronoun.

> **Example:** That book <u>by Dickens</u> is a historical novel. The settings <u>of the novel</u> are London and Paris.
> **Answer:** <u>Dickens'</u> book is a historical novel. <u>Its</u> settings are London and Paris.

1. The Marquis imprisons the father <u>of Lucie Manette</u>. Mr. Lorry arranges for the release <u>of the father</u>.
2. The book depicts the anger <u>the peasants felt</u> during the French Revolution. The wrath <u>of the peasants</u> led to violence.
3. Cruel deeds <u>committed by Madame Defarge</u> reflect this violence. The knitting <u>of Madame Defarge</u> even records a coded list of victims.
4. What were the goals <u>of the Revolution</u>? What was the outcome <u>of it</u>?

EXERCISE B: Rewrite each sentence, streamlining it through the use of possessive nouns or possessive pronouns.

> **Example:** The performance by Mozart astonished everyone.
> **Answer:** <u>Mozart's</u> performance astonished everyone.

1. The originality of the music pleased the Emperor.
2. The play *Amadeus* is based on the life of Mozart.
3. An enemy of his was the rival composer Salieri.
4. The expenditures of the Mozarts drove them into bankruptcy.
5. Mozart was given the burial of a pauper.

EXERCISE C: Rewrite the paragraph, streamlining it by using ten possessive nouns or possessive pronouns.

> **Example:** The conductor of the orchestra bowed toward the audience.
> **Answer:** The <u>orchestra's</u> conductor bowed toward the audience.

The role of the drums signaled the beginning of the overture. The blast from the trumpeters nearly drowned out the solo of the flutist. The conductor noticed the nervousness of the soloist and waved the baton he held more slowly. No one noticed the inexperience in the clarinetists. The applause given by the audience thrilled the young performers. This concert of theirs represented practice of many hours.

Prepositions

Identifying and Using Prepositions and Prepositional Phrases

EXERCISE A: Make two columns. In the first column, write the adjective phrases from the sentences and the word that each phrase modifies. In the second column, write the adverb phrases and the word that each modifies. Underline each preposition.

Example: Some paintings by Mary Cassatt are displayed in that museum.
Answer: Adjective Phrase   Adverb Phrase
            by Mary Cassatt (paintings)   in that museum (are displayed)

1. Mary Cassatt, a leader among American painters, was born in 1844.
2. When she was a child, she toured Europe extensively with her family.
3. Art museums in France and Germany enchanted her.
4. By the age of seventeen, Cassatt had chosen a career as a painter.
5. In 1874, a Cassatt painting in an exhibition was seen by Edgar Degas.
6. Degas introduced Cassatt to several impressionist painters.

EXERCISE B: Complete each sentence with a prepositional phrase. Label each new phrase as *adjective* or *adverb*.

Example: I often think about the playground _____.
Answer: I often think about the playground <u>on Oak Street</u>. (adjective)

1. One afternoon _____, I visited the playground again.
2. _____, several children were playing a noisy game of tag.
3. I watched _____ and shouted encouragement.
4. Suddenly, children _____ felt raindrops.
5. The busy playground emptied _____.
6. I wish I could return _____.
7. Some stories _____ let me relive those days.
8. Sometimes a photograph _____ will bring back memories.
9. I can still remember the laughter _____.
10. The happiness displayed _____ the greatest I have ever known.

Using Prepositions Correctly

EXERCISE A: Write the letter of the sentence in each pair that uses prepositions correctly.

    Example: a. Who did you give the gift to?

                b. To whom did you give the gift?

    Answer: b

  1. a. Who did you attend the party with?
      b. With whom did you attend the party?
  2. a. Are birthdays different from other celebrations?
      b. Are birthdays different than other celebrations?
  3. a. Can you compare a birthday to a rite of passage?
      b. Can you compare a birthday with a rite of passage?
  4. a. Where was the party at?
      b. Where was the party?
  5. a. Please let the guests in.
      b. Please let in the guests.

EXERCISE B: Rewrite the sentences so that each one reflects the correct use of prepositions.

    Example: I would compare him with a snarling tiger.
    Answer: I would compare him <u>to</u> a snarling tiger.

  1. Who did Raymond express his rage to?
  2. Where was the logic of his argument at?
  3. Did he compare his opponent with a clown?
  4. The dispute was different than any I'd heard.
  5. Do you remember what the original lecture was about?

EXERCISE C: Proofread this paragraph, correcting any errors in preposition usage.

    Example: Did you see where the bats went to?
    Answer: Did you see where the bats went?

    Where do bats hibernate at? This is what tonight's show is about. The host compares bats with sonar and other location devices. Bats have a sense of place different than that of most other mammals. What do they live on?

Developing Your Style: Using Prepositional Phrases in Descriptions

EXERCISE A: Expand each sentence by adding a prepositional phrase.

Example: What is the most famous tower _____?
Answer: What is the most famous tower <u>in the world</u>?

1. I believe it is the Leaning Tower _____.
2. Galileo used the Leaning Tower _____.
3. Magda saw it _____.
4. I keep my souvenir pictures _____.
5. This book illustrates the Seven Wonders _____.

EXERCISE B: Combine the information in each pair of sentences to write one sentence containing a prepositional phrase.

Example: "Guys and Dolls" is a title song. The song is from a musical comedy.
Answer: "Guys and Dolls" is the title song <u>of a musical comedy</u>.

1. I have read several books. They are by Margaret Mead.
2. We found the book. It was on the top shelf.
3. My favorite version stars that famous English actor. It is of Charles Dickens' *A Christmas Carol.*
4. The two boys were frightened. Their fright was caused by the dinosaurs.
5. *Jurassic Park* has special effects. They are quite realistic.

EXERCISE C: Rewrite this choppy paragraph, adding prepositional phrases or combining sentences with prepositional phrases to create a clear description. Try to use ten prepositional phrases in all.

Example: We followed the narrow road. It went upward.
Answer: We followed the narrow road <u>up a hill</u>.

The road led inward. There was a thicket of trees. Underbrush lined the road. You could see wildflowers. Weeds formed a carpet. The wildflowers dotted the carpet. They were colorful. Birds and insects flew around. They pollinated the flowers. The pollination was a ritual. It occurs every spring.

Developing Your Style: Using Prepositional Phrases in Transitions

EXERCISE A: Rewrite each sentence, replacing the underlined transition with a prepositional phrase that is more precise.

> **Example:** <u>Soon</u> we will dress for the party.
> **Answer:** <u>In a few minutes</u> we will dress for the party.

1. My friend Donna gave a party <u>recently</u>.
2. <u>First,</u> she sent out fancy invitations.
3. <u>Next,</u> she planned an elaborate menu.
4. The first guests arrived <u>early</u>.
5. <u>Then,</u> several cars pulled into the driveway.
6. The five-piece band began to play <u>next.</u>
7. <u>Afterward,</u> dinner was served in the sunroom.
8. <u>Then,</u> people began dancing again.
9. Most of the guests stayed <u>late</u>.
10. <u>Finally,</u> Donna collapsed, exhausted but happy.

EXERCISE B: Rewrite each sentence, adding a transitional prepositional phrase to indicate the passage of time.

> **Example:** I set up a birdhouse.
> **Answer:** <u>In early spring</u> I set up a bird house.

1. I selected a tree on which to hang my bird house.
2. I saw two tree swallows swooping past the house.
3. One of the swallows stopped and peered inside.
4. The other swallow watched from a high branch.
5. I kept the dogs as far from the bird house as possible.

EXERCISE C: Rewrite the paragraph, adding ten transitional prepositional phrases to indicate the passage of time.

> **Example:** I paid for his ticket and my own.
> **Answer:** <u>After that,</u> I paid for his ticket and my own.

I took my nephew to the movies. He wanted to see *Aladdin.* I had already seen it. Nevertheless, we stood in line together. We went into the theater. He picked a seat near the front. I sat him on my lap. He wanted his own seat. He scrambled into the seat next to mine. His seat folded up with him inside!

Pronouns

Identifying and Using Personal Pronouns

EXERCISE A: Write the personal pronoun or pronouns in each sentence. If a sentence has an incorrect pronoun, rewrite the sentence correctly. If a sentence contains no errors, write *Correct*.

Examples: The first speaker will be him.

Between you and I, I'm bored by this meeting.

Answers: him   The first speaker will be <u>he</u>.

me   Between you and <u>me</u>, I'm bored by this meeting.

1. Colleen gave him a pen-and-pencil set for his birthday.
2. A new student will be sitting between him and I.
3. Brenda and her will be studying together for our economics test.
4. The guests of honor are them and me.
5. The most spirited students are we tenth graders.
6. Our's are the gray-and-white striped beach blankets by their umbrella.
7. How the beauty of the surroundings pleased Anna and she.
8. Kim wants to go the basketball game as much as them.
9. Watching him act, they felt as if the actor were speaking directly to them.
10. Please show she and them the science laboratory.

EXERCISE B: Rewrite the sentences, completing each with an appropriate pronoun.

Example: Kenneth enjoys fishing as much as _____.
Answer: Kenneth enjoys fishing as much as <u>I</u>.

1. Arthur and _____ are the best anglers in the Fishing Club.
2. Leilani and Todd are almost as good at casting as _____.
3. Barney gave _____ a new computerized rod and reel as a birthday present.
4. Hearing about our fun, the Turners and _____ became avid anglers, too.
5. _____ prefer drift fishing because _____ takes so little work.

Identifying and Using Interrogative and Relative Pronouns

EXERCISE A: Write and label the interrogative and relative pronouns in the sentences.

> **Example:** Whom did you see at the skating rink?
> **Answer:** Whom (interrogative)

1. Jane is the girl whose answer is correct.
2. The parkway that Dad takes to work is being repaired.
3. Will you do whatever is necessary to finish the job on time?
4. Whose science experiment won first prize?
5. Marilyn's boots, which are genuine leather, must have cost a fortune!
6. Whoever heard of such an outlandish place as Gooligulch?
7. Who is the family for whom Alma baby-sits?
8. The name of the girl who is giving the party is Sharon—or is it Sherry?
9. Are you so sure that you can run the errands and still get home on time?

EXERCISE B: Rewrite this retelling of the opening scene from the classic fairy tale "The Twelve Dancing Princesses" by completing the sentences with an appropriate interrogative or relative pronoun.

Once there were twelve lovely princesses _____ mysterious evening antics were driving their royal father crazy—and broke. Every day for months, the princesses had awakened to find their slippers worn clear through—a circumstance _____ forced the king to buy his daughters new slippers. "_____ happens to your slippers every night?" asked the king, _____ was perplexed and annoyed. The girls replied _____ they had no idea, for they slept soundly every night through.

At his wit's end, and with bankruptcy staring him in the face, the king decreed, "_____ shall solve the mystery of the princesses' slippers shall marry the princess of his choice." However, the princesses objected. Cried the eldest, "How will you know if the person to _____ you give one of us is worthy—or just lucky?"

"But, my dears," replied the king, "_____ can I do? The treasury is nearly empty!"

"Our happiness, about _____ you claim to care, will be ruined!"

"Very well," sighed the beleagured father, "I'll do _____ you suggest."

EXERCISE C: Use each pair of pronouns in an original sentence.

1. what/that
2. which/who
3. whom/whose
4. whomever/that
5. that/whatever

Identifying and Using Demonstrative Pronouns

EXERCISE A: Write the demonstrative pronoun in each sentence.

> **Example:** Those are Matt's favorite trucks.
> **Answer:** Those

1. This is my favorite painting in the entire exhibit.
2. Might these be the earliest works of the artist?
3. Those are cubist paintings from an early period in her career.
4. I wonder if that is especially representative of her painting technique.
5. Those are the last three works of her career, as far as we know.

EXERCISE B: Write each demonstrative pronoun and antecedent from the sentences. If no antecedent is given, write *None.*

> **Example:** This is the year's most anticipated fashion show.
> **Answer:** This   (show)

1. That may be the show's most unusual suit, with its combination of turquoise and pink.
2. The hats are over there—look at this!
3. Of all the belts displayed, these appear to be the most popular.
4. Those are the pairs of shoes that don't match hats and gloves with which they're supposed to be worn.
5. How can you be sure that this is the jacket that belongs to this dress?

EXERCISE C: Rewrite each sentence by supplying the demonstrative pronoun indicated in parentheses.

> **Example:** (Near, plural) are well-formed crystals of exquisite beauty and great rarity.
> **Answer:** These are well-formed crystals of exquisite beauty and great rarity.

1. (Near, singular) is a perfect topaz crystal, one of many found in Siberia.
2. Azurite, a copper mineral, is always a blue shade. (Far, singular) will be crushed and used as pigment.
3. Quartz is an ideal gemstone for carving and cutting. (Near, plural) will become part of pins, rings, earrings, and pendants.
4. Diamonds are crystals of pure, immensely hard carbon. (Far, plural) of outstanding luster and brilliant cut are highly prized.
5. Of the beryl gems, emeralds and aquamarines are the best known. (Near, plural) are popular as gemstones due to their durability and deep, rich color.

Identifying and Using Indefinite Pronouns

EXERCISE A: Write the indefinite pronoun or pronouns in each sentence. Then rewrite the sentence, using another indefinite pronoun that could substitute in each case. (In some cases, you may need to make other changes to accommodate the new pronoun.)

   Example: Each of the boys plays soccer.
   Answer: Each   <u>One</u> of the boys plays soccer.

   1. Someone has eaten my banana!
   2. No one believed his alibi; something remained a mystery.
   3. Many reported seeing the eclipse, but everyone was careful not to look directly at the sun.
   4. I have two choices, and neither is attractive.
   5. Did you get everything on the list?
   6. Theresa knows all of my cousins—except one whom she's never met.
   7. Most of the stores in the mall are still open.
   8. Several of my friends walk to school, but a few take the bus.
   9. Nobody is available to help you; all of the workers are repaving the main road.
   10. Have both of the twins finished their homework?
   11. One of the streetlights is broken; another is sputtering badly.
   12. Did everyone in our class go to the Halloween party?
   13. Some of these newspapers are torn; others are poorly folded.

EXERCISE B: Write an indefinite pronoun in each sentence. If the pronoun has an antecedent, write it in parentheses after the pronoun.

   Example: _____ of the items remain to be found.
   Answer: Some (job)

   1. When I saw the ambulance, I knew that _____ was wrong.
   2. _____ of the neighbors were outside watching, just as I was.
   3. _____ of us knew what had happened.
   4. As we watched, a _____ of paramedics sped into the McMurtry house.
   5. "I hope it's _____ serious," I heard _____ say.
   6. "I don't think that _____ in the house has been sick," _____ added.
   7. Soon, the medics came out, accompanied by _____ of the McMurtry family.
   8. "_____ is all right," Mrs. McMurtry called to us. Colin has just gotten his hand stuck in a drainpipe he was trying to clean!"

Identifying and Using Reflexive and Intensive Pronouns

EXERCISE A: Write and label each reflexive and intensive pronoun in the sentences.

>   **Example:** Abby made herself a scarf.
>   **Answer:**   herself (reflexive)

1. We should buy ourselves some potatoes for the cookout.
2. The Secretary of State himself attended the ceremony.
3. Letitia carved the pumpkin face herself.
4. Nora convinced herself that victory was in reach.
5. Have assembly members voted themselves a raise?

EXERCISE B: Rewrite the sentences, using the reflexive or intensive form of the pronoun in parentheses. Label your answer as *reflexive* or *intensive*.

>   **Example:** The little town was _____ four hundred years old. (it)
>   **Answer:**   The little town was <u>itself</u> four hundred years old. (intensive)

1. The townsfolk decided to restore many historical buildings _____. (them)
2. The president of the town council appointed _____ the director of the historical society. (him)
3. Mrs. MacGillicuddy, _____ a descendant of one of the town's founders, donated many original documents. (her)
4. We congratulated _____ when the project was finished. (our)

EXERCISE C: Rewrite the passage, adding ten reflexive or intensive pronouns where appropriate. (You may need to make some minor changes.)

   I decided to redecorate my office. I knew I could do it, but my family wasn't so sure. I sat down to listen.
   "You broke your leg the time you tried to hang wallpaper," my mother pointed out when I stood and took books from the shelves. "Here, let me help you carry those."
   "You had a smashed thumb when we built shelves," my brother reminded me. "Here, let me lift that."
   "Remember when you got cut with the yardstick?" my sister asked. "Ask if you want to go through that again."
   "Some people, you know," my dad remarked kindly, "aren't made to do it themselves," and he and my brother began to mix the paint.
   I got positioned on the bottom stair to direct the crew I had handpicked.

Pronouns and Antecedents

EXERCISE A: Write each underlined pronoun in parentheses; then write its antecedent. If no antecedent appears in the same sentence, write *None*.

> **Example:** <u>Each</u> of the guests brought <u>him</u> a wonderful present.
> **Answer:** Each (guests) him (None)

1. When <u>all</u> of <u>his</u> relatives had arrived, Denis sighed.
2. Julie and Scott <u>themselves</u> had told <u>him</u> about the surprise party.
3. Scott served <u>everyone</u> dinner and then gave <u>himself</u> a rest.
4. When Denis saw the cake, <u>whose</u> candles glowed, <u>he</u> managed a smile.
5. <u>Those</u> of the guests <u>who</u> stood nearby chuckled, for *Denis* had been misspelled *Denise!*

EXERCISE B: Complete each sentence, using a pronoun that has a clear antecedent in the sentence and that makes sense. Underline the antecedent.

> **Example:** _____ is Michael's violin.
> **Answer:** That is Michael's <u>violin</u>.

1. The music teacher forgot _____ instrument.
2. I wonder _____ of the instruments she will be able to borrow.
3. Ted said, "Ms. Hill, _____ would be glad to lend you my violin."
4. Now the orchestra is ready for _____ rehearsal to begin.
5. The students are playing better today than _____ did yesterday.

EXERCISE C: Rewrite each sentence, completing it by adding both a pronoun and its antecedent.

> **Example:** _____, will _____ have lunch with me?
> **Answer:** <u>Ed</u>, will <u>you</u> have lunch with me?

1. _____ is the team's favorite _____.
2. _____ of the _____ are eating hot dogs.
3. _____ and _____ ordered meals for _____.
4. Only _____ of the _____ wants dessert.
5. _____ of the _____ will pay for this meal?
6. Either _____ or _____ has _____ money.
7. The _____ has lost _____ pen.
8. _____, have _____ been able to find it?
9. No; in fact, _____ is Caleb's _____.
10. It is a writing _____ _____ will have to make do for now.

Using Personal Pronouns Correctly

EXERCISE A: Write the pronoun in parentheses that correctly completes each sentence.

    Example: The principal advised Toby and (he, him) to apply.
    Answer: him

1. (Me, My) driving a long distance concerns Dad.
2. Three track stars—April, Lauren, and (she, her)—have been on the team since last year.
3. Uncle Clifton always jokes with Darry and (me, I).
4. The doctor's assistants are (them, they).
5. The teacher's demonstrations intrigued (we, us) observers.

EXERCISE B: Write the pronoun in parentheses that correctly completes each sentence. Then write the function of that pronoun.

    Example: The supervisor praised (us, we) trainees for our efforts.
    Answer: us   appositive to a direct object

1. The producer of the movie is (him, he).
2. Ms. Wilder showed Tom and (I, me) the new microscope.
3. Everyone studied more than Zack and (I, me).
4. (We, Us) voters supported her more than (he, him).

EXERCISE C: Write a sentence that includes the pronoun function identified

    Example: pronoun as part of compound subject
    Answer: Marie and <u>she</u> sat in front of the fire.

1. pronoun   as appositive to a subject
2. pronoun   as part of compound direct object
3. pronoun   as predicate nominative
4. pronoun   as object of a preposition
5. pronoun   as part of compound indirect object
6. pronoun   as subject of understood clause
7. pronoun   as modifier of a gerund
8. pronoun   as appositive to a direct object
9. pronoun   as part of compound indirect object
10. pronoun   as part of compound object of a preposition

Using Interrogative and Relative Pronouns Correctly

EXERCISE A: Write whether each sentence is correct or incorrect in its use of interrogative and relative pronouns.

Example: Whom designed this building?
Answer: Incorrect

1. With whom are you meeting this afternoon?
2. Whose standing next to Benjamin?
3. Give these copies to whoever he desires.
4. The principal of this school is who?
5. The telegram which you sent last night hasn't been delivered yet!

EXERCISE B: Rewrite the sentences, correcting any misuse of interrogative and relative pronouns. If a sentence needs no changes, write *Correct*.

Example: Carol will train whoever she selects for the job.
Answer: Carol will train <u>whomever</u> she selects for the job.

1. Whomever is the last one to leave, please shut the door.
2. Who's gray scarf is this?
3. I'll reward whoever finds my lost cat.
4. The weather report, which you heard, must have been inaccurate.
5. Ms. Martin is an actress who's career we should follow carefully.

EXERCISE C: Rewrite the paragraph, correcting any interrogative and relative pronouns that are used incorrectly.

A sword embedded in stone? Whom would take on the challenge? Whoever did—and was successful—would become High King. Most believed that he who's arm had strength enough to draw the sword would be a famous knight—someone whose great deeds were known near and far. Thus, when young Wart, a skinny lad whom everyone knew could hardly lift the kettle from over the fire, faced the strange phenomenon, no crowd gathered round. He stood alone, this scrawny boy who the sword called, and he studied the weapon angled in the rock. Perhaps, reasoned Wart, whomever was destined to draw out the sword didn't need strength. Perhaps the challenger simply needed faith.

Using Indefinite and Reflexive Pronouns Correctly

EXERCISE A: Write whether each sentence is correct or incorrect in its use of indefinite and reflexive pronouns.

> **Example:** Each of the women brought her own materials.
> **Answer:** correct

1. One of the biologists spoke about her research.
2. Few of the actors knew his lines.
3. Neither Leon nor myself have met the ambassador.
4. Both of the groups distributed their pamphlets.
5. Several of the students read their poems aloud theirselves.

EXERCISE B: Rewrite each sentence, correcting any misuse of pronouns.

> **Example:** Hector doesn't know the way hisself.
> **Answer:** Hector doesn't know the way <u>himself</u>.

1. Eliza and her entered the dimly lit room.
2. Was this article written by Verity and yourself?
3. Most of the pie were still left.
4. Brian decided to check the safety lock hisself.
5. Somebody on the boys' team left their bat.
6. Either of the critics will be glad to give you their opinion.
7. Richard and she planned the entire program theirselves.
8. Someone with a large dog by their side is waiting for her.
9. Most of the workers donated some of his or her earnings.
10. Each of my friends brought their CD's to the party.

EXERCISE C: Rewrite the paragraph, correcting any errors relating to indefinite and reflexive pronouns.

The gardens once had been the finest in the land, even though now none was cared for or pruned or cultivated. All the trees grew riotously, its branches intertwined. Many of the plants spread its roots above ground, completely covering the gardens' walks in places. Each of the rosebushes had lost their blooms years ago; the plants' brambles twisted back around theirselves in sharp, wicked knots.

Grammar, Usage, Mechanics • Pronouns   **201**

Developing Your Style: Pronouns

EXERCISE A: Revise sentences 1-2 by substituting the correct personal pronoun for the underlined noun. Revise sentences 3-4 by clarifying the pronoun's antecedent.

>**Example:** Mike reported that <u>Mike's</u> car insurance was based on <u>Mike's</u> safe-driver record.
>**Answer:**   Mike reported that <u>his</u> car insurance was based on <u>his</u> safe-driver record.

1. Sheila can't believe that <u>Sheila</u> has won the state's Superspeller Award.
2. The last four contestants couldn't spell *opalescence,* but Sheila spelled *opalescence* easily.
3. Pete told Jamal that he wouldn't last a round.
4. Many losing students said they studied word lists and dictionaries, which didn't help.

EXERCISE B: Rewrite each sentence so that it answers the question in parentheses.

>**Example:** Bob asked his father if he would be finished in the garage soon. (Who would be finished in the garage soon?)
>**Answer:**   "Do you think I'll be finished in the garage soon?" Bob asked his father.

1. Davis told Willis that he had to complete the assignment before the end of the day. (Who had to complete the assignment?)
2. Joan asked Terry whether she could go to the movies. (Who wants to go to the movies?)
3. We moved all the desks from the first-floor rooms, which was hard work. (What was hard work?)
4. The neighbors told them that they would need help to get the house in shape for selling. (Who needs help? Whose home needs to be put in shape?)

EXERCISE C: Rewrite the paragraph, using pronouns to streamline the writing, to avoid repetition, and to clarify any vague antecedents.

Detective Donovan pulled up a chair, opened Detective Donovan's notebook and then sat down. Donovan looked at the suspects around the table, one by one. As Donovan eyed Pasty-faced Pete, Pete straightened. Donovan looked at Awful Alice, which made her shiver and look away. It had an adverse effect on Conniving Colette as well, and she refused to meet it. Donovan motioned to his sidekick, Ensign Ed, and he pushed a folder at him. Opening the folder, he quickly read the report that it contained; then he left it on the table as he stood up. When he surreptitiously jerked his head at Ed, he left the room.

Question Marks

Using Question Marks Correctly

EXERCISE A: Rewrite each sentence, punctuating it correctly. Use question marks where they are needed.

> **Example:** Did you witness the solar eclipse
> **Answer:** Did you witness the solar eclipse?

1. In a lunar eclipse, does the earth block the sun
2. Is your confusion because we call it "lunar"
3. "Think of it this way, won't you" Dr. Po suggested.
4. "Don't both eclipses involve the sun" I asked.
5. It is a bit confusing, isn't it

EXERCISE B: Rewrite the sentences, adding any missing question marks and periods.

> **Example:** Leo Rosten wrote a funny book Don't you agree
> **Answer:** Leo Rosten wrote a funny book. Don't you agree?

1. Have you ever read *The Joys of Yiddish*
2. For a dictionary, it's a lot of fun, isn't it
3. It has a lexicon, but aren't the definitions unusual
4. Mr. Roston includes many jokes, doesn't he
5. What do people mean when they use the word *farblondjet*.
6. Did you read this example: "He drove toward New Rochelle but got so *farblondjet* that he ended up in White Plains"
7. Rosten seems to ask, "Why should a dictionary be dull"
8. Something should liven it up—but what
9. He asks the reader to take an interest in culture
10. "Why not," says Rosten, "make learning fun"

EXERCISE C: Follow the rules below to write a dialogue. Use question marks and periods correctly.

> **Example:** Have Hiro ask a question about an English phrase.
> **Answer:** "What do you mean by 'get a life'?" asked Hiro.

1. Have Dinah introduce Hiro to Sally, using a question.
2. Have Sally ask Hiro about his interests.
3. Have Hiro answer Sally and ask her a polite question.
4. Have Sally respond with a question ending "don't you?"
5. Have Hiro answer and then ask about a quotation that he had heard.

Quotation Marks

Using Quotation Marks with Direct Quotations

EXERCISE A: Rewrite each sentence so that it becomes a correctly punctuated direct quotation.

    Example: Mary exclaimed Look at all these old paint cans!
    Answer: Mary exclaimed, "Look at all these old paint cans!"

1. The former owner's hobby must have been collecting old paint cans, complained Mary. Why couldn't he clean out the basement?
2. We could make the cans into lamps or buckets I joked.
3. Wait a minute! Mary said suddenly. What's this? She picked up a box.
4. Let's get a screwdriver and try to open it I suggested.
5. After ten minutes of effort, Mary pried open the box and shouted Wow! Just look at all this money—Monopoly money, that is!

EXERCISE B: Rewrite each sentence as a direct quotation. Follow the instructions in parentheses. Be sure to use quotation marks and other punctuation correctly.

    Example: Gene noted here is a convenient place to stop. (declarative)
    Answer: Gene noted, "Here is a convenient place to stop."

1. The official stated we have difficult decisions to make. (declarative)
2. When is your next piano lesson Daphne asked me. (interrogative)
3. I think the inspector declared that the mystery is solved. (divided quotation) (declarative)
4. The coach said with conviction we can definitely win. (declarative)
5. Stand back the policeman ordered. (imperative)
6. Our prices are the lowest in town the salesman claimed. (declarative)
7. Let's get out of here the burglar yelled before we get caught. (divided quotation) (imperative)
8. This appliance he warned cannot be immersed in water. (divided quotation) (declarative)
9. Is it time I asked. Should I call the meeting to order? (divided quotation) (interrogative, interrogative)
10. What an outrage this is he stormed. I will never work until midnight again. (divided quotation) (exclamatory, declarative)

Other Uses of Quotation Marks

EXERCISE A: Identify the ten items in the sentences that should appear within quotation marks. Write each item correctly.

> **Example:** I've written a poem to my town; it's modeled after Carl Sandburg's Chicago.
> **Answer:** "Chicago"

1. Yes, I like the song, but I don't want to hear Bohemian Rhapsody all day long!
2. Which of these tales by Ray Bradbury do you prefer—The Veldt or Hail and Farewell?
3. Chapter 2, Europeans Reach the Americas, includes an excerpt from Joaquin Miller's poem Columbus.
4. The guest, Pete Jazzman Wilkins, sat down at the piano and played an impromptu rendition of Deep Purple.
5. I believe that *impromptu* means without previous preparation.

EXERCISE B: Rewrite each sentence, adding any missing quotation marks.

> **Example:** Tonight's episode is entitled A Dangerous Encounter.
> **Answer:** Tonight's episode is entitled "A Dangerous Encounter."

1. Is tonight's assignment to read Chapter 14—The Civil War Begins?
2. Alone on the stage, Todd picked up a guitar and played Cat's in the Cradle.
3. An *antihero* is commonly defined as a protagonist who lacks the strengths of a heroic figure; I guess that makes the title character of Melville's story Bartleby the Scrivener an antihero.
4. In the 1969 play, characters with nicknames like Moonbeam and Dr. Peace told the audience what a bad trip their life had been.
5. Two famous poems by Emily Dickinson, The Belle of Amherst, are It Dropped So Low and My Life Closed Twice.

EXERCISE C: Write several sentences about a film festival. Include six titles of stories, songs, or other short works relating to films; two examples of slang and/or nicknames; and two definitions of terms related to filmmaking. You may use more than one item in a sentence. (Remember: Titles of movies should be underlined.)

Quotations

Distinguishing Between Direct and Indirect Quotations

EXERCISE A: Write whether each sentence includes a *direct quotation* or an *indirect quotation*.

> **Example:** Aimee remarked that Scott Hamilton has been an innovative figure skater.
> **Answer:** indirect

1. "I agree with you, Aimee," Allen said. "He really 'broke the ice' as far as what male skaters were expected to do at the Olympics."
2. Brad groaned at Allen's pun but added that the requirements for amateur competitors are even more difficult now than in the 1980's.
3. "Remember that men were doing a couple of triple jumps," he explained, "and women weren't expected to do more than one."
4. Pam pointed out that Peggy Fleming had changed the direction of women's competition by displaying a flowing, graceful skating style.

EXERCISE B: If a sentence includes a direct quotation, rewrite it as an indirect quotation. If a sentence includes an indirect quotation, rewrite it as a direct quotation. Label the *new* sentence as including a *direct* or *indirect* question.

> **Example:** Standing in the middle of the room, the decorator remarked that he wasn't sure that the chosen colors would make the room look larger.
> **Answer:** Standing in the middle of the room, the decorator remarked, "I'm not sure that your choice of colors will make the room look larger." (direct)

1. "I can complete this experiment alone," Alfonso announced.
2. Nia warned Doug that driving in heavy rain was dangerous.
3. "I don't want to hear one more word about what other kids get to do," Mrs. Diller said, shaking her finger at her son.
4. "We should have chosen to do a play with more substance," complained Geneva.
5. "Let's change some of the recipe ingredients," suggested Tanner.
6. Eric watched, startled, as the baseball hopped over the bat, and then asked to know what trick Tim was using to produce the effect.
7. Mr. Grady gathered the bedraggled kitten into his arms, crooning softly, "I'll have you warm, dry, and fed in a jiffy, little fella."
8. Margot announced defiantly that she didn't believe in ghosts and that, furthermore, she insisted on sleeping in the "haunted" room.
9. Jason raced after the puppy, screaming at the top of his lungs for it to stop, frightening the poor little thing even more.
10. "Well," squealed Maude, pointing across the lawn. "those two must have made up."

Speaker Tags and Divided Quotations

EXERCISE A: Rewrite each sentence. Add the correct punctuation or capitalization and change the verb *said* in each speaker tag to a more specific or appropriate verb.

> **Example:** That is an impertinent inquiry said Mrs. Peters and I refuse to answer.
> **Answer:** "That is an impertinent inquiry," sniffed Mrs. Peters, "and I refuse to answer."

1. My mood is always more positive Bette Jones said after my morning run.
2. She is a brilliant poet who combines warmth and intellect said Professor Vanister.
3. Within five years, ten at the most, said editor T. Hawks, every magazine in this country will be publishing on-line computer editions.
4. I've given up trying to keep squirrels from stuffing themselves at my birdfeeder said amateur naturalist Franklin Grandy.
5. Some astounding pieces of journalism have recounted the sinking of the *Titanic* said news reporter E. D. Chang.

EXERCISE B: Write an introductory, concluding, or interrupting expression on the blank line. Identify the speaker of the sentence. Add punctuation and capitalization as needed.

> **Example:** I really dig archaeology _____. You turn up the most interesting objects.
> **Answer:** "I really dig archaeology," chuckled the amateur archaeologist. "You turn up the most interesting objects."

1. this is the best collection of antique motorcycles I've ever seen _____
2. my gosh _____ look at that vintage Harley-Davidson motorcycle
3. the first Harleys were produced in 1903 _____ but Daimler built one even earlier
4. about 1885 I think _____ that makes motorcycles about the same age as cars _____ give or take a couple of years
5. older or younger _____ motorcycles have always been prized for their purchase prices, considerably lower than those of cars
6. don't forget their manuevering ease and their low running costs _____
7. that's interesting _____ looking up from a brochure did you know that streamlining a motorcycle not only reduces wind resistance but also increases the machine's stability
8. _____ does Harley-Davidson dominate the motorcycle market
9. between the world wars, it did _____
10. now, of course, Japanese models lead the market _____

Using Quotations in Essays and Research Papers

EXERCISE A: For each statement, write the letter of the quotation that better supports it.

> **Example:** Change is vital to the growth of a nation.
> a. "A nation without the means of reform is without the means of survival."
> b. "It is a dangerous thing to reform anyone."
>
> **Answer:** a

1. Revolution is a reaction against tyranny.
   a. "It is essential to the triumph of reform that it shall never succeed."
   b. "The times pounded at me. I pounded back at the times."
2. A sole revolutionary may effect great change.
   a. "By gnawing through a dike, even a rat may drown a nation."
   b. "Riots are the voices of the unheard."

EXERCISE B: Use each quotation as the focus of a paragraph.

> **Example:** "Architecture is inhibited sculpture." (Constantin Brancusi)
> **Answer:** The best architecture joins the aesthetic to the practical. As Brancusi told us, "Architecture is inhibited sculpture." An architect must not give up art for mundane concerns, nor forget people in the interest of making art.

1. "The waste basket is a writer's best friend." (Isaac Bashevis Singer)
2. "One must care about a world one will not see." (Bertrand Russell)
3. "Most people have to talk so they won't hear." (May Sarton)
4. "No gains without pains." (Adlai Stevenson)

EXERCISE C: Interview two adults and two classmates on this topic: "Why Vote?" Write down their statements and use their quotations in a paragraph about the topic.

Writing Dialogue

EXERCISE A: Rewrite the dialogue below, using quotation marks, other punctuation marks, and paragraph indention as needed.

    Example: Why Brenda asked does he need a folding bicycle?
    Answer: "Why," Brenda asked, "does he need a folding bicycle?"

    What's inside that blue bag asked Brenda. It looks so lumpy. I was waitng for you to ask replied Jed. This bag he continued contains a bicycle. Brenda stared skeptically at the bag. What condition is it in? Oh, it functions quite well answered Jed. It's my dad's folding bicycle. How convenient remarked Brenda. Yes, he takes it everywhere said Jed. My dad calls himself the 'celebrated city cyclist of Cincinnati.'

EXERCISE B: In the dialogue below, each number indicates a new speaker. Write the dialogue, adding quotation marks, single quotation marks, capital letters, other punctuation marks, and paragraph indents. For each set of dashes, write your own dialogue.

    Example: do you have hiking boots Robert asked
    Answer: "Do you have hiking boots?" Robert asked.

    (1) why are you examining this tent asked Robert (2) well said Wesley I remember you said let's go hiking this fall (3) I was kidding cried Robert I'm the type who prefers a lush and luxurious hotel (4) —Wesley insisted (5) sitting quietly in the shade is preferable replied Robert (6) just imagine the morning sunrise where, as they say the deer and the antelope play said Wesley enticingly. (7) — replied his friend (8) don't be ridiculous said Wesley I know that you will change your mind (9) don't be so sure answered Robert I rarely change my mind about things that are fundamentally against my principles (10) —said Wesley—

Semicolons

Using Semicolons Correctly

EXERCISE A: Rewrite the sentences, adding semicolons where needed. (In some cases, you may need to replace a comma with a semicolon.)

> **Example:** The audience applauded enthusiastically they enjoyed the show.
> **Answer:** The audience applauded enthusiastically; they enjoyed the show.

1. Arthur enjoys caring for animals he wants to be a veterinarian.
2. In the morning, they completed tasks in the evening they relaxed.
3. William loves all kinds of winter sports I prefer the sand and sun.
4. I've visited Cumberland Island, Georgia, Sitka National Historical Park, Alaska, and Montezuma Castle National Monument, Arizona.
5. Once we almost missed our vacation deciding where to go was so hard!
6. Arlene is inexperienced in fact, this is only her second job.
7. My cousin sends for many catalogs she loves to shop by mail.
8. I take notes after I read otherwise, I forget some important points.
9. We discussed pros and cons after the game it helps with future planning.
10. I ordered a hamburger, broiled and served on a bun, a large salad topped with Italian dressing, and peach sorbet, cool and refreshing.

EXERCISE B: Rewrite the paragraph. Add semicolons or replace incorrect punctuation with semicolons, where needed.

A balloon can be used as an aircraft a passenger sits in a basket-like structure. Helium is used to lift some balloons other balloons use hot air. A hot-air balloon can be controlled by heating the air with a propane burner, an action that makes the craft ascend. Balloons are used by sports enthusiasts, having fun in the air scientists, studying weather patterns, and military personnel, protecting areas from low-level attack. An amazing balloon flight was made by Ben Abruzzo he flew from Japan to California in November 1981.

Name _____ Class _____ Date _____

Sentences: Structure and Types

Identifying and Using Complete Subjects and Predicates

EXERCISE A: Write and label the complete subject (CS) and the complete predicate (CP) in each sentence.

> **Example:** Electrical energy is produced from three main sources.
> **Answer:** Electrical energy (CS) / is produced from three main sources (CP)

1. Huge generators convert mechanical energy into electricity and thus provide most of our electrical energy.
2. A single generator may provide enough electrical power for a community of half a million people.
3. Batteries, consisting of one or more electric cells, change chemical energy into electricity.
4. The electric power for artificial satellites and space capsules comes from solar cells.

EXERCISE B: Rewrite the inverted sentences so that the complete subject comes first. Then underline each complete subject.

> **Example:** Is copper wire a good conductor of electricity?
> **Answer:** <u>Copper wire</u> is a good conductor of electricity.

1. Can metals such as lead and tin act as superconductors?
2. Has our class discussed the properties of insulators?
3. Are insulators made from materials such as glass and rubber?
4. Was the experiment involving the photo cells fascinating?

EXERCISE C: Use either a complete subject or a complete predicate to complete each sentence. Then underline the complete subject in each sentence.

> **Example:** Electrical energy
> **Answer:** <u>Electrical energy</u> runs many appliances in our home.

1. tape players, washing machines, and light bulbs
2. uses more electricity per person than any other country
3. computers and digital watches
4. the uses of electrical energy

Identifying and Using Simple and Compound Subjects and Predicates

EXERCISE A: Write whether each sentence contains a simple subject (SS) or a compound subject (CS), and whether it contains a simple predicate (SP) or a compound predicate (CP).

> **Example:** Eduardo and Selina were playing computer chess.
> **Answer:** (CS) (SP)

1. Danielle was sketching and planning a painting.
2. John and Paul were practicing a song and writing new lyrics.
3. Flowers were provided by the Parents' Group and the Garden Club.
4. Sewing and knitting are two of Naomi's favorite hobbies.
5. Did the President and Congress disagree over policy?
6. Panting and staggering, the messenger entered the fort.
7. Neither rain nor snow can keep the mail from getting through.
8. Auditions for the play are scheduled for today and tomorrow.
9. Dayna and Mike will dance together and perform a brief skit.
10. Lee tells jokes and is always looking for new ones.

EXERCISE B: Combine each pair of sentences. Write whether each new sentence contains a *compound subject*, a *compound predicate*, or *both*.

> **Example:** Larry was building a shelf. Lorraine was building a shelf.
> **Answer:** Larry and Lorraine were building a shelf. (compound subject)

1. The tornado wrecked the barn. The tornado flattened the house.
2. Ryan entered the talent show. Jeff entered, too.
3. Scott was watching the game. Scott was eating a hot dog.
4. Computers provide access to information. Telephones improve communication.

EXERCISE C: Complete each sentence as directed.

> **Example:** (CS) bought new sneakers.
> **Answer:** <u>Donny and his two older brothers</u> bought new sneakers.

1. (SS) were playing catch and listening to the stereo.
2. Joanna and Geraldine (CP)
3. the penguins at the zoo (CP)
4. an enormous dish of ice cream (SP)
5. (CS) know how to play lacrosse

Identifying and Using Complements

EXERCISE A: Write the complement in each sentence. Then label each one as an *indirect object*, a *direct object*, an *object complement*, or a *subject complement*.

    Example: Warren tells the best jokes in the class.
    Answer: jokes (direct object)

1. Grandma planted daffodils in her garden.
2. Airplanes brought the earthquake victims supplies.
3. The governor made the lawyer her advisor.
4. The iced tea tasted refreshing.
5. Please order us some dessert.
6. Sitting in his seat for the lecture made Antonio restless.

EXERCISE B: Rewrite the sentences, adding the complements named in parentheses.

    Example: Uncle Roy is a tremendous (subject complement) of baseball.
    Answer: Uncle Roy is a tremendous <u>fan</u> of baseball.

1. Uncle Roy gave (indirect object) tickets to the game.
2. Uncle Roy thought that the game would be (subject complement).
3. It turned out that the game was (subject complement).
4. We bought (direct object) as soon as we arrived.
5. The team designated the game (object complement).
6. The manager gave (indirect object) the game ball.
7. He showed (indirect object) where the pitchers warm up.
8. From the upper deck, the stadium looked (subject complement).
9. They had just painted the clubhouse (object complement).
10. A last inning rally made the home team (object complement).

EXERCISE C: Think about a place that is special to you. Write five sentences. Include and label at least one *direct object, indirect object, object complement,* and *subject complement.*

    Example: The Rocky Mountains give <u>me</u> (indirect object) <u>goosebumps</u> (direct object).

Identifying and Using Sentence Patterns

EXERCISE A: Complete each sentence with a word or phrase that fits the pattern in parentheses. Write the new sentences.

> **Example:** Kara showed (indirect object) slides of her vacation.
> **Answer:** Kara showed <u>us</u> slides of her vacation.

1. She (action verb) (direct object) with beautiful scenery.
2. (Subject) (linking verb) the most unusual that I have ever seen.
3. Kara (action verb) (indirect object) several (direct object) while hiking.
4. With her knowledge of underwater life and forestry, she (linking verb) (predicate nominative) one day.
5. (Subject) was very (predicate adjective) to us.

EXERCISE B: Write whether each sentence matches or does not match the sentence pattern in parentheses. If it does not match, rewrite it so that it matches.

> **Example:** An epidemic spreads disease rapidly. (S + LV + PN)
> **Answer:** An epidemic is an outbreak of a disease that spreads rapidly.

1. Germs are the cause of epidemic diseases. (S + AV + DO)
2. Animals and other people spread disease unknowingly. (S + S + LV + PN)
3. Did the bubonic plague cause the deaths of nearly 60 million people? (S + AV + IO + DO)
4. The battle against epidemics remains an exciting story. (S + LV + PN)
5. Diseases are better understood today, so scientists are more effective fighters of epidemics. (S + AV + S + AV + DO)

EXERCISE C: Write four sentences about a hobby, using the sentence patterns in parentheses. (You may add other words, but do not change the pattern.) Unless an item directs otherwise, write declarative sentences.

> **Example:** (S + LV + PN; question)
> **Answer:** Does baking bread seem an unusual hobby?

1. (S + AV + DO + DO)
2. (S + S + LV + PN)
3. (S + S + AV + DO; exclamation)
4. (S + AV + DO + S + AV + IO + DO; question)

Identifying and Using Types of Sentences

EXERCISE A: Label each sentence as *declarative, interrogative, imperative,* or *exclamatory.* In parentheses, write the appropriate end mark.

Example: Please buy a ticket to our Glee Club's spring presentation
Answer: imperative (.)

1. We're offering Gilbert and Sullivan's *The Mikado* this year
2. What a spectacular show it will be
3. My sister is singing in the trio "Three Little Maids from School"
4. Don't forget the dates—May 15, 16, and 17
5. Why would anyone ever miss a show like this, especially since I'm the Lord High Executioner

EXERCISE B: Rewrite each sentence as the type of sentence named in parentheses.

Example: The Cold War lasted almost fifty years. (interrogative)
Answer: Didn't the Cold War last almost fifty years?

1. It was a relief to everyone when the Cold War ended. (exclamatory)
2. Leaders on both sides are more frank and open now. (interrogative)
3. Is there nothing to be gained by recalling the tensions of those years? (declarative)
4. It is now time to forget about the past and to build a better future. (imperative)

EXERCISE C: Write a dialogue, using the types of sentences named in parentheses.

Example: RITA: (declarative) (interrogative)
Answer: RITA: There's nothing to do around here. Do you want to go shopping?

PAT: (interrogative) (declarative) (imperative)
RITA: (declarative) (exclamatory)
PAT: (declarative) (interrogative)
RITA: (exclamatory) (declarative) (imperative)

Name _____ Class _____ Date _____

Identifying and Using Simple Sentences

EXERCISE A: If a group of words is a simple sentence, write and label its simple subject and predicate. If it is not a simple sentence, rewrite it so that it becomes one.

Example: Australia is an island, a country, and a continent.
Answer: Australia/is

1. Most of Australia's population lives along the country's east coast.
2. Settled by deported British criminals.
3. The Australian island-state of Tasmania lies off the southeastern coast.
4. Many of Australia's unique animal species belong to the marsupial family.
5. Great Coral Reef world's largest natural coral reef.
6. Aborigines continent's earliest inhabitants.
7. Australians participate in many kinds of sports.
8. About one third of Australia is covered by deserts.
9. Permanent lakes artificially created.
10. Acacias and eucalyptus shrubs dominate Australia's landscape.

EXERCISE B: Write whether each group of words is a *subject* or a *predicate*. Then write a complete sentence using the group of words.

Example: dress casually
Answer: predicate   Most Americans <u>dress casually</u>.

1. T-shirts and jeans
2. do require at least shirts and shoes
3. must be easy to care for, too
4. working attire
5. is almost unheard of today
6. gloves and hats
7. people
8. may polish their shoes once or twice a year
9. very few functions
10. bright colors and simple designs

EXERCISE C: Rewrite the two paragraphs, changing the incomplete sentences to complete simple sentences.

Bats truly amazing, remarkable animals. Of all mammals, only bats have wings and fly. Bats' natural behavior often alienates them from people. Live in dark caves, hanging upside down when at rest. Only at night. Much incorrect information about bats makes the small, timid creatures unpopular with humans.

Too, a bat's appearance does not endear it to people. Furry but not cuddly. A bat's wings are leathery rather than feathery. Face bear, hog, or dog.

Identifying and Using Compound Sentences

EXERCISE A: Write *C* if a sentence is compound and *NC* if it is not. If a sentence is compound, write its compound parts and underline the coordinating conjunction.

> **Example:** Originally, all flowers were wild flowers, but through the centuries, gardeners have cultivated many kinds.
> **Answer:** C; Originally, all flowers were wild flowers, <u>but</u> through the centuries, gardeners have cultivated many kinds.

1. About 350,000 species of plants exist, and 250,000 of those have flowering plants.
2. Flowers are prized for their lovely shapes, their exquisite colors, and their delightful fragrances.
3. Most flowers provide decoration, but some are used in cooking and for perfume.
4. Many flower lovers follow the hobbies of flower arranging, or flower breeding.
5. A flower may have more than one common name, or two or more flowers may be known by the same common name.

EXERCISE B: Combine each pair of independent clauses into one compound sentence. Use a comma and the coordinating conjunction in parentheses.

> **Example:** Calypso songs of nonsense are called *bracket*. Serious calypso songs are called *ballode*. (but)
> **Answer:** Calypso songs of nonsense are called *bracket*, <u>but</u> serious calypso songs are called *ballode*.

1. Singer Harry Belafonte popularized calypso music in the 1950's. Calypso music had developed several centuries earlier. (yet)
2. Enslaved Africans in Trinidad were not allowed to talk to each other. They communicated information and emotions through music. (so)
3. The lyrics of a calypso tune may express the singer's philosophy. Verses may comment on local political events or gossip. (for)
4. Brass instruments are not used a great deal in playing calypso music. Except for the guitar, stringed instruments are not employed in calypso. (nor)
5. Would you like to go to a live calypso concert? Is listening to recordings enough for now? (or)

Identifying and Using Complex Sentences

EXERCISE A: If a sentence is complex, write *C* and the subordinate clause of the sentence. Write *NC* if a sentence is not complex.

> **Example:** Music, which is a series of sounds arranged in patterns, plays an important part in cultural and social activities.
> **Answer:** C; which is a series of sounds arranged in patterns

1. Music can express ideas and emotions as it relaxes and entertains the listener.
2. Classical music, which is composed according to strict rules, and popular music are the two main kinds of Western music.
3. Although most pieces of popular music do not retain their popularity for long, classical music compositions can remain popular for centuries.
4. Rock music mixes blues, jazz, country music, and British and American entertainment music.
5. Because Asian music uses different standards and instruments, it sounds much different from Western music.

EXERCISE B: Rewrite each complex sentence, changing the subordinate clause.

> **Example:** The films that I find most entertaining study personal relationships.
> **Answer:** The films <u>that win the most awards</u> study personal relationships.

1. Would you please tell me what is going on?
2. Look both ways before you cross the street.
3. Did you know that many people collect early twentieth-century fruit crate labels as an art form?
4. While the cake bakes, we can decorate the dining room.
5. After Janice and Kate had sold all their raffle tickets, they walked along the midway.

EXERCISE C: Expand each subordinate clause into a complex sentence.

> **Example:** since he wasn't wearing his uniform
> **Answer:** <u>Since he wasn't wearing his uniform</u>, no one recognized the doorman.

1. after she finishes the illustrations
2. which we have written ourselves
3. whose house is always spotless
4. if you recommend it
5. although Matt practiced
6. before she finalizes the arrangements
7. whenever his face gets that look
8. because Mom went to the office early
9. while they visit the aquarium
10. since Jack was so tall

Identifying and Using Compound-Complex Sentences

EXERCISE A: Write each compound-complex sentence. Put parentheses around each conjunction; then bracket and label the clauses—*M* for main clauses and *S* for subordinate clauses.

> **Example:** Director Stephen Spielberg is best-known for adventure epics, but he also directed serious films, which include the critically acclaimed *Schindler's List.*
>
> **Answer:** M
> [Director Stephen Spielberg is best-known for adventure epics,]
> M   S
> (but) [he also directed serious films,] [which include the critically acclaimed
>
> *Schindler's List.*]

1. During the 1970s, Spielberg captured audiences with *Star Wars,* which was his first trilogy; and in the 1980s, he produced the *Indiana Jones* and *Back to the Future* series.
2. The heroes of *Star Wars* were aided by a mysterious power called "The Force," but the protagonist of *Indiana Jones,* who was an archaeology professor, relied upon his quick wits and courage.
3. For *Star Wars* and *Indiana Jones,* Spielberg chose settings that took the audience around the world and the cosmos; yet the *Back to the Future* movies take place in a small American town.
4. Spielberg can wow audiences with special effects, as he did in *Jurassic Park,* or he can touch them profoundly, as he did in *Schindler's List.*

EXERCISE B: Create compound-complex sentences by combining each set of clauses.

> **Example:** Painting is a very old, important art. Painting was developed by people in prehistoric times. They wanted to share their ideas and feelings.
>
> **Answer:** Painting, which is a very old, important art, was developed by people in prehistoric times because they wanted to share their ideas and feelings.

1. Some people simply enjoy the color in a painting. They also like the arrangement of objects. Others make a demand. They want paintings to express a deep human emotion.
2. Paintings can skillfully portray the majesty of nature. A storm raging is an example. Paintings can capture the joy and verve of everyday occurrences.
3. Artists often comment on their times. Some paintings teach about social injustice. Others reveal much about an era.
4. No one painting produces exactly the same response in every person. The artist doesn't expect that. Each viewer brings his or her own unique ideas to the painting.

Spelling

Adding Prefixes

EXERCISE A: Add a prefix to each base word given. Write the new word.

    Example: ___assemble
    Answer: <u>dis</u>assemble

  1. ___moral
  2. ___necessary
  3. ___advantage
  4. ___circle
  5. ___match
  6. ___violent
  7. ___commend
  8. ___septic
  9. ___marine
10. ___approved

EXERCISE B: Rewrite each sentence, adding the prefix in parentheses to the underlined word in the sentence.

    Example: I considered it <u>natural</u> for Leslie to be upset. (un-)
    Answer: I considered it <u>unnatural</u> for Leslie to be upset.

  1. When Leslie walked off the stage in the middle of her soliloquy, Ms. Barnes looked after her in <u>belief</u>. (dis-)
  2. Later, Ms. Barnes said that Leslie's behavior was <u>responsible</u>. (ir-)
  3. She asked for Leslie's <u>conditional</u> resignation from the cast. (un-)
  4. Even the most <u>aggressive</u> student wanted to take Leslie's part, in spite of feeling let down by her action. (non-)
  5. Leslie stayed in bed for a week, remaining almost <u>mobile</u> during that time. (im-)
  6. Dr. Willis diagnosed Leslie's condition as <u>tension</u> and prescribed medication for her. (hyper-)
  7. We <u>estimated</u> the medicine's power; Leslie recovered quickly. (under)
  8. Leslie said that there was also an <u>balance</u> in her body chemistry. (im-)
  9. We all learned a lesson—not to <u>judge</u> anyone until all the facts are available. (pre-)
10. Sometimes a person's real problems are <u>visible</u> at first glance. (in-)

Adding Suffixes

EXERCISE A: Rewrite the sentences, adding the suffix in parentheses to the underlined word. Be sure to spell the new word correctly.

    Example: Because of his <u>avaricious</u>, Andrew could not be trusted. (-ness)
    Answer: Because of his <u>avariciousness</u>, Andrew could not be trusted.

1. Andrew <u>breezy</u> dismissed the charges against him. (-ly)
2. No one wanted to oppose Andrew, whose <u>stubborn</u> was legendary. (-ness)
3. <u>Adventure</u> Alicia decided to challenge his poor behavior. (-ous)
4. Fearful of this <u>occur</u>, Andrew begged Alicia not to be <u>pity</u>. (-less, ence)
5. Alicia found it very difficult to talk to Andrew because of his <u>disagree</u> ways. (-able)

EXERCISE B: Write two base words that could be combined with each suffix. Then write the resulting words, taking care to spell them correctly.

    Example: -able
    Answer: depend, dependable; negotiate, negotiable

1. -ly
2. -ness
3. -ish
4. -ing
5. -ment
6. -ed
7. -less
8. -ous
9. -like
10. -ence

EXERCISE C: Add the suffix in parentheses to each word. Then write at least ten sentences that include the new words, spelling each word correctly (You must use every word, but you may use more than one word in a sentence.)

    Example: guide (-ance)
    Answer: I've just finished a long meeting with my <u>guidance</u> counselor.

1. rely (-ance)	8. study (-ed)	15. acknowledge (-ment)
2. outrage (-ous)	9. depend (-ence)	16. love (-able)
3. comfort (-able)	10. complete (-ly)	17. travel (-ed)
4. infer (-ing)	11. weary (-ness)	18. mighty (-ly)
5. heart (-less)	12. believe (-ing)	19. pertain (-ence)
6. merry (-ment)	13. ignore (-ance)	20. treachery (-ous)
7. dog (-ed)	14. regard (-less)	

Choosing Correct Homophones

EXERCISE A: Write the choice in parentheses that correctly completes the sentence. Then write a sentence that includes the other choice.

> **Example:** Your work (complements, compliments) mine.
> **Answer:** complements; I appreciate the <u>compliments</u> you just gave me.

1. Ms. Day plays the (base, bass) fiddle in the civic orchestra.
2. Sheila was not (idle, idol) while she worked.
3. Stella was up to her (waist, waste) in chicken feathers.
4. (Your, You're) welcome to spend the (night, knight) with us.
5. Phil slammed his foot on the (knew, new) (brake, break).
6. (There, They're) never late (four, for) physical education class.
7. General Jimmy Doolittle (lead, led) the (air, heir) attack over Tokyo in World War II.
8. Alex (pride, pried) open the crate and (pared, paired) the potatoes inside it.
9. The (too, two) life-long enemies (made, maid) (piece, peace) with each other before they left.
10. The charts are (all ready, already) to be (sent, scent) by express mail to the publisher.

EXERCISE B: Write a sentence for each pair of homophones.

> **Example:** discrete/discreet
> **Answer:** Arrange the coins in three <u>discrete</u> piles, and be <u>discreet</u> about where you hide them.

1. groan/grown
2. ascent/assent
3. through/threw
4. passed/past
5. coarse/course
6. its/it's
7. alter/altar
8. whose/who's
9. wail/whale
10. capital/Capitol

Applying Other Spelling Rules and Tips

EXERCISE A: Complete the words in each sentence with the correct combination of letters, *ei* or *ie*. Write another sentence with the completed words.

> **Example:** He hadn't meant to dec__ve his friend.
> **Answer:** deceive; Did you purposely try to <u>deceive</u> me?

1. Jane's n__ghbor enjoyed working in her garden.
2. An ambassador from a for__gn country has diplomatic immunity.
3. Some people never ach__ve their goals.
4. Ned lay there staring at the c__ling of his bedroom.
5. The team was forced to forf__t the game.

EXERCISE B: Choose the appropriate ending in parentheses to add to each word base. Write another sentence with each completed word.

> **Example:** This memo will super_____ all previous information about the project.
> **Answer:** supersede; This report <u>supersedes</u> the one I gave last week.

1. Let's pro_____ without further interruption. (cede, ceed)
2. Angela had to con_____ that her brother was right about her team. (cede, sede)
3. After the spring floods, the waters began to re_____. (cede, ceed)
4. The American Revolu_____ caused strained relations with England. (sion, tion)
5. Clay's expul_____ from school was not unexpected. (sion, tion)

EXERCISE C: Rewrite each word, spelling it correctly.

> **Example:** Unknown: frug?l
> **Answer:** Correct Spelling: <u>frugal</u>

Unknown Spelling   Correct Spelling

1. rap?d   _____
2. resid?nce   _____
3. barb?rous   _____
4. avar?ce   _____
5. lux?ry   _____

Spelling Commonly Misspelled Words Correctly I

EXERCISE A: Rewrite the passage, correcting any spelling errors.

   Example: To be eligable for the trip, one had to pass many tests.
   Answer: To be <u>eligible</u> for the trip, one had to pass many tests.

   One Feburary, I accompanied a group of fourty students on an artic expedition. The goal of
the expedition was to asend an ice-covered mountain in a hostile enviroment. The trip required
much special appuratus and large amounts of food. Each hiker carried biscuts, cheese, boullion,
and canned meat.

   The expedition was led by a concientous colonel who demanded good disipline and hygene
from the group. One day, a boy accidently fell into a crevasse. His absense was soon noticed; the
other hikers spread out and began calling his name. Everyone was greatly relieved when he
ansered. Not only did we know where he was, but we also knew that he was still conscous. The
colonel immediatly dropped a rope into the crevasse, and the boy climbed out. He was
embarassed but not injured. The colonel took the opportunity to lecture the group on the
dangers of crevasses. He said that he could not guarante anyone's safety—that each person was
responsible.

EXERCISE B: Spell each word correctly; then use it in an original sentence. If a word is spelled
correctly, write Correct before the sentence. (You may use more than one word in a sentence.)

   Example: genious
   Answer: Everyone thinks that Rob is a real <u>genius</u>.

   1. attendent
   2. inaguration
   3. extasy
   4. chauffeur
   5. jewelery
   6. calendar
   7. comittee
   8. discipline
   9. consciounce
  10. goverment

Spelling Commonly Misspelled Words Correctly II

EXERCISE A: Rewrite the passage, correcting any spelling errors. (There are 20 errors in all.)

> **Example:** His stooped silhuette cast a shadow against the wall.
> **Answer:** His stooped <u>silhouette</u> cast a shadow against the wall.

On Wednsdays, I visit my accomplished friend, Mr. Ortega. Mr. Ortega is a ninty-year-old millionare who lives in a house that looks like a midievel castle. Mr. Ortega greets me at the door with a mischevious smile. He is wearing a plaid shirt, tan slacks, and mocassins. He manuvers his wheelchair down the hall to the sitting room. He looks forward to these ocassions because he knows that I am truely interested in the stories he has to tell.

Mr. Ortega made his fortune mining nickle. Before that, he was a sargent and then a lietenant in the Air Force. He has many momentos from his years in the military. One day, he told me about getting his pilot's licence. He likes to remenisce about the past, but he also has many pasttimes that keep him busy in the present. A playwrite, he has had several of his plays produced. He likes to read books about phychology and sociology. He continues to have remarkable perseverence and imagination. I consider it a great priviledge to know someone as interesting as Mr. Ortega.

EXERCISE B: Choose the correctly spelled word in each pair and use it in an original sentence. (You many use more than one word in a sentence.)

1. parliament/parlament
2. unecessary/unnecessary
3. unanimous/unanamous
4. turnament/tournament
5. righteous/rightous
6. referrence/reference
7. sincerely/sinserely
8. warrantee/warranty
9. labrotory/laboratory
10. versatile/versitile
11. parallel/parralel
12. predictable/predictible
13. vacuum/vaccuum
14. liquify/liquefy
15. muscle/mussle
16. maintennence/maintenance
17. paraphanalia/paraphernalia
18. miscellaneous/miscelaneous
19. occasion/occassion
20. paralyzed/parallysed

Underlining/Italics

Using Underlining/Italics in Titles and Names

EXERCISE A: Rewrite the sentences, underlining or italicizing any titles and names that should be printed in italics.

Example: Have you read The Red Badge of Courage?
Answer: Have you read *The Red Badge of Courage*?

1. I read the article in yesterday's New York Times.
2. Will 60 Minutes be interviewing the senator?
3. The U.S.S. Missouri has been named a national monument.
4. The artist claimed that he was inspired by Michelangelo's sculpture the Pieta.
5. When I was younger, my favorite book was Dear Mr. Henshaw.
6. I have a poster of Monet's Waterlilies in my room.
7. The animator used Beethoven's Symphony No. 9 as background music.
8. The Orient Express once ran between Paris and Istanbul.
9. There was a full-page ad about the sale in The Shopper's News.
10. Did you know that My Fair Lady was based on George Bernard Shaw's play Pygmalion?

EXERCISE B: Rewrite the paragraph, adding underlining or italics where needed.

Example: Have you read That Was Then, This Is Now by S. E. Hinton?
Answer: Have you read *That Was Then, This Is Now* by S. E. Hinton?

The "Books" section of the Times interviewed her recently. Inside Edition ran a story about her life in Tulsa, Oklahoma. Hinton wrote her most popular work, The Outsiders, when she was only sixteen! Hinton's works remind me of the film Grease. Her descriptive writing style and ear for dialogue are distinctive.

EXERCISE C: Write a sentence for each piece of information designated in parentheses. Be sure to use underlining correctly.

Example: (film)
Answer: One of my favorite old movies is Hitchcock's *Rear Window*.

1. (book)
2. (newspaper)
3. (television series)
4. (painting)
5. (opera)

Other Uses of Underlining/Italics

EXERCISE A: Rewrite the sentences. Use underlining or italics to mark the words or groups of words that should be italicized.

Example: There are three 5's in my address.
Answer: There are three <u>5</u>'s in my address.

1. The expression et cetera literally means "and other things."
2. Where does the saying "Mind your p's and q's" come from?
3. The word right has more than one meaning—right?
4. Put a : after the greeting in your letter.
5. Do you spell judgment with one e or two?
6. D, when used as a Roman numeral, represents 500.
7. The sign had Danger written in huge red letters!
8. How many O's are there in a trillion?
9. Many historians cite the policy of detente with China as Richard Nixon's greatest achievement as President.
10. The two sides settled their dispute with a quid pro quo arrangement.

EXERCISE B: Rewrite the paragraph, adding underlining or italics where needed.

Example: Is terrific spelled with one r or two?
Answer: Is <u>terrific</u> spelled with one r or two?

Always use italics when writing words as words, as in this example: "Foul has many meanings." Use italics to write numerals, as in this case: "These 7's look like 1's." When referring to specific marks of punctuation, such as ! or ?, be sure to use italics. Of course, foreign phrases, such as au demain, should be set off in italics.

EXERCISE C: Write four sentences as directed. Be sure to use underlining correctly.

Example: (letters used as letters)
Answer: In some styles of calligraphy, <u>s</u>'s look like <u>f</u>'s.

1. (word used as word)
2. (foreign phrase)
3. (number used as number)
4. (letter used as letter)

Verbals

Identifying and Using Participles and Participial Phrases

EXERCISE A: Write the participle or participial phrase in each sentence. Then write the word that each one modifies.

> **Example:** Shivering in the cold room, she soothed the crying baby.
> **Answer:** Shivering in the cold room, she; crying, baby

1. The exhausted players sat glumly on the sidelines.
2. Burdened with many books, I couldn't wave to my departing friends.
3. The rescue team, having searched for hours, finally located the stranded survivors.
4. With a pleased smile, Lynn accepted the award.
5. You sound like a laughing hyena or a wheezing horse!
6. The new sergeant, beaming proudly, showed us his stripes.
7. The First Lady gave a televised tour of the White House.
8. Did Miranda buy the dress decorated with bows?
9. Glancing over his shoulder, the distracted young man tripped over a rock.
10. Delighted by the scene, I stopped to watch a father playing with his children.
11. Known around the world, the talented performer is a show-business legend.
12. The award-winning restaurant specializes in fresh fish flown in daily from the seacoast.

EXERCISE B: Write each participle or participial phrase and the word that it modifies. Then rewrite the sentence, replacing the participle or participial phrase with another that makes sense.

> **Example:** Having lost her gloves, Louise bought herself a new pair.
> **Answer:** Having lost her gloves, Louise
>
> Having worn out her running shoes, Louise bought herself a new pair.

1. Embarrassed by his mistake, Peter slouched in his seat.
2. Concentrating deeply on my work, I didn't hear her question.
3. Startled, the flock of sparrows fluttered off the wire.
4. I wrote my report on the exciting history of spaceflight.
5. Stunned, I could offer no answer.
6. The stolen property was promptly returned.
7. Having been tempted, I helped myself to another bowl of soup.
8. The dinner, cooked to perfection, was delicious.
9. Falling to his knees, he begged for forgiveness.
10. Our smiling host met us at the door.

Identifying and Using Gerunds and Gerund Phrases

EXERCISE A: Write the gerund or gerund phrase in each sentence. Label whether it functions as a *subject, direct object, indirect object, predicate nominative, object of a preposition,* or *appositive.*

> **Example:** Shooting the rapids is a dangerous sport.
> **Answer:** Shooting the rapids (subject)

1. Riding the cable cars is part of a visit to San Francisco.
2. Sal's only exercise is walking to school and, occasionally, swimming.
3. Only by trying will you know for sure what you are capable of doing.
4. The skunk protects itself by emitting an offensive smell.
5. Rochelle's career goal, engineering, seems a good one for her.
6. The architect began including more windows in his plans.
7. Both walking and dancing are good forms of exercise.
8. Many teenagers earn money from baby-sitting or mowing lawns.
9. Joel gives studying the bulk of his free time.
10. The child's first task, feeding the chickens, delighted her.
11. After the announcement, everyone started grumbling.
12. The chorus enjoys singing, but rehearsing can be a chore.
13. There's no pleasure like that of having done a difficult job well!
14. The twins' habit of making animal noises brought them disparaging looks.
15. How can I give practicing my undivided attention?

EXERCISE B: Write a sentence that uses each gerund or gerund phrase as indicated in parentheses.

> **Example:** fishing in the pond (direct object)
> **Answer:** The children went <u>fishing in the pond</u>.

1. writing poetry (subject)
2. whining (direct object)
3. collecting coins (predicate nominative)
4. starting an argument (object of a preposition)
5. making the salad (appositive)
6. studying for the test (subject)
7. doing your homework (direct object)
8. crying (object of a preposition)
9. building a robot (appositive)
10. finishing on time (predicate nominative)

Identifying and Using Infinitives and Infinitive Phrases

EXERCISE A: Write the infinitive or infinitive phrase in each sentence. Then label it as a *noun,* an *adjective,* or an *adverb.*

> **Example:** Jane promised to tell me all about it.
> **Answer:** to tell me all about it (noun)

1. Mount Rushmore is the place to see.
2. To flee seemed his only hope.
3. My parents have promised to take us to Canada this year.
4. I'll be very happy to attend.
5. The main road to take to Centerville is under repair.

EXERCISE B: Write the ten infinitives or infinitive phrases in the sentences. Then label the function of each as an *adjective, adverb, subject, direct object, predicate nominative, object of a preposition,* or *appositive.*

> **Example:** To play guitar, Nan decided to cut her fingernails.
> **Answer:** To play guitar, adverb; to cut her fingernails, direct object

1. My attempt to speak was pitiful to hear.
2. Halley's Comet was too dim to see clearly without binoculars.
3. To translate, one must understand the sense as well as the words.
4. To misuse the apostrophe is considered a serious error.
5. Angela will be home for several months to recuperate.
6. My plan is to complete all assignments by Friday.
7. To photograph a night scene, you will need to use a tripod.
8. Calvin Coolidge decided not to seek reelection in 1928.

EXERCISE C: Write a sentence that uses each infinitive or infinitive phrase as indicated in parentheses.

> **Example:** to go home (adjective)
> **Answer:** He decided it was time <u>to go home</u>.

1. to master the violin (subject)
2. to study (direct object)
3. to be done (adjective)
4. to complete (adverb)
5. to understand this book (subject)
6. to go to the zoo (direct object)
7. to lose (adjective)
8. to return home (adverb)
9. to write a poem (subject)
10. to seek her fortune (direct object)

Using Verbals Correctly

EXERCISE A: Rewrite each sentence to correct any errors in the use of verbals or verbal phrases. If a sentence needs no changes, write *Correct.*

> **Example:** You can begin to, if you wish, choose your partners.
> **Answer:** You can begin, *if you wish, to choose* your partners.

1. Fred losing his way came as quite a surprise.
2. Finding our compass, the voyage turned out all right in the end.
3. By studying hard, your test scores can increase dramatically.
4. After moving, they expected to never again see their old friends.
5. Seeming not to fear for their own safety, the fire fighters battled the blaze.
6. His mother asked him to quickly finish his homework.
7. Reading the new thriller, Chapter 4 was very exciting.
8. Charles's singing leaves a great deal to be desired.
9. The boys planned to somehow raise enough money to buy the tickets.
10. Having graduated with honors, a good job was practically guaranteed.

EXERCISE B: Write whether each sentence demonstrates a split infinitive (I), a dangling participle or participial phrase (P), or a failure to use the possessive case before a gerund (G). Then rewrite the sentence to correct the error. If a sentence needs no changes, write *Correct.*

> **Example:** Robert losing the directions caused us to be late.
> **Answer:** (G) *Robert's losing the directions* caused us to be late.

1. Having taken our seats, the concert began.
2. My little sister likes to always play the same silly games.
3. The fact that Gillian was invited has nothing to do with me deciding not to go.
4. Our receiving the reward money came as a delightful surprise.
5. Having lost her gloves, Betty's hands were very cold.
6. The students were asked to promptly take their seats and to pay close attention.
7. Having heard all the evidence, a guilty verdict is almost certain.
8. Reading about history, the cultures of Africa were especially intriguing.
9. Having traveled all day, we would like to, if possible, take a brief rest.
10. The judge deciding for the plaintiff was a disappointment to the defendant.

Developing Your Style: Verbals

EXERCISE A: Combine each pair of sentences by using a verbal phrase of the type indicated in parentheses.

Example: That woman wears a green dress. She is my mother. (participial)
Answer: That woman <u>wearing a green dress</u> is my mother.

1. Mayor Jefferson shook hands with the governor. The mayor looked proud. (participial)
2. Hillary collects stamps. It is her favorite hobby. (gerund)
3. The boys were playing in the park. They spotted a rare bird. (participial)
4. The prospectors traveled to California. They were looking for gold. (infinitive)
5. Silk Moonstone writes poetry. It helps her express her feelings. (gerund)

EXERCISE B: Rewrite each sentence, making it more interesting by adding at least one verbal phrase of the type indicated in parentheses.

Example: Tamara took a class. (infinitive)
Answer: Tamara took a class <u>to learn how to play tennis</u>.

1. The girls were eager. (infinitive)
2. The campers quickly grew tired. (participial)
3. Jon tried. (gerund)
4. They used different kinds of bait. (infinitive)
5. Reggie ran as fast as he could. (participial)

EXERCISE C: Write ten sentences, using the combination of verbal phrases given below.

Example: gerund, infinitive
Answer: <u>Playing basketball</u> is a great way <u>to enjoy a sunny afternoon</u>.

1. gerund, infinitive
2. infinitive, participial
3. infinitive, infinitive
4. participial, participial
5. participial, infinitive
6. gerund, gerund
7. gerund, infinitive
8. infinitive, infinitive
9. gerund, participial
10. gerund, gerund

Verbs

Verb-Forming Suffixes

EXERCISE A: Rewrite the sentences, using a verb-forming suffix (-ate, -en, -er, -ify, -ize) to change the word in parentheses to a verb.

> **Example:** Before you seal the envelope, (moist) the adhesive flap.
> **Answer:** Before you seal the envelope, <u>moisten</u> the adhesive flap.

1. Mom's face (soft) when she smiles.
2. If you don't cover that pan, grease will (splat) everywhere.
3. Could anyone possibly (false) these records?
4. We students in the chorus sometimes (vocal) and even (harmony) after school.
5. Please (note) the secretary if you plan to be absent on Friday.
6. I don't think you should (short) this skirt; it looks just right to me.
7. How well that speaker can (motive) a crowd!
8. If you (public) that information, you will (humility) the entire family.
9. I don't know where you learned to (decor) a room like this, but those colors really (bright) up this dingy space.
10. Maybe that movie (fright) you, but it didn't (horror) me one bit.

EXERCISE B: Change each word into a verb by adding the verb-forming suffix given. Use a dictionary to check spelling, if needed. Then use the resulting word in a sentence.

> **Example:** critic + ize
> **Answer:** If all you can do is <u>criticize</u>, you might as well keep quiet.

1. theory + ize
2. stiff + en
3. peace + ify
4. pat + er
5. tranquil + ize
6. liquid + ate
7. liquid + ify
8. eulogy + ize
9. ripe + en
10. pollen + ate

Identifying Action Verbs and Linking Verbs

EXERCISE A: Write each verb and label it as an *action verb* or *linking verb*. If the verb is an action verb, write whether the action is *physical* or *mental*. If the verb is a linking verb, write which words are linked by the verb.

> **Example:** The coach seemed happy with the team's performance.
> **Answer:** seemed, linking verb (coach, happy)

1. The coach praised the players for their effort.
2. The captain led the team through the new plays.
3. The cheerleaders were skillful and enthusiastic.
4. The manager thought of a new slogan for the team.
5. The bleachers looked full of the team's supporters.

EXERCISE B: Fill in each blank with one of these verbs—*feel, grow, look, sound, or taste*—using each of these verbs as a linking verb and as an action verb. Then label each verb as *linking* or *action*.

> **Example:** The barbecue sauce _____ too sweet.
> **Answer:** The barbecue sauce <u>tastes</u> too sweet. (linking)
>
> <u>Taste</u> this barbecue sauce. (action)

1. Cindy has _____ fond of her baby brother.
2. Mrs. Goldstein _____ geraniums in her flower boxes.
3. Please help me _____ for the softball, Lewis.
4. The car _____ unsafe for the road.
5. Principal Hansen _____ the alarm for a fire drill.
6. Rod _____ surprisingly nervous about the track meet.
7. Terry _____ disappointed after striking out.
8. Pam _____ the sheep's thick woolly coat.
9. Don't you think the beef stew _____ a bit too salty?
10. _____ these cookies and tell me if you like them.

EXERCISE C: Write a brief anecdote about a sporting event. Include the verbs *seem, appear, look, sound, feel;* you may add other verbs, as well. Underline each verb and label it *action verb* or *linking verb*.

> **Example:** As spectators <u>took</u> (action) their seats, they appeared (linking) hopeful of a victory for the home team.

Identifying Transitive Verbs and Intransitive Verbs

EXERCISE A: Write the verb in each sentence and label it as *transitive* or *intransitive*. If a verb is transitive, write its object.

Example: We enjoyed our camping trip last fall.
Answer: enjoyed (transitive), trip

1. Has Susan picked a name for her puppy yet?
2. The waves crashed upon the shore.
3. The letter carrier looked warily at the vigilant collie.
4. A few embers flickered in the fireplace.
5. Our neighbor whittles wooden animals for children in the hospital.
6. Bradley crawled across the room, toward the kitchen.
7. The distant thunder disturbed my sleep.
8. Two mysterious packages have just arrived in the mail.
9. Will Aunt Mamie drive us to the airport?
10. The astronauts performed several experiments during their mission.

EXERCISE B: Rewrite the sentences, using each intransitive verb as transitive and each transitive verb as intransitive. Beside each answer, write *transitive* or *intransitive*.

Example: The playful child hid behind the tree.
Answer: The playful child hid the ball behind the tree. (transitive)

1. The scientist read her lecture.
2. She spoke clearly.
3. Some listeners cheered the scientist's genius.
4. She stood on a platform.
5. Please leave through the rear doors.

EXERCISE C: Complete each sentence by following the directions given in parentheses.

Example: The moonlight reflected (intranstive).
Answer: The moonlight reflected <u>on the water</u>.

1. The tide washed (transitive).
2. How the wet sand stuck (intransitive).
3. A mild breeze blew (transitive).
4. When did clouds form (intransitive)?
5. Huge waves crashed (intransitive).

Identifying Main Verbs and Helping Verbs

EXERCISE A: Write the helping verb or verbs in each phrase.

    Examples: should be seen

               should have been considered
    Answers: should be

               should have been

  1. may be talking
  2. has opposed
  3. might have seen
  4. could help
  5. am reconsidering
  6. does appreciate
  7. had begun
  8. could have planned
  9. will be finishing
10. should have suggested

EXERCISE B: Add appropriate main verbs and helping verbs to complete the sentences.

    Example: Liana _____ _____ _____ a lot of time at the library.
    Answer: Liana <u>has been spending</u> a lot of time at the library.

  1. I _____ not _____ her, but my brother spotted her there twice last week.
  2. I wonder—_____ she _____ _____ _____ research for the biology report?
  3. Certainly no one _____ _____ a report like Liana!
  4. If you _____ not _____ me, then you _____ _____ her grades this past year.
  5. She _____ _____ _____ on that report for two months.

Identifying Verb Forms, Number, and Person

EXERCISE A: Write the verbs in each sentence and give the person and number of each subject.

> **Example:** We usually spend three or four weekends at the coast each year because my parents love the ocean.
> **Answer:** spend, first-person plural; love, third person plural

1. My brother enjoys the beach as much as I do.
2. I swim often; my brother's favorite activity is fishing.
3. Sally, would you come with us the next time we go?
4. If the cousins join us, you (all) could rent the condo next to ours.
5. We usually eat breakfast and lunch in the condo, but dinnertime usually means a trip to a restaurant.

EXERCISE B: Rewrite the sentences, correcting any verbs that do not agree with their subjects. If a sentence needs no changes, write *Correct.* Then write the person and number of each subject and verb in the sentence.

> **Example:** My little brother, Will, attend kindergarten.
> **Answer:** My little brother, Will, <u>attends</u> kindergarten. (third-person singular)

1. He likes kindergarten, but he doesn't likes taking naps.
2. When I observe his class, he gets very excited.
3. The children spend a lot of time on computers, they also listens to many tapes.
4. What does you remember about kindergarten, Jim?
5. We spent a lot of time playing and painting.

EXERCISE C: Complete the dialogue, using sentences whose subjects and verbs show the person and number designated in parentheses.

> **Example:** Antonio: (first-person singular)
> **Answer:** Antonio: May I speak to Jorge?

JORGE: (first-person singular) (third-person singular)
ANTONIO: (third-person plural) (second-person singular)
JORGE: (first-person singular) (second-person singular)
ANTONIO: (first-person plural) (first-person plural)

Identifying and Using Simple Tenses

EXERCISE A: Write the verbs from the sentences and give the tense of each. Some verbs may have contractions.

Example: The window on the old house has some cracked glass.
Answer: has   present

1. The young man swaggers down the sidewalk and clicks his fingers to the beat.
2. He will blush if Joanie talks to him at the party.
3. Cary studied himself in the mirror, made a face, and grinned.
4. The match scrapes against the box and then catches fire.
5. Did you see the old cupboard in the corner?
6. I once visited Mexico with my parents; but I was very young and don't remember much about it.
7. I will sleep on the twin bed.
8. There are a few pieces of fruit in the refrigerator.
9. If you want Earl, I think that he's in the kitchen.
10. I also think he's with Lacy.

EXERCISE B: Rewrite the sentences, putting the verb in the tense designated in parentheses.

Example: We (go-past) to a rock concert last weekend.
Answer: We <u>went</u> to a rock concert last weekend.

1. The young singer (step-past) into the spotlight.
2. After the concert, he probably (sign-future) autographs.
3. Now the sounds of guitars, drums, and trumpets (swirl-present) around the auditorium.
4. The lead singer (nod-present) to the drummer, who (respond-present) with a machine-like drum roll.
5. The singer (become-present) animated, dancing about the stage.
6. Our ears (ring-future) for hours from all this loud music!
7. Later, we (laugh-past) about the wonderful evening.
8. Still, if we ever (attend-present) an event like that again, we probably (take-future) earplugs!
9. I really (like-present) this music, even though I (complain-present) about the noise.
10. By the way, my favorite group (be-present) the Deltas, although in the past it (be-past) the Kentuckians.

Identifying and Using Perfect Tenses

EXERCISE A: Rewrite each sentence, using the verb and tense designated in parentheses.

Example: A dog always (be-present perfect) one of the easiest animals to train.
Answer: A dog always <u>has been</u> one of the easiest animals to train.

1. The dog's intelligence (help-past perfect) it to learn quickly.
2. You (learn-future perfect) some general rules about training a dog.
3. Their owners (be-past perfect) firm with their dogs.
4. A trained dog (obey-present perfect) its owner even when it (feel-present perfect) playful or inattentive.
5. A good owner (taught-future perfect) only one command at a time.
6. Owners (use-present perfect) the same command words, repeating the lesson daily until the dog learns.
7. A dog (receive-future perfect) praise often when it (do-present perfect) well.
8. The dog trainer (insist-present perfect) that a dog's owner always be present.
9. You (watch-present perfect) a dog trainer work, I presume.
10. My dog (finish-future perfect) his course before your dog Elsie begins hers.

EXERCISE B: Rewrite the paragraph, using the form of the verb indicated in parentheses.

Example: Martha (finish-past perfect) making the biscuits by the time I began the fruit salad.
Answer: Martha <u>had finished</u> making the biscuits by the time I began the fruit salad.

1. Traditionally, the favorite pie at this time of year (be-present perfect) always my grandmother's gooseberry pie.
2. You (pick-future perfect) all the strawberries you need by noon.
3. No one who (be-present perfect) a guest at our dinners ever goes away hungry.
4. Ned just (set-past perfect) the table as the first guest arrived.
5. Adam (offer-past perfect) his services as dishwasher even before I (finish-past perfect) eating.

Identifying and Using Progressive Forms of Verb Tenses

EXERCISE A: Write the progressive verb form in each of the sentences. Then label its tense.

> **Example:** Were you painting scenery yesterday after school?
> **Answer:** <u>Were painting</u> (past progressive)

1. Everyone has been working very hard in preparation for the spring play.
2. Each student will be inviting his or her family to the play.
3. Last week, Mrs. Yamamoto was hoping that all the sets would be finished on time.
4. Even today she is approving the designer's sketches.
5. At Saturday's rehearsal, a few actors were still memorizing their lines.
6. "How am I feeling right now?" she fumed at them.
7. "I won't be giving you more than one guess about that!"
8. We've all been anticipating opening night.
9. By next Monday we will all be breathing a deep sigh of relief.
10. By opening night we will have been rehearsing for six weeks.

EXERCISE B: Rewrite the sentences, using the progressive form of each verb tense in parentheses. Then use a different verb, keeping the same tense and form, in a sentence of your own. If a sentence contains two progressive verbs, use both in the new sentence.

> **Example:** I (submit-present) a story to the school literary magazine.
> **Answer:** I <u>am submitting</u> a story to the school literary magazine.
> My friend Mariana <u>is living</u> in Europe for a year.

1. Most of my friends (work-present perfect) on something for the *Aerie.*
2. Mr. Cunningham (promote-past perfect) the magazine for about a week before I became interested.
3. I (discuss-past) my writer's portfolio with Ben and Jolene.
4. "Ben," I asked, "you (give-future) the editors a story, won't you?"
5. "Walt," he joked. "I (clear-future perfect) my desk before you (revise-present) your first drafts!"
6. Jolene said that the two of us (be-past) too competitive.
7. "The editor-in-chief (invite-present perfect) everyone to enter," she reminded us.
8. "I (look-future) for both of your names in the *Aerie,*" she said, "because I am confident you can win."

Identifying and Using Irregular Verbs I

EXERCISE A: Rewrite the sentences, using the correct form of each verb in parentheses.

Example: The clock had been (broke, broken) for several months.
Answer: The clock had been <u>broken</u> for several months.

1. Carlos (became, become) upset upon hearing the cost for fixing the clock.
2. He had (driven, drove) twenty miles to this clock repair shop.
3. "When I (began, begun) the trip," he thought, "I hoped it would be cheap."
4. "I (heared, heard) from a friend that your costs are reasonable," he said.
5. "The clock has (hanged, hung) on my grandfather's wall for fifty years."
6. "During an earthquake," Carlos explained, "It had somehow (fallen, fell)."
7. Carlos's grandfather had (given, give) it to him.
8. "It means a lot to me," Carlos added, "since it (was, be) my grandpa's."
9. On hearing all this, the shopkeeper (grew, growed) sympathetic.
10. "I will see what can be (did, done) with it as cheaply as possible," the shopkeeper sighed.

EXERCISE B: Rewrite the sentences, using the correct past or present participle form of each verb in parentheses.

Example: Sachi (freeze) in her tracks and (drink) in the preposterous scene.
Answer: Sachi <u>froze</u> in her tracks and <u>drank</u> in the preposterous scene.

1. Sachi (burst) through the door and (fling) herself on the sofa.
2. "I have never (feel) so awful," she cried as she (fight) back tears.
3. "I have never (have) such a humiliating experience!"
4. She (catch) a glimpse of herself in a mirror, laughed, and (bite) her lip.
5. "I should have (go) back and explained what happened," she said to herself.
6. "Instead, I (fly) into a panic; now, I'm afraid, it has (cost) me my self-respect."
7. "If Marta has (find) out what happened, she'll make me grovel!"
8. Sachi (blow) back some hair from her eyes and vowed, "I've (eat) crow in the past—but not this time!"
9. "I've not yet been (beat)," Sachi said, continuing her pep talk.
10. She would not be (break) by this, either!

Identifying and Using Irregular Verbs II

EXERCISE A: Rewrite each sentences, using the correct form of the verb in parentheses.

> **Example:** William had (rose, risen) early to get to the bus on time.
> **Answer:** William had <u>risen</u> early to get to the bus on time.

1. William (rang, rung) the bell and waited for someone to come to the door.
2. He had (rode, ridden) the bus across town to visit this unique museum.
3. A tall, thin woman who (worn, wore) a gray smock came to the door.
4. She opened her mouth and would have (spoke, spoken) to William.
5. Before she could utter a word, however, a man (threw, throwed) open the door.
6. He reached out and enthusiastically (shook, shaken) William's hand.
7. "Welcome!" the man said. "I (knowed, knew) you'd be here today."
8. He clapped William on the back with such force that it (stinged, stung).
9. William was (taken, took) aback by the man's overly friendly manner.
10. "I (seen, saw) the flyer advertising your museum," William stammered.

EXERCISE B: Rewrite the sentences, using the correct past or present participle form of each verb in parentheses.

> **Example:** William had not (sing) for days, but he (tell) the pianist that he'd try.
> **Answer:** William had not <u>sung</u> for days, but he <u>told</u> the pianist that he'd try.

1. After William had (pay) the admission fee, the curator (tear) the ticket in two, handing William the stub.
2. William (put) the stub in his pocket and (make) his way to the exhibits.
3. A hallway (lead) to his left; a sign (say) that it went to the exhibits.
4. He stepped into a gallery where a dozen flutes (lie) on a table.
5. William's uncle had (lend) him a flute once and had even (teach) William to play a few simple tunes.
6. Then his uncle had (tell) William that it was useless; he was tone deaf.
7. William (sit) on the piano bench that had been (set) against the wall.
8. He (rise) to examine a clavichord and a steam-powered organ that William (think) would surely shake the museum to pieces if played.
9. He picked up a score that someone had (leave)—and that had been (write) by Chopin.
10. The curator's booming voice (split) the air; "Put that down," he commanded.

Identifying and Using Active and Passive Voice

EXERCISE A: Make two columns. Label them <u>Active Voice</u> and <u>Passive Voice</u>. Then read the paragraph below. Under each heading, write the numbers of the sentences that contain a verb in that voice.

> **Example:** 1. A story by Mark Twain was read to us by Anita.
> **Answer:** <u>Active Voice</u>   <u>Passive Voice</u>
>   1

(1) Mark Twain is loved by many people as one of our nation's greatest writers and humorists. (2) His humorous stories and novels are especially admired by readers. (3) Twain grew up in Hannibal, Missouri. (4) In his youth, he was hired by several employers for a number of jobs. (5) He served as a printer, a steamboat pilot, an editor, and a foreign correspondent.

(6) Twain based many of his stories on personal experiences. (7) Life along the Mississippi River was described by him. (8) In addition, everyday speech was frequently included. (9) Besides all this writing, Twain completed an around-the-world lecture tour. (10) How American literature has been enriched by Mark Twain!

EXERCISE B: Rewrite each sentence, changing verbs in the passive voice to the active voice and vice-versa. Label each new sentence as *active* or *passive*. If there is not enough information to rewrite a sentence, write *No Change.*

> **Example:** The picture in our living room was painted by Ellen.
> **Answer:** Bridget <u>painted</u> the picture in our living room. (active)

1. My favorite dessert, pineapple upside-down cake, was prepared by my mother.
2. Last summer I obtained a part-time job at Frank's Fine Furniture.
3. The cooking class is taught by David Jones.
4. The environmental bumper sticker on our car was made by my best friend, Hattie.
5. John gave the surprise party for Alana.
6. Jacqueline made the poster.
7. The newspaper was delivered by a boy on a bicycle.
8. Your questions will be answered by a team of experts.
9. It has been said not only that "absence makes the heart grown fonder" but also that sometimes "out of sight [is] out of mind."
10. The director gave Claudio a starring role.

Identifying and Using the Subjunctive Mood

EXERCISE A: Write the verb in parentheses that correctly completes each sentence.

> **Example:** We recommend that he (buy, buys) now.
> **Answer:** buy

1. If I (was, were) you, I would invest in real estate.
2. It is necessary that a buyer (keep, keeps) alert.
3. Do you recommend that he (view, views) several sites?
4. The bank may demand that he (cosign, cosigns) the loan.
5. I suggest that you (are, be) honest about your income.

EXERCISE B: Rewrite each sentence, using the correct form of the verb in parentheses.

> **Example:** It is best that you _____ alert. (to remain)
> **Answer:** It is best that you <u>remain</u> alert.

1. We recommend that he _____ our directions. (to follow)
2. I insist that any map _____ both clear and readable. (to be)
3. Is it necessary that I _____ the whole way? (to drive)
4. We would prefer that Gwen _____ for a few hours. (to rest)
5. If she _____ a truck driver, would she rest? (to be)
6. I would demand that any driver _____ some time off. (to take)
7. It is recommended that each car _____ down at the tunnel. (to slow)
8. Dad is insisting that Mom _____ the freeway. (to leave)
9. If you _____ she, would you need a break? (to be)
10. I suggested that Dad _____ less domineering. (to be)

EXERCISE C: Complete each sentence by using the subjunctive mood correctly.

> **Example:** It is important that _____.
> **Answer:** It is important that <u>a teacher be wise</u>.

1. Would you recommend that _____?
2. I would prefer that _____.
3. It might be better if _____.
4. He insists that _____!
5. We suggest that _____.

Using Easily Confused Verbs Correctly

EXERCISE A: Rewrite each sentence so that the verb is in the correct form. If a sentence needs no changes, write *Correct*.

> **Example:** The sun had raised over the farm where we rose chickens.
> **Answer:** The sun had <u>risen</u> over the farm where we <u>raised</u> chickens.

1. Most people had taken us biscuits or cakes; many had brought them away again.
2. A metal roof lays over the coop where the chickens lay their eggs.
3. Leave us let the young chicks alone until later.
4. That hen would have laid more eggs if you had not sat down to watch her.
5. I plan to set here until the sun has sat.

EXERCISE B: Rewrite each sentence, using the correct form of the correct verb in parentheses.

> **Example:** The sun usually has (raise/rise) by six o'clock.
> **Answer:** The sun usually has <u>risen</u> by six o'clock.

1. I will (sit/set) the table for breakfast.
2. Dad should have (raise/rise) the camp flag by now.
3. Yesterday Bart (lie/lay) the tablecloth out to dry.
4. Aunt Evelyn will (bring/take) the baby down here.
5. Mom told Bart, "(Let/Leave) the muffins alone!"
6. After Mom has (sit/set) down, everyone else may, too.
7. The temperature already has (raise/rise) to 70 degrees.
8. We plan to (lie/lay) outside in the sunshine.
9. Haven't you (bring/take) too many muffins at once?
10. After Evelyn has (let/leave), we will clean up.

EXERCISE C: Use a form of each pair of words in a sentence that shows you know the meaning of each word.

> **Example:** sit/set
> **Answer:** I <u>sat</u> there for an hour, waiting for the sun to set.

1. bring/take
2. leave/let
3. lie/lay
4. raise/rise
5. sit/set

Using Principal Parts of Verbs Correctly

EXERCISE A: Write the form of the verb in parentheses that correctly completes each sentence.

Example: Brandon has (saw, seen) that movie already.
Answer: seen

1. We have been (waited, waiting) in line for tickets.
2. Have previews of coming attractions been (shown, shared)?
3. Willie has (buyed, bought) a bag of buttered popcorn.
4. Jennifer (like, likes) the cartoons.
5. Who was (feature, featured) in that picture?
6. Dina is always (read, reading) movie magazines!
7. These tickets are (become, becoming) more expensive.
8. It bothers me when people (are, be) talking during the show.
9. Lance has (save, saved) two seats on the aisle.
10. The show will (begin, began) any minute now.

EXERCISE B: Rewrite each sentence, using correct verb forms.

Example: Marcie and her friends had decide on a play.
Answer: Marcie and her friends had <u>decided</u> on a play.

1. Ronnie and Davie has been working on a script.
2. Nicole is design special costumes for the play.
3. Graham had setted up microphones and speakers around the stage.
4. Juliette and Tom was rehearsed their parts backstage.
5. The tickets has been printing and sold by Ricky.

EXERCISE C: Rewrite each sentence, using the correct form of the verb in parentheses.

Example: An everyday scene was (depict) on canvas.
Answer: An everyday scene was <u>depicted</u> on canvas.

1. The artist had (try) to present the scene as it was.
2. She has (use) dark colors to enhance the mood.
3. Do the people (appear) happy or sad?
4. I have (see) other paintings like this in the city museum.
5. This artist has always (impress) me with her ability to capture emotions on canvas.

Using Tense Sequence Correctly

EXERCISE A: Rewrite each sentence, correcting any problems in tense by changing the second verb.

  Example: He walked home with me and tells me the latest news.
  Answer: He walked home with me and <u>told</u> me the latest news.

1. We usually stay after school and worked on our science project.
2. Although I tried to listen, I will fall asleep—much to my embarrassment!
3. The customer complained about the service and says that he wouldn't return.
4. Manuel had not finished playing the piano, but the audience applauds anyway.
5. First we sang a folk song; then we continue with a lullably.
6. We were editing the story while she draws an illustration.
7. When Susan offered to help me paint the scenery, I accept with a heartfelt "Thanks!"
8. We had gotten home by the time Josh will arrive.
9. Has Nina explained the problem and asking Nancy's opinion?
10. When he asked you a question, do you immediately reply?

EXERCISE B: Rewrite the paragraph, correcting inappropriate shifts in tense.

  Example: Patty meets Anton and tried to help him.
  Answer: Patty meets Anton and <u>tries</u> to help him.

Having recently finished reading the novel *The Summer of My German Soldier,* I will be recommending it highly. The events took place in Arkansas during World War II. Patty Bergen narrated the story. She has described the arrival of German prisoners of war. These prisoners will be sent to Arkansas to work in the cotton fields. Their arrival has been less exciting than Patty expected. One day, however, Patty has met one of the prisoners in her father's store. He and the other prisoners came to the store to buy hats to protect themselves from the strong sun. Patty befriended this prisoner and learns about his past. While I am reading the book, I wondered whether this friendship will prove dangerous for both Patty and the soldier.

Developing Your Style: Using Vivid, Precise Verbs

EXERCISE A: Rewrite each sentence, replacing each underlined verb or verb phrase with a more vivid, precise verb.

> **Example:** "That young man <u>walks</u> like a soldier!" she <u>said</u>.
> **Answer:** "That young man <u>marches</u> like a soldier!" she <u>exclaimed</u>.

1. Each fashion model <u>walked</u> gracefully down the runway but then <u>went</u> to the dressing room without a second to waste.
2. Photographers <u>used</u> their cameras the minute they <u>saw</u> the models.
3. At the last minute, the designer <u>changed</u> a velvet sash for the silk one and then <u>changed</u> it to a scarf.
4. One bold reporter secretly <u>went</u> backstage and <u>listened in</u> on private conversations.
5. After the show, the designer <u>places</u> the one-of-a-kind clothes in plastic bags in order to <u>care for</u> them.

EXERCISE B: Complete each sentence with a vivid, precise verb. Write each sentence.

> **Example:** At Teen Camp, some squeamish campers _____ at the sight of snakes, but many nature lovers _____.
> **Answer:** At Teen Camp, some squeamish campers <u>squeal</u> at the sight of snakes, but many nature lovers <u>cheer</u>.

1. The thermometer _____ that the temperature _____ ten degrees in the past hour.
2. After a morning swim, the hungry campers _____ their lunch and _____ in their cabins until early afternoon.
3. A bugle call _____ the campers to the flagpole where they _____ the Pledge of Allegiance.
4. The campers _____ so noisily that the counselor _____ the direction three times.
5. After the two teams _____ out an agreement, they _____ to the lake.

EXERCISE C: Rewrite the paragraph, replacing ten vague verbs or verb phrases with more vivid, precise verbs.

The sheriff put his hands above his eyes as he looked at the horizon. Quickly he got on his horse and took the reins. The horse's hoofbeats sounded as the rider rode after the bandit. The horse moved clouds of dust that hid the sheriff's face. At this point, the movie audience yelled and wanted their money back.

Developing Your Style: Choosing the Active Voice

EXERCISE A: Rewrite each sentence, changing any passive verbs to active verbs.

   Example: Space travel was advanced by pioneers of science.
   Answer: Pioneers of science <u>advanced</u> space travel.

1. Liquid rocket fuel first was tested by Robert Goddard in 1926.
2. A prototype of a helicopter had been sketched by Leonardo da Vinci.
3. Alternatives to the use of gasoline have been explored by scientists.
4. Electric cars, for example, have been advocated by environmentalists.

EXERCISE B: Write whether the verb in each sentence is in the *active* or *passive* voice. If a verb is in the passive voice, rewrite the sentence, changing the passive verb to an active verb.

   Example: The home-run king finally was defeated by a relief pitcher.
   Answer: passive; A relief pitcher finally defeated the home-run king.

1. The National League has been outdone for the third straight year by the American League.
2. The title role in *The Lou Gehrig Story* was played by Gary Cooper.
3. He played it strictly by the script.
4. Was any kind of award received by this talented actor?

EXERCISE C: Rewrite the paragraph, changing passive verbs to active verbs where appropriate. If there is not sufficient information to change a passive verb, keep it as it is.

   In the past, college-bound students were advised by the teaching staff. However, graduates who were entering the job force were not given any special treatment. The need for professional career counseling was recogized by students and teachers. Soon, the Board of Education was bombarded with petitions by concerned educators. Special counselors were hired by the board to satisfy this need. These counselors wisely sought the help of the business community. Eventually, a summer internship program for graduates was underwritten by several business executives. The special student meeting at school was attended by an overflowing crowd. Since that time, many students have taken advantage of the internship program. They have been successfully trained by their business mentors.

Answer Key

Grammar, Usage, and Mechanics

Abbreviations

Abbreviating Names and Titles, Exercise A
1. NATO
2. Lt. Angelo Pareti
3. Supt. Mary Fuller
4. Meredith Helm, D.D.S.
5. Irwin Kroll, M.S.
6. FDR
7. Sen. Claudia Pappas
8. Rosalie Cooper, M.B.A.
9. FDIC
10. Gov. Miguel Fuentes

Abbreviating Names and Titles, Exercise B
1. CBS; My favorite program is on CBS at 7:00 P.M.
2. Prof., Rm.; Prof. Chang's history class meets in Rm. 184.
3. Inc.; Bill applied for a job at Bentwood Manufacturing, Inc.
4. Atty., FBI; Atty. Veronica Chávez works for the FBI.
5. M.F.A.; You can see the art of Ana Ríos, M.F.A., at the gallery.
6. Jr.; Daniel Parker, Jr., has opened his own accounting firm.
7. Rev.; Sgt.; The Rev. Percy Maddux has an appointment to see Sgt. Edward Ames.

Abbreviating Names and Titles, Exercise C
Sentences will vary; possible sentences are given.
1. Sr.; M.D.; I dread my visit to Benjamin Parks, Sr., M.D.
2. Atty.; UAW; Atty. Carl Baker is representing the UAW.
3. Ph.D.; Piri Villanueva, Ph.D., is lecturing at the conference.
4. Hon.; AFT; The Hon. Helen Drake ruled on the case involving the AFT.
5. Amb.; VOA; UN; Amb. Kyoko Mizumura spoke at VOA headquarters and then at the UN.

Other Types of Abbreviations, Exercise A

1. <u>Mon.,</u> June 11
2. <u>Mt.</u> Olive
3. Boston, <u>MA</u>
4. 8 <u>hr.</u>
5. 11:05 <u>A.M.</u>
6. 1349 <u>N.</u> Berry Rd.
7. St. Charles <u>Co.</u>
8. milk, eggs, salt, <u>etc.</u>
9. 100 <u>km</u>
10. 37 degrees <u>C</u>
11. 5 <u>L</u> of milk
12. Lansing, <u>MI</u>
13. 6421 Lindell <u>Blvd.</u>
14. 14 g
15. 10 <u>min.,</u> 40 <u>sec.</u>
16. <u>Ft.</u> Union
17. <u>e.g.,</u> books, pencils, chalk
18. <u>Sept.</u> 4, 1947
19. 3.6 <u>cm</u>
20. Logan <u>Bros.</u> Moving <u>Co.</u>

Other Types of Abbreviations, Exercise B

1. A.D.; In A.D. 1066, the Normans conquered England.
2. Ave., IL; Mark lives at 216 Lincoln Ave., Springfield, IL.
3. tsp., tbsp.; Add 2 tsp. of salt and 3 tbsp. of butter.
4. Co., MO; My grandfather lives in Franklin Co., in MO.
5. gal., L; Which is larger: 1 gal. or 1 L?
6. D.C., A.M.; Our flight arrives in Washington, D.C., at 9:00 A.M.
7. et al.; Tanya Denton et al. edited this book.
8. km, CA, WY; How many km is it from Los Angeles, CA, to Cheyenne, WY?
9. gal. qt.; My car holds 14 gal. of gasoline and 4 qt. of oil.
10. i.e., P.M.; The aurora borealis—i.e., the northern lights—appeared at 11:30 P.M.
11. B.C.; These flint tools were made in the year 8000 B.C.

Addresses

Writing Addresses Correctly, EXERCISE A

1. 186 Forest Dr.
   Camden<u>,</u> AR 71701
2. 76 <u>19th</u> St.
   Suite <u>7</u>-A
3. <u>102</u> Mountain View Rd.
   Milwaukee<u>,</u> WI 53202
4. They live in Laconia Township<u>,</u> Belknap County.
5. Send the poster to me at <u>15</u> Adams <u>Street,</u> Grand Forks<u>, North Dakota</u> 58201.

Writing Addresses Correctly, EXERCISE B
  1. 145 <u>12th</u> St. (or <u>Twelfth Street</u>)
     Charleston, SC 29401;
     145 <u>12th Street</u> (or <u>Twelfth Street</u>), Charleston, <u>South Carolina</u> 29401
  2. 672 Mellon Ave.
     Bountiful, UT 84010;
     672 Mellon <u>Avenue</u>, Bountiful, <u>Utah</u> 84010
  3. Washburn
     Bayfield County, WI;
     Washburn, Bayfield County, <u>Wisconsin</u>
  4. 12 Bay Blvd., Apartment <u>8</u>
     Providence, RI 02904;
     12 Bay <u>Boulevard</u>, Apartment <u>8</u>, Providence, <u>Rhode Island</u> 02904
  5. Village of Madison
     Boone County, WV;
     Village of Madison, Boone County, <u>West Virginia</u>

Writing Addresses Correctly, EXERCISE C
Letters will vary; correct address and body forms are given.
  1. <u>95</u> Cedar La.; <u>95</u> Cedar <u>Lane</u>
  2. Atchison, KS 66002; Atchison, <u>Kansas</u> 66002
  3. Goshen, IN 46526; Goshen, <u>Indiana</u> 46526
  4. <u>18</u> Alder St., Apartment <u>2</u>; <u>18</u> Alder <u>Street</u>, Apartment <u>2</u>
  5. Pierre, SD 57501; Pierre, <u>South Dakota</u> 57501

Adjectives

Adjective-Forming Suffixes, EXERCISE A
Answers will vary; possible answers are given.
  1. portable, lovable
  2. dependent, reverent
  3. harmful, useful
  4. economical, satirical
  5. foolish, selfish
  6. administrative, protective
  7. careless, homeless
  8. zealous, furious
  9. fearsome, burdensome
 10. witty, shifty

Adjective-Forming Suffixes, EXERCISE B
  1. The Irish potato famine had a <u>historical</u> background.
  2. Absentee <u>English</u> landlords owned the land.
  3. The <u>landless</u> Irish tenants lived <u>miserable</u> lives.
  4. They earned a <u>marginal</u> existence by growing potatoes and other foods on tiny plots of land.
  5. A potato blight destroyed the potato crop, and a <u>horrible</u> famine was <u>disastrous</u>.
  6. They traveled under <u>loathsome</u> conditions to the United Stated on overcrowded, <u>filthy</u> boats.
  7. Up to twenty percent of the immigrants died on the <u>terrible</u> journey.

Adjective-Forming Suffixes, EXERCISE C

Marianne Moore's poetry is not especially <u>musical</u>, but it is not <u>artless</u>. It definitely is <u>paradoxical</u>. She wrote <u>introspective</u> poetry that often examines how people survive the never <u>predictable</u> hazards and always <u>perilous</u> difficulties of life. However, her poems are also <u>playful</u>, well crafted, and <u>witty</u>. She was a <u>careful</u> observer of nature. In "The Wood-Weasel," for example, Moore creates a <u>delightful</u> image of a skunk.

Identifying Adjectives and Their Functions, EXERCISE A
1. All, the, out-of-the-way, muddy, narrow
2. An, old, iron, the, vast
3. A, dusty, the, farm
4. The, rugged, the, aged, many
5. The, green, the, yellow, the, dangerous

Identifying Adjectives and Their Functions, EXERCISE B
1. opposite (side)
2. two (steps), bulletlike (missile)
3. three (times), more (times), every (serve)
4. Four (aces), one (serve)
5. nice (performance), nuclear-powered (racket)

Identifying Adjectives and Their Functions, EXERCISE C
1. Two, how many; mysterious-looking, what kind; third, which one; train, what kind
2. tall, what kind; thin, what kind; brown, what kind; one, which one
3. other, which one; well-worn, what kind; leather, what kind
4. second, which one; short, what kind; stout, what kind; black, what kind; grizzled, what kind
5. third, which one; young, what kind
6. stylish, what kind; tall, what kind
7. strange, what kind; opposite, which one; another, which one
8. keen-eyed, what kind; police, what kind; clandestine, what kind

Positioning Adjectives Effectively, EXERCISE A
Answers may vary; possible answers are given.
1. The morning was misty.
2. Fog, cool and damp, had settled on the river.
3. The yellow, weak sun shone through the mist.
4. the lovely, dreamlike river
5. chilly and quiet canoeists
6. nervous canoeists
7. Rapids, noisy and white, thundered.
8. Rocks protruding from the water were vicious.
9. the ominous day
10. the no-longer-peaceful morning.

Positioning Adjectives Effectively, EXERCISE B

Answers will vary; possible answers are given.
 1. Polly O'Keefe, red-haired and adventuresome, is the main character.
 2. Polly lives with her grandparents; the home is large and rambling.
 3. Polly finds a gate in time and passes through to a world, strange and exotic.
 4. The Celtic era she enters is ancient and magical.
 5. It is the time of the Druids and their lore, mysterious and forgotten.
 6. Many leaders of the People of the Wind that Polly meets are admirable.
 7. Karralys, who is peace loving, is a healer and religious leader of his tribe.
 8. Courageous and wise, Tav is the chief of the warriors.
 9. Polly has adventures that are dangerous in the land of the Celts.
10. Another tribe captures her, planning to sacrifice her to a god who is angry.

Positioning Adjectives Effectively, EXERCISE C

Paragraphs will vary; a possible paragraph is given.

John had trained for months for this <u>arduous</u> marathon. The gun fired, and a thousand runners, <u>hopeful and determined</u>, were off. A dozen runners <u>were more experienced</u>, and they pulled ahead. John kept them in sight for the first ten miles, <u>which were easy</u>. His goal was simply to finish. The test would be Heartbreak Hill, a two-mile-long hill that runners, <u>already tired</u>, had to conquer at mile nineteen.

Identifying and Using Proper Adjectives, EXERCISE A

 1. European
 2. English
 3. French, Italian
 4. Germanic
 5. African-American
 6. British, American
 7. Australian, Dutch
 8. Brazilian
 9. West Indian
10. African

Identifying and Using Proper Adjectives, EXERCISE B

Sentences will vary; possible answers are given.
 1. My favorite <u>Elizabethan</u> play is *Romeo and Juliet*.
 2. The Beatles began as <u>Liverpudlian</u> performers.
 3. The <u>Roman</u> empire lasted for about one thousand years.
 4. The <u>Indian</u> subcontinent supports one of the largest populations in the world.
 5. The <u>Victorian</u> Era began with Queen Victoria's ascent to the throne of England.
 6. Let's go to a <u>Chinese</u> restaurant tonight.
 7. The <u>Hindu</u> religion is one of the largest in the world.
 8. The story was told with <u>Dickensian</u> detail.
 9. The <u>Ugandan</u> president visited the United States.
10. A new <u>Shavian</u> Club has been formed to study and perform George Bernard Shaw's plays.

Identifying and Using Demonstrative and Indefinite Adjectives, EXERCISE A

 1. those   demonstrative
 2. Each   indefinite
 3. this   demonstrative
 4. Every   indefinite
 5. any   indefinite

Identifying and Using Demonstrative and Indefinite Adjectives, EXERCISE B
Answers will vary; possible answers are given.
 1. David Muench is one of <u>these</u> photographers who concentrate on landscapes.
 2. <u>This</u> photograph shows <u>several</u> kinds of wildflowers.
 3. <u>Another</u> picture shows the rocky bluffs of <u>some</u> mountains.
 4. In <u>many</u> photographs, Muench shows colorful subjects, such as <u>that</u> laurel, set in neutral surroundings, such as gray rocks.
 5. Ansel Adams prefers <u>those</u> subjects, too, but <u>all</u> photographs I've seen of his have been in black and white.
 6. <u>Each</u> photograph shows texture or the contrast of shadow and light.

Identifying and Using Demonstrative and Indefinite Adjectives, EXERCISE C
Answers will vary; possible answers are given.
 1. indefinite, demonstrative; <u>Most</u> people like <u>that</u> cartoon with Calvin and Hobbes.
 2. indefinite, demonstrative; Does <u>any</u> person think the idea behind <u>this</u> cartoon makes sense?
 3. indefinite, demonstrative; It happens <u>every</u> time a child plays with one of <u>those</u> stuffed animals.
 4. demonstrative, indefinite; <u>These</u> imaginary adventures, which <u>all</u> children have, are real to them.
 5. indefinite, demonstrative; <u>Few</u> things are more real than <u>those</u> conversations with a teddy bear.

Comparing with Adjectives, EXERCISE A
 1. <u>worse</u> health
 2. <u>most distant</u> city
 3. <u>wider</u> truck
 4. <u>most unusual</u> clothing
 5. <u>more forgetful</u> son
 6. <u>best</u> news
 7. <u>farthest</u> star
 8. <u>remoter</u> chance
 9. <u>more bizarre</u> sense of humor
10. <u>less</u> opportunity
11. <u>earliest</u> class
12. <u>funnier</u> comedian
13. <u>more</u> vegetables
14. <u>most fundamental</u> baseball
15. <u>more sought-after</u> actor
16. <u>most available</u> player
17. <u>cleverest</u> performer
18. <u>more serious</u> discussion
19. <u>most predictable</u> behavior
20. <u>most awful</u> taste

Comparing with Adjectives, EXERCISE B

1. Was Albert Einstein or Isaac Newton the <u>more brilliant</u> physicist?
2. Einstein developed the theory of relativity, one of the two or three <u>most important</u> concepts ever developed in physics.
3. However, Newton developed the theory of gravity; was it <u>more insightful</u>?
4. Both theories are used to explain black holes, which may be the <u>most mysterious</u> of all celestial phenomena.
5. Black holes form when <u>larger</u> stars than our sun burn out and collapse in on themselves.
6. <u>Smaller</u> stars do not have enough mass to form black holes.
7. Our sun has <u>less</u> mass than is required to form a black hole.
8. Black holes have the <u>strongest</u> gravitational pull of any object in space, attracting all nearby matter and energy, including light.
9. No light escapes, so even our <u>best</u> telescopes cannot see them.
10. Some scientists say that black holes don't exist, but a <u>better</u> guess is that there are thousands in our galaxy alone.

Avoiding Double and Illogical Comparisons, EXERCISE A

1. happier
2. writer's
3. stronger
4. earlier
5. hardest

Avoiding Double and Illogical Comparisons, EXERCISE B

1. less
2. schools'
3. more eager
4. easiest
5. bluebird's

Avoiding Double and Illogical Comparisons, EXERCISE C

1. Do you think Ramona is <u>smarter</u> than Lois?
2. Randy's car is in <u>worse</u> condition than <u>Arthur's</u>.
3. The pitch of a piccolo is higher than a <u>flute's</u>.
4. Which of those three stereo systems has the <u>best</u> sound?
5. If the ending were different, this novel would be <u>perfect</u>.
6. Who has traveled the <u>farthest</u> distance to be here?
7. Correct
8. This month's telephone bill is lower than last <u>month's</u>.
9. John's visits are more <u>often</u> during the summer.
10. That diamond, the only one of its kind in the world, is a <u>unique</u> gem.

Avoiding Incomplete Comparisons, EXERCISE A

1. Isaac has more foreign stamps than <u>any other member</u> of our club.
2. Ursula knows more about gardening than <u>anyone else</u> I know.
3. Complete
4. Your apple pie is better than <u>anyone else's</u> in this state, so it's sure to win first prize.
5. A diamond is harder than <u>any other</u> natural substance.
6. Complete
7. My sister Whitney is better at fixing bicycles than <u>anyone else</u> I know.
8. <u>No other scientist</u> in the twentieth century was as famous as Albert Einstein.
9. Are his pitches harder to hit than <u>anyone else's</u> in the entire league?
10. Complete

Avoiding Incomplete Comparisons, EXERCISE B
Answers will vary; possible answers are given.
1. Lawrence's science project is better than <u>anyone else's in the school</u>.
2. They spent more time talking about their boyfriends than <u>any other topic</u>.
3. Carol's story was longer than <u>anyone else's in the class</u>; in fact, it almost put me to sleep!
4. Is she a better musician than <u>any other member of the band</u>?
5. Their house is bigger than <u>any other house on the block</u>.
6. The committee's new plan is better than <u>any other plan they have proposed</u>.
7. The pizza at that restaurant is more delicious than <u>any other pizza I've ever tasted</u>.
8. Brad spends more time on the basketball court than <u>anywhere else</u>.
9. Because Julio sings better than <u>anyone else in the chorus</u>, he probably will get a leading role in the spring play.
10. Taller than <u>anyone else on our street</u>, my dad can be spotted in any crowd.

Developing Your Style: Using Precise Adjectives, EXERCISE A
Answers will vary; possible answers are given.
1. Jacob Fields, a <u>fabulous</u> new baseball stadium, came with a <u>costly</u> price tag.
2. The Cleveland Indians were <u>excited</u> when they finally moved into their <u>state-of-the-art</u> stadium.
3. At their first home game, however, the ballplayers seemed somewhat <u>edgy</u> in their <u>unfamiliar</u> surroundings.
4. The <u>mild</u> weather brought out a(n) <u>overflowing</u> crowd on opening day.
5. I took my <u>freshly painted</u> seat and pulled out a pair of <u>powerful</u> binoculars.
6. The President threw out the first ball with <u>admirable</u> style on that <u>historic</u> day.
7. Then the <u>popular</u> announcer called to the <u>enthusiastic</u> crowd, "Play ball!"
8. We all gave a <u>tumultuous</u> greeting to the first batter—and we went crazy when his bat connected with the ball with a <u>resounding</u> CRACK!
9. The smell of <u>roasted</u> peanuts and <u>tart</u> lemonade added to the <u>festive</u> atmosphere.
10. After the <u>exciting</u> game, we talked in the <u>jam-packed</u> corridors, agreeing that the team was looking <u>professional</u> and <u>promising</u>.

Developing Your Style: Using Precise Adjectives, EXERCISE B
Answers will vary; possible answers are given.
1. The <u>sudden</u> snowstorm dumped six inches of <u>granular</u> snow in the city.
2. In the mountains, the already <u>snow-laden</u> slopes looked like <u>vanilla</u> ice-cream cones.
3. In a snow avalanche, <u>trained</u> huskies are used to rescue the survivors.
4. The sudden, <u>rumbling</u> noise that signals an avalanche is both <u>unmistakable</u> and <u>terrifying</u>.
5. As tons of snow crash down the mountainside, the <u>crushing</u> weight serves as a truly <u>destructive</u> force.

Developing Your Style: Avoiding Overuse of Adjectives, EXERCISE A
1. b
2. a

Developing Your Style: Avoiding Overuse of Adjectives, EXERCISE B
1. If a company or government doesn't <u>economize</u> on expenses, it will go into debt.
2. A company may <u>protect</u> its investments with strict spending policies.
3. Another firm may <u>educate</u> its staff on how to cut costs.
4. Such a policy <u>promises success</u> in the future.

Developing Your Style: Avoiding Overuse of Adjectives, EXERCISE C
Answers will vary; possible answers are given.
1. The upholsterer <u>redecorated</u> the chair with colorful fabric.
2. The old chair looked like new with this <u>improvement</u>.
3. This fabric hides all <u>imperfections</u> in the chair.
4. The special fabric also <u>resists</u> dirt and stains.

Adverbs

Identifying and Using Adverbs That Modify Verbs, EXERCISE A
Replacement verbs will vary; possible answers are given.
1. narrowly (escaped); barely
2. gracefully (moved); delicately
3. completely (was covered); totally
4. late (arrived); tardily
5. never (could be seen) not

Identifying and Using Adverbs That Modify Verbs, EXERCISE B
Answers will vary; possible answers are given.
1. tomorrow (must be submitted)
2. slowly (dictated); legibly (wrote)
3. everywhere (looked)
4. early (arrived)
5. carefully (cleaned)

Identifying and Using Adverbs That Modify Verbs, EXERCISE C
Answers will vary; possible answers are given
1. quickly (had sold [out]); completely (had sold [out])
2. not (did have); outside (waited)
3. impatiently (clapped)
4. late (arrived); somewhat (grumbled)
5. Then (dimmed); suddenly (dimmed)

Identifying and Using Adverbs That Modify Adjectives and Other Adverbs, EXERCISE A
Replacement adverbs will vary; possible answers are given.
1. quite (diligently - adverb); very
2. nearly (exhausting - adjective); rather
3. almost (never - adverb); usually
4. quite (capably - adverb); extremely
5. most (admirably - adverb), quite
6. rather (enthusiastically - adverb), very
7. very (visible - adjective), most
8. truly (amazing - adjective), quite; quite (able - adjective), especially
9. unusually (forceful - adjective), remarkably

Identifying and Using Adverbs That Modify Adjectives and Other Adverbs, EXERCISE B
Answers will vary; possible answers are given.
1. The people in line felt <u>very</u> excited. (adjective)
2. The fans were <u>surprisingly</u> polite after such a long wait. (adjective)
3. The crowd reacted <u>most</u> happily when the ticket booth opened. (adverb)
4. The line moved <u>rather</u> quickly. (adverb)
5. The tickets to the game were <u>incredibly</u> expensive! (adjective)
6. The fans at the end of the line were <u>notably</u> patient. (adjective)
7. The ticket sales went <u>very</u> smoothly. (adverb)
8. That girl was <u>totally</u> thrilled when she got her tickets. (adjective)
9. The ticket-sellers are <u>not</u> busy now. (adjective)
10. The fans who lost out on tickets acted <u>understandably</u> upset. (adverb)

Distinguishing Adverbs From Adjectives and Prepositions, EXERCISE A
1. preposition
2. adverb
3. preposition
4. adjective
5. preposition
6. adverb
7. preposition
8. adjective
9. adverb
10. preposition

Distinguishing Adverbs From Adjectives and Prepositions, EXERCISE B
Answers will vary; possible answers are given.
1. The children were playing all <u>around</u> the house.
2. Somebody was hiding <u>under</u> the bed, making not a sound.
3. A few children had sneaked <u>outside</u>.
4. They were playing enthusiastically <u>in</u> the snow.
5. The nurse walked <u>into</u> the playroom.
6. She ran <u>around</u>, intent on finding her missing charges.
7. The children hid <u>behind</u> the tool shed, but the nurse spotted them.
8. The nurse yelled, "Come <u>out</u> right now!"
9. As the children ran, they fell <u>down</u> in the snow and got <u>into</u> a snowball fight.
10. Soon the children came <u>inside</u> the house and sat <u>down</u> at the kitchen table for milk or fruit.

Comparing with Adverbs, EXERCISE A
1. Brendan Walsh did <u>better</u> than any other player.
2. <u>Most amazingly</u>, he won three school championships in a row.
3. No one trained <u>harder</u> than Walsh.
4. His records will last <u>longer</u> than many others.
5. Walsh will be remembered as one of the <u>greatest</u> high-school basketball players of all time.

Comparing with Adverbs, EXERCISE B
Some answers may vary; possible answers are given.
1. cleanly, positive
2. most skillfully, superlative
3. less awkwardly, comparative
4. farther, comparative
5. best, superlative

Comparing with Adverbs, EXERCISE C
Answers will vary: possible answers are given.
 1. more quickly, comparative
 2. happily, positive
 3. more radiantly, comparative
 4. quickly, positive
 5. more deeply, comparative

Using Adverbs Correctly, EXERCISE A
 1. badly
 2. surely
 3. very, well
 4. swiftly

Using Adverbs Correctly, EXERCISE B
 1. She practiced <u>very</u> hard all year.
 2. Skaters must be in <u>amazingly</u> good shape, to be sure.
 3. Correct
 4. How <u>quickly</u> the skaters must rotate in their jumps!
 5. Correct
 6. The audience sits <u>nervously</u> as the skaters do their routines.
 7. People applaud <u>loudly</u> as each contestant finishes.
 8. The contestant's parents jumped up and down <u>wildly</u>.
 9. Her routine was <u>nearly</u> perfect.
10. She smiles <u>proudly</u> and waves as she receives a medal.

Using Adverbs Correctly, EXERCISE C
Answers will vary; possible answers are given.
 1. At one time, the Pony Express delivered mail <u>more quickly</u> than any other service.
 2. Pony Express riders <u>speedily</u> took the mail across the country.
 3. People <u>surely</u> felt that their mail would be delivered <u>promptly</u>.
 4. That pony ran <u>fastest</u> of all.
 5. Riders stopped <u>regularly</u> to get supplies and a fresh horse.

Developing Your Style: Adverbs, EXERCISE A
 1. quietly   6. steadfastly
 2. effectively   7. responsibly
 3. seriously   8. courageously
 4. carefully   9. eloquently
 5. eventually   10. Unfortunately

Developing Your Style: Adverbs, EXERCISE B
Answers will vary; possible answers are given.
 1. Thomas Jefferson <u>thoughtfully</u> went about his task.
 2. He did not want to write <u>hastily</u>.
 3. Jefferson knew that his words must be written <u>deliberately</u>.
 4. <u>Suddenly</u>, he picked up a pen.
 5. Jefferson wrote <u>very patiently</u>.

Apostrophes

Using Apostrophes in Possessives anbd Contractions, EXERCISE A
1. children's
2. Who's
3. Phyllis'
4. won't
5. jury's, witness's

Using Apostrophes in Possessives and Contractions, EXERCISE B
1. The <u>baroness's</u> schedule was changed.
2. Please let us know if you've changed <u>your</u> mind.
3. Correct
4. Considering the alternatives, <u>theirs</u> would appear to be the best plan.
5. Will you or <u>won't</u> you be coming home for dinner?
6. The <u>teachers'</u> meeting for all staff will be held at three o'clock.
7. <u>It's</u> getting late, and you won't want to miss the last bus.
8. These <u>boys'</u> book reports were handed in a week late.
9. Correct
10. I wouldn't say that <u>their</u> project has achieved all <u>its</u> objectives.

Using Apostrophes in Possessives and Contractions, EXERCISE C
Sentences will vary; possible sentences are given.
1. Debbi <u>hasn't</u> asked for <u>everybody's</u> opinion yet.
2. <u>Chris's</u> suitcases will take up too much space; <u>he's</u> overpacking again!
3. The <u>girls'</u> complaints <u>haven't</u> kept them from improving the situation.
4. My <u>sister-in-law's</u> father <u>wouldn't</u> see a doctor, even though he didn't feel well.
5. The <u>Joneses'</u> plans are ambitious; <u>they've</u> decided to learn skydiving!
6. <u>Aren't</u> those <u>mechanics'</u> abilities incredible?
7. The <u>treasurer's</u> report <u>hadn't</u> been distributed before the meeting began.
8. Since everything is prepared, the <u>guests'</u> early arrival <u>won't</u> be a problem.
9. The <u>boss's</u> memo <u>wasn't</u> well written, nor was it particularly well received.
10. If the <u>children's</u> group has arrived, <u>I'll</u> begin my lecture.

Other Uses of Apostrophes, EXERCISE A
1. The <u>x's</u> at the bottom of the letter stand for kisses.
2. William Shakespeare died in the early <u>1600's</u>.
3. "I reckon I'll be <u>goin'</u> now," he said.
4. This contract contains an awful lot of <u>whereas's</u>.
5. Have our <u>C.O.D.'s</u> arrived from the Post Office?

Other Uses of Apostrophes, EXERCISE B
1. I promised to arrive by seven <u>o'clock</u>.
2. The children tried counting to 100 by <u>3's</u>.
3. "I never was much good at <u>writin'</u>," he muttered.
4. That veterinary school graduates more <u>D.V.M.'s</u> every year than any other in the world.
5. How many <u>g's</u> are there in your name?
6. Boeing <u>747's</u> are very large airplanes.
7. That child is old enough to learn her <u>ABC's</u>.
8. "Get <u>'em</u> while they're hot!" called the cook.
9. My aunt was born in the late <u>1950's</u>.
10. Those <u>%'s</u> in the ad are called *percent signs*.

Other Uses of Apostrophes, EXERCISE C

Sentences will vary; possible sentences are given.

1. My telephone number has three <u>4</u>'s in it.
2. The United States became a major world power in the late <u>1800</u>'s.
3. Those <u>S</u>'s look a lot like <u>$</u>'s.
4. Can't you offer any clear solutions instead of presenting a string of <u>if</u>'s?
5. Use <u>;</u>'s to separate the main clauses in these compound sentences.
6. Sentences that have too many <u>and</u>'s should be rephrased.
7. Putting four <u>?</u>'s at the end of a sentence is really a bit much!
8. A line of <u>+</u>'s across the top of a page makes an interesting border.
9. How many <u>m</u>'s are there in recommend?
10. Although I try hard, I have trouble writing <u>&</u>'s.

Appositives

Identifying and Punctuating Appositives, EXERCISE A

1. Ford (car)
2. Sean (brother)
3. engineer (employee)
4. William Faulkner (novelist)
5. cardiopulmonary resuscitation, CPR

Identifying and Punctuating Appositives, EXERCISE B

1. Her destination, <u>Cincinnati</u>, seemed farther away than ever.
2. I don't know much about the songwriter <u>Irving Berlin</u>.
3. The new rug, <u>a rag rug woven in Kentucky</u>, made the room look great.
4. Our dog <u>Rover</u> truly lives up to his name.
5. The new teacher, <u>Mrs. Mansfield</u>, coaches softball.
6. Hercule Poirot, <u>a Belgian detective</u>, was created by Agatha Christie.
7. The poet begged assistance of Orpheus, <u>the Greek god of music</u>.
8. Is the lamp, <u>that brass piece</u>, Victorian?
9. Their anniversary party, <u>a catered affair</u>, was a huge success.
10. The Olivers won a marvelous prize, <u>a weekend at a country inn</u>.

Identifying and Punctuating Appositives, EXERCISE C

Sentences will vary; possible sentences are given.

1. Samantha's hobby, <u>stamp collecting</u>, is making her rich.
2. I am sure that James's friend <u>Leslie</u> can explain that to you.
3. The composer <u>Wolfgang Amadeus Mozart</u> became famous at an early age.
4. I used the money to buy a book, <u>a collection of short stories</u>.
5. Rhode Island, <u>the smallest state</u>, is not the least populous.
6. Is Richard's sister, <u>the captain of the team</u>, the top scorer?
7. Have you read Poe's poem <u>"The Raven"</u>?
8. The Drama Club's first production, <u>a comedy</u>, was a great success.
9. With a smile, the waiter handed me a menu, <u>a six-page listing of luscious foods</u>.
10. Jupiter, <u>the fifth planet from the sun</u>, has faint rings around it.

Developing Your Style: Appositives, EXERCISE A

Answers may vary slightly; possible answers are given.

1. My sister, a doctor, explained the examination procedure to me.
2. Our neighbors just bought a tiny dog, a Chihuahua.
3. The new teacher, Mr. Roberts, is a strict disciplinarian.
4. Mt. Everest, the highest mountain in the world, is in Asia.
5. Please ask Mr. Trask, the sophomore class advisor, about the change.
6. Albany, the capital of New York, is much smaller than New York City.
7. This poem, a sonnet, was written by Elizabeth Barrett Browning.
8. A dictator, Joseph Stalin, ruled Russia from 1922 to 1953.
9. Mars, a planet smaller than Earth, has two moons, Deimos and Phobos.
10. Franklin Delano Roosevelt, the thirty-second president, had three vice presidents: John Garner, Henry Wallace, and Harry Truman.

Developing Your Style: Appositives, EXERCISE B

Answers may vary slightly; possible answers are given.

1. Our cat Marmalade won second prize in the cat show. (Commas are optional.)
2. We gave Pedro and Carmen, our cousins, a tour of the city.
3. Our favorite restaurant, Dilietro's, is closed for renovations.
4. My sister Sara was elected class president. (Commas are optional.)
5. Everyone agrees that Walter, my iguana, is a very unusual pet.
6. The rescue squad arrived in time to save Chester, our neighbor.
7. Zebras, graceful striped beasts, grazed on the grassy plain.
8. William Shakespeare, one of England's greatest writers, was born in 1564.
9. Africa, a continent, is a leading producer of gold, diamonds, and uranium.
10. Isn't the famous novelist James Michener one of her favorites?

Using Brackets Correctly, Exercise A

1. With his mentor (Dr. Mary Li [formerly of the University of Pennsylvania]), Chet studies rabbits.
2. They recently published a paper in *Biology Today* (in the April issue [volume VII]).
3. According to Chet (who is only [hard to believe] a junior), rabbits make an ideal subject of study.
4. Chet (with his co-workers [most of whom are seniors]) will attend a symposium at Cold Spring Harbor.

Using Brackets Correctly, EXERCISE B

1. Did you read Roth's book on dreams (similar to Freud's theories [although much easier to understand])?
2. Dreams (which are interesting [as long as they're your own]) are the subject of much speculation.
3. Roth has written often on dreams. (See *Superego Monthly*, May 1993 [volume XII]).
4. Roth works with victims of insomnia. (Sleep disorders [especially psychologically based ones] are her focus).

Using Brackets Correctly, EXERCISE C

Answers will vary; possible answers are given.

1. I grow all my own vegetables <u>(fresh vegetables being so much better [as my grandmother once told me])</u>.
2. Zucchini <u>(a green squash [good in stews])</u> is easy to grow.
3. A fresh <u>(by which I mean right off the vine [and unbesieged by bugs])</u> tomato is a work of art.
4. How do you keep the pests <u>(meaning [in our area, at least] rabbits and groundhogs)</u> away?

Capitalization

Capitalizing Names and Titles of People, EXERCISE A

1. Amy McDonnel
2. Morris
3. Republicans, Democrats, Senate
4. Helen Keller, Radcliffe College
5. Helen, Ann Sullivan Macy, American Foundation of the Blind
6. Christopher Columbus, Queen Isabella, King Ferdinand
7. Christianity, Hinduism, Islam, Judaism
8. Americans, Koreans, Pakistanis
9. Professor, Roosevelt High School
10. Galileo, Copernicus, Curies

Capitalizing Names and Titles of People, EXERCISE B

Sentences will vary; possible sentences are given.

1. Dr. Martin Luther King, Jr., was assassinated in 1968.
2. Is <u>Judge Carlton</u> running for re-election?
3. I haven't seen <u>Aunt Sarah</u>, who lives in Omaha, for many years.
4. When I arrived, I reported to <u>Colonel Soto</u>.
5. The <u>Vice President of the United States</u> has many responsibilities.
6. Our family doctor is <u>Dr. Florence Rosenberg</u>.
7. Aaron's favorite baseball team is the <u>Atlanta Braves</u>.
8. <u>Lana Landry</u> is a talented actress and director.
9. <u>Senator John Glenn</u> is a former astronaut.
10. The <u>Reverend John Michaels</u> presided at Betty and Lou's wedding.

Capitalizing Names of Places, EXERCISE A

1. One of the world's largest cities is <u>São Paolo, Brazil</u>.
2. Many industries have left the <u>Northeast</u> and moved south.
3. The second largest planet in the solar system is <u>Saturn</u>.
4. The <u>English Channel</u> separates <u>England</u> and <u>France</u>.
5. The <u>Sears Tower</u>, in <u>Chicago</u>, is a very tall building.

Capitalizing Names of Places, EXERCISE B

1. Correct
2. Riverside Drive, Pine Lake
3. Cape Cod, Nantucket
4. Atlantic Ocean, India, Saudi Arabia, Egypt
5. Empire State Building, New York City

Capitalizing Names of Places, EXERCISE C
Answers will vary; possible answers are given.
1. After studying the Civil War, my class went to <u>Gettysburg</u>, <u>Pennsylvania</u>./ After studying
   the Civil War, my class visited <u>Fort Sumter</u>, <u>South Carolina</u>.
2. Can you spot the <u>Big Dipper</u>, the <u>Little Dipper</u>, and <u>Orion</u>? / Can you spot <u>Sagittarius</u>,
   <u>Sirius</u>, and <u>Cassiopeia</u>?
3. I am going to <u>Yellowstone National Park</u> this summer. / I am going to <u>Acadia National Park</u>
   this summer.
4. Someday I'd like to climb <u>Mt. Rainier</u>, or maybe go rafting down the <u>Colorado River</u>. /
   Someday I'd like to climb <u>Mt. Everest</u>, or maybe go rafting down the <u>Rio Grande</u>.
5. I'd also love to see the <u>Rocky Mountains</u>.
   I'd also love to see the <u>Swiss Alps</u>.

Capitalizing Other Names, EXERCISE A
1. Magna Carta, World History 101
2. July, August, Tanglewood Music Festival
3. Battle of New Orleans, War of 1812
4. Correct
5. Spanish, French
6. Thursday, November
7. Capitol
8. "The Most Dangerous Game"
9. *Queen Mary*
10. World Civilization, Bronze Age, Industrial Revolution

Capitalizing Other Names, EXERCISE B
   During the first week of <u>June</u>, my history class will be taking a trip to Washington, D.C. We
will be visiting the <u>Washington Monument</u>, the <u>Lincoln Memorial</u>, and <u>Arlington National</u>
<u>Cemetery</u>. At the <u>Smithsonian Institution</u>, we'll see the <u>Apollo</u> spacecraft and a replica of the
Wright Brothers' plane *Kitty Hawk*. My <u>English</u> teacher, Mrs. Quinn, will be a chaperone on this
trip. I knew she was my favorite teacher when I saw her driving a *Firebird* and eating in <u>Burgers,</u>
that fast-food restaurant.

Capitalizing Proper Adjectives, EXERCISE A
1. Colombian, Danish
2. Japanese, Spanish
3. Swiss, American
4. Korean, Italian
5. Russian, Polish

Capitalizing Proper Adjectives, EXERCISE B
1. Is this silk <u>Japanese</u>, <u>Indian</u>, or <u>Chinese</u>?
2. My brother travels on various <u>American</u> airlines for his <u>North American</u> trips.
3. An <u>English</u> guide led the <u>Canadian</u> and <u>Australian</u> tourists in Guatemala.
4. Have you seen the new <u>Swedish</u> stamps or the old <u>Roman</u> coins?

Capitalizing Proper Adjectives, EXERCISE C
Sentences will vary; possible sentences are given.
 1. An <u>Israeli scientist</u> is working on a cure for cancer.
 2. <u>Mexican citizens</u> can request a translator at the government office.
 3. Would you like to sample some <u>Italian cuisine</u> tonight?
 4. Gail went to a <u>Cypriot resort</u> on her honeymoon.
 5. The orchestra performed an <u>English symphony</u>.
 6. When John arrived in London, he converted his money into <u>British pounds</u>.
 7. Have you ever seen a <u>Shakespearean comedy</u>?
 8. Her nomination will be considered by a <u>Congressional committee</u>.
 9. The gift of a box of <u>Belgian chocolates</u> was an appreciated—if fattening—gesture.
10. Gavin is a <u>San Franciscan</u>.

Using Capitals to Mark Beginnings of Sentences and Direct Quotations, EXERCISE A
 1. "<u>T</u>omorrow we will try some new experiments," announced Phil.
 2. "<u>A</u>fter dinner," asked my brother, "<u>w</u>ill you help me with my homework?"
 3. <u>W</u>onderful! <u>H</u>ow soon can you begin?
 4. <u>I</u> know what will please her: <u>S</u>he adores the classical guitar.
 5. <u>T</u>ruman said, "<u>I</u>f you can't stand the heat, stay out of the kitchen."
 6. "<u>I</u> stopped to talk to Tom," Adele said, "and that's why I was late for school."
 7. <u>L</u>et's ride our bicycles. <u>W</u>here?
 8. "<u>S</u>urprisingly," she remarked, "no one has noticed it."
 9. <u>L</u>isten carefully! <u>I</u> won't repeat these directions.
10. "<u>T</u>he highest of distinctions is service to others."—King George VI
11. <u>D</u>id you see Georgie yesterday? <u>W</u>hen?
12. <u>O</u>h, no! <u>W</u>e missed the 9:00 train to Philadelphia!
13. Correct
14. "<u>I</u> will win," he boasted. "<u>T</u>his time <u>I</u> am ready."
15. "<u>W</u>hen you call me that, smile!"—Owen Wister
16. Correct
17. <u>F</u>red told us the news: <u>A</u> frog had escaped from the laboratory.
18. <u>A</u> slogan of the U.S. Air Force was "<u>K</u>eep 'em flying."
19. Correct
20. "<u>L</u>iberty, like charity, must begin at home."—James Bryant Conant

Using Capitals to Mark Beginnings of Sentences and Direct Quotations, EXERCISE B
  <u>When</u> we first moved to New York from Puerto Rico, I had difficulty adjusting to my new home. <u>Although</u> my aunt and uncle were kind to me, I felt like a visitor on an alien planet. <u>My</u> uncle told me, "<u>You</u> belong in this country now. <u>Give</u> yourself time; you'll fit in." <u>It</u> was strange to be living with so many people. <u>After</u> we got our own apartment, though, I felt more relaxed. "<u>Home</u>, sweet home," I sang to myself, as I unpacked my special things. <u>I</u> began to make more friends and invite them to my house. <u>Now</u> I can admit that I enjoy my life in the United States.

Using Capitals to Mark Other Beginnings, EXERCISE A
1. <u>D</u>ear <u>S</u>ir or <u>M</u>adam:
2. <u>I</u>n sympathy
3. "<u>T</u>he music that can deepest reach,/<u>A</u>nd cure all ill, is cordial speech."
   —Ralph Waldo Emerson
4. <u>D</u>earest Adrienne,
5. <u>S</u>incerely yours,
6. <u>D</u>ear <u>S</u>uperintendent <u>M</u>iller:
7. "<u>T</u>he world no longer let me love,/<u>M</u>y hope and treasure lie above." —Anne Bradstreet
8. <u>M</u>y best regards,
9. "<u>H</u>e met a pilgrim shadow—/'<u>S</u>hadow,' said he,/'<u>W</u>here can it be—/<u>T</u>his land of Eldorado?'"—Edgar Allan Poe
10. I. <u>Q</u>ualities needed for training a dog
    A <u>I</u>ntelligence
    B. <u>D</u>esire to please

Using Capitals to Mark Other Beginnings, EXERCISE B
<u>D</u>ear <u>A</u>lexandra,

   I'm sending you a writer's magazine because you're interested in writing. Notice the article entitled "<u>R</u>eading <u>L</u>ike a <u>W</u>riter," by Dennis S. Anders. I think he gives good advice when he says to "read in order to understand how the writer has worked." I especially enjoy Shakespeare's comment: "<u>W</u>ords, words, mere words, no matter from the heart."

   The magazine may give you some good ideas for your English report, following this sample outline:
   I. American Poets
     A. Walt Whitman
     B. Langston Hughes
   Let me know what you think of the magazine!

                                   <u>W</u>ith much love,
                                   <u>A</u>unt <u>L</u>ee

Clauses

Identifying and Using Main and Subordinate Clauses, EXERCISE A
1. <u>I'll count the money</u> if you'll drive me home afterward.
2. <u>Glynis bought the coat</u>, although it was really too expensive.
3. When Keith made honor roll, <u>his father bought him the promised bike</u>.
4. <u>Your offer</u>, which comes as a surprise, <u>could make the difference</u>.

Identifying and Using Main and Subordinate Clauses, EXERCISE B
Sentences will vary; possible sentences are given.
1. Greece is a country <u>that I have always wanted to visit</u>.
2. Stacy had to bake the cookies <u>because two volunteers reneged on their promise</u>.
3. The National Audubon Society, <u>which works to protect birds</u>, has bought this land for a bird sanctuary.
4. <u>Since Florida is a semi-tropical state</u>, delicious oranges can be grown there.

Identifying and Using Main and Subordinate Clauses, EXERCISE C

Sentences will vary; possible answers are given.
1. <u>Tina played a trumpet solo at the concert</u>, and the audience responded enthusiastically. / <u>When Tina played a trumpet solo at the concert</u>, she didn't hit a single sour note.
2. <u>Dave is a terrific softball player</u>, because he practices a great deal. / I'm proud of my brother <u>because Dave is a terrific softball player</u>.
3. Mom hid your present, but <u>you can find it easily</u>. / I left the book on the table, <u>where you can find it easily</u>.
4. Do you want to play a game, or <u>would you rather take a walk</u>? / <u>If you would rather take a walk</u>, I'll get my jacket.

Identifying and Using Adjective Clauses, EXERCISE A

New sentences will vary; possible answers are given.
1. Our wood <u>stove</u>, which was installed last year, has saved us a lot of money.
2. Yes, this is the <u>place</u> where I would like to spend my vacation.
3. Mrs. Nakamura is a <u>teacher</u> whom the state has recently awarded.
4. <u>Bo</u>, who loves his job as a veterinarian's assistant, has some wonderful stories to tell.
5. Trigonometry is one class <u>that</u> I want to take next year.

Identifying and Using Adjective Clauses, EXERCISE B

Answers may vary slightly; possible answers are given.
1. Lincoln's family moved to Indiana, which had no slavery, in 1816.
2. In 1837 Lincoln, who was only twenty-five years of age, was elected to the Illinois General Assembly.
3. Lincoln, who was the candidate for the Whig Party, was elected to the U.S. House of Representatives in 1846.
4. Lincoln, whom Stephen A. Douglas defeated in the 1858 Senate race, was elected President of the United States in 1860.

Identifying and Using Adjective Clauses, EXERCISE C

Sentences will vary; possible answers are given.
1. Many good deeds, <u>which helped a great many people</u>, were done within those walls.
2. Grandmother was a talkative woman <u>who often spoke about her childhood</u>.
3. The door <u>that my grandfather carved out of oak</u> stood open to friends as well as to family.
4. These wonderful people, <u>whose lives have left such an impression on my own</u>, taught me the importance of hospitality.

Distinguishing Between Restrictive and Nonrestrictive Clauses, EXERCISE A

1. nonrestrictive
2. nonrestrictive
3. restrictive
4. not a clause
5. restrictive

Distinguishing Between Restrictive and Nonrestrictive Clauses, EXERCISE B

1. which was attended by hundreds of students (nonrestrictive)
2. that our committee designed (restrictive)
3. who came dateless (restrictive)
4. whom I knew (restrictive)
5. whose graciousness was acknowledged (nonrestrictive)

Distinguishing Between Restrictive and Nonrestrictive Clauses, EXERCISE C
Answers will vary; possible answers are given.
  1. The sculptor <u>whom I most appreciate</u> is Rodin.
  2. His work<u>, which you can see anywhere,</u> is in stone.
  3. I worked with a hammer and chisel <u>that my father had once used</u>.
  4. My teacher, Mr. Dexter<u>, who teaches privately,</u> assisted me.
  5. Dexter<u>, whose work is on display at the Rhodes Gallery,</u> was commissioned to build a
     monument.

Identifying and Using Adverb Clauses, EXERCISE A
  1. observes
  2. identifies
  3. reacts
  4. enthusiastic
  5. curious

Identifying and Using Adverb Clauses, EXERCISE B
  1. <u>Before</u> Eisenhower was elected President (served)
  2. <u>When</u> you feel rested (call)
  3. <u>After</u> we finished our breakfast (read)
  4. <u>than</u> it was a year ago (better)
  5. <u>as if</u> she had been burned (jumped)

Identifying and Using Adverb Clauses, EXERCISE C
Sentences will vary; possible answers are given.
  1. <u>Because he could not afford a receptionist</u>, the detective answered the phone.
  2. He would take any case offered <u>unless it involved criminal action</u>.
  3. He swung into action <u>as soon as he hung up the phone</u>.
  4. In his bag he packed a spyglass <u>so that he could watch the suspect from afar</u>.
  5. <u>Although he enjoyed his work</u>, he rarely made much money on his cases.

Identifying and Using Noun Clauses, EXERCISE A
  1. Whomever the board picks
  2. How they select a winner
  3. what Linda wishes to study
  4. that she will win

Identifying and Using Noun Clauses, EXERCISE B
  1. <u>How the storm began</u> makes an interesting story. (subject)
  2. The news was <u>that a hurricane was coming</u>. (predicate nominative)
  3. I don't remember <u>who alerted the town</u>. (direct object)
  4. I'm not sure about <u>what occurred after that</u>. (object of a preposition)
  5. I told <u>whoever was in charge</u> <u>that I would help</u>. (indirect object, direct object)

Identifying and Using Noun Clauses, EXERCISE C
Sentences will vary; possible answers are given.
  1. <u>Whoever joins the class</u> will learn about the movements of the planets.
  2. It seems clear to me <u>that astronomy offers fantastic opportunities</u>.
  3. Most astronomers agree on <u>whatever the theory of the day might be</u>.
  4. Read this article on black holes to <u>whomever you like</u>.
  5. The author can teach you <u>what she knows about black holes</u>.

Using Clauses Correctly, EXERCISE A
1. faulty subordination; they may get sicker
2. faulty subordination; these people need help
3. Correct
4. faulty subordination; many homeless children fall behind in their education

Using Clauses Correctly, EXERCISE B
Positions of subordinate clauses may vary.
1. Most students will dress lightly tomorrow since the air conditioning won't be repaired for a couple of days.
2. Correct
3. Because they were uncomfortable and irritable from the heat, the principal dismissed the students early.
4. Whenever the science teacher talked about the physical composition of snow, the class moaned.

Using Clauses Correctly, EXERCISE C
Answers may vary slightly; possible answers are given.
1. Because we breathe the air, we shouldn't pollute it.
2. When cars burn fuel, they emit carbon dioxide into the atmosphere.
3. Temperatures begin to rise if there is too much carbon dioxide in the air.
4. You help fight pollution when you use your bicycle instead of your car.

Colons

Using Colons Correctly, EXERCISE A
1. My watch must be running fast; it can't be 10:00 already!
2. Correct
3. Caution: The next five miles are under construction.
4. If I miss the 2:45 bus, I'll have to wait until 3:20 for the next one.
5. To begin this project, gather these materials: two cups of flour, a bowl of water, and several newspapers.
6. The letter from Acme Manufacturing said, in part, "Dear Ms. Bryant: We were quite impressed with your letter of March 14."
7. Teaching kindergarten calls for several important traits: organizational skills, the ability to explain things well, and patience.
8. Correct
9. The announcement began as follows: "To all sophomores: Congratulations on a job well done!"
10. Attention: We will close at 7:30 P.M. to prepare for tomorrow's sale.

Using Colons Correctly, EXERCISE B
Dear Mr. and Mrs. Harper:

Thank you for your letter of November 18, in which you expressed concern about several important issues: health-care reform, rising taxes, and gun control. As your new representative, I am concerned about these issues, too. During my campaign, I set these goals: to make the issues clear to the community, to know how people feel about them, and to act in the people's best interest. To begin fulfilling those goals, I have scheduled a series of "Explore the Issues" meetings. They will be held from 7:30 to 9:00 P.M. at Town Hall on the following dates: November 24, December 1, and December 8. There also will be a Saturday morning meeting—from 9:45 to 11:15—on December 10. These meetings will be attended by a variety of community leaders: Mayor Dunn, members of the City Council, law-enforcement officials, and local businesspeople.

Please note: A list of scheduled topics is enclosed. I hope to meet you there.

Sincerely,

Jeremy Ortega

Commas

Using Commas with Coordinating Conjunctions, EXERCISE A
Answers may vary slightly; possible answers are given.
1. Radio waves travel great distances, for they can pass through air and some solid objects.
2. The military depends upon rapid communications, so military planes and ships are equipped with radios.
3. Radio was once the leading form of entertainment, but it has been surpassed by television.
4. Many people get their news from the radio, or they listen to its music.
5. There are about 10,000 radio stations in the United States, and Americans own some 500 million radios.

Using Commas with Coordinating Conjunctions, EXERCISE B
New sentences will vary; possible answers are given.
1. "Baby boomers" enjoy listening to the radio, so "oldies" stations remain popular.
2. Some stations are fierce competitors, and "air wars" frequently take the form of contests and giveaways.
3. Kareem never listens to "Top Ten" radio, but he loves the all-sports station.
4. Amber loves soccer and softball, so she listen to that station, too.
5. Myra stays turned to weather reports, for she always wants to be prepared.
6. I listen to the radio after school, or I turn it on right after dinner.
7. This station plays classical music until 8:00 P.M., but it switches to alternative rock after that.
8. My city has two classical music stations, and a third is ready to go on the air.
9. KHIP, the all-jazz station, seemed an unlikely choice for this market, yet it has attracted many listeners.
10. No one station can play all my favorite songs, nor can the choice of stations please everyone.

Using Commas with Subordinating Conjunctions, EXERCISE A
Answers may vary slightly; possible answers are given.
1. After he graduated from college, "Dutch" Reagan got a job as a sports announcer.
2. Because he had impressed some Hollywood producers, he was later signed to a movie contract.
3. Reagan first served in public office in 1966, when he was elected governor of California.
4. Although his campaign for the Presidency in 1976 was unsuccessful, he did attract great support from conservatives.
5. When Reagan campaigned again in 1980, he gathered even more support and defeated Jimmy Carter, the incumbent.

Using Commas with Subordinating Conjunctions, EXERCISE B
Sentences will vary; possible answers are given.
1. If you want to explain the country's policy, you should know about our political leadership.
2. When you read the daily newspaper, look for information about local politics.
3. As Election Day approaches, candidates can always use volunteers.
4. After a major news story breaks, political commentators offer valuable insights.
5. While they discuss the facts of the story, they may suggest the legislative effects of the news.
6. Because issues of personal confidence mean a great deal, voters are attracted by many personal qualities.
7. Since the voter turnout is less than one hundred percent, some people obviously seem to take for granted their right to vote.
8. When they open, the polls are rarely busy.
9. If you were running for President, what kind of campaign would you organize?
10. Although the choice of President may reflect the nation's mood, many Presidents try to build support among diverse groups.

Using Commas with Adjectives, EXERCISE A

1. Their parents, anxious yet relieved, greeted them at the gate.
2. From the start, the rusted, greasy ship had not seemed seaworthy.
3. Its sails had been ripped apart by fierce, howling, hurricane-like winds.
4. The ordeal, both frightening and interminable, ended with a daring rescue.
5. Correct

Using Commas with Adjectives, EXERCISE B

Towering, graceful palms ringed the island. The interior, cool and shady, offered a welcome relief from the hot, humid afternoon. Banana trees, fragrant and filled with ripe fruit, bent under their heavy loads. Green, snakelike vines hung suspended across the forest canopy. Even the surrounding coral reef supported various species of plants.

Using Commas with Adjectives, EXERCISE C

New sentences will vary; possible answers are given.

1. The small, picturesque hotel was located near the beach.
2. The manager, friendly and polite, was standing in the lobby.
3. The new guest, eager but shy, spoke Spanish fluently.
4. His postcard home said, "Having a wonderful, carefree time. Wish you were here."
5. No one wanted to leave the pleasant, restful vacation resort.

Using Commas with Introductory Words and Phrases, EXERCISE A

1. Before the next major snowstorm, I
2. Trimming the front hedges, Dad
3. In spite of the cool temperature, the
4. Actually, I've
5. In the beginning of the story, Gene
6. Indeed, he
7. Instead of waiting until tomorrow, let
8. As always, Grandma
9. Rushing to catch the bus, Donald
10. After four or five days, the

Using Commas with Introductory Words and Phrases, EXERCISE B

1. In a bold transaction, the United States bought land from France.
2. From the Mississippi River to the Rocky Mountains, this land spread.
3. Almost doubling the area of the country, the land cost $15 million.
4. Finally, word came that Spain had ceded the land to France.
5. Correct

Using Commas with Introductory Words and Phrases, EXERCISE C

In 1725, Peter the Great of Russia sent Vitus Bering to explore the North Pacific. Oddly enough, he wanted to know whether Asia was connected to North America by land. On his second expedition, Bering sighted the Alaskan mainland. After proving that Asia and North America were not connected, Bering returned to Russia. Establishing Russia's claim to Alaska, a Russian fur trader began the first European settlement there in 1784.

Using Commas with Interrupters, EXERCISE A

1. The show was, however, an immediate success.
2. She became, as you know, a great star.
3. I will play, Philip, if you will accompany me.
4. Isabelle's essay, not mine, won an award.
5. Faye Doran, the well-known actress, hosted the program.

Using Commas with Interrupters, EXERCISE B

(1) John Quincy Adams, the sixth President of the United States, was the son of a former President. (2) This, as you can imagine, was an unusual situation. (3) It had never occurred before and has not occurred since, as the records show. (4) His father was John Adams, the second President of the United States. (5) John Quincy Adams was an experienced diplomat, as history attests, before he took office. (6) Essential (7) Essential (8) This doctrine, which warned Europe against interfering in the Americas, was quite important. (9) As President, not as Secretary of State, Adams had to deal with a hostile Congress. (10) Adams, who was not re-elected, became the only former President to serve in Congress.

Using Commas with Interrupters, EXERCISE C

Sentences will vary; possible answers are given.

1. Jon Goddard, the goalkeeper, plays a pivotal role on our soccer team.
2. Goalkeepers, if they do their job well, can win or lose a game for their team.
3. The forwards, for example, must be shifty and very fast to score most of the goals.
4. The defenders, on the other hand, seldom score, but their teamwork sets up the goals for the forwards.
5. Soccer, needless to say, is a game of endurance for the busy midfielders.

Using Commas in Series, EXERCISE A

1. I can travel to school by car, by private bus, or by subway.
2. A French bakery, a pizzeria, a kosher delicatessen, and a Korean restaurant are just a few of the dining spots in my neighborhood.
3. Do you want this picture near the sofa, above the fireplace, or opposite your desk?
4. We will be looking for energetic, eager, and cooperative trainees.
5. The author told us about her latest novel, described its major characters, read us a short selection, and then answered questions.
6. Correct
7. We serve three kinds of sandwiches: bologna and cheese, peanut butter and jelly, and lettuce and tomato.
8. "Which explorer," Capt. Reynolds asked, "has traveled along the Amazon River, climbed Mt. Everest, and excavated ruins in Egypt?"
9. Correct
10. Among William Butler Yeats's best-known poems are "The Wild Swans at Coole," "Easter 1916," "Lapis Lazuli," and "Sailing to Byzantium."

Using Commas in Series, EXERCISE B

Sentences will vary; possible sentences are given.

1. Ken likes bacon and eggs, juice, and whole-wheat toast for breakfast.
2. Vanessa searched for her dog in the yard, under the porch, and at the park.
3. Mary Chan, Enrique Sanchez, Paul Sullivan, and Donna Adams have been chosen to serve on the the Entertainment Committee.
4. Jill hopes to visit Italy, Japan, Brazil, and maybe even Australia when she is older.
5. Memorial Day, Thanksgiving, and New Year's Day are among the federal holidays.
6. The weather today is hazy, hot, and more humid than I would have imagined possible!
7. Thomas Jefferson is remembered as a strong President and statesman, a keen scholar, and an enthusiastic inventor.
8. Phil Collins, Brooks & Dunn, Mariah Carey, and En Vogue are my favorite musical performers.
9. I find out about my favorite performers by reading magazines, talking to my friends, and watching MTV and VH-1.
10. If I had a recording contract, I would want "Somewhere Out There," "Unchained Melody," and "Could It Be Magic?" on my first CD.

Using Commas with Direct Quotations, EXERCISE A

1. The coach said, "You had to signal for a replacement."
2. "Wait on the sidelines for a stretcher," the referee directed.
3. Rita announced, "That shouldn't have happened to our star player."
4. "I can't imagine a star player leaving the game," Linda sighed.
5. "Forget the melodramatics," Maria complained, "and get on with the game!"

Using Commas with Direct Quotations, EXERCISE B

1. Andrew Jackson declared, "One man with courage makes a majority."
2. "Neither current events nor history show that the majority rules, or ever did rule," wrote Jefferson Davis.
3. "What is history," Napolean asked, "but a fable agreed upon?"
4. "Love is space and time measured by the heart," penned Proust.
5. "Better die once for all," noted Aesop, "than live in continual terror."
6. Albert Einstein advised, "Let every man be respected as an individual."
7. "I will back the masses," said Gladstone, "over the classes."
8. Bertrand Russell wrote, "Men fear thought as they fear nothing else."
9. "Whatever you cannot understand," explained Goethe, "you cannot possess."
10. "'My country right or wrong' is a thing no patriot would think of saying," G. K. Chesterton affirmed.

Using Commas with Direct Quotations, EXERCISE C

Sentences will vary; possible answers are given.

1. "Why?" asked Dmitri. "What do we need?"
2. "We're out of milk," Kay replied, "and I need tomatoes for our salad."
3. "How I wish we'd grown our own tomatoes!" she added.
4. Laughed Dmitri, "Do you wish we had our own cow, too?"
5. "Yes," Kay shot back, "if you would be the one to milk it."

Other Uses of Commas, EXERCISE A
1. Hanoi, Vietnam
2. Tuesday, June 7, 1994
3. Act III, scene ii
4. Dear Mr. Markova,
5. Yours truly,
6. 1,000,000 pounds
7. Correct
8. Volume 2, page 24
9. Correct
10. Akron, Ohio

Other Uses of Commas, EXERCISE B
1. We had planned our trip to New York for Thanksgiving, 1994.
2. On November 21, 1994, we were finally on our way.
3. Marc read from *Tour Guide to NYC*, Chapter 5, page 230.
4. It said that in 1988, 7,000,000 people lived here.
5. We visited the Convention and Visitors Bureau, 2 Columbus Circle, New York, New York.
6. Sunday, November 27, was a great day for us.
7. We went to see *Ah, Wilderness!* by Eugene O'Neill.
8. During Act I, scene i, I recognized a friend.
9. Kristy had come all the way from Lubbock, Texas.
10. My postcard home said, "Dear Mom, What a great place!"

Other Uses of Commas, EXERCISE C

                                                          May 1, 1995

Dear Uncle Leo,
     Please come see my school play on Saturday, May 20, at 7:00 P.M. I'm not the star, but I have a big scene in Act II, scene ii, that I know you will love. For a clue, look at your copy of *Favorite Plays for Children*, page 235. The play will be given at Harold Dawes School, Route 20. The auditorium seats 1,500, so there should be no problem getting tickets.
                                                   Your niece,
                                                   Dorrie

Using Comma Sense, EXERCISE A
1. We filed out solemnly.
2. He spoke solemnly.
3. We dispersed into the room.
4. The woman stumbled into the room.

Using Comma Sense, EXERCISE B
1. Sharon, Martin studies the novels of Scott Paul.
2. Sharon Martin studies the novels of Scott, Paul.
3. After studying Scott for years, in England I began to work on a book.
4. After studying Scott for years in England, I began to work on a book.

Using Comma Sense, EXERCISE C
     Intrigued by dog training, P.J. talked to breeders. After studying books on several breeds, he decided on an Irish setter. He talked to a breeder, Ms. Jane Fried, on a trip to Pennsylvania. Ms. Fried promised him the pick of the litter, the best puppy in the batch.

Commonly Confused or Misused Words

Commonly Confused or Misused Words I, EXERCISE A

1. alluded
2. already
3. badly
4. accept
5. illusion
6. a while
7. besides
8. adverse
9. advice
10. all right

Commonly Confused or Misused Words I, Exercise B

Yoko loves to <u>accept</u> every challenge. She has a few mistaken <u>illusions</u> about herself; thus, we were <u>all ready</u> for Yoko to fail. <u>Among</u> the three finalists, Yoko was certainly the most enthusiastic. In the end, I guess, she didn't do too <u>badly</u>.

Commonly Confused or Misused Words I, Exercise C

Sentences will vary; possible are given.

1. The store will <u>accept</u> every coupon <u>except</u> that one.
2. If you are going to <u>adopt</u> that strategy you'll need to <u>adapt</u> it to fit your circumstances.
3. People who like to <u>advise</u> others may have trouble receiving <u>advice</u>.
4. The minister's <u>allusion</u> to good and evil was considered an <u>illusion</u> by some listeners.
5. The farm was divided <u>between</u> the two brothers; the money was distributed <u>among</u> all the people of the valley.

Commonly Confused or Misused Words II, Exercise A

1. You <u>may</u> take notes if you wish so that you <u>can</u> review your "James Bond" assignment later.
2. The dictator's <u>capital</u> city is in a hot, dry <u>desert</u>.
3. <u>Choose</u> <u>clothes</u> that are inconspicuous but cool.
4. Did you <u>choose</u> a trench coat to <u>complement</u> that outfit?
5. Don't go to sleep; your <u>continuous</u> vigilance is essential.
6. No government is <u>disinterested</u> when it comes to intelligence gathering.
7. Be <u>discreet</u> when inquiring about <u>discrete</u> events.
8. <u>Take</u> a camera with you; <u>bring</u> back photographs.
9. The <u>council</u> is planning something; my <u>counsel</u> is to proceed cautiously.
10. With you on this assignment, I can <u>breathe</u> more easily.
11. Our actions are a <u>capital</u> crime—so don't fail!
12. Our informant will <u>emigrate</u> to Brazil when the mission is completed.
13. Keep me posted; I am not <u>uninterested</u> in your progress.

Commonly Confused or Misused Words II, Exercise B

1. Welcome to our country. Are you <u>immigrating</u> or visiting?
2. Ah! I see from your passport that you are an <u>eminent</u> doctor.
3. Why did you <u>choose</u> to come to the desert on your vacation?
4. Did you bring a camera here to photograph our beautiful <u>capital</u>?
5. I like your <u>clothes</u>, but you will not need a trench coat in the desert.
6. <u>May</u> I have your permission to open your suitcase so that I can look inside?
7. Bring it here, please. Why do you <u>breathe</u> so fast? Are you hiding something?
8. I <u>compliment</u> you on your camera. What a long lens it has!
9. Did you choose to stay in the capital, or will you go <u>farther</u> inland?
10. Take my counsel and try the <u>dessert</u> in the hotel cafe; it's capital!

Commonly Confused or Misused Words III, EXERCISE A
1. teach
2. ingenuous
3. infer
4. formally
5. indigenous
6. imply
7. formerly
8. indigent
9. ingenious
10. oral

Commonly Confused or Misused Words III, EXERCISE B

In <u>less</u> than three weeks, I could play songs. I can play some popular songs <u>well</u>, but I am also learning how to make up my own songs, too. Now I <u>pick out tunes by ear</u>. I don't mean to <u>imply</u> that I am any kind of musical genius; <u>it's</u> just that I enjoy music and I practice every chance that I get.

Commonly Confused or Misused Words III, EXERCISE C
Definitions will vary slightly; possible definitions are given.
1. indigent: poor; lacking money or property
2. formerly: in earlier times
3. ingenious: creative and clever, intelligent
4. loose: opposite of *tight*
5. oral: having to do with the mouth

Commonly Confused or Misused Words IV, EXERCISE A
1. The park <u>personnel</u> told us how to <u>proceed</u> to find Druid Arch, our <u>principal</u> objective.
2. Rather <u>than</u> start immediately, we found a very nice campground and <u>set</u> up our new tent.
3. We decided to <u>rise</u> early the next day and get started.
4. The <u>weather</u> was hot, so we stopped often to <u>sit</u>.
5. We didn't know <u>whether</u> we were going in the right direction.
6. Many other people had <u>preceded</u> us, leaving prints in the sand.
7. We didn't know <u>whose</u> footprints they were.
8. Druid Arch is a <u>real</u> arch; <u>you're</u> going to love it.
9. I couldn't <u>set</u> down the camera; there were so many great views!
10. We returned to camp just as the sun began to <u>set</u>.

Commonly Confused or Misused Words IV, EXERCISE B
1. The park is really managed by <u>personnel</u> from the National Parks Department.
2. The responsibility is <u>theirs</u> to protect the park's natural resources.
3. <u>Regardless</u> of whether <u>you're</u> traveling by car or on foot, Canyonlands National Park is as really breathtaking place to explore.
4. If you <u>proceed</u> on your trip by foot, carry plenty of water.
5. In the <u>past</u>, people who have hiked there have suffered from dehydration.
6. Rather <u>than</u> risk a tragedy, tell park personnel where you are hiking.
7. Whoever explores by car should also think about <u>their</u> safety.
8. <u>Weather</u> can change quickly; violent thunderstorms may cause water to <u>rise</u> suddenly in the canyons, washing out roads.

Conjunctions

Identifying and Using Coordinating Conjunctions, EXERCISE A
1. for
2. and, so
3. or
4. yet
5. but

Identifying and Using Coordinating Conjunctions, EXERCISE B
Sentences may vary slightly; possible sentences are given.
1. The airline will sell discount tickets, <u>but</u> people need to make reservations early.
2. Nancy <u>and</u> Kelly brought Molly birthday gifts, <u>but</u> Linda forgot hers.
3. Lucy lost her library card, <u>so</u> she couldn't take out books and complete her assignment.
4. One hundred years ago, farmers used horses for power, <u>but</u> today they utilize tractors.
5. Cindy <u>or</u> Matt may baby-sit for us Saturday night.
6. Each year the cost of cassette tapes and CD's increases, <u>yet</u> teenagers are the largest group of music consumers.
7. Tony cannot take the job, <u>nor</u> is Bob available.
8. At the campground, the family secured their food supply in locked coolers, <u>for</u> they had spotted black bears <u>and</u> raccoons in the area.
9. Camping is so much fun, <u>and</u> it's also an inexpensive way to spend a vacation.
10. Mountain climbing is similar to spending a few days in the woods, <u>but</u> it's more expensive.

Identifying and Using Correlative Conjunctions, EXERCISE A
1. <u>Neither</u> Anita <u>nor</u> Marti will be at the dance Friday because they both have to work.
2. <u>Both</u> corn <u>and</u> beans are common ingredients in Southwest cuisine.
3. <u>Either</u> Garth <u>or</u> Gloria will go fishing with us.
4. We don't know <u>whether</u> to schedule the class picnic for May <u>or</u> to wait until June.
5. <u>Not only</u> Gary <u>but also</u> Jan and Merle went to the game early to get good seats.

Identifying and Using Correlative Conjunctions, EXERCISE B
Sentences may vary slightly; possible sentences are given.
1. <u>Neither</u> Andy's mother <u>nor</u> his brother was at the opening performance of his play.
2. <u>Both</u> Teresa <u>and</u> Carlos love Latin American music.
3. <u>Either</u> lasagna <u>or</u> spaghetti makes a good inexpensive meal.
4. The teacher hasn't decided <u>whether to</u> test us on Thursday or to have another review.
5. <u>Both</u> new homes <u>and</u> a shopping mall will be built on the west side of town.
6. <u>Neither</u> bad weather <u>nor</u> illness will stop Jody from going home for Thanksgiving, since <u>not only</u> Ray <u>but also</u> Sarah will be coming home.
7. <u>Whether</u> Diana <u>or</u> Ellen comes, the party is sure to be a success.
8. <u>Not only</u> the twins <u>but also</u> their parents will be arriving in Boston <u>either</u> tonight <u>or</u> tomorrow morning.
9. <u>Both</u> a hurricane <u>and</u> floods are expected (or predicted).
10. <u>Neither</u> a bad day at the office <u>nor</u> a poor performance review will cause Duane to quit.

Identifying and Using Subordinating Conjunctions and Conjunctive Adverbs, EXERCISE A
1. however, conjunctive adverb
2. While, subordinating conjunction
3. in addition, conjunctive adverb
4. After, subordinating conjunction
5. furthermore, conjunctive adverb; since, subordinating conjunction

Identifying and Using Subordinating Conjunctions and Conjunctive Adverbs, EXERCISE B
Sentences may vary slightly; possible sentences are given.
1. That movie received bad reviews; <u>however</u>, many people went to see it./<u>Although</u> the movie received bad reviews, many people went to see it.
2. The bus was very slow; <u>therefore</u>, we were late for our dance lessons./<u>Since</u> the bus was very slow, we were late for our dance lessons.
3. Tom was failing geometry; <u>consequently</u>, he needed a tutor./Tom needed a tutor <u>because</u> he was failing geometry.
4. Lionel is a gifted singer; <u>in addition</u>, he plays piano well./<u>While</u> Lionel is a gifted singer, he also plays piano well.
5. Lisa arrived ten minutes late; <u>furthermore</u>, she did not have her homework./<u>Although</u> Lisa arrived ten minutes late, she did not have her homework.
6. The Murrays waited three months for their new CD player; <u>finally</u>, it was delivered to their apartment./<u>After</u> the Murrays waited three months for their new CD player, it was delivered to their apartment.
7. Terry's car is not dependable; <u>for example</u>, it rarely starts on cold mornings./<u>Because</u> Terry's car rarely starts on cold mornings, it is not dependable.
8. Cats will drink water; <u>however</u>, they prefer milk./<u>Although</u> cats will drink water, they prefer milk.
9. The singer had many fans; <u>consequently</u>, tickets for her concerts were hard to get./<u>Since</u> the singer had many fans, tickets for her concerts were hard to get.
10. Our car would not start; <u>therefore</u>, Dad called a towing service./<u>When</u> our car would not start, Dad called a towing service.

Distinguishing Between Conjunctions and Prepositions, EXERCISE A
1. since   conjunction
2. after   preposition
3. as   conjunction
4. as   preposition
5. until   conjunction
6. since   conjunction
7. before   conjunction
8. until   preposition
9. since   preposition; before   preposition

Distinguishing Between Conjunctions and Prepositions, EXERCISE B
Answers may vary; possible answers are given.
1. Candice accepted the trophy <u>after</u> she was introduced as captain. (conjunction)
2. <u>After</u> lunch, we will drive to the airport. (preposition)
3. <u>As</u> I've said, the typewriter will be in the repair shop <u>until</u> Friday. (conjunction, preposition)
4. <u>Before</u> Graciela begins college, she will visit Spain, <u>as</u> a graduation present. (conjunction, preposition)
5. <u>After</u> the soccer game, I will drive Victor home <u>since</u> his mother is working late. (preposition, conjunction)
6. Joey has been sick <u>since</u> Saturday and he'll have to stay in bed <u>until</u> he sees the doctor on Wednesday. (preposition, conjunction)

Distinguishing Between Conjunctions and Prepositions, EXERCISE C

Sentences will vary; possible sentences are given.

1. The pool will be open in the evenings only <u>until</u> school ends on June 24./The park will be open to the public <u>until</u> dark.
2. <u>Since</u> Pablo is going to the local community college, he will be living at home./Joan's allergies have been bothering her <u>since</u> March.
3. Wendy will fly to Florida <u>after</u> she takes her last exam on Friday./<u>After</u> dinner, we'll take the baby to the playground.
4. Some babies learn how to walk <u>before</u> they reach their first birthday./Most high school seniors are notified of college acceptance <u>before</u> April 1.
5. <u>As</u> I headed for math class, I bumped into Briana./I treated my little brother to lunch and a movie, <u>as</u> a surprise.

Using Conjunctions Correctly, EXERCISE A

1. incorrect
2. incorrect
3. correct
4. incorrect
5. incorrect

Using Conjunctions Correctly, EXERCISE B

Answers will vary; possible answers are given.

1. Josh was disappointed <u>because</u> his team lost the game.
2. <u>While</u> Dad bought some gas, Mom and I finished shopping.
3. Bobby is not only my cousin, <u>but</u> he is also my best friend.
4. Nicky looks <u>as though</u> he is ready to fall asleep.
5. <u>Although</u> Carlos has little experience, he is a hard worker.
6. We could go to a movie <u>or</u> head for the roller rink.
7. Nina missed the dress rehearsal for the concert <u>because</u> she had a stomach virus.
8. Ted still enjoys playing with trains, <u>even though</u> he is almost twenty.
9. The clerk apologized, <u>for</u> he had kept us waiting a long time.
10. The coach yelled at Lily <u>as if</u> she had gone deaf.

Developing Your Style: Conjunctions, EXERCISE A

Answers may vary; possible answers are given.

1. A recent book by Maya Angelou tells of her African travels, <u>but</u> it also describes her search for a sense of belonging.
2. Angelou has written, produced, and directed television productions and movies <u>so that</u> she might voice her experiences as an African American.
3. <u>Before</u> Maya Angelou received an award for a television documentary, she also had earned awards for her books.
4. She hosted a thirty-part study course for public television, <u>and</u> she wrote a television script for *I Know Why the Caged Bird Sings*.
5. Angelou shares her personal story intimately in her books, <u>where</u> she has greater room for details. (or, where)

Developing Your Style: Conjunctions, EXERCISE B

Answers may vary; possible answers are given.

1. <u>Although</u> people have been looking for gold for centuries, they have not found much gold.
2. Properties of gold that make it valuable are its beautiful color <u>and</u> its softness.
3. Pure gold can be worked into various shapes <u>or</u> can be minted as coins.
4. <u>When</u> gold is used in jewelry, it is usually combined with other metals to make it harder <u>and</u> more durable.
5. Jewelers use the term *karat* to measure the purity of gold, <u>and</u> a twenty-four-karat gold ring is one hundred percent gold.
6. <u>While</u> eighteen-karat gold is often used in jewelry, it is equal to eighteen parts of gold <u>and</u> six parts of another metal.
7. Finding gold in a jewelry store is easier <u>than</u> finding it in its natural state, <u>for</u> gold is found far below the earth's surface in veins of ore.
8. In 1848 gold was struck in California, <u>and</u> hundreds of thousands of people flocked to the gold fields.
9. A little later, gold was found in the Yukon Territory, <u>and</u> the gold rush was on!
10. <u>Because</u> the famous author Jack London went to the gold fields of the Yukon, he wrote about his thrilling adventures.

Contractions

Identifying and Forming Contractions, EXERCISE A

1. she's
2. who'd
3. won't
4. where's
5. he'll
6. they're
7. doesn't
8. should've
9. haven't
10. she hasn't (or she's not)

Identifying and Forming Contractions, EXERCISE B

<u>I am</u> planning a trip to the Hayden Planetarium. <u>It's</u> located on 81st Street in New York City. I <u>cannot</u> wait to see the seventy-five-foot dome that forms the setting for the sky shows. <u>There's</u> also a space theater that presents slides on twenty-two screens simultaneously. After I see each presentation, <u>I will</u> (or <u>I shall</u>) look at the exhibits. <u>Will</u> it <u>not</u> be exciting to see a 14-ton meteorite? <u>Who'd</u> want to miss it? Of course, <u>I would</u> also like to see the library, where <u>they have</u> accumulated an impressive collection of books on astonomy. <u>I've</u> set aside an entire day for this excursion.

Identifying and Forming Contractions, EXERCISE C

Paragraphs will vary; a possible paragraph is given.

<u>Randy's</u> in Kansas for the summer. <u>He's</u> learning about that state as he travels through it. Before he left he <u>didn't</u> know much about Kansas. Now, <u>you'd</u> be surprised how informative his letters are. He surprised me by writing that the land in Kansas <u>isn't</u> all prairie.

Distinguishing Between Possessive Pronouns and Contractions, EXERCISE A

1. It's
2. Your
3. who's
4. You're
5. Whose

Distinguishing Between Possessive Pronouns and Contractions, EXERCISE B
1. Correct
2. In my family, <u>everybody's</u> favorite meal is Chicago-style pizza.
3. <u>Who's</u> the man in the gray suit, holding the portfolio?
4. Our race is finished, but they have not yet run <u>theirs</u>.
5. This museum is known for <u>its</u> collection of pre-Columbian art.
6. How eagerly we listened to <u>your</u> stories!
7. Correct
8. Correct
9. Have you seen <u>their</u> design for the cover?
10. Correct

Distinguishing Between Possessive Pronouns and Contractions, EXERCISE C
Answers may vary; suggested answers are given.
1. Does <u>your</u> cabin face west?
2. <u>They're</u> building a highway around the lake.
3. Can you tell me <u>whose</u> bike that is?
4. The truck made <u>its</u> way through the mountains.
5. <u>Who's</u> in charge here?

Dashes

Using Dashes Correctly, EXERCISE A
1. This fruit—Have you ever seen one?—grows in the tropics.
2. The story—a fable that I always enjoy—has an important moral.
3. Precious jewels—for example, diamonds—are appraised here.
4. Some cities—Cleveland, Pittsburgh, Detroit—have a distinctive flavor.
5. The ending was a real surprise—but that's enough for now.
6. The woman—an actress of great talent—lives in Cincinnati.
7. The violinist—Have you ever heard such a stunning performance?—bowed before the enthusiastic audience.
8. Flour, honey, and raisins—these are the basic ingredients.
9. Is the costume—a traditional folk-dancing outfit—valuable?
10. The inventor—a pioneer in the development of video recording equipment—was honored by her colleagues.

Using Dashes Correctly, EXERCISE B
Some answers may vary slightly; possible answers are given.
1. Tides—Have you ever observed them?—are beneficial in many ways.
2. The moon's gravity—A theory that may be hard to understand—creates two high tides each day.
3. During high tides, ocean boats—which might otherwise become stuck in the shallow waters—enter or leave the harbor.
4. High tide—the moon's pulling of the solid earth through the ocean—takes place on the opposite side of the earth.
5. Spring tides—which are extremely dramatic—are caused by the pull of the moon combined with the pull of the sun.

Dates

Writing Dates Correctly, EXERCISE A
1. the seventeenth century
2. December 1, 1917
3. Friday
4. Thanksgiving
5. fall and winter
6. Wednesday
7. March 1, 1991
8. the Elizabethan Age
9. Saturday
10. Memorial Day

Writing Dates Correctly, EXERCISE B
1. Eleanor was born in the summer of 1932.
2. From that date until May 2, 1948, she lived in Chicago.
3. She lived in Hollywood until Labor Day.
4. One Sunday she was playing volleyball on the beach.
5. She broke her leg and returned to Chicago in the fall.
6. Eleanor attended the University of Chicago from September 5, 1948, until sometime in 1951.
7. On November 1, 1952, she married a classmate.
8. Correct
9. They settled in New York State in the latter half of the twentieth century.
10. Eleanor retired on June 15, 1995, from the social services job she had held since the 1970's.

Writing Dates Correctly, EXERCISE C

July 3, 1995

Dear Uri,

I will be lecturing around the country from August 19 until Columbus Day or Halloween. I hope to be in your area on Tuesday or Wednesday of the week of September 18, 1995. Would you like to attend my talk? The title is "The Victorian Era." Afterward, you might show me the autumn colors in New Hampshire.

Sincerely,
Derek

Double Negatives

Avoiding Double Negatives, EXERCISE A
1. anyone
2. anything
3. ever
4. anything
5. anyone

Avoiding Double Negatives, Exercise B
Some answers may vary; suggested answers are given.
 1. Gene <u>had never</u> seen such a colorful parade./ Gene <u>hadn't ever</u> seen such a colorful parade.
 2. You <u>shouldn't do anything</u> until next week./ You <u>should do nothing</u> until next week.
 3. Phillip <u>wouldn't</u> admit his mistake to <u>anybody</u>./ Phillip <u>would</u> admit his mistake to <u>nobody</u>.
 4. Correct
 5. Claire and I <u>haven't made any</u> decisions yet./ Claire and I <u>have made no</u> decisions yet.
 6. <u>Can't</u> Roberta find her notebook <u>anywhere</u>?/ <u>Can</u> Roberta find her notebook <u>nowhere</u>?
 7. These reports <u>don't mention anything</u> about it. / These reports <u>mention nothing</u> about it.
 8. We <u>won't place anyone</u> in a dangerous situation./ We <u>will place no one</u> in a dangerous situation.
 9. Correct
10. Nancy <u>has never been</u> to Los Angeles, so she <u>can hardly wait</u> to go./ Nancy <u>hasn't ever been</u> to Los Angeles, so she <u>can't wait</u> to go.

Avoiding Double Negatives, Exercise C
Sentences and corrections will vary; possible answers are given.
 1. When I <u>hardly understood</u> the material, I arranged for a tutor.
 2. The police <u>never found any evidence</u>; the case remains a mystery to this day.
 3. Stefan <u>couldn't buy anything</u> at the auction, for he had left his checkbook at home.
 4. The wall <u>was scarcely completed</u> before someone spray-painted it.
 5. If you'll let me come with you, I promise that I <u>won't bother anybody</u>.

Ellipsis

Using Ellipsis Points Correctly, EXERCISE A
 1. Correct
 2. A wag wrote, "If it moves, salute it. . . . If you can't pick it up, paint it."
 3. Jefferson insisted, "For a people who are free . . . a well-organized . . . militia is their best security."
 4. Washington states, "Discipline is the soul of an army. It . . . procures . . . esteem to all."
 5. Did you . . . pardon my asking . . . did you read the writings of Sun Tze on strategy?

Using Ellipsis Points Correctly, EXERCISE B
 1. Willa . . . grew up in Nebraska.
 2. Cather wrote novels. . . . A few were set in the Southwest.
 3. Her work . . . well, she is one of my favorite authors.
 4. Honestly . . . excuse me . . . you should read *O Pioneers!*
 5. Her main theme is the . . . settlement of the . . . Middle West.

Exclamation Points

Using Exclamation Points Correctly, EXERCISE A
 1. What a pity<u>!</u>
 2. Watch out<u>!</u>
 3. Stop, Doreen<u>!</u>
 4. How beautiful you look<u>!</u>
 5. What an awesome movie<u>!</u>
 6. Just in time<u>!</u> Whew<u>!</u>
 7. Ugh<u>!</u> How disgusting that is<u>!</u>
 8. That was a close call<u>!</u>
 9. Ivy said, "This is my lucky day!"
10. Did Ed say, "Let's get out of here<u>!</u>"?

Using Exclamation Points Correctly, EXERCISE B
Answers will vary; possible answers are given.
1. Quiet! Don't startle the birds!
2. This painting is spectacular! Such colors!
3. That pathway is a little uneven. Watch how you walk!
4. Kids, move away from the railing!
5. Mind your own business! I'll do as I please!
6. Look at that! It's incredible!
7. You made the finals? Wow!
8. How spectacular that is! I wish I could afford it!
9. Chocolate syrup and birdseed—what a sight I must look!
10. The baby is asleep. Shh!

Using Exclamation Points Correctly, EXERCISE C
Answers will vary; possible answers are given. Exclamation points are underlined.
1. Good grief!
2. How delicious this pizza tastes!
3. Listen to me!
4. Phooey!
5. Such talent!
6. Don't you dare go in there!
7. Hallelujah!
8. What a mistake that was!
9. Sit down right this moment and be quiet!
10. How wonderful it all sounds to me!

Gender

Using Gender References Correctly, EXERCISE A
1. incorrect, or she
2. correct
3. incorrect, it
4. incorrect, they
5. incorrect, he or she

Using Gender References Correctly, EXERCISE B
1. Mario's mother lent him <u>her</u> car when he took <u>his</u> driving test.
2. Her car was very small, so it was easier for <u>him</u> to park <u>it</u>.
3. Everyone worries when <u>he or she</u> is about to take the test if <u>his or her</u> tester will be Officer Mary Ott.
4. Officer Ott never smiles when <u>she</u> tests teenagers, who are nervous when <u>they</u> are tested.
5. Mark and Jennifer got <u>their</u> licenses; each claimed that <u>he or she</u> had scored higher.

Using Gender References Correctly, EXERCISE C
1. *Lyddie* is about Lyddie, a girl who has to earn <u>her</u> own way in the 1840's.
2. *Lyddie* begins when a bear gets into her family's home, and <u>it</u> tears the place apart.
3. Lyddie's father has left home, and all <u>he</u> has left the family is a poor farm.
4. Everyone in the family is trying <u>his or her</u> best to pay the farm's debts.
5. Taking the youngest children with <u>her</u>, Lyddie's mother moves to a city.
6. Lyddie and her brother stay on their farm, trying to pay off <u>its</u> debts.
7. Neither of them is happy when they are sent for by <u>their</u> mother.
8. Each wants to stay and do <u>his or her</u> part in saving the family home.
9. Lyddie goes to work in a mill; no employee is happy with <u>his or her</u> situation there.
10. Lyddie and many other employees are forced to leave <u>their</u> job.

Hyphens

Using Hyphens for Syllabification and Line Breaks, EXERCISE A
1. trade-
2. bil-
3. de-
4. fury
5. self-
6. even
7. brought
8. back-
9. Finland
10. part-

Using Hyphens for Syllabification and Line Breaks, EXERCISE B
1. Correct
2. spend-ing
3. left-handed
4. iden-tity or identi-ty
5. brother-in-law

Using Hyphens for Syllabification and Line Breaks, EXERCISE C
Some answers may vary slightly; possible answers are given.
1. Did your pack- / age arrive on time?
2. When he winked, / I understood.
3. Our trip to / Washington was postponed.
4. Correct
5. Please don't be so self / ish anymore.

Other Uses of Hyphens, EXERCISE A
1. so-called friend
2. African-American literature
3. self-reliant
4. sister-in-law
5. mid-February snowstorm
6. three-quarters empty
7. step-by-step approach
8. three-hour meeting
9. how-to book
10. our ex-governor

Other Uses of Hyphens, EXERCISE B
1. The president-elect will take office in January.
2. Are those three four-year-olds triplets?
3. My friend's parents went on a six-day cruise of the Caribbean.
4. No technical jargon is used in these easy-to-understand directions.
5. His great-grandparents are in very good health.

Other Uses of Hyphens, EXERCISE C
1. They left home early in the morning and arrived by <u>mid-afternoon</u>.
2. That nation was already <u>semi-independent</u> even before the revolution.
3. She took a <u>part-time</u> job teaching crafts at the after-school center.
4. Is it more economical to buy a new sofa or to <u>re-cover</u> the old one?
5. The union is demanding higher wages and a <u>35-hour</u> week.
6. Our ex-mayor did not show much <u>self-control</u> in the recent election campaign.
7. The fraction <u>twenty-three</u> <u>thirty-sixths</u> cannot be further reduced.
8. Correct.
9. We usually meet on Mondays, but it's not a <u>hard-and-fast</u> rule.
10. Many businesses prospered in the <u>post-World War II</u> economic boom.

Interjections

Identifying and Punctuating Interjections, EXERCISE A
1. Hey
2. Oh
3. uh
4. Hurray
5. Ouch
6. Wow
7. Ah
8. Well
9. Ugh
10. No

Identifying and Punctuating Interjections, EXERCISE B
Answers will vary; possible answers are given.
1. <u>Wow</u>! That was a wonderful performance.
2. I can't believe that Elisa's eating snails! <u>Ugh</u>!
3. Maybe it would be better if you, <u>uh</u>, resigned.
4. <u>Uh, oh</u>! I think I flunked the exam.
5. <u>Ah</u>! How I wish that this night could last forever!
6. <u>Whew</u>! These suitcases must weigh a ton!
7. I learned to set the VCR. <u>Cool</u>!
8. <u>Ouch</u>! I think that I've sprained my ankle!
9. <u>Well</u>, you'll just have to try harder next time, won't you?
10. <u>Ooh</u>! You make me so angry sometimes!

Identifying and Punctuating Interjections, EXERCISE C
Sentences will vary; appropriate interjections are given.
1. oh
2. so
3. well
4. phooey
5. gosh
6. um
7. ugh
8. wow
9. alas
10. aha

Nouns

Noun-Forming Suffixes, EXERCISE A
1. coincidence, lawyer, pianist
2. internist
3. director, friendship, neighborhood
4. tendency, predicaments
5. Democracy

Noun-Forming Suffixes, EXERCISE B
Sentences will vary; possible sentences are given.
1. The parents were charged with the <u>abandonment</u> of their children.
2. The two merchants decided to form a <u>partnership</u>.
3. <u>Feminism</u> has tried to improve working conditions for women.
4. They were not ready for <u>parenthood</u> until they had been married for five years.
5. When the <u>contractions</u> increased, Mrs. Salinas knew that it was time to go to the hospital.
6. The <u>widower</u>, an anthropologist, studied peoples of the Pacific.
7. The <u>prisoner</u> learned a trade while serving his time.
8. I have papers that will prove my <u>residency</u>.
9. The depressed teenager sought <u>guidance</u> from a counselor.
10. That <u>kingdom</u> was famous for its diamonds and rubies.

Noun-Forming Suffixes, EXERCISE C
Answers will vary; possible answers are given.
1. It was a marriage of great <u>happiness</u>.
2. The college <u>commencement</u> will be held on May 25.
3. During the Middle Ages, a lord commonly ruled a <u>fiefdom</u>.
4. My mother called it <u>idiocy</u> to drive on the icy roads.
5. She was awarded a <u>scholarship</u> for her excellent grades.
6. The services of an <u>exterminator</u> were required to get rid of the huge nest of wasps.
7. The renowned <u>violinist</u> will play here on Friday.
8. Lydia accused her mother of <u>favoritism</u>.
9. There is a good <u>likelihood</u> that he will be the next senator.
10. The child's sudden <u>obedience</u> was a surprise to her parents.

Identifying and Using Common and Proper Nouns, EXERCISE A
Answers may vary; possible answers are given.
1. team
2. Atlanta
3. poet
4. holiday
5. continent
6. Kennedy International Airport
7. Atlantic Ocean
8. state
9. planet
10. Uncle Rudolfo

Identifying and Using Common and Proper Nouns, EXERCISE B
Answers will vary; possible answers are given.
1. Our teacher can speak <u>French</u>.
2. I asked <u>Cousin Ernest</u> if I could borrow the car.
3. Next month our class will travel to <u>Trenton</u>.
4. <u>Pittsburgh</u> is located on a river.
5. <u>*The Taming of the Shrew*</u> received a good review in the newspaper.

Identifying and Using Common and Proper Nouns, EXERCISE C
Answers will vary; possible answers are given.

July 12, 1995

Dear <u>Boris</u>,

   I am writing you from <u>Montana</u>. <u>Mom</u> and <u>I</u> are staying at the <u>Eagle Inn</u>. On <u>Saturday</u> we visited <u>Hunter Pass</u>. It reminded me of a scene in *True Grit*—you know, something in which <u>John Wayne</u> might have been seen.

Love,
Mariah

Identifying and Using Collective Nouns, EXERCISE A
1. group, singular
2. pair, plural
3. crowd, singular
4. assembly, singular
5. committee, plural

Identifying and Using Collective Nouns, EXERCISE B
Some answers may vary; possible answers are given.
1. committee, Correct
2. staff, The <u>staff visits</u> schools across the nation.
3. team, They watch each <u>team</u> as <u>it plays</u> basketball.
4. panel, Correct
5. family, One <u>family prefers</u> Michigan to Wisconsin.
6. family, Another <u>family disagree</u> about <u>their</u> desires.
7. public, Sometimes the <u>public is</u> concerned with the choice.
8. audience, After all, the <u>audience needs</u> to be entertained.
9. crowd, The <u>crowd determines</u> the revenue.
10. group, Correct

Identifying and Using Collective Nouns, EXERCISE C
Answers will vary; a possible sentence for each collective noun is given.
1. The <u>army</u> is launching a new enlistment campaign this month. (singular)
2. Has <u>Congress</u> voted on the proposed legislation? (singular)
3. The <u>squad</u> could not agree about their next move. (plural)
4. This volunteer <u>association</u> does fine work in this community. (singular)
5. After the ship dropped anchor, the <u>crew</u> went about their maintenance tasks. (plural)
6. The <u>Senate</u> is meeting in special session during the holidays. (singular)
7. The <u>band</u> are unpacking their instruments. (plural)
8. Has the <u>jury</u> asked to review the evidence? (singular)
9. The <u>trio</u> asked me to help them put away their music. (plural)

Identifying and Using Concrete and Abstract Nouns, EXERCISE A

1. concrete	11. concrete
2. concrete	12. concrete
3. abstract	13. abstract
4. concrete	14. abstract
5. concrete	15. concrete
6. abstract	16. concrete
7. concrete	17. abstract
8. abstract	18. abstract
9. concrete	19. concrete
10. abstract	20. concrete

Identifying and Using Concrete and Abstract Nouns, EXERCISE B
1. Hilda (promotion)
2. Matthew (memories), (childhood)
3. mayor (compassion), families
4. economists (recession)
5. boxer (cunning), (agility)

Identifying and Using Concrete and Abstract Nouns, EXERCISE C
Answers will vary; possible answers are given. Required nouns are underlined.

We meet to honor a <u>worker</u> who has shown us <u>loyalty</u> and <u>humanity</u>. His <u>family</u> should feel great <u>pride</u> in his <u>success</u>. This <u>man</u> has worked hard in the <u>factory</u>, demonstrating <u>talent</u> and <u>judgment</u> in everything that he has done.

Spelling Plural Nouns Correctly, EXERCISE A
1. nickels
2. witches
3. superheroes
4. foxes
5. moose
6. donkeys
7. qualities
8. calves
9. attorneys-at-law
10. crises
11. juries
12. branches
13. schoolbuses
14. Fridays
15. wisdom teeth
16. chefs
17. contraltos
18. oxen
19. sons-in-law
20. spoons

Spelling Plural Nouns Correctly, EXERCISE B
1. The <u>libraries</u> opened as the <u>clocks</u> struck.
2. Outside, along the <u>walkways</u>, the <u>women</u> waited.
3. I balanced my <u>boxes</u> near my <u>feet</u>.
4. The <u>doors</u> opened, and the <u>First Ladies</u> entered.
5. My <u>armfuls</u> spilled across the <u>counters</u>.
6. The <u>computers</u> connected me to the <u>encyclopedias</u>.
7. Your <u>analyses</u> of the <u>data</u> seemed correct.
8. Did your <u>sisters-in-law</u> send you the <u>tables of contents</u>?
9. I read the <u>speeches</u> by the Revolutionary <u>heroes</u>.
10. Then I checked out The <u>Lives</u> of Our <u>Children</u>.

Spelling Plural Nouns Correctly, EXERCISE C
Many <u>families</u> met yesterday to discuss the recent increases in <u>taxes</u>. Our <u>beliefs</u> were represented by June and Jeb Ellery. The <u>Ellerys</u> made <u>speeches</u> about the need for better <u>utilities</u>. Even the <u>children</u> listened to the discussions on their <u>radios</u>. <u>Several</u> <u>handfuls</u> of <u>attorneys-at-law</u> called for a vote.

Developing Your Style: Choosing Specific, Concrete Nouns, EXERCISE A
Answers will vary; possible answers are given.
1. Jamie sipped her <u>soda</u> while Manuel spoke to <u>Rita</u>.
2. "Heart-shaped <u>balloons</u> are exactly what your <u>basement</u> needs!"
3. Jamie's <u>mother</u> came in, carrying a <u>bowl</u> that Jamie's pet eyed with interest as well as with eagerness.
4. As they ate, Ryan talked about his <u>surprise</u> at recognizing <u>Bob Kerry</u> at <u>Silverado's</u> last month.
5. As <u>Ryan and Rita</u> set out for the <u>library</u> on their <u>bicycles</u>, they looked forward to the next meeting.

Developing Your Style: Choosing Specific, Concrete Nouns, EXERCISE B
Answers will vary; possible answers are given.

We arrived at <u>the stadium</u> early and went in at <u>the gate</u>. Was that place ever crowded—just full of <u>women</u> and <u>men</u>, <u>teenagers</u> and <u>adults</u>! I looked at the <u>souvenirs</u> that were for sale; then I bought <u>T-shirts</u> and <u>a program</u>. <u>An usher</u> helped us find our <u>seats</u> just as the lights dimmed.

A <u>murmur</u> swept the <u>arena</u>; every <u>ticket-buyer</u> looked toward the <u>stage</u>. Then <u>spotlights</u> filled the stage with color, and <u>cheers</u> filled the air. <u>Fans</u> danced in the aisles when <u>the Windwalkers</u> began to play <u>"Glad We're Together."</u> The band performed for <u>three hours</u>. During the last <u>song</u>, <u>fireworks</u> shot into the air, and the crowd went wild. What <u>a thrill</u> fills our hearts when we remember that <u>evening</u>!

Numerals

Ways of Writing Cardinals and Ordinals, EXERCISE A
 1. ninety-one, cardinal
 2. twenty-third, ordinal
 3. four hundred forty, cardinal
 4. four thousand four hundred four, cardinal
 5. two hundred eighty-seventh, ordinal
 6. six hundred twelve, cardinal
 7. seven thousand fifteenth, ordinal
 8. three thousand three hundred twenty-second, ordinal
 9. fifty thousand five, cardinal
10. eleven million, cardinal

Ways of Writing Cardinals and Ordinals, EXERCISE B
Peat Moss would be in town for <u>two</u> shows only. <u>One</u> day before tickets went on sale at Blue Tiger Music, <u>three</u> of my friends and I thought about camping in front of the store—from about <u>ten</u> o'clock or so—to make sure that we got good seats. Mr. Adams told me that tickets cost (<u>$32.00</u>) each, plus a (<u>$4.00</u>) service charge, that he could sell only <u>six</u> per customer—and that each customer's place in line would be determined by a lottery!

"You mean, we could be <u>first</u> in line but <u>fiftieth</u> at the cash register?" I gasped.

"You even could be <u>one hundredth</u>—this'll be a popular gig," he replied.

Sure of our strategy, we met the next morning and took the (<u>#10</u>) bus to the mall. <u>Thirty-five</u> people were already standing outside Blue Tiger Music! "Swell," Melanie complained. "I knew we should have been here by <u>eight</u> o'clock!"

"It doesn't matter," I reminded her. "We have just as good a chance of being <u>first</u> as they do.

<u>Two</u> hours later, we were congratulating ourselves. The person <u>four</u> places ahead of Melanie was pulled in the lottery, giving her the <u>fifth</u> position for buying tickets. We were poorer—but we had <u>twelfth</u>-row tickets to see Peat Moss!

Using Numerals Correctly, EXERCISE A

1. Apartment <u>19</u>-C
2. I have <u>three</u> rolls of quarters.
3. <u>5:25</u> P.M.
4. Is this <u>93</u> Morningstar Circle?
5. B. Camels
    <u>1</u>. Dromedary
    <u>2</u>. Bactrian
6. about <u>500</u> B.C.
7. <u>1700</u> Beach Drive
8. 6525 <u>Fifth</u> Avenue North
9. I've collected <u>370</u> aluminum cans.
10. For the party, we'll need <u>10</u> pizzas, <u>30</u> cans of pop, and about 180 minutes of music.

Using Numerals Correctly, EXERCISE B

<u>290</u> Griswold Street
Waldo, OH 43356
October <u>3</u>, <u>1994</u>

Pampered Pets, Inc.
<u>1411</u> Lane Avenue
Suite <u>20</u>-A
Solana Beach, CA 92075

Dear Sir or Madam:

On September <u>16</u> I placed a mail order with Pampered Pets, Inc. Here's what I ordered:

A. Accessories
    <u>1</u>. <u>three</u> dog collars
    <u>2</u>. a "fire hydrant" bandana

B. Health-care products
    <u>1</u>. a box of NutriTreats
    <u>2</u>. <u>two</u> bottles of Flea Free Dip

The order arrived only <u>nine</u> days after I'd mailed it (about <u>3:30</u> P.M.). The collars, the bandana, and the shampoo were fine.

However, I have <u>one</u> complaint about the NutriTreats. According to the catalog, a box of NutriTreats is supposed to contain "<u>150</u> nutritious nibbles." The box I received contained not <u>150</u>, not <u>149</u>, but <u>146</u> pieces! Pepper (my dog) and I would appreciate your sending those <u>four</u> missing NutriTreats. I've enclosed a self-addressed, stamped (<u>29¢</u>) envelope for that purpose.

Thank you for your cooperation.

Sincerely,

Zane Wilkins

Parentheses

Using Parentheses Correctly, EXERCISE A

1. The dorm was draped with bougainvillea <u>(</u>tropical vines with bright flowers<u>)</u>.
2. Gabrielle <u>(</u>What a good student she is!<u>)</u> loves Keats.
3. John Keats <u>(</u>1795-1821<u>)</u> wrote "Lamia."
4. Gaby reads aloud to me. <u>(</u>She does have a nice voice.<u>)</u> Hearing the poetry helps me understand it.

Using Parentheses Correctly, EXERCISE B

1. He wore a lugubrious <u>(</u>very mournful<u>)</u> expression.
2. Sixty percent of the boys <u>(</u>25<u>)</u> joined the club.
3. Humphrey Bogart <u>(</u>1899-1957<u>)</u> won an Academy Award.
4. Few people liked the film <u>(</u>The subtitles did not help.<u>)</u>
5. Dwight raised his hand <u>(</u>Does he never give up?<u>)</u> The class tried to ignore him.

Using Parentheses Correctly, EXERCISE C
1. The punishment was ostracism (banishment or exclusion).
2. Carla (She is such a world traveler!) spent two weeks in Switzerland.
3. The house rents for five hundred dollars ($500) a month.
4. Tennis is a tricky (and occasionally hazardous) game.

Periods

Using Periods at the Ends of Sentences and Direct Quotations, EXERCISE A
1. In May, however, a friend introduced her to Jim.
2. Although she still liked Tony, she started thinking a lot about Jim.
3. Other
4. Patty said that she really didn't know.
5. Other
6. "Yes! He's asked me to go to a movie with him," Stephanie replied.
7. Other
8. "It would be great—if I knew what to do," Stephanie sighed.
9. "Tell Tony that you want to date other guys," Patty advised.
10. "After all, you're not married, you know."

Using Periods at the Ends of Sentences and Direct Quotations, EXERCISE B
   We had a wonderful time, but we should have planned our trip better. The park opens at 10:00, but we didn't get there until 12:30. As we bought our tickets, the clerk said, "Take this map." By that time, we were starving. We found a restaurant and ordered lunch. Meanwhile, we studied the map. I explained, "This shows where all the attractions are and what time the various shows start." A show called "Symphony of the Sea" began at 1:30 at the White Whale and Dolphin Stadium. Unfortunately, the restaurant was crowded, and it took us a long time to be served. We missed the 1:30 show, so we decided to go and see the sharks being fed.

Using Periods at the Ends of Sentences and Direct Quotations, EXERCISE C
Sentences will vary; possible sentences, for the second topic, are given.
1. We advertised a 9:00 A.M. opening, but shoppers started showing up at 7:45.
2. One of them cheerfully called to me, "The early bird gets the worm."
3. Michelle, please write down the purchases as you watch the cash box.
4. Two customers argued over a few old pieces of milk glass.
5. "Please be patient," I urged them. "I'm sure that we can make everybody happy."

Other Uses of Periods, EXERCISE A
1. 4.5 miles
2. $7.35
3. P. A. Reyes
4. 7.8 liters
5. $21.80
6. 11.3 kilograms
7. J. E. Kingsland
8. $170.52
9. 90.04 meters
10. H. K. Brown

Other Uses of Periods, EXERCISE B
I am writing to complain about the service I have received from your company. On June 4, 1994, I ordered a tote bag from your catalog. I wanted to use it when I went swimming at the YMCA this summer. The bag cost $5.95. I sent a check for that amount and signed it S. A. Beecher.

I waited a month but heard nothing from your company. When I called, the salesperson said that since the bag weighed 1.2 pounds, I should have sent $1.04 extra for postage. How was I supposed to know that? Please cancel my order and refund my money.

Sincerely yours,
S. A. Beecher

Other Uses of Periods, EXERCISE C
Sentences will vary; possible sentences are given.
1. We visited the store owned by A. D. Gardner.
2. We bought 2.5 pounds of oranges there.
3. The total bill for our groceries came to $57.58.
4. My mother signed the check C. M. Anderson.
5. We forgot that the recipe called for 1.75 pounds of apples, as well.

Phrases

Identifying and Using Types of Phrases, EXERCISE A
1. infinitive phrase
2. adjective phrase
3. appositive phrase
4. adverb phrase
5. participial phrase
6. infinitive phrase
7. gerund phrase
8. verb phrase
9. infinitive phrase
10. adverb phrase

Identifying and Using Types of Phrases, EXERCISE B
New sentences will vary; possible sentences are given.
1. is known, verb phrase; as a poet, adverb phrase; Christina Rossetti is remembered best for her poetry, but she also was a painter.
2. Lacking self-confidence, participial phrase; to become a famous poet, infinitive phrase; Being unsure of herself, Rossetti didn't try to achieve fame.
3. Having a melancholy nature, gerund phrase; to her potential, adjective phrase; Suffering bouts of melancholy also was a roadblock for her.
4. a voluminous poet, appositive phrase; of poor and uneven quality, adjective phrase; Rossetti, that busy author, wrote some poems with poor, uneven features.
5. At her best, adjective phrase; Like the greatest writers, however, she penned exquisitely beautiful poems.

Identifying and Using Types of Phrases, EXERCISE C
Answers will vary; a possible paragraph is given.
　Laughing hysterically, the alien, a strange, other-worldly creature, bounced out of its space capsule. Looking about gleefully was all the creature with green skin could do for a long time. Then the alien, eyeing the ground, fell on its back and rolled luxuriously in the long grass. Then it suddenly leaped up and ran to get a camera from the capsule. "I am required to take pictures," it cried, "or no one will believe me when I tell them what I did on my summer vacation!" What a strange dream that was!

Identifying Functions of Phrases, EXERCISE A
1. adverb
2. adjective, adverb
3. adjective
4. adjective
5. noun, noun
6. adjective, adjective
7. noun

Identifying Functions of Phrases, EXERCISE B
New sentences will vary: possible sentences are given.
1. noun; <u>Keeping up with the opposing guard</u>, Jevon burned out quickly.
2. adverb; The coach's motive for bringing in the substitute was <u>to gain an advantage</u>.
3. noun; Stanley was the player <u>shooting a three-point basket</u>.
4. adjective; The player stood <u>at the free-throw line</u>.
5. adjective; <u>Shooting a free-throw</u> was more difficult in the final minute.

Identifying Functions of Phrases, EXERCISE C
Answers will vary; possible answers are given.

<u>Looking out her window</u>, Marie noticed something unusual about the sunlight. <u>Stepping onto the lawn</u> gave her a feeling of <u>eerie misgiving</u>. She moved to <u>return to the house</u>, but something held her <u>against her will</u>. Something peculiar was happening. The sun, <u>shining from a blue sky</u>, didn't beat down <u>with its usual intensity</u>. Shadows <u>falling on the ground</u> were not as deep. Then she realized <u>with a sigh of relief</u> that she was experiencing a solar eclipse! <u>Witnessing this astronomical phenomenon</u> was an exciting event!

Using Commas with Phrases, EXERCISE A
1. correct
2. incorrect
3. incorrect
4. correct
5. incorrect
6. incorrect
7. incorrect
8. correct
9. incorrect
10. correct

Using Commas with Phrases, EXERCISE B
1. Knowing that the loser died, the strongest trembled, having little hope of victory.
2. Looking for a fight, Heracles, the greatest hero of all, visited Antaeus.
3. Correct
4. By touching the earth, Antaeus grew stronger, laughing as Heracles tired.
5. Heracles, discovering the secret, lifted Antaeus into the air, keeping him off the ground.

Using Commas with Phrases, EXERCISE C
Homer, the most famous ancient Greek storyteller, is more mythic than his stories. According to legend, he was blind. To claim that he lived around 1000 B.C. is only a guess, though a reasonable one. The stories that Homer told are much older, having been passed down orally by generations of storytellers. Homer's two best-known poems, the *Iliad* and the *Odyssey*, date from hundreds of years before Homer lived.

Using Phrases Correctly, EXERCISE A
 1. correct
 2. incorrect; Designed to explore the planets, <u>the spacecraft were prepared by NASA</u> to exit our system.
 3. incorrect; Carrying with them a gold-coated copper phonograph record, <u>the spacecraft can share information about Earth.</u>
 4. incorrect; The record has audio and video messages to tell any alien life about Earth.
 5. correct
 6. incorrect; To identify our location, <u>a map</u> of our solar system and galaxy <u>is included</u>.
 7. correct
 8. incorrect; <u>Extraterrestrials finding the spacecraft</u> will know exactly where we are.
 9. correct
10. incorrect; The message to any alien life forms also includes <u>music from around the world</u>.

Using Phrases Correctly, EXERCISE B
Paragraphs may vary slightly; a possible paragraph is given.

<u>Appearing in 1740,</u> the English novel has a peculiar history. Its origin can be traced to a social gathering <u>of young women</u> in Samuel Richardson's London home. Serving as a sort of eighteenth-century *Dear Abby,* <u>Richardson gave the young ladies advice</u> on personal matters. <u>Going even further,</u> he often wrote letters to suitors on their behalf. Writing the letters frequently, <u>Richardson was successful with them. It occurred to Richardson that perhaps writing an entire book of universal letters about specific problems might be popular. Someone needing a good letter could choose one from the book, copy it, and send it.</u> Richardson wrote the book, and it was a hit. <u>Inspired by his success,</u> Richardson then wrote *Pamela,* the first English novel. It was written <u>as a series of letters</u> to and from a young woman, Pamela. Pamela, <u>being aggressively pursued by a man,</u> desperately needed advice.

Developing Your Style: Phrases, EXERCISE A
Answers may vary; possible answers are given.
 1. Iris had been walking for hours <u>in the 100-degree heat</u>.
 2. To get to that cold bottle <u>of orange juice</u> was all she could imagine.
 3. <u>Although knowing better,</u> Iris had gone for a walk without carrying water.
 4. She had become lost in the arroyo, <u>wandering aimlessly</u>.
 5. Iris had followed the wrong side-canyon, <u>a dry, sandy dead-end</u>.
 6. Heat bounced <u>in palpable waves</u> off the arroyo's walls.
 7. She stumbled along, <u>tripping in the deep sand</u>.
 8. Finally, <u>rounding a bend,</u> she saw the trail.
 9. <u>In a stupor of exhaustion,</u> Iris climbed the bank of the arroyo.
10. Her car, <u>shimmering in the heat,</u> stood a few yards away.

Developing Your Style: Phrases, EXERCISE B
Answers will vary; possible answers are given.
 1. Lyle Medwick, <u>a sophomore,</u> wants to become a novelist.
 2. <u>Writing a novel</u> with the power of Dickens is his goal.
 3. Like Dickens, he tries <u>to create characters in expansive detail.</u>
 4. He creates characters <u>for his stories</u> from people in his neighborhood.
 5. <u>With their exaggerated personalities,</u> his characters seem rather unrealistic.
 6. Lyle writes <u>with a great sense of humor</u>.
 7. <u>Compared to Dickens' writing,</u> Lyle's focuses on less serious subjects.
 8. <u>To make serious subjects humorous</u> is very difficult for Lyle, who has trouble mixing serious themes and high comedy.
 9. Lyle shares one other characteristic <u>with Dickens</u>.
10. He describes events <u>in such detail</u> that his stories become lengthy.

Possessives

Identifying and Forming Possessive Nouns and Pronouns, EXERCISE A
1. <u>Its</u> Oval Office has been the work area of many Presidents.
2. This <u>office's</u> furniture changes with each President.
3. Abigail <u>Adams'</u> laundry was hung in the unfinished East Room.
4. The Kennedy <u>children's</u> antics once enlivened the White House.
5. Do you ever wish that <u>someone else's</u> room was <u>yours</u>?

Identifying and Forming Possessive Nouns and Pronouns, EXERCISE B
1. Frances was beautiful—and <u>Fran's</u> popularity won Grover Cleveland many votes.
2. The distress in Congress after President <u>Wilson's</u> stroke was understandable.
3. Afterward, the <u>President's</u> signature did not resemble those on earlier documents.
4. One of <u>Mrs. Kennedy's</u> contributions was to change upholstery.
5. Landscaping requires a full-time <u>gardener's</u> attention.
6. During the Wilson administration, the <u>sheep's</u> grazing kept the lawn trimmed.
7. The Tafts lived in the White House in 1908; the <u>Tafts'</u> cow was named Pauline.
8. Correct
9. The <u>Clintons'</u> <u>cat's</u> name is Socks.
10. Correct

Identifying and Forming Possessive Nouns and Pronouns, EXERCISE C
Answers will vary; possible answers are given.
1. The <u>roses'</u> aroma from the nearby garden drifts into the Oval Office.
2. <u>President Hayes's</u> wife initiated the White House Egg Hunt.
3. The <u>diplomat's</u> car bore flags on its fenders.
4. Their pictures, taken inside, were too dark; <u>ours</u>, however, were perfect.
5. Look at this glass; <u>its</u> rim is chipped.

Using Possessive Forms Correctly, EXERCISE A
1. The Spanish, <u>whose</u> treasure ship sank in 1622, were stunned.
2. <u>Its</u> name was the *Atocha*.
3. <u>It's</u> said that in <u>its</u> hold were forty-seven tons of gold and silver.
4. Mel Fisher and his sons Dirk and Kim wanted the gold to be <u>theirs</u>.
5. <u>Mel's and Dirk's</u> boats sailed in different directions.
6. Unfortunately, <u>Dirk and his wife's</u> boat sank.
7. Lyon, a friend of <u>Fisher's</u>, helped research the ship's location.
8. <u>Fisher and Lyon's</u> research paid off.
9. Fisher located the <u>*Santa Margarita's* and the *Atocha's*</u> treasures.
10. <u>Who's</u> responsible for deciding <u>whose</u> treasure it is?

Using Possessive Forms Correctly, EXERCISE B
1. The shovels were <u>theirs</u>.
2. They lifted the box and found <u>its</u> contents heavy.
3. <u>Jason and Erik's</u> dog began to howl.
4. <u>Whose</u> brother is calling?
5. A brother of <u>Jack's</u> is calling. *or* <u>Jack's</u> brother is calling.

Using Possessive Forms Correctly, EXERCISE C

Answers will vary; possible answers are given.
1. William Clark helped educate <u>Sacajawea and Charbonneau's</u> son.
2. The expedition used <u>Clark's</u> raft.
3. The Shoshones gave their information, and the Mandans gave <u>theirs</u>.
4. <u>Marquette and Joliet's</u> earlier expedition took place in 1673.
5. <u>Whose</u> death is a mystery because he was found shot to death in an inn?

Developing Your Style: Streamlining Sentences with Possessive Forms, EXERCISE A
1. The Marquis imprisons <u>Lucie Manette's</u> father. Mr. Lorry arranges for <u>his</u> release.
2. The book depicts <u>the peasants'</u> anger during the French Revolution. <u>Their</u> wrath led to violence.
3. <u>Madame Defarge's</u> cruel deeds reflect this violence. <u>Her</u> knitting even records a coded list of victims.
4. What were <u>the Revolution's</u> goals? What was <u>its</u> outcome?

Developing Your Style: Streamlining Sentences with Possessive Forms, EXERCISE B

Answers will vary; possible answers are given.
1. The <u>music's</u> originality pleased the Emperor.
2. The play *Amadeus* is based on <u>Mozart's</u> life.
3. <u>His</u> enemy was the rival composer Salieri.
4. The <u>Mozarts'</u> expenditures drove them into bankruptcy.
5. Mozart was given a <u>pauper's</u> burial.

Developing Your Style: Streamlining Sentences with Possessive Forms, EXERCISE C

Answers will vary; possible answers are given.

The <u>drums'</u> roll signaled the <u>overture's</u> beginning. The <u>trumpeters'</u> blast nearly drowned out the <u>flutist's</u> solo. The conductor noticed the <u>soloist's</u> nervousness and waved <u>his</u> baton more slowly. No one noticed the <u>clarinetists'</u> inexperience. The <u>audience's</u> applause thrilled the young performers. <u>Their</u> concert represented many <u>hours'</u> practice.

Prepositions

Identifying and Using Prepositions and Prepositional Phrases, EXERCISE A

Adjective Phrase	Adverb Phrase
1. <u>among</u> American painters (leader)	<u>in</u> 1844 (was born)
2.	<u>with</u> her family (toured)
3. <u>in</u> France and Germany (museums)	
4. <u>of</u> seventeen (age)	<u>By</u> the age (had chosen)
<u>as</u> a painter (career)	
5. <u>in</u> an exhibition (painting)	<u>In</u> 1874 (was seen)
	<u>By</u> Edgar Degas (was seen)
6.	<u>to</u> several impressionist painters (introduced)

Identifying and Using Prepositions and Prepositional Phrases, EXERCISE B

Answers will vary; possible answers are given.
1. One afternoon <u>in September,</u> I visited the playground again. (adjective)
2. <u>In one corner,</u> several children were playing a noisy game of tag. (adverb)
3. I watched <u>with amusement</u> and shouted encouragement. (adverb)
4. Suddenly, children <u>around the playground</u> felt raindrops. (adjective)
5. The busy playground emptied <u>within two minutes</u>. (adverb)
6. I wish I could return <u>to my youth</u>. (adverb)
7. Some stories <u>about children</u> let me relive those days. (adjective)
8. Sometimes a photograph <u>of my childhood</u> will bring back memories. (adjective)
9. I can still remember the laughter <u>of children</u>. (adjective)
10. The happiness displayed <u>in that playground</u> was the greatest I have ever known. (adverb)

Using Prepositions Correctly, EXERCISE A

1. b
2. a
3. a
4. b
5. b

Using Prepositions Correctly, EXERCISE B

1. <u>To whom</u> did Raymond express his rage?
2. <u>Where</u> was the logic of his argument?
3. Did he compare his opponent <u>to</u> a clown?
4. The dispute was different <u>from</u> any I'd heard.
5. Do you remember <u>the topic of</u> the original lecture?

Using Prepositions Correctly, EXERCISE C

Answers may vary slightly; possible answers are given.

<u>Where</u> do bats hibernate? This is <u>the topic of</u> tonight's show. The host compares a bat's echolocation abilities <u>to</u> sonar and other location devices. Bats have a sense of place different <u>from</u> that of most other mammals. <u>On what</u> do they live?

Developing Your Style: Using Prepositional Phrases in Descriptions, EXERCISE A

1. I believe it is the Leaning Tower <u>of Pisa</u>.
2. Galileo used the Leaning Tower <u>for his experiments</u>.
3. Magda saw it <u>during her European vacation</u>.
4. I keep my souvenir pictures <u>in this album</u>.
5. This book illustrates the Seven Wonders <u>of the Ancient World</u>.

Developing Your Style: Using Prepositional Phrases in Descriptions, EXERCISE B

1. I have read several books <u>by Margaret Mead</u>.
2. We found the book <u>on the top shelf</u>.
3. My favorite version <u>of Dickens' *A Christmas Carol*</u> stars that famous English actor.
4. The two boys were frightened <u>by the dinosaurs</u>.
5. The special effects <u>in *Jurassic Park*</u> are quite realistic.

Developing Your Style: Using Prepositional Phrases in Descriptions, EXERCISE C

Answers will vary; possible answers are given.

The road <u>up the hill</u> was narrow, winding <u>through the trees</u>. Thick underbrush lined <u>each side of the road</u>. Wildflowers peeked <u>through the thick carpet of weeds</u>, dotting it <u>with color</u>. Birds and insects flew <u>among the flowers</u> <u>in their springtime ritual of pollination</u>.

Developing Your Style: Using Prepositional Phrases in Transitions, EXERCISE A

Answers will vary; possible answers are given.

1. My friend Donna gave a party <u>in early May</u>.
2. <u>On April 15</u> she sent out fancy invitations.
3. <u>During late April</u> she planned an elaborate menu.
4. <u>At six o'clock</u> the first guests arrived <u>early</u>.
5. <u>After that</u>, several cars pulled into the driveway.
6. The five-piece band began to play <u>at six-thirty</u>.
7. <u>Around eight</u>, dinner was served in the sunroom.
8. <u>After dinner</u>, people began dancing again.
9. Most of the guests stayed <u>until midnight</u>.
10. <u>After their departure</u>, Donna collapsed, exhausted but happy.

Developing Your Style: Using Prepositional Phrases in Transitions, EXERCISE B

Answers will vary; possible answers are given.

1. <u>In April</u> I selected a tree on which to hang my bird house.
2. <u>During the first week of May</u>, I saw two tree swallows swooping past the house.
3. <u>After a short time</u>, one of the swallows stopped and peered inside.
4. <u>During this time</u>, the other swallow watched from a high branch.
5. <u>From that moment</u>, I kept the dogs as far from the bird house as possible.

Developing Your Style: Using Prepositional Phrases in Transitions, EXERCISE C

Answers will vary; possible answers are given.

    <u>In August</u> I took my nephew to the movies. <u>At that time</u>, he wanted to see *Aladdin.* I had already seen it <u>about a year ago</u>. Nevertheless, we stood in line together <u>for an hour</u>. <u>After a long wait</u>, we went into the theater. <u>In no time at all</u>, he picked a seat near the front. I sat him on my lap <u>for a while</u>. <u>After that</u>, he wanted his own seat. <u>During a quiet scene</u>, he scrambled into the seat next to mine. <u>In an instant</u>, his seat folded up with him inside!

Pronouns

Identifying and Using Personal Pronouns, EXERCISE A

1. him, his; Correct
2. him, I; A new student will be sitting between him and <u>me</u>.
3. her, our; Brenda and <u>she</u> will be studying together for our economics test.
4. them, me; The guests of honor are <u>they</u> and <u>I</u>.
5. we; Correct
6. Ours, their; <u>Ours</u> are the gray-and-white striped beach blankets by their umbrella.
7. she; How the beauty of the surroundings pleased Anna and <u>her</u>.
8. them; Kim wants to go the basketball game as much as <u>they</u>.
9. him, they, them; Correct
10. she, them; Please show <u>her</u> and them the science laboratory.

Identifying and Using Personal Pronouns, EXERCISE B

Answers will vary; possible answers are given.

1. Arthur and <u>I</u> are the best anglers in the Fishing Club.
2. Leilani and Todd are almost as good at casting as <u>they</u>.
3. Barney gave <u>her</u> a new computerized rod and reel as a birthday present.
4. Hearing about our fun, the Turners and <u>they</u> became avid anglers, too.
5. <u>I</u> prefer drift fishing because <u>it</u> takes so little work.

Identifying and Using Interrogative and Relative Pronouns, EXERCISE A

1. whose (relative)
2. that (relative)
3. whatever (relative)
4. Whose (interrogative)
5. which (relative)
6. Whoever (interrogative)
7. Who (interrogative); whom (relative)
8. who (relative)
9. that (relative)

Identifying and Using Interrogative and Relative Pronouns, EXERCISE B
Some answers may vary; possible answers are given.

Once there were twelve lovely princesses <u>whose</u> mysterious evening antics were driving their royal father crazy—and broke. Every day for months, the princesses had awakened to find their slippers worn clear through—a circumstance <u>that</u> forced the king to buy his daughters new slippers. "<u>Whatever</u> happens to your slippers every night?" asked the king, <u>who</u> was perplexed and annoyed. The girls replied <u>that</u> they had no idea, for they slept soundly every night through.

At his wit's end, and with bankruptcy staring him in the face, the king decreed, "<u>Whoever</u> shall solve the mystery of the princesses' slippers shall marry the princess of his choice." However, the princesses objected. Cried the eldest, "How will you know if the person to <u>whom</u> you give one of us is worthy—or just lucky?"

"But, my dears," replied the king, "<u>What</u> can I do? The treasury is nearly empty!"

"Our happiness, about <u>which</u> you claim to care, will be ruined!"

"Very well," sighed the beleagured father, "I'll do <u>whatever</u> you suggest."

Identifying and Using Interrogative and Relative Pronouns, EXERCISE C
Sentences will vary; possible sentences are given.
1. <u>What</u> do you think <u>that</u> I should do?
2. These packages, <u>which</u> have been sitting here for two days, must be picked up by someone <u>who</u> will take responsibility for them.
3. To <u>whom</u> did you give the report, and <u>whose</u> signature appears on it?
4. <u>Whomever</u> will you approach for advice about the plans <u>that</u> must be made?
5. Kurt agreed <u>that</u> you were right, and he promised to do <u>whatever</u> you thought best.

Identifying and Using Demonstrative Pronouns, EXERCISE A
1. This
2. these
3. Those
4. that
5. Those

Identifying and Using Demonstrative Pronouns, EXERCISE B
1. That, suit
2. this, None
3. these, belts
4. Those, pairs
5. this, jacket

Identifying and Using Demonstrative Pronouns, EXERCISE C
1. <u>This</u> is a perfect topaz crystal, one of many found in Siberia.
2. Azurite, a copper mineral, is always a blue shade. <u>That</u> will be crushed and used as pigment.
3. Quartz is an ideal gemstone for carving and cutting. <u>These</u> will become part of pins, rings, earrings, and pendants.
4. Diamonds are crystals of pure, immensely hard carbon. <u>Those</u> of outstanding luster and brilliant cut are highly prized.
5. Of the beryl gems, emeralds and aquamarines are the best known. <u>These</u> are popular as gemstones due to their durability and deep, rich color.

Identifying and Using Indefinite Pronouns, EXERCISE A
New sentences will vary; possible sentences are given. Indefinite pronouns are underlined.
1. Someone; <u>No one</u> has eaten my banana!
2. No one, something; <u>Few</u> believed his alibi; <u>everything</u> remained a mystery.
3. Many, everyone; <u>Several</u> reported seeing the eclipse, but <u>all</u> were careful not to look directly at the sun.
4. neither; I have two choices, and <u>both</u> are unattractive.
5. everything; Did you get <u>all</u> that was on the list?
6. all, one; Theresa knows <u>most</u> of my cousins—except a <u>few</u> whom she's never met.
7. Most; <u>All</u> the stores in the mall are still open.
8. Several, few; <u>Many</u> of my friends walk to school, but <u>others</u> take the bus.
9. Nobody, all; <u>No one</u> is available to help you; <u>several</u> of the workers are repaving the main road.
10. both; Has <u>either</u> of the twins finished his (or her) homework?
11. One, another; <u>Some</u> of the streetlights are broken; <u>others</u> are sputtering badly.
12. everyone; Did <u>someone</u> in our class go to the Halloween party?
13. Some, others; A <u>few</u> of these newspapers are torn; <u>many</u> are poorly folded.

Identifying and Using Indefinite Pronouns, EXERCISE B
Some answers may vary; possible answers are given.
1. something
2. Some (neighbors)
3. None (us)
4. couple (paramedics)
5. nothing (it); somebody
6. anyone; another
7. some (family)
8. Everything

Identifying and Using Reflexive and Intensive Pronouns, EXERCISE A
1. ourselves (reflexive)
2. himself (intensive)
3. herself (intensive)
4. herself (reflexive)
5. themselves (reflexive)

Identifying and Using Reflexive and Intensive Pronouns, EXERCISE B
1. The townsfolk decided to restore many historic buildings <u>themselves</u>. (intensive)
2. The president of the town council appointed <u>himself</u> the director of the historical society. (reflexive)
3. Mrs. MacGillicuddy, <u>herself</u> a descendent of one of the town's founders, donated many original documents. (intensive)
4. We congratulated <u>ourselves</u> when the project was finished. (reflexive)

Identifying and Using Reflexive and Intensive Pronouns, EXERCISE C
Answers may vary; possible answers are given.

I decided to redecorate my office <u>myself</u>. I knew I could do it, but my family wasn't so sure. I sat <u>myself</u> down to listen.

"You broke your leg the time you tried to hang wallpaper <u>yourself</u>," my mother pointed out when I stood and took books from the shelves. "Here, let me help you carry those."

"You gave <u>yourself</u> a smashed thumb when we built shelves <u>ourselves</u>," my brother reminded me. "Here, let me lift that."

"Remember when you cut <u>yourself</u> with the yardstick?" my sister asked. "Ask <u>yourself</u> if you want to go through that again."

"Some people, you know," my dad remarked kindly, "aren't made to do it themselves," and he and my brother began to mix the paint <u>themselves</u>.

I positioned <u>myself</u> on the bottom stair to direct the crew I had handpicked <u>myself</u>.

Pronouns and Antecedents, EXERCISE A
1. all (relatives); his (Denis)
2. themselves (Julie, Scott); him (None)
3. everyone (None); himself (Scott)
4. whose (cake); he (Denis)
5. Those (guests); who (guests)

Pronouns and Antecedents, EXERCISE B
Answers will vary; possible answers are given.
1. The music <u>teacher</u> forgot <u>her</u> instrument.
2. I wonder <u>which</u> of the <u>instruments</u> she will be able to borrow.
3. <u>Ted</u> said, "Ms. Hill, <u>I</u> would be glad to lend you my violin."
4. Now the <u>orchestra</u> is ready for <u>its</u> rehearsal to begin.
5. The <u>students</u> are playing better today than <u>they</u> did yesterday.

Pronouns and Antecedents, EXERCISE C
Some answers may vary; possible answers are given.
1. <u>This</u> is the team's favorite <u>restaurant</u>.
2. <u>Some</u> of the <u>players</u> are eating hot dogs.
3. <u>Jesse</u> and <u>Tim</u> ordered meals for <u>themselves</u>.
4. Only <u>one</u> of the <u>diners</u> wants dessert.
5. <u>Which</u> of the <u>students</u> will pay for this meal?
6. Either <u>Tab</u> or <u>Ravi</u> has <u>his</u> money.
7. The <u>waitress</u> has lost <u>her</u> pen.
8. <u>Ravi</u>, have <u>you</u> been able to find it?
9. No; in fact, <u>this</u> is Caleb's <u>marker</u>.
10. It is a writing <u>instrument that</u> will have to make do for now.

Using Personal Pronouns Correctly, EXERCISE A
1. My
2. she
3. me
4. they
5. us

Using Personal Pronouns Correctly, EXERCISE B
 1. he, predicate nominative
 2. me, indirect object
 3. I, subject (of understood clause)
 4. We, appositive of a subject; he, subject (of understood clause)

Using Personal Pronouns Correctly, EXERCISE C
Sentences will vary; possible sentences are given.
 1. <u>We</u> carpenters are proud of our work.
 2. Can I reach Vince and <u>them</u> at the store?
 3. My tennis instructor is <u>she</u>.
 4. In physics class, I sit in front of Jan and <u>her</u>.
 5. Randy sent both Valerie and <u>you</u> an invitation to his party.
 6. Does it surprise you that Al cooks as well as <u>I</u>?
 7. <u>Our</u> talking in the library earned us a reprimand.
 8. Mr. Pappas is very patient as he trains <u>us</u> gymnasts.
 9. Jeanne handed my sister and <u>me</u> the mail.
10. Between you and <u>me</u>, I think that Tara deserves to win.

Using Interrogative and Relative Pronouns Correctly, EXERCISE A
 1. Correct
 2. Incorrect
 3. Incorrect
 4. Correct
 5. Incorrect

Using Interrogative and Relative Pronouns Correctly, EXERCISE B
 1. <u>Whoever</u> is the last one to leave, please shut the door.
 2. <u>Whose</u> gray scarf is this?
 3. Correct
 4. The weather report <u>that</u> you heard must have been inaccurate.
 5. Ms. Martin is an actress <u>whose</u> career we should follow carefully.

Using Interrogative and Relative Pronouns Correctly, EXERCISE C
   A sword embedded in stone? <u>Who</u> would take on the challenge? Whoever did—and was successful—would become High King. Most believed that he <u>whose</u> arm had strength enough to draw the sword would be a famous knight—someone whose great deeds were known near and far. Thus, when young Wart, a skinny lad <u>who</u> everyone knew could hardly lift the kettle from over the fire, faced the strange phenomenon, no crowd gathered round. He stood alone, this scrawny boy <u>whom</u> the sword called, and he studied the weapon angled in the rock. Perhaps, reasoned Wart, <u>whoever</u> was destined to draw out the sword didn't need strength. Perhaps the challenger simply needed faith.

Using Indefinite and Reflexive Pronouns Correctly, EXERCISE A
 1. Correct
 2. Incorrect
 3. Incorrect
 4. Correct
 5. Incorrect

Using Indefinite and Reflexive Pronouns Correctly, EXERCISE B
1. Eliza and <u>she</u> entered the dimly lit room.
2. Was this article written by Verity and <u>you</u>?
3. Most of the pie <u>was</u> still left.
4. Brian decided to check the safety lock <u>himself</u>.
5. Somebody on the boys' team left <u>his</u> bat.
6. Either of the critics will be glad to give you <u>his</u> (or <u>her</u>) opinion.
7. Richard and she planned the entire program <u>themselves</u>.
8. Someone with a large dog by <u>her</u> (or <u>his</u>) side is waiting for her.
9. Most of the workers donated some of <u>their</u> earnings.
10. Each of my friends brought <u>his or her</u> CD's to the party.

Using Indefinite and Reflexive Pronouns Correctly, EXERCISE C

The gardens once had been the finest in the land, even though now none <u>were</u> cared for or pruned or cultivated. All the trees grew riotously, <u>their</u> branches intertwined. Many of the plants spread <u>their</u> roots above ground, completely covering the gardens' walks in places. Each of the rosebushes had lost <u>its</u> blooms years ago; the plants' brambles twisted back around <u>themselves</u> in sharp, wicked knots.

Developing Your Style: Pronouns, EXERCISE A
Some answers may vary; possible answers are given.
1. Sheila can't believe that <u>she</u> has won the state's Superspeller Award.
2. The last four contestants couldn't spell *opalescence,* but Sheila spelled <u>it</u> easily.
3. <u>"I wouldn't last a round,"</u> Pete told Jamal.
4. Many losing students said that <u>studying word lists and dictionaries</u> didn't help.

Developing Your Style: Pronouns, EXERCISE B
Sentences will vary; possible sentences are given.
1. <u>"I have to complete the assignment before the end of the day,"</u> Davis told Willis.
2. Joan asked Terry, <u>"Can you go to the movies?"</u>
3. <u>Moving</u> all the desks from the first-floor rooms was hard work.
4. <u>The Smiths told the Johnsons, who were getting their home ready to sell, that help might be needed</u> to get the house in shape for selling.

Developing Your Style: Pronouns, EXERCISE C
Answers will vary; possible answers are given.

Detective Donovan pulled up a chair, opened <u>his</u> notebook and then sat down. <u>He</u> looked at the suspects around the table, one by one. As <u>he</u> eyed Pasty-faced Pete, Pete straightened. <u>When Donovan looked at Awful Alice, she</u> <u>shivered and looked away.</u> <u>Donovan's piercing look</u> had an adverse effect on Conniving Colette as well, and she refused to meet <u>the detective's eyes.</u> Donovan motioned to his sidekick, Ensign Ed, <u>who</u> pushed a folder at him. Opening the folder, <u>Donovan</u> quickly read the report that it contained; then he left <u>both</u> on the table as he stood up. When he surreptitiously jerked his head<u>, Ed left the room.</u>

Question Marks

Using Question Marks Correctly, EXERCISE A
1. In a lunar eclipse, does the earth block the sun<u>?</u>
2. Is your confusion because we call it "lunar"<u>?</u>
3. "Think of it this way, won't you<u>?</u>" Dr. Po suggested.
4. "Don't both eclipses involve the sun<u>?</u>" I asked.
5. It is a bit confusing, isn't it<u>?</u>

Using Question Marks Correctly, EXERCISE B
1. Have you ever read *The Joys of Yiddish?*
2. For a dictionary, it's a lot of fun, isn't it?
3. It has a lexicon, but aren't the definitions unusual?
4. Mr. Roston includes many jokes, doesn't he?
5. What do people mean when they use the word *farblondjet?*
6. Did you read this example: "He drove toward New Rochelle but got so farblondjet that he ended up in White Plains"?
7. Rosten seems to ask, "Why should a dictionary be dull?"
8. Something should liven it up—but what?
9. He asks the reader to take an interest in culture.
10. "Why not," says Rosten, "make learning fun?"

Using Question Marks Correctly, EXERCISE C
Answers will vary; possible answers are given.
1. "Sally, have you met Hiro?" asked Dinah.
2. Sally asked, "Hiro, what do you like to read?"
3. "I like to read stories and novels by Ernest Hemingway and F. Scott Fitzgerald. Who is your favorite author?"
4. "I like Dickens, don't you?" asked Sally.
5. "I have heard of him," said Hiro. "Could you explain to me what he meant when he wrote, 'It was the best of times, it was the worst of times'"?

Quotation Marks

Using Quotation Marks with Direct Quotations, EXERCISE A
1. "The former owner's hobby must have been collecting old paint cans," complained Mary. "Why couldn't he clean out the basement?"
2. "We could make the cans into lamps or buckets," I joked.
3. "Wait a minute!" Mary said suddenly. "What's this?" She picked up a box.
4. "Let's get a screwdriver and try to open it," I suggested.
5. After ten minutes of effort, Mary pried open the box and shouted, "Wow! Just look at all this money—Monopoly money, that is!"

Using Quotation Marks with Direct Quotations, EXERCISE B
Some answers will vary slightly; possible answers are given.
1. The official stated, "We have difficult decisions to make."
2. "When is your next piano lesson?" Daphne asked me.
3. "I think," the inspector declared, "that the mystery is solved."
4. The coach said with conviction, "We can definitely win."
5. "Stand back!" the policeman ordered.
6. "Our prices are the lowest in town," the salesman claimed.
7. "Let's get out of here," the burglar yelled, "before we get caught."
8. "This appliance," he warned, "cannot be immersed in water."
9. "Is it time?" I asked. "Should I call the meeting to order?"
10. "What an outrage," he stormed, "this is!" "I will never work until midnight again."

Other Uses of Quotation Marks, EXERCISE A
1. "Bohemian Rhapsody"
2. "The Veldt"; "Hail and Farewell"
3. "Europeans Reach the Americas"; "Columbus"
4. "Jazzman"; "Deep Purple"
5. "without previous preparation"

Other Uses of Quotation Marks, EXERCISE B

1. Is tonight's assignment to read Chapter 14—"The Civil War Begins"?
2. Alone on the stage, Todd picked up a guitar and played "Cat's in the Cradle."
3. An antihero is commonly defined as "a protagonist who lacks the strengths of a heroic figure"; I guess that makes the title character of Melville's story "Bartleby the Scrivener" an antihero.
4. In the 1969 play, characters with nicknames like "Moonbeam" and "Dr. Peace" told the audience what a "bad trip" their life had been.
5. Two famous poems by Emily Dickinson, "The Belle of Amherst," are "It Dropped So Low" and "My Life Closed Twice."

Other Uses of Quotation Marks, EXERCISE C
Answers will vary; possible answers are given.

1. The festival began with a musical salute to Disney—everything from "A Dream Is a Wish Your Heart Makes," from *Cinderella*, to "A Whole New World," from *Aladdin*.
2. Then the host read an original poem, called "Dizzying Disney," as a humorous tribute to the great animator.
3. I think that <u>animator</u> means something like "one who gives life," right?
4. Octavian ("the Emperor") DeGrassi invited us to see his film, loosely based on Annie Dillard's essay "Total Eclipse," at the cinematheque.
5. He assured us that the film would be "fabuloso."
6. A <u>cinematheque</u> is defined as "a theater that shows vintage or experimental films."
7. How I wish that someone would make a film version of Alfred Noyes's poem "The Highwayman"; it could be incredibly romantic!
8. Of course, it would have to have a love theme—something like "Everything I Do, I Do for You," from *Robin Hood: Prince of Thieves*.

Quotations

Distinguishing Between Direct and Indirect Quotations, EXERCISE A

1. direct
2. indirect
3. direct
4. indirect

Distinguishing Between Direct and Indirect Quotations, EXERCISE B
Answers will vary; possible answers are given.

1. Alfonso announced that he could complete the experiment alone. (indirect)
2. Nia warned, "Doug, driving in heavy rain is dangerous." (direct)
3. Mrs. Diller shook her finger at her son, saying that she didn't want to hear one more word about what other kids got to do. (indirect)
4. Geneva complained that they should have chosen to do a play with more substance. (indirect)
5. Tanner suggested that we change some of the recipe ingredients. (indirect)
6. As the baseball hopped over the bat, Eric watched, startled, and then asked, "Tim, what trick are you using to produce the effect?" (direct)
7. Mr. Grady gathered the bedraggled kitten into his arms, crooning softly to the little fella that he'd have it warm, dry, and fed in a jiffy. (indirect)
8. "I don't believe in ghosts," announced Margot defiantly. "Furthermore, I insist on sleeping in the 'haunted' room." (direct)
9. "Stop!" screamed Jason at the top of his lungs as he raced after the puppy, frightening the poor little thing even more. (direct)
10. Maude pointed across the lawn and squealed that those two must have made up. (indirect)

Speaker Tags and Divided Quotations, EXERCISE A
1. "My mood is always more positive," Bette Jones informed us, "after my morning run."
2. "She is a brilliant poet who combines warmth and intellect," claimed Professor Vanister.
3. "Within five years, ten at the most," asserted editor T. Hawks, "every magazine in this country will be publishing on-line computer editions."
4. "I've given up trying to keep squirrels from stuffing themselves at my birdfeeder," sighed amateur naturalist Franklin Grandy.
5. "Some astounding pieces of journalism have recounted the sinking of the *Titanic*," maintained news reporter E. D. Chang.

Speaker Tags and Divided Quotations, EXERCISE B
1. "This is the best collection of antique motorcycles I've ever seen," announced motorcycle expert Joe Morris.
2. "My gosh!" cried one woman. "Look at that vintage Harley-Davidson motorcycle!"
3. "The first Harleys were produced in 1903," stated Joe, "but Daimler built one even earlier."
4. "About 1885 I think," broke in Judge Sam Adamson. "That makes motorcycles about the same age as cars," he continued, "give or take a couple of years."
5. "Older or younger," his wife claimed, "motorcycles have always been prized for their purchase prices, considerably lower than those of cars."
6. "Don't forget their manuevering ease and their low running costs," asserted Joe.
7. "That's interesting," said Mrs Adamson, looking up from a brochure. "Did you know that streamlining a motorcycle not only reduces wind resistance but also increases the machine's stability?"
8. Asked the man, "Does Harley-Davidson dominate the motorcycle market?"
9. "Between the wars, it did," Joe nodded.
10. "Now, of course, Japanese models lead the market," he added.

Using Quotations in Essays and Research Papers, EXERCISE A
1. b
2. a

Using Quotations in Essays and Research Papers, EXERCISE B
Answers will vary; possible answers are given.
1. Part of the secret of becoming an efficient writer is knowing when to let go of ideas that aren't working. As Isaac Bashevis Singer said, "The waste basket is the writer's best friend." As I've learned from my own experience, it's easier to develop a fresh idea than to flog a dead horse.
2. I wonder how different the world would be if we followed this advice from Bertrand Russell: "One must care about a world one will not see"? For one thing, we'd take better care of the environment; and we'd work harder to cure diseases. I think we'd treat children better, too. In short, we'd do the things that would make for a better future.
3. Isn't it amazing that so many people don't know how to be quiet and listen? As soon as we enter a room, we switch on the TV or radio to keep us company. If we find ourselves in a quiet space, we start to get jumpy after only a few minutes. In fact, as May Sarton has noted, "Most people have to talk so they won't hear."
4. Adlai Stevenson's famous proverb, "No gains without pains," has many applications. For example, athletes must train hard to perform well, and students sometimes must put aside other pleasures so that they can focus on their studies. Even within a family or a circle of friends, one often must make sacrifices for the welfare of the group.

Using Quotations in Essays and Research Papers, EXERCISE C
Answers will vary, but quotations should work together to support a single main idea.

Writing Dialogue, EXERCISE A
"What's inside that blue bag?" asked Brenda. "It looks so lumpy."
"I was waiting for you to ask," replied Jed. "This bag," he continued, "contains a bicycle."
Brenda stared skeptically at the bag. "What condition is it in?"
"Oh, it functions quite well," answered Jed. "It's my dad's folding bicycle."
"How convenient!" remarked Brenda.
"Yes, he takes it everywhere," said Jed. "My dad calls himself the 'celebrated city cyclist of Cincinnati.'"

Writing Dialogue, EXERCISE B
New dialogue will vary. Possible answers are given.
"Why are you examining this tent?" asked Robert.
"Well," said Wesley, "I remember you said, 'Let's' go hiking this fall!'"
"I was kidding!" cried Robert. "I'm the type who prefers a lush and luzurious hotel!"
"You'll love hiking on a crisp, clear day," Wesley insisted.
"Sitting quietly in the shade is preferable," replied Robert.
"Just imagine the morning sunrise where, as they say, 'the deer and the antelope play,'" said Wesley enticingly.
"I never rise before ten," replied his friend.
"Don't be ridiculous," said Wesley. "I know that you will change your mind.
"Don't be so sure," answered Robert. "I rarely change my mind about things that are fundamentally against my principles.
"I must say," said Wesley, "that you don't know what you're missing."

Semicolons

Using Semicolons Correctly, EXERCISE A
1. Arthur enjoys caring for animals; he wants to be a veterinarian.
2. In the morning, they completed tasks; in the evening they relaxed.
3. William loves all kinds of winter sports; I prefer the sand and sun.
4. I've visited Cumberland Island, Georgia; Sitka National Historical Park, Alaska; and Montezuma Castle National Monument, Arizona.
5. Once we almost missed our vacation; deciding where to go was so hard!
6. Arlene is inexperienced; in fact, this is only her second job.
7. My cousin sends for many catalogs; she loves to shop by mail.
8. I take notes after I read; otherwise, I forget some important points.
9. We discussed pros and cons after the game; it helps with future planning.
10. I ordered a hamburger, broiled and served on a bun; a large salad topped with Italian dressing; and peach sorbet, cool and refreshing.

Using Semicolons Correctly, EXERCISE A
A balloon can be used as an aircraft; a passenger sits in a basket-like structure. Helium is used to lift some balloons; other balloons use hot air. A hot-air balloon can be controlled by heating the air with a propane burner, an action that makes the craft ascend. Balloons are used by sports enthusiasts, having fun in the air; scientists, studying weather patterns; and military personnel, protecting areas from low-level attack. An amazing balloon flight was made by Ben Abruzzo; he flew from Japan to California in November 1981.

Sentences: Structure and Types

Identifying and Using Complete Subjects and Predicates, EXERCISE A
1. Huge generators (CS) / convert mechanical energy into electricity and thus provide most of our electrical energy (CP)
2. A single generator (CS) / may provide enough electrical power for a community of half a million people (CP)
3. Batteries, consisting of one or more electric cells (CS)/ change chemical energy into electricity (CP)
4. The electric power for artificial satellites and space capsules (CS) / comes from solar cells (CP)

Identifying and Using Complete Subjects and Predicates, EXERCISE B
Answers may vary slightly; possible answers are given.
1. Metals such as lead and tin can act as superconductors.
2. Our class has discussed the properties of insulators.
3. Insulators are made from materials such as glass and rubber.
4. The experiment involving the photo cells was fascinating.

Identifying and Using Complete Subjects and Predicates, EXERCISE C
Answers will vary; possible answers are given.
1. Tape players, washing machines, and light bulbs depend upon electric power.
2. The United States uses more electricity per person than any other country.
3. Computers and digital watches require integrated circuits.
4. The uses of electrical energy are still being explored.

Identifying and Using Simple and Compound Subjects and Predicates, EXERCISE A
1. (SS) (CP)   6.   (SS) (SP)
2. (CS) (CP)   7.   (CS) (SP)
3. (SS) (SP)   8.   (SS) (SP)
4. (CS) (SP)   9.   (CS) (CP)
5. (CS) (SP) 10. (SS) (CP)

Identifying and Using Simple and Compound Subjects and Predicates, EXERCISE B
1. The tornado wrecked the barn and flattened the house. (compound predicate)
2. Ryan and Jeff entered the talent show. (compound subject)
3. Scott was watching the game and eating a hot dog. (compound predicate)
4. Computers and telephones provide access to information and improve communication. (both)

Identifying and Using Simple and Compound Subjects and Predicates, EXERCISE C
Answers will vary; possible answers are given.
1. The boys were playing catch and listening to the stereo.
2. Joanna and Gerladine raced through the house and climbed into the attic.
3. The penguins at the zoo swim in the tank and eat fish on the rocks.
4. An enormous dish of ice cream stood waiting for me on the counter.
5. Both Carl and his cousin Ernie know how to play lacrosse.

Identifying and Using Complements, EXERCISE A
1. daffodils (direct object)
2. victims (indirect object); supplies (direct object)
3. lawyer (direct object); advisor (object complement)
4. refreshing (subject complement)
5. us (indirect object); dessert (direct object)
6. Antonio (direct object); restless (object complement)

Identifying and Using Complements, EXERCISE B
Answers will vary; possible answers are given.
1. Uncle Roy gave <u>Bobby</u> and <u>Donny</u> tickets to the game.
2. Uncle Roy thought that the game would be a <u>treat</u>.
3. It turned out that the game was a <u>sellout</u>.
4. We bought <u>programs</u> as soon as we arrived.
5. The team designated the game <u>Kids' Day</u>.
6. The manager gave <u>us</u> the game ball.
7. He showed <u>Bobby</u> where the pitchers warm up.
8. From the upper deck, the stadium looked <u>enormous</u>.
9. They had just painted the clubhouse <u>green</u>.
10. A last inning rally made the home team the <u>winners</u>.

Identifying and Using Complements, EXERCISE C
Sentences will vary; possible sentences are given.
1. The mountains look as if they are touching the <u>sky</u>. (direct object)
2. With the movement of the sun, the scene looks <u>different</u> at different times of the day. (subject complement)
3. Their height and sheer mass make <u>them</u> (direct object) <u>majestic</u>. (object complement)
4. As I view <u>them</u> (direct object), I make <u>myself</u> (indirect object) a <u>promise</u> (direct object).
5. Someday, I will make the <u>Rockies</u> (direct object) my <u>home</u> (object complement).

Identifying and Using Sentence Patterns, EXERCISE A
Answers will vary; possible answers are given.
1. She <u>displayed postcards</u> with beautiful scenery.
2. <u>The underwater photographs are</u> the most unusual that I had ever seen.
3. Kara <u>gave us</u> several <u>lectures</u> while hiking.
4. With her knowledge of underwater life and forestry, she <u>may become a scientist</u> one day.
5. This <u>information</u> was very <u>helpful</u> to us.

Identifying and Using Sentence Patterns, EXERCISE B
New sentences will vary; possible answers are given.
1. does not match; Germs cause epidemic diseases.
2. does not match; Animals and other people can be unknowing spreaders of disease.
3. does not match; Did the bubonic plague cause nearly 60 million people their deaths?
4. matches
5. does not match; Diseases are better understood today, so scientists can fight epidemics more effectively.

Identifying and Using Sentence Patterns, EXERCISE C
Sentences will vary; possible sentences are given.
1. I bake whole-wheat rolls or pumpernickel bread at least once a month.
2. Kneading and punching the bread are good ways of releasing tension.
3. How my friends and I enjoy eating those freshly baked goodies!
4. Would you like a slice of bread, or shall I give you a whole loaf?

Identifying and Using Types of Sentences, EXERCISE A
1. declarative (.)
2. exclamatory (!)
3. declarative (.)
4. imperative (.)
5. interrogative (?)

Identifying and Using Types of Sentences, EXERCISE B
Answers may vary slightly; possible answers are given.
1. What a relief it was to everyone when the Cold War ended!
2. Are leaders on both sides more frank and open now?
3. There's nothing to be gained by recalling the tensions of those years.
4. Let's forget about the past and build a better future.

Identifying and Using Types of Sentences, EXERCISE C
Answers will vary; possible answers are given.
PAT: What am I going to use for money. I'm completely broke. If you want to go shopping, go without me.
RITA: Maybe we could go to the park. What fun it is to watch the children playing there!
PAT: That's a good idea. Should we invite Chris to come with us?
RITA: How clever you are to think of that! I'll call her right now. Let's go!

Identifying and Using Simple Sentences, EXERCISE A
Revisions will vary; possible revisions are given.
1. Most/lives
2. Australia was settled by deported British criminals.
3. island-state/lies
4. Many/belong
5. The Great Coral Reef remains the world's largest natural coral reef.
6. Aborigines are the continent's earliest inhabitants.
7. Australians/participate
8. one third/is covered
9. Many of Australia's permanent lakes have been artificially created.
10. Acacias, eucalyptus shrubs/dominate

Identifying and Using Simple Sentences, EXERCISE B
Sentences will vary; possible sentences are given.
1. subject; <u>T-shirts and jeans</u> are favorites with people everywhere.
2. predicate; Most places, however, <u>do require at least shirt and shoes</u>.
3. predicate; Today's clothing <u>must be easy to care for, too</u>.
4. subject; <u>Working attire</u> is often casual and comfortable as well.
5. predicate; Ironing clothes <u>is almost unheard of today</u>.
6. subject; <u>Gloves and hats</u> are not worn often by women today.
7. subject; <u>People</u> once dressed formally for almost every occasion.
8. predicate; Many people <u>may polish their shoes once or twice a year</u>.
9. subject; <u>Very few functions</u> demand formal dress.
10. subject; <u>Bright colors and simple designs</u> are the outstanding features of contemporary clothing.

Identifying and Using Simple Sentences, EXERCISE C
Revisions will vary; possible revisions are given.

Bats <u>are</u> truly amazing, remarkable animals. Of all mammals, only bats have wings and fly. Bats' natural behavior often alienates them from people. <u>The little fliers</u> live in dark caves, hanging upside down when at rest. <u>Most come out</u> only at night. Much incorrect information about bats makes the small, timid creatures unpopular with humans.

Too, a bat's appearance does not endear it to people. <u>It is</u> furry but not cuddly. A bat's wings are leathery rather than feathery. <u>In addition, a bat's</u> face <u>often resembles that of a</u> bear, a hog, or a dog.

Identifying and Using Compound Sentences, EXERCISE A
1. C; About 350,000 species of plants exist, <u>and</u> 250,000 of those have flowering plants.
2. NC
3. C; Most flowers provide decoration, <u>but</u> some are used in cooking and for perfume.
4. NC
5. C; A flower may have more than one common name, <u>or</u> two or more flowers may be known by the same common name.

Identifying and Using Compound Sentences, EXERCISE B
Answers may vary slightly; possible answers are given.
1. Singer Harry Belafonte popularized calypso music in the 1950's, <u>yet</u> calypso music had developed several centuries earlier.
2. Enslaved Africans in Trinidad were not allowed to talk to one another, <u>so</u> they communicated information and emotions through music.
3. The lyrics of a calypso tune may express the singer's philosophy, <u>for</u> verses may comment on local political events or gossip.
4. Brass instruments are not used a great deal in playing calypso music, <u>nor</u> are stringed instruments employed, except for the guitar.
5. Would you like to go to a live calypso concert, <u>or</u> is listening to recordings enough for now?

Identifying and Using Complex Sentences, EXERCISE A
1. C; as it relaxes and entertains the listener
2. C; which is composed according to strict rules
3. C; Although most pieces of popular music do not retain their popularity for long
4. NC
5. C; Because Asian music uses different standards and instruments

Identifying and Using Complex Sentences, EXERCISE B
1. Would you please tell me <u>when I can expect our guests</u>?
2. Look both ways <u>as you back into a parking place</u>.
3. Did you know <u>that there are many examples of graphic art</u>?
4. <u>After we clean the house</u>, we can decorate the dining room.
5. <u>While Janice and Kate ate their hot dogs</u>, they walked along the midway.

Identifying and Using Complex Sentences, EXERCISE C

Sentences will vary; possible sentences are given.

1. Sally plans to mail the book to the publisher <u>after she finishes the illustrations</u>.
2. We're performing the play, <u>which we have written ourselves</u>, next Saturday.
3. Ralph's aunt, <u>whose house is always spotless</u>, rarely has visitors.
4. We'll certainly take in the natural history museum, <u>if you recommend it</u>.
5. <u>Although Matt practiced</u>, he didn't make the junior varsity team.
6. <u>Before she finalizes the arrangements</u>, Robin needs to know the number of people attending.
7. <u>Whenever his face gets that look</u>, he's planning some sort of mischief.
8. Dad fixed breakfast <u>because Mom went to the office early</u>.
9. He'll go to the gym <u>while they visit the aquarium</u>.
10. <u>Since Jack was so tall</u>, he could easily reach the box on the top shelf.

Identifying and Using Compound-Complex Sentences, EXERCISE A M

1.   M   S
   [During the 1970s, Spielberg captured audiences with Star Wars,] [which was his first
             M
   trilogy;] (and) [in the 1980s, he produced the Indiana Jones and Back to the Future series.]

2. [The heroes of Star Wars were aided by a mysterious power called "The Force,"] (but) [the
     M   S
   protagonist of Indiana Jones, [who was an archaeology professor,] relied upon his quick wits

   and courage.]
              M
3. [For Star Wars and Indiana Jones, Spielberg chose settings] [that took the audience around
   S   M
   the world and the cosmos;] (yet) [the Back to the Future movies take place in a small

   American town.]
          M   S
4. [Spielberg can wow audiences with special effects,] [as he did with Jurassic Park,] (or) [he
         M   S
   can touch them profoundly,] [as he did with Schindler's List.]

Identifying and Using Compound-Complex Sentences, EXERCISE B

Sentences may vary; possible sentences are given.

1. Some people simply enjoy the color or arrangement of objects in a painting, but others demand that paintings express a deep human emotion.
2. Paintings can skillfully portray the majesty of nature, as when a storm rages, or they can capture the joy and verve of everyday occurrences.
3. Because artists often comment on their times, some paintings teach about social injustice, and others reveal much about an era.
4. No one painting produces exactly the same response in every person, nor does the artist expect that, since each viewer brings his or her unique ideas to the painting.

Spelling

Adding Prefixes, EXERCISE A
Some answers will vary; possible answers are given.
1. immoral
2. unnecessary
3. disadvantage
4. semicircle
5. mismatch
6. nonviolent
7. recommend
8. antiseptic
9. submarine
10. preapproved

Adding Prefixes, EXERCISE B
1. When Leslie walked off the stage in the middle of her soliloquy, Ms. Barnes looked after her in disbelief.
2. Later, Ms. Barnes said that Leslie's behavior was irresponsible.
3. She asked for Leslie's unconditional resignation from the cast.
4. Even the most nonaggressive student wanted to take Leslie's part, in spite of feeling let down by her action.
5. Leslie stayed in bed for a week, remaining almost immobile during that time.
6. Dr. Willis diagnosed Leslie's condition as hypertension and prescribed medication for her.
7. We underestimated the medicine's power; Leslie recovered quickly.
8. Leslie said that there was also an imbalance in her body chemistry.
9. We all learned a lesson—not to prejudge anyone until all the facts are available.
10. Sometimes a person's real problems are invisible at first glance.

Adding Suffixes, EXERCISE A
1. Andrew breezily dismissed the charges against him.
2. No one wanted to oppose Andrew, whose stubbornness was legendary.
3. Adventurous Alicia decided to challenge his poor behavior.
4. Fearful of this occurrence, Andrew begged Alicia not to be pitiless.
5. Alicia found it very difficult to talk to Andrew because of his disagreeable ways.

Adding Suffixes, EXERCISE B
Answers will vary; possible answers are given.
1. irresponsible, irresponsibly; wary, warily
2. kind, kindness; open, openness
3. girl, girlish; clan, clannish
4. trip, tripping; grieve, grieving
5. punish, punishment; establish, establishment
6. precede, preceded; defy, defied
7. flavor, flavorless; limit, limitless
8. courage, courageous; thunder, thunderous
9. child, childlike; ghost, ghostlike
10. excel, excellence; abstain, abstinence

Adding Suffixes, EXERCISE C

Sentences will vary; possible sentences are given.

1. When Lucy received no <u>acknowledgment</u> for her hard work, she cried, "This is <u>outrageous</u>!"
2. With <u>dogged</u> devotion, Adam followed the group leader up the <u>treacherous</u> cliff.
3. Just what should I be <u>inferring</u> from that remark?
4. My <u>reliance</u> on that <u>lovable</u> old dog is amazing.
5. Jeannette got <u>comfortable</u> on the sofa and soon was <u>completely</u> rested.
6. <u>Believing</u> that they deserved a reward for their good grades, Yohgi and Pat spent a day of <u>merriment</u> at the amusement park.
7. <u>Dependence</u> upon good advice is no sign of weakness.
8. I've <u>studied</u> the question, but I don't see its <u>pertinence</u> to the issue at hand.
9. Dr. Harris <u>traveled</u> around the world but managed to remain in almost complete <u>ignorance</u> about the cultures he encountered.
10. Your decision seems rather <u>heartless</u>, and I'll work <u>mightily</u> to change your mind.
11. <u>Regardless</u> of Mindy's encouragement, we surrendered and sank in <u>weariness</u> along the side of the road.

Choosing Correct Homophones, EXERCISE A

New sentences will vary; possible answers are given.

1. bass; How I enjoy playing first <u>base</u>!
2. idle; The movie <u>idol</u> was mobbed by her fans.
3. waist; Please don't <u>waste</u> that paper.
4. You're, night; What are <u>your</u> ideas about a costume for the <u>knight</u> in this play?
5. new, brake; I <u>knew</u> I'd <u>break</u> this dish if I had to wash it!
6. They're, for; <u>There</u> are the <u>four</u> skirts that need to be hemmed.
7. led, air; Ramona just became an <u>heir</u> to a <u>lead</u> mine owned by her uncle.
8. pried, pared; I've been <u>paired</u> with Cheryl for the science project, and we take great <u>pride</u> in our work.
9. two, made, peace; The <u>maid</u> was never <u>too</u> busy to offer a guest a <u>piece</u> of advice.
10. all ready, sent; Change your cologne; I've <u>already</u> had enough of that <u>scent</u>!

Choosing Correct Homophones, EXERCISE B

Answers will vary; possible answers are given. Designated words are underlined.

1. Aunt Amy said with a <u>groan</u>, "How you've <u>grown</u> this year!"
2. David's <u>ascent</u> to the presidency had the council's full <u>assent</u>.
3. We <u>threw</u> out garbage until the work was <u>through</u>.
4. The <u>past</u> has <u>passed</u>; let it go!
5. The running <u>course</u> was covered with <u>coarse</u> sand.
6. <u>It's</u> a fine day for a dog to take <u>its</u> master for a walk.
7. This design for the new church is wonderful; in particular, don't <u>alter</u> that <u>altar</u> design!
8. <u>Who's</u> most likely to know <u>whose</u> sweater this is?
9. With a <u>wail</u> of delight, the <u>whale</u>-watchers started clicking their cameras.
10. Will we tour the <u>Capitol</u> when we visit the nation's <u>capital</u>?

Applying Other Spelling Rules and Tips, EXERCISE A

New sentences will vary; possible answers are given.

1. neighbor; My <u>neighbor</u> shares none of my interests.
2. foreign; The President must become involved in <u>foreign</u> affairs, even when he would rather be concerned with domestic problems.
3. achieve; Goals are usually <u>achieved</u> after much work and dedication.
4. ceiling; You have to put a <u>ceiling</u> on your expenditures.
5. forfeit; Kazuko knew that if she refused the offer, she would <u>forfeit</u> her dreams of success.

Applying Other Spelling Rules and Tips, EXERCISE B
New sentences will vary; possible answers are given.
1. proceed; You may <u>proceed</u> with the auction, Ms. Clark.
2. concede; Mitchell knew that it was time to <u>concede</u>.
3. recede; The walls <u>recede</u> at this point.
4. Revolution; The setting of the *A Tale of Two Cities* was the time of the French <u>Revolution</u>.
5. expulsion; The <u>expulsion</u> of Conrad as Police Commissioner was long overdue.

Applying Other Spelling Rules and Tips, EXERCISE C
Alternate words will vary; possible answers are given.
1. rapid
2. residence
3. barbarous
4. avarice
5. luxury

Spelling Commonly Misspelled Words Correctly I, EXERCISE A
   One <u>February</u>, I accompanied a group of <u>forty students</u> boys on an <u>arctic</u> expedition. The goal of the expedition was to <u>ascend</u> an ice-covered mountain in a hostile <u>environment</u>. The trip required much special <u>apparatus</u> and large amounts of food. Each hiker carried <u>biscuits</u>, cheese, <u>bouillon</u>, and canned meat.
   The expedition was led by a <u>conscientious</u> colonel who demanded good <u>discipline</u> and <u>hygiene</u> from the group. One day, a boy <u>accidentally</u> fell into a crevasse. His <u>absence</u> was soon noticed; the other hikers spread out and began calling his name. Everyone was greatly relieved when he <u>answered</u>. Not only did we know where he was, but we also knew that he was still <u>conscious</u>. The colonel <u>immediately</u> dropped a rope into the crevasse, and the boy climbed out. He was <u>embarrassed</u> but not injured. The colonel took the opportunity to lecture the group on the dangers of crevasses. He said that he could not <u>guarantee</u> anyone's safety—that each person was responsible.

Spelling Commonly Misspelled Words Correctly I, EXERCISE B
Sentences will vary; possible answers are given.
1. attendant; The store <u>attendant</u> greeted us.
2. inauguration; We attended the governor's <u>inauguration</u>.
3. ecstasy; I was in <u>ecstasy</u> when I ate the chocolate eclair.
4. correct; I would enjoy being a <u>chauffeur</u>.
5. jewelry; Is this <u>jewelry</u> fake?
6. calendar; Let me mark that date on my <u>calendar</u>.
7. committee; Yes, I am on the <u>committee</u>.
8. correct; <u>Discipline</u> is important in any military unit.
9. conscience; People who injure animals have no <u>conscience</u>.
10. government; The legislative branch of the <u>government</u> is the Congress.

Spelling Commonly Misspelled Words Correctly II, EXERCISE A
Corrections are underlined.

On <u>Wednesdays</u>, I visit my accomplished friend, Mr. Ortega. Mr. Ortega is a ninety-year-old <u>millionaire</u> who lives in a house that looks like a <u>medieval</u> castle. Mr. Ortega greets me at the door with a <u>mischievous</u> smile. He is wearing a plaid shirt, tan slacks, and <u>moccasins</u>. He <u>maneuvers</u> his wheelchair down the hall to the sitting room. He looks forward to these <u>occasions</u> because he knows that I am <u>truly</u> interested in the stories he has to tell.

Mr. Ortega made his fortune mining <u>nickel</u>. Before that, he was a <u>sergeant</u> and then a <u>lieutenant</u> in the Air Force. He has many <u>mementos</u> from his years in the military. One day, he told me about getting his pilot's <u>license</u>. He likes to <u>reminisce</u> about the past, but he also has many <u>pastimes</u> that keep him busy in the present. A <u>playwright</u>, he has had several of his plays produced. He likes to read books about <u>psychology</u> and sociology. He continues to have remarkable <u>perseverance</u> and imagination. I consider it a great <u>privilege</u> to know someone as interesting as Mr. Ortega.

Spelling Commonly Misspelled Words Correctly II, EXERCISE B
1. It is <u>unnecessary</u> to <u>vacuum</u> every day.
2. The <u>righteous</u> politician was a member of <u>parliament</u>.
3. I <u>sincerely</u> hope you win the golf <u>tournament</u>.
4. She made a <u>reference</u> to the <u>unanimous</u> vote.
5. That appliance is supposed to be very <u>versatile</u> and useful, but I would ask for a <u>warranty</u>, anyway.
6. Part of his job in the <u>laboratory</u> is to <u>liquefy</u> the gas.
7. For a few moments after the accident, every <u>muscle</u> in my leg felt <u>paralyzed</u>.
8. The behavior of the <u>maintenance</u> worker was very <u>predictable</u>.
9. Draw a set of <u>parallel</u> lines on your paper.
10. On that <u>occasion</u>, the technician found <u>miscellaneous</u> <u>paraphernalia</u> in the laboratory.

Underlining/Italics

Using Underlining/Italics in Titles and Names, EXERCISE A
1. I read the article in yesterday's <u>New York Times</u>.
2. Will <u>60 Minutes</u> be interviewing the senator?
3. The U.S.S. <u>Missouri</u> has been named a national monument.
4. The artist claimed that he was inspired by Michelangelo's sculpture the <u>Pieta</u>.
5. When I was younger, my favorite book was <u>Dear Mr. Henshaw</u>.
6. I have a poster of Monet's <u>Waterlilies</u> in my room.
7. The animator used Beethoven's <u>Symphony No. 9</u> as background music.
8. The <u>Orient Express</u> once ran between Paris and Istanbul.
9. There was a full-page ad about the sale in <u>The Shopper's News</u>.
10. Did you know that <u>My Fair Lady</u> was based on George Bernard Shaw's play <u>Pygmalion</u>?

Using Underlining/Italics in Titles and Names, EXERCISE B
The "Books" section of the <u>Times</u> interviewed her recently. <u>Inside Edition</u> ran a story about her life in Tulsa, Oklahoma. Hinton wrote her most popular work, <u>The Outsiders</u>, when she was only sixteen! Hinton's works remind me of the film <u>Grease</u>. Her descriptive writing style and ear for dialogue are distinctive.

Using Underlining/Italics in Titles and Names, EXERCISE C
Sentences will vary; possible sentences are given.
1. Have you ever read the novel <u>Moby-Dick</u>?
2. The <u>Miami Herald</u> ran a story about the high school game.
3. Episodes of <u>I Love Lucy</u> are in the Museum of Modern Art.
4. Grant Wood's <u>American Gothic</u> is frequently parodied.
5. Last night I saw a wonderful production of <u>Carmen</u>.

Other Uses of Underlining/Italics, EXERCISE A
1. The expression <u>et cetera</u> literally means "and other things."
2. Where does the saying "Mind your <u>p</u>'s and <u>q</u>'s" come from?
3. The word <u>right</u> has more than one meaning—right?
4. Put a <u>:</u> after the greeting in your letter.
5. Do you spell <u>judgment</u> with one e or two?
6. <u>D</u>, when used as a Roman numeral, represents 500.
7. The sign had <u>Danger</u> written in huge red letters!
8. How many <u>O</u>'s are there in a trillion?
9. Many historians cite the policy of <u>detente</u> with China as Richard Nixon's greatest achievement as President.
10. The two sides settled their dispute with a <u>quid pro quo</u> arrangement.

Other Uses of Underlining/Italics, EXERCISE B
Always use italics when writing words as words, as in this example: "<u>Foul</u> has many meanings." Use italics to write numerals, as in this case: "These <u>7</u>'s look like <u>1</u>'s." When referring to specific marks of punctuation, such as <u>!</u> or <u>?</u>, be sure to use italics. Of course, foreign phrases, such as <u>à demain</u>, should be set off in italics.

Other Uses of Underlining/Italics, EXERCISE C
Sentences will vary; possible sentences are given.
1. The sign read <u>Exit</u> in large letters.
2. <u>Entre nous</u>, I doubt if this alliance will last a week!
3. Did you say that there was a <u>6</u> in your address?
4. The city named <u>Juneau</u> begins with a capital <u>J</u>.

Verbals

Identifying and Using Participles and Participial Phrases, EXERCISE A
1. exhausted, players
2. Burdened with many books, I; departing, friends
3. having searched for hours; team; stranded, survivors
4. pleased, smile
5. laughing, hyena; wheezing, horse
6. beaming proudly, sergeant
7. televised, tour
8. decorated with bows, dress
9. Glancing over his shoulder, man; distracted, man
10. Delighted by the scene, I, playing with his children, father
11. Known around the world, performer; talented, performer
12. award-winning, restaurant; flown in daily from the seacoast, fish

Identifying and Using Participles and Participial Phrases, EXERCISE B

Sentences will vary; possible sentences are given.
1. Embarrassed by his mistake, Peter; <u>Surprised to be observed</u>, Peter slouched in his seat.
2. Concentrating deeply on my work, I; <u>Failing to pay attention</u>, I didn't hear her question.
3. Startled, flock; <u>Hearing the noise</u>, the flock of sparrows fluttered off the wire.
4. exciting, history; I wrote my report on the <u>intriguing</u> history of spaceflight.
5. Stunned, I; <u>Having forgotten to study</u>, I could offer no answer.
6. stolen, property; The <u>borrowed</u> property was promptly returned.
7. Having been tempted, I; <u>Still feeling hungry</u>, I helped myself to another bowl of soup.
8. cooked to perfection, dinner; The dinner, <u>prepared by a master chef</u>, was delicious.
9. Falling to his knees, he; <u>Crying aloud</u>, he begged for forgiveness.
10. smiling, host; Our <u>charming</u> host met us at the door.

Identifying and Using Gerunds and Gerund Phrases, EXERCISE A
1. Riding the cable cars, subject
2. walking to school, predicate nominative; swimming, predicate nominative
3. trying, object of a preposition; doing, object of a preposition
4. emitting an offensive smell, object of a preposition
5. engineering, appositive
6. including more windows in his plans, direct object
7. walking, subject; dancing, subject
8. baby-sitting, object of a preposition; mowing lawns, object of a preposition
9. studying, indirect object
10. feeding the chickens, appositive
11. grumbling, direct object
12. singing, direct object; rehearsing, subject
13. having done a difficult job well, object of a preposition
14. making animal noises, object of a preposition
15. practicing, indirect object

Identifying and Using Gerunds and Gerund Phrases, EXERCISE B

Sentences will vary; possible sentences are given.
1. <u>Writing poetry</u> is fun.
2. Her mother dislikes <u>whining</u>.
3. Mae's favorite hobby is <u>collecting coins</u>.
4. Chuck ruined the picnic by <u>starting an argument</u>.
5. She completed her assignment, <u>making the salad</u>.
6. <u>Studying for the test</u> required a great deal of time.
7. Please begin <u>doing your homework</u> right after dinner.
8. What will you accomplish by <u>crying</u>?
9. His science project, <u>building a robot</u>, was quite impressive.
10. The toughest part of this project is <u>finishing on time</u>.

Identifying and Using Infinitives and Infinitive Phrases, EXERCISE A
1. to see (adjective)
2. To flee (noun)
3. to take us to Canada this year (noun)
4. to attend (adverb)
5. to take to Centerville (adjective)

Identifying and Using Infinitives and Infinitive Phrases, EXERCISE B
 1. to speak, adjective; to hear, adverb
 2. to see clearly without binoculars, adverb
 3. to translate, adverb
 4. to misuse the apostrophe, subject
 5. to recuperate, adverb
 6. to complete all assignments by Friday, predicate nominative
 7. to photograph a night scene, adverb; to use a tripod, direct object
 8. not to seek reelection in 1928, direct object

Identifying and Using Infinitives and Infinitive Phrases, EXERCISE C
 1. <u>To master the violin</u> takes years of practice.
 2. I think that Helen needs <u>to study</u>.
 3. The jobs <u>to be done</u> are described in this memo.
 4. Our mission will be difficult <u>to complete</u>.
 5. <u>To understand this book</u> may not be easy.
 6. Would you like <u>to go to the zoo</u>?
 7. We have nothing <u>to lose</u>.
 8. He was glad <u>to return home</u>.
 9. <u>To write a poem</u> can be very satisfying.
10. She decided <u>to seek her fortune</u>.

Using Verbals Correctly, EXERCISE A
Corrections may vary; possible corrections are given.
 1. <u>Fred's</u> losing his way came as quite a surprise.
 2. <u>Once we found our compass</u>, the voyage turned out all right in the end.
 3. By studying hard, <u>you can increase your test scores</u> dramatically.
 4. After moving, they expected <u>never to see their old friends again</u>.
 5. Correct
 6. His mother asked him <u>to finish</u> his homework <u>quickly</u>.
 7. <u>Reading the new thriller, I thought</u> Chapter 4 was very exciting.
 8. Correct
 9. The boys planned <u>to raise enough money somehow</u> to buy the tickets.
10. Having graduated with honors, <u>he was practically guaranteed a good job</u>.

Using Verbals Correctly, EXERCISE B
Corrections may vary; possible corrections are given.
 1. (P) Having taken our seats, <u>we heard the concert begin</u>.
 2. (I) My little sister <u>always likes to play</u> the same silly games.
 3. (G) The fact that Gillian was invited has nothing to do with <u>my</u> deciding not to go.
 4. Correct
 5. (P) Having lost her gloves, <u>Betty</u> had very cold hands.
 6. (I) The students were asked <u>to take their seats promptly</u> and to pay close attention.
 7. (P) Having heard all the evidence, <u>the jury is almost certain to bring in a guilty verdict</u>.
 8. (P) Reading about history, <u>I found the cultures of Africa to be</u> especially intriguing.
 9. (I) Having traveled all day, <u>we would like, if possible, to take</u> a brief rest.
10. (G) The <u>judge's</u> deciding for the plaintiff was a disappointment to the defendant.

Developing Your Style: Verbals, EXERCISE A
Answers may vary; possible answers are given.
 1. Shaking hands with the governor, Mayor Jefferson looked proud.
 2. Collecting seashells is Hillary's favorite hobby.
 3. Playing in the park, the boys spotted a rare bird.
 4. The prospectors traveled to California to look for gold.
 5. Writing poetry helps Silk Moonstone express her feelings.

Developing Your Style: Verbals, EXERCISE B
Answers will vary; possible answers are given.
1. The girls were eager <u>to get started</u>.
2. <u>Climbing the mountain</u>, the campers quickly grew tired.
3. Jon tried <u>helping the lost child</u>.
4. They used different kinds of bait <u>to tempt the giant bass</u>.
5. <u>Ignoring the pain in his knee</u>, Reggie ran as fast as he could.

Developing Your Style: Verbals, EXERCISE C
Sentences will vary; possible sentences are given.
1. Glad <u>to help her friend</u>, Joanne began <u>sweeping the kitchen</u>.
2. <u>To see the museum</u>, the girls <u>taking the tour</u> woke up early.
3. <u>To lose a loved one</u> is <u>to experience grief</u>.
4. <u>Walking down the street</u>, they saw a man <u>sleeping on the sidewalk</u>.
5. Edna, <u>having studied until midnight</u>, started <u>to fall asleep</u>.
6. <u>Being overly cautious</u> is better than <u>taking unnecessary risks</u>.
7. <u>Washing your hands</u> is a good way <u>to prevent infections</u>.
8. <u>To get to the park</u>, you should plan <u>to take the bus</u>.
9. <u>Having lost her slipper</u>, Cinderella considered <u>returning to the castle</u>.
10. Mr. Nguyen likes <u>watching television</u>, but his wife prefers <u>going to the movies</u>.

Verbs

Verb-Forming Suffixes, EXERCISE A
1. Mom's face <u>softens</u> when she smiles.
2. If you don't cover that pan, grease will <u>splatter</u> everywhere.
3. Could anyone possibly <u>falsify</u> these records?
4. We students in the chorus sometimes <u>vocalize</u> and even <u>harmonize</u> after school.
5. Please <u>notify</u> the secretary if you plan to be absent on Friday.
6. I don't think you should <u>shorten</u> this skirt; it looks just right to me.
7. How well that speaker can <u>motivate</u> a crowd!
8. If you <u>publicize</u> that information, you will <u>humiliate</u> the entire family.
9. I don't know where you learned to <u>decorate</u> a room like this, but those colors really <u>brighten</u> up this dingy space.
10. Maybe that movie <u>frightens</u> you, but it doesn't <u>horrify</u> me one bit.

Verb-Forming Suffixes, EXERCISE B
Sentences will vary; possible sentences are given.
1. The astronomers <u>theorized</u> about the cause of the strange phenomenon.
2. A little starch will <u>stiffen</u> that lace just fine.
3. No one could <u>pacify</u> little Keith when his mother left the nursery.
4. Baby Danielle <u>patters</u> around the house.
5. We must <u>tranquilize</u> the lion before we can treat its wounds.
6. "I will <u>liquidate</u> those mosquitoes," Pedro vowed, scratching.
7. For a refreshing drink, <u>liquefy</u> some pineapple and apples in a blender.
8. At the funeral, the mayor herself will <u>eulogize</u> the late president of the school board.
9. These tomatoes will <u>ripen</u> quickly if you put them in a paper bag.
10. How busily the bees are <u>pollinating</u> the garden!

Identifying Action Verbs and Linking Verbs, EXERCISE A
1. praised, action (physical)
2. led, action (physical)
3. were, linking (cheerleaders/skillful, enthusiastic)
4. thought, action (mental)
5. looked, linking (bleachers/full)

Identifying Action Verbs and Linking Verbs, EXERCISE B
Answers may vary; possible answers are given.
1. Cindy has <u>grown</u> fond of her baby brother. (linking)
2. Mrs. Goldstein <u>grows</u> geraniums in her flower boxes. (action)
3. Please help me <u>look</u> for the softball, Lewis. (action)
4. The car <u>looks</u> unsafe for the road. (linking)
5. Principal Hansen <u>sounded</u> the alarm for a fire drill. (action)
6. Rod <u>sounded</u> surprisingly nervous about the track meet. (linking)
7. Terry <u>felt</u> disappointed after striking out. (linking)
8. Pam <u>felt</u> the sheep's thick woolly coat. (action)
9. Don't you think the beef stew <u>tastes</u> a bit too salty? (linking)
10. <u>Taste</u> these cookies and tell me if you like them. (action)

Identifying Action Verbs and Linking Verbs, EXERCISE C
Paragraphs will vary; a possible paragraph is given.

As the teams <u>ran</u> (action) onto the field, the announcer's voice <u>sounded</u> (action) over the loudspeaker. "Our team <u>looks</u> (linking) really good today," Juan <u>grinned</u> (action) as he <u>looked</u> (action) through his binoculars. "A win <u>seems</u> (linking) a sure thing," I <u>replied</u> (action). During the first two innings, our team <u>scored</u> (action) three runs, and my prophecy <u>appeared</u> (linking) ready for fulfillment. In the third inning, however, dark clouds <u>appeared</u> (action) on the horizon and <u>drifted</u> (action) over the stadium. "Oh, no!" <u>groaned</u> (action) Juan as we <u>felt</u> (action) the first drops of rain. "Oh, well," I <u>shrugged</u> (action)." I <u>guess</u> (action) our win must <u>wait</u> (action) for another day."

Identifying Transitive Verbs and Intransitive Verbs, EXERCISE A
1. Has picked (transitive), a name
2. crashed (intransitive)
3. looked (intransitive)
4. flickered (intransitive)
5. whittles (transitive), animals
6. crawled (intransitive)
7. disturbed (transitive), sleep
8. have arrived (intransitive)
9. Will drive (transitive), us
10. performed (transitive), experiments

Identifying Transitive Verbs and Intransitive Verbs, EXERCISE B
Answers will vary, possible answers are given.
1. The scientist read from notes. (intransitive)
2. She spoke her words clearly. (transitive)
3. Some listeners cheered as she spoke. (intransitive)
4. She stood her ground as questions were asked. (transitive)
5. The audience left the hall quietly. (transitive)

Identifying Transitive Verbs and Intransitive Verbs, EXERCISE C

Answers will vary; possible answers are given.

1. The tide washed <u>the sandcastle away</u>.
2. How the wet sand stuck <u>to my toes</u>!
3. A mild breeze blew <u>the toy sailboats out into the water</u>.
4. When did clouds form <u>in the sky</u>?
5. Huge waves crashed <u>into the seawall</u>.

Identifying Main Verbs and Helping Verbs, EXERCISE A

1. may be
2. has
3. might have
4. could
5. am
6. does
7. had
8. could have
9. will be
10. should have

Identifying Main Verbs and Helping Verbs, EXERCISE B

Answers will vary; possible answers are given.

1. I <u>have</u> not <u>seen</u> her, but my brother spotted her there twice last week.
2. I wonder—<u>might</u> she <u>have been doing</u> research for the biology report?
3. Certainly no one <u>can prepare</u> a report like Liana!
4. If you <u>do</u> not <u>believe</u> me, then you <u>should review</u> her grades this past year.
5. She has been working on that report for two months.

Identifying Verb Forms, Number, and Person, EXERCISE A

1. enjoys (third-person singular); do (first-person singular)
2. swim (first-person singular); is (third-person singular)
3. would come (second-person singular); go (first-person plural)
4. join (third-person plural); could rent (second-person plural)
5. eat (first-person plural); means (third-person singular)

Identifying Verb Forms, Number, and Person, EXERCISE B

1. He likes kindergarten, but he doesn't <u>like</u> taking naps. (third-person singular; third-person singular)
2. Correct (first-person singular; third-person singular)
3. The children spend a lot of time on computers; they also <u>listen</u> to many tapes. (third-person plural; third-person plural)
4. What <u>do</u> you remember about kindergarten, Jim? (second-person singular)
5. Correct (first-person plural)

Identifying Verb Forms, Number, and Person, EXERCISE C

Dialogues will vary; a possible dialogue is given.

Jorge: How glad <u>I am</u> to hear your voice! <u>What's</u> new?
Antonio: <u>Things</u> at our house <u>are</u> always dull. What <u>are you doing</u>?
Jorge: <u>I'm watching</u> TV. <u>Can you come</u> over?
Antonio: <u>We have</u> a science project to do. Maybe <u>we should work</u>.

Identifying and Using Simple Tenses, EXERCISE A
 1. swaggers, present; clicks, present
 2. will blush, future; talks, present
 3. studied, past; made, past; grinned, past
 4. scrapes, present; catches, present
 5. Did see, past
 6. visited, past; was, past; do remember, present
 7. will sleep, future
 8. are, present
 9. want, present; think, present; is, present
10. is, present

Identifying and Using Simple Tenses, EXERCISE B
 1. The young singer <u>stepped</u> into the spotlight.
 2. After the concert, he probably <u>will sign</u> autographs.
 3. Now the sounds of guitars, drums, and trumpets <u>swirl</u> around the auditorium.
 4. The lead singer <u>nods</u> to the drummer, who <u>responds</u> with a machine-like drum roll.
 5. The singer <u>becomes</u> animated, dancing about the stage.
 6. Our ears <u>will ring</u> for hours from all this loud music!
 7. Later, we <u>laughed</u> about the wonderful evening.
 8. Still, if we ever <u>attend</u> an event like that again, we probably <u>will take</u> earplugs!
 9. I really <u>like</u> this music, even though I <u>complain</u> about the noise.
10. By the way, my favorite group <u>is</u> the Deltas, although in the past, it <u>was</u> the Kentuckians.

Identifying and Using Perfect Tenses, EXERCISE A
 1. The dog's intelligence <u>had helped</u> it to learn quickly.
 2. You <u>will have learned</u> some general rules about training a dog.
 3. Their owners <u>had been</u> firm with their dogs.
 4. A trained dog <u>has obeyed</u> its owner even when it <u>has felt</u> playful or inattentive.
 5. A good owner <u>will have taught</u> only one command at a time.
 6. Owners <u>have used</u> the same command words, repeating the lesson daily until the dog learns.
 7. A dog <u>will have received</u> praise often when it <u>has done</u> well.
 8. The dog trainer <u>has insisted</u> that a dog's owner always be present.
 9. You <u>have watched</u> a dog trainer work, I presume.
10. My dog Fido <u>will have finished</u> his course before your dog Elise begins hers.

Identifying and Using Perfect Tenses, EXERCISE B
Answers will vary; possibles answers are given.
 1. Traditionally, the favorite pie at this time of year <u>has</u> always <u>been</u> my grandmother's gooseberry pie.
 2. You <u>will have picked</u> all the strawberries you need by noon.
 3. No one who <u>has been</u> a guest at our dinner ever goes away hungry.
 4. Ned <u>had</u> just <u>set</u> the table as the first guest arrived.
 5. Adam <u>had offered</u> his services as dishwasher even before I <u>had finished</u> eating.

Identifying and Using Progressive Forms of Verb Tenses, EXERCISE A
 1. has been working (present perfect progressive)
 2. will be inviting (future progressive)
 3. was hoping (past progressive)
 4. is approving (present progressive)
 5. were memorizing (past progressive)

6. am feeling (present progressive)
7. will be giving (future progressive)
8. have been anticipating (present perfect progressive)
9. will be breathing (future progressive)
10. will have been rehearsing (future perfect progressive)

Identifying and Using Progressive Forms of Verb Tenses, EXERCISE B
New sentences will vary; possible sentences are given.
1. Most of my friends <u>have been working</u> on something for the *Aerie.*
   I <u>have been missing</u> Mariana terribly.
2. Mr. Cunningham <u>had been promoting</u> the magazine for about a week before I became interested.
   She <u>had been writing</u> me a letter a week before school started over there.
3. I <u>was discussing</u> my writer's portfolio with Ben and Jolene.
   She <u>was telling</u> me all kinds of things about life in and around Amsterdam.
4. "Ben," I asked, "you <u>will be giving</u> the editors a story, won't you?"
   Mariana <u>will be studying</u> in Europe until the middle of July.
5. "Walt," he joked. "I <u>will have been clearing</u> my desk before you even write your first drafts!"
   By that time, her dad <u>will have been teaching</u> in Amsterdam for almost a year.
6. Jolene said that the two of us <u>were being</u> too competitive.
   I <u>was waiting</u> for a letter today.
7. "The editor-in-chief <u>has been inviting</u> everyone to enter," she reminded us.
   Perhaps she <u>has been finding</u> a whole new group of friends in the Netherlands!
8. "I <u>will be looking</u> for both your names in the *Aerie*," she said, "because I am confident you can win."
   She <u>will be seeing</u> her before too long.

Identifying and Using Irregular Verbs I, EXERCISE A
1. Carlos <u>became</u> upset upon hearing the cost for fixing the clock.
2. He had <u>driven</u> twenty miles to this clock repair shop.
3. "When I <u>began</u> the trip," he thought, "I hoped it would be cheap."
4. "I <u>heard</u> from a friend that your costs are reasonable," he said.
5. "The clock has <u>hung</u> on my grandfather's wall for fifty years."
6. "During an earthquake," Carlos explained, "It had somehow <u>fallen</u>."
7. Carlos's grandfather had <u>given</u> it to him.
8. "It means a lot to me," Carlos added, "since it <u>was</u> my grandpa's."
9. On hearing all this, the shopkeeper <u>grew</u> sympathetic.
10. "I will see what can be <u>done</u> with it as cheaply as possible," the shopkeeper sighed.

Identifying and Using Irregular Verbs I, EXERCISE B
1. Sachi <u>burst</u> through the door and <u>flung</u> herself on the sofa.
2. "I have never <u>felt</u> so awful," she cried as she <u>fought</u> back tears.
3. "I have never <u>had</u> such a humiliating experience!"
4. She <u>caught</u> a glimpse of herself in a mirror, laughed, and <u>bit</u> her lip.
5. "I should have <u>gone</u> back and explained what happened," she said to herself.
6. "Instead, I <u>flew</u> into a panic; now, I'm afraid, it has <u>cost</u> me my self-respect."
7. "If Marta has <u>found</u> out what happened, she'll make me grovel!"
8. Sachi <u>blew</u> back some hair from her eyes and vowed, "I've <u>eaten</u> crow in the past—but not this time!"
9. "I've not yet been <u>beaten</u>," Sachi said, continuing her pep talk.
10. She would not be <u>broken</u> by this, either!

Identifying and Using Irregular Verbs II, EXERCISE A
1. William <u>rang</u> the bell and waited for someone to come to the door.
2. He had <u>ridden</u> the bus across town to visit this unique museum.
3. A tall, thin woman who <u>wore</u> a gray smock came to the door.
4. She opened her mouth and would have <u>spoken</u> to William.
5. Before she could utter a word, however, a man <u>threw</u> open the door.
6. He reached out and enthusiastically <u>shook</u> William's hand.
7. "Welcome!" the man said. "I <u>knew</u> you'd be here today."
8. He clapped William on the back with such force that it <u>stung</u>.
9. William was <u>taken</u> aback by the man's overly friendly manner.
10. "I <u>saw</u> the flyer advertising you museum," William stammered.

Identifying and Using Irregular Verbs II, EXERCISE B
1. After William had <u>paid</u> the admission fee, the curator <u>tore</u> the ticket in two, handing William the stub.
2. William <u>put</u> the stub in his pocket and <u>made</u> his way to the exhibits.
3. A hallway <u>led</u> to his left; a sign <u>said</u> that it went to the exhibits.
4. He stepped into a gallery where a dozen flutes <u>lay</u> on a table.
5. William's uncle had <u>lent</u> him a flute once and had even <u>taught</u> William to play a few simple tunes.
6. Then his uncle had <u>told</u> William that it was useless; he was tone deaf.
7. William <u>sat</u> on the piano bench that had been <u>set</u> against the wall.
8. He <u>rose</u> to examine a clavichord and a steam-powered organ that William <u>thought</u> would surely shake the museum to pieces if played.
9. He picked up a score that someone had <u>left</u>—and that had been <u>written</u> by Chopin.
10. The curator's booming voice <u>split</u> the air; "Put that down," he commanded.

Identifying and Using Active and Passive Voice, EXERCISE A

<u>Active Voice</u>	<u>Passive Voice</u>
3, 5, 6, 9	1, 2, 4, 7, 8, 10

Identifying and Using Active and Passive Voice, EXERCISE B
Answers may vary; possible answers are given.
1. My mother <u>prepared</u> my favorite dessert, pineapple upside-down cake. (active)
2. Last summer a part-time job at Frank's Fine Furniture <u>was obtained</u> by me. (passive)
3. David Jones <u>teaches</u> the cooking class. (active)
4. My best friend, Hattie, <u>made</u> the environmental bumper sticker on our car. (active)
5. The surprise party for Alana <u>was given</u> by John. (passive)
6. The poster <u>was made</u> by Jacqueline. (passive)
7. A boy on a bicycle <u>delivered</u> the newspaper. (active)
8. A team of experts <u>will answer</u> your questions. (active)
9. No change
10. Claudio <u>has been given</u> a starring role by the director. (passive)

Identifying and Using the Subjunctive Mood, EXERCISE A
1. were
2. keep
3. view
4. cosign
5. be

Identifying and Using the Subjunctive Mood, EXERCISE B
1. We recommend that he <u>follow</u> our directors.
2. I insist that any map <u>be</u> both clear and readable.
3. Is it necessary that I <u>drive</u> the whole way?
4. We would prefer that Gwen <u>rest</u> for a few hours.
5. If she <u>were</u> a truck driver, would she rest?
6. I would demand that any driver <u>take</u> some time off.
7. It is recommended that each car <u>slow</u> down at the tunnel.
8. Dad is insisting that Mom <u>leave</u> the freeway.
9. If you <u>were</u> she, would you need a break?
10. I suggested that Dad <u>be</u> less domineering.

Identifying and Using the Subjunctive Mood, EXERCISE C
Answers will vary; possible answers are given.
1. Would you recommend that <u>they arrive a little early</u>?
2. I would prefer that <u>Garry leave those muddy shoes on the porch</u>.
3. It might be better if <u>you perform right after the intermission</u>.
4. He insists that <u>we let him in on our secret</u>.
5. We suggest that <u>he not be so nosy</u>!

Using Easily Confused Verbs Correctly, EXERCISE A
1. Most people <u>had brought</u> us biscuits or cakes; many <u>had taken</u> them away again.
2. A metal roof <u>lies</u> over the coop where the chickens lay their eggs.
3. <u>Let</u> us <u>leave</u> the young chicks alone until later.
4. Correct
5. I plan to <u>sit</u> here until the sun has set.

Using Easily Confused Verbs Correctly, EXERCISE B
1. I will <u>set</u> the table for breakfast.
2. Dad should have <u>raised</u> the camp flag by now.
3. Yesterday Bart <u>lay</u> the tablecloth out to dry.
4. Aunt Evelyn will <u>bring</u> the baby down here.
5. Mom told Bart, "<u>Leave</u> the muffins alone!"
6. After Mom has <u>sat</u> down, everyone else may, too.
7. The temperature already has <u>risen</u> to 70 degrees.
8. We plan to <u>lie</u> outside in the sunshine.
9. Haven't you <u>taken</u> too many muffins at once?
10. After Evelyn has <u>left</u>, we will clean up.

Using Easily Confused Verbs Correctly, EXERCISE C
Sentences will vary; possible answers are given.
1. You may <u>take</u> the cooler to the picnic, but be sure to <u>bring</u> it back sometime this next week.
2. <u>Let</u> us be very quiet as we <u>leave</u>; Regan has fallen asleep.
3. I <u>laid</u> down my backpack and now have <u>lain</u> down beside it.
4. Cordell <u>raises</u> vegetables in his garden, and he <u>rises</u> early to take care of them before school.
5. Hey, Cordelia—<u>set</u> that work aside; <u>sit</u> and talk with me!

Using Principal Parts of Verbs Correctly, EXERCISE A

1. waiting
2. shown
3. bought
4. likes
5. featured
6. reading
7. becoming
8. are
9. saved
10. begin

Using Principal Parts of Verbs Correctly, EXERCISE B

Answers may vary slightly; possible answers are given.

1. Ronnie and Davie have been working on a script.
2. Nicole is designing special costumes for the play.
3. Graham has set up microphones and speakers around the stage.
4. Juliette and Tom were rehearsing their parts backstage.
5. The tickets have been printed and sold by Ricky.

Using Principal Parts of Verbs Correctly, EXERCISE C

1. The artist had tried to present the scene as it was.
2. She has used dark colors to enhance the mood.
3. Do the people appear happy or sad?
4. I have seen other paintings like this in the city museum.
5. This artist has always impressed me with her ability to capture emotions on canvas.

Using Tense Sequence Correctly, EXERCISE A

1. We usually stay after school and work on our science project.
2. Although I tried to listen, I fell asleep—much to my embarrassment!
3. The customer complained about the service and said that he wouldn't return.
4. Manuel had not finished playing the piano, but the audience applauded anyway.
5. First we sang a folk song; then we continued with a lullably.
6. We were editing the story while she drew (was drawing) an illustration.
7. When Susan offered to help me paint the scenery, I accepted with a heartfelt "Thanks!"
8. We had gotten home by the time Josh arrived.
9. Has Nina explained the problem and asked Nancy's opinion?
10. When he asked you a question, did you immediately reply?

Using Tense Sequence Correctly, EXERCISE B

Answers may vary slightly; possible answers are given.

Having recently finished reading the novel *The Summer of My German Soldier,* I can recommend it highly. The events take place in Arkansas during World War II. Patty Bergen narrates the story. She describes the arrival of German prisoners of war. These prisoners have been sent to Arkansas to work in the cotton fields. Their arrival is less exciting than Patty expected. One day, however, Patty meets one of the prisoners in her father's store. He and the other prisoners have come to the store to buy hats to protect themselves from the strong sun. Patty befriends this prisoner and learns about his past. While I was reading the book, I wondered whether this friendship would prove dangerous for both Patty and the soldier.

Developing Your Style: Using Vivid, Precise Verbs, EXERCISE A

Answers will vary; possible answers are given.

1. Each fashion model <u>sauntered</u> gracefully down the runway but then <u>scampered</u> to the dressing room without a second to waste.
2. Photographers <u>clicked</u> their cameras the minute they <u>spotted</u> the models.
3. At the last minute, the designer <u>substituted</u> a velvet sash for the silk one and then <u>converted</u> it to a scarf.
4. One bold reporter secretly <u>slipped</u> backstage and <u>eavesdropped</u> on private conversations.
5. After the show, the designer <u>packs</u> the one-of-a-kind clothes in plastic bags to <u>preserve</u> them.

Developing Your Style: Using Vivid, Precise Verbs, EXERCISE B

Answers will vary; possible answers are given.

1. The thermometer <u>revealed</u> that the temperature had <u>climbed</u> ten degrees in the past hour.
2. After a morning swim, the hungry campers <u>devoured</u> their lunch and <u>dawdled</u> in their cabins until early afternoon.
3. A bugle call <u>summoned</u> the campers to the flagpole where they <u>recited</u> the Pledge of Allegiance.
4. The campers <u>babbled</u> so noisily that the counselor <u>repeated</u> the direction three times.
5. After the two teams <u>hammered</u> out an agreement, they <u>raced</u> to the lake.

Developing Your Style: Using Vivid, Precise Verbs, EXERCISE C

Answers will vary; possible answers are given.

The sheriff <u>cupped</u> his hands above his eyes as he <u>scanned</u> the horizon. Quickly he <u>leaped</u> on his horse and <u>seized</u> the reins. The horse's hoofbeats <u>thundered</u> as the rider <u>galloped</u> after the bandit. The horse <u>raised</u> clouds of dust that <u>obscured</u> the sheriff's face. At this point, the movie audience <u>booed</u> and <u>demanded</u> their money back.

Developing Your Style: Choosing the Active Voice, EXERCISE A

1. Robert Goddard first <u>tested</u> liquid rocket fuel in 1926.
2. Leonardo da Vinci <u>had sketched</u> a prototype of a helicopter.
3. Scientists <u>have explored</u> alternatives to the use of gasoline.
4. Environmentalists <u>have advocated</u> electric cars, for example.

Developing Your Style: Choosing the Active Voice, EXERCISE B

1. passive; The American League has outdone the National League for the third straight year.
2. passive; Gary Cooper played the title role in *The Lou Gehrig Story.*
3. active
4. passive; Did this talented actor receive any kind of award?

Developing Your Style: Choosing the Active Voice, EXERCISE C

Answers will vary; possible answers are given. In the past, the teaching staff advised college-bound students. However, graduates who were entering the job force were not given any special treatment. Students and teachers recognized the need for professional career counseling. Soon, concerned educators bombarded the Board of Education with petitions. The board hired special counselors to satisfy this need. These counselors wisely sought the help of the business community. Eventually, several business executives underwrote a summer internship program for graduates. An overflowing crowd attended the special student meeting at school, Since that time, many students have taken advantage of the internship program. Their business mentors have successfully trained them.

Overview

Throughout their scholastic careers, most students are expected to take a variety of standardized tests. Developing skill in taking standardized tests will be of great value to students as they proceed through the grades and encounter such tests.

Most standardized tests, including the Scholastic Aptitude Test (SAT), include a verbal component that tests students' knowledge of vocabulary. In order to perform up to their potential and achieve competitive scores on these tests of verbal skills, students need substantive preparation.

To achieve success on standardized tests, students must be able to apply their knowledge of vocabulary to the types of items encountered on these tests. Therefore, in addition to developing their vocabularies, students should learn the format of standardized tests and practice answering the various types of items included on the tests.

Description of the Vocabulary Practice Tests

The following pages are designed to familiarize students with standardized test formats and to give students practice in taking the verbal portions of these tests. Each of the practice tests includes one or more of the following types of questions: synonyms, antonyms, verbal analogies, and sentence completions.

Organization

The vocabulary practice tests are structured so that the tests become increasingly challenging as students progress from grade to grade. This progression will enable students to continue developing their vocabulary and test-taking skills throughout their scholastic careers and will prepare them for the pivotal standardized tests they are likely to encounter in their last few years of high school.

The structure of the Vocabulary Practice Tests for Grade 10 enables you to devote the first part of the school year to developing students' vocabulary skills before testing their skills in simulated-test situations. The first three tests are each divided into sections that focus on a single vocabulary skill. For example, the first section of Test 1 consists entirely of antonyms. You have the option of administering the first three tests in their entirety or using each of the sections as a separate test. Test 5, which is similar in structure to the first three tests, provides you with the same option. Test 4, on the other hand, consists of only one section and is limited to sentence-completion items. The final two tests are both modeled after a typical standardized test and include all three types of vocabulary questions. These tests make it possible for you to create simulated-test situations in which students are required to use all of their vocabulary skills.

The Vocabulary Practice Tests for Grade 10 are as follows:

Test 1	Antonyms
	Verbal Analogies
Test 2	Sentence Completions
	Antonyms
Test 3	Verbal Analogies
	Antonyms
	Sentence Completions
Test 4	Sentence Completions

Test 5	Antonyms
	Sentence Completions
	Verbal Analogies
Test 6	20 Antonyms
	15 Verbal Analogies
	10 Sentence Completions
Test 7	25 Antonyms
	20 Verbal Analogies
	15 Sentence Completions

How to Use the Vocabulary Practice Tests

Before you begin administering the Vocabulary Practice Tests to your students, give each of them a copy of Test-Taking Strategies for Students, page 335.

This section provides students with proven test-taking strategies that should help to improve their performance on standardized tests.

We urge you to use these vocabulary tests for practice, not for grades, in order to allow students to develop comfort and facility with test items and situations. Although you may choose to provide students with a limited amount of time in which to complete each test, try to allow at least one minute for each item on the test. If you choose to administer Tests 6 and 7 as simulated standardized tests, you should divide each test into two parts and allow students thirty minutes to complete each part. The first part should consist of all antonym items and the first ten verbal analogies; the second part should include the remaining verbal analogies and all the sentence completions.

Answer Sheet

The answer sheet included here (page 381) is a blackline master. You may duplicate copies for your classes. Please be aware that these blackline copies cannot be read in a scanner.

Test-Taking Strategies for Students

General Strategies

Over the course of your school career, you will probably encounter many standardized tests. To perform well on these tests, you must be well-prepared and have a solid background in the subjects being tested. In addition, you will benefit from using the following proven test-taking strategies.

1. Before taking any standardized test, you should learn about the types of items included on the test. Familiarize yourself with the instructions and examples for each type of item on the test. When you take the test, avoid wasting valuable time reading the instructions and examples. You should know what is required with each type of item, and one glance should tell you which type of items you are about to tackle.

2. Difficult questions often take much more time to answer than easier questions. If you cannot answer a question quickly, skip over it and focus on answering easier ones. Once you have reached the end of the section, return to the questions you passed over and try to answer them.

3. Avoid making wild guesses. If you are unsure of the correct answer to a question, examine the choices to see if any can be eliminated. Once you have eliminated two or more choices, you can make an educated guess.

4. Trust your first instincts. Avoid going back and changing your answers, unless you are reasonably certain that your original answer was incorrect.

5. Make sure that you enter each of your answers beside the appropriate number on your answer sheet. If you pass over a question, make sure that you do not forget to skip over the corresponding number on your answer sheet.

Taking Standardized Vocabulary Exams

Standardized vocabulary examinations generally include three types of items: antonyms, verbal analogies, and sentence completions. In each of the antonym items, you are given one word and asked to select the word most opposite in meaning. In each of the verbal analogies, you are given a pair of words and asked to determine the relationship between the two words and then select the word pair with the most similar relationship. Finally, the sentence completions provide a sentence with one or two blank spaces for which the most appropriate word or words must be selected.

Antonyms

Antonym items require you to choose the best opposite of a given word. Before you begin a group of antonym items, you will encounter the following instructions. Read them thoroughly now and study the example.

Directions: Each question below consists of a word in CAPITAL LETTERS, followed by five lettered words or phrases. Choose the word or phrase that is most nearly *opposite* in meaning to the word in CAPITAL LETTERS. Blacken the letter of your answer on the answer sheet. Because some of the choices are close in meaning, consider all the choices before deciding which is best.

Example:

TEPID:

(A) bold
(B) cool
(C) curious
(D) rancid
(E) engaging

Cool is the correct answer. You would have filled in the circle marked B on your answer sheet.

Answering Antonym Items

Having familiarized yourself with these instructions, you will be able to avoid wasting valuable time reading them on an actual test. Instead, you will be able to glance at the instructions, and if you see the underlined word *opposite,* you will know what is required.

To give you some insight into antonym items, we will discuss the following example:

WHISPER:

(A) shout
(B) murmur
(C) mutter
(D) speak
(E) praise

Because the word WHISPER can be either a noun or a verb and has several possible meanings, you must first determine the form in which the word is being used. Note that in antonym items the word in capital letters and the answer always belong to the same word group: all nouns, all verbs, all adjectives, or all adverbs. So while WHISPER by itself could be a noun or a verb, you can tell from the answer choices that it is the verb WHISPER for which the best antonym is required here. Once you have concluded that WHISPER is being used as a verb, you should focus on defining it. The verb WHISPER is most often used mean "to speak very softly." Given this definition, it should be apparent that the best opposite is *shout,* which means "to cry out loudly."

If you were not completely sure of the meaning of WHISPER, it would have also been possible for you to come up with the correct answer by eliminating the other choices. To do so, you would look at the opposite for each of the choices. For *murmur,* it would be *articulate.* For *mutter,* it would be *enunciate.* For speak it would be *keep silent.* The word *blame* might be one antonym for *praise.* But for *shout,* the best antonym is WHISPER, the original word.

Tips for Answering Antonym Questions

1. Be aware that many words have more than one meaning. Before choosing an antonym for a given word, read the word and the word choices, and determine the meaning of the given word in relation to the choices.

2. If you are not completely sure of the given word's meaning, try using it in a sentence. This technique may help trigger a contextual meaning for the word.

3. If necessary, try using the given word's root, prefix, or suffix to unlock its meaning.

4. Make sure that you choose the word or phrase that is *opposite* to the given word. Take care that you do not mistakenly choose a word that is *similar* to the original word.

5. Many words do not have exact opposites, or antonyms. Therefore, consider the choices carefully. Always choose the word *most nearly* opposite in meaning to the given word.

6. If the correct answer is not immediately apparent, try to eliminate as many choices as possible by looking at their opposites.

Verbal Analogies

Verbal analogies require you to determine a relationship between a given pair of words and then look at five other word pairs and select the pair with the relationship most similar to the original pair. Before you begin a group of verbal analogies, you will encounter directions similar to the following. Read these directions thoroughly now and study the example.

Directions: Each question below consists of a related pair of words in CAPITAL LETTERS, followed by five lettered pairs of words. Choose the pair that best expresses a relationship similar to that expressed in the pair in CAPITAL LETTERS. Blacken the letter of your answer on the answer sheet.

Example:

PHYSICS : CHEMISTRY ::
(A) rock 'n' roll : music
(B) building : architect
(C) philosophy : logic
(D) prose : literature
(E) swimming : tennis

Swimming : tennis is the correct answer. You would have filled in the circle marked E on your answer sheet. When looking at the example, did you notice the single colon between the two words in each pair? And the double colon after the original pair? They are a kind of shorthand. The single colon stands for the words *is to,* and the double colon stands for the word *as.*

Answering Verbal Analogies

To answer a verbal analogy, you must first determine the relationship between the two words in the original pair. In the preceding example you would look at the relationship between the words *physics* and *chemistry.* You should note that both physics and chemistry are types of science. In other words, the two words fit into the same category. Next, you should look through the possible answers and find two words with a similar relationship. Choices A, C, and D all include a general category and a more specific genre or subject that fits into this category: *rock 'n' roll* is a type of *music, logic* is a branch of *philosophy,* and *prose* is a type of *literature.* Therefore, all three of these choices can be eliminated. Choice B can also be eliminated because the word *building* refers to either an activity or an object, while the word *architect* refers to a type of person. If you look at choice E, however, you will note that the two words fit into the same category: both *swimming* and *tennis* are sports. So the correct answer is E.

You may find it helpful to formulate a sentence expressing the relationship between the original pair. Use the words *first* and *second* in your sentence, showing the order in which the words appear in the item. For example, if the two words were *rocket* and *soars,* you might write the following sentence: The first word is an object and the second word is the action it performs. This technique can be extremely helpful because the order in which the two words appear is often vital. For instance, if the relationship between the original pair is cause/effect, you must choose a pair of words whose relationship is cause/effect, not effect/cause.

Typical Relationships

The following are some of the most common types of relationships used in verbal analogies:

Same Meaning

    grammatically equal

            START : BEGIN
            ANNOYED : ANGRY

    grammatically unequal

            EARLY : PREMATURE
            WEALTH : AFFLUENT

Opposite Meanings

    grammatically equal

            LOUD : QUIET
            SATISFY : DISSATISFY

    grammatically unequal

            STRONG : WEAKLY
            QUICKLY : SLOW

Relationship	Example
Cause/Effect	FIRE : SMOKE
Effect/Cause	DEVASTATION : WAR
Lesser/Greater	ANNOYED : FURIOUS
Greater/Lesser	DASH : WALK
Whole/Part	FOOT : TOE
Part/Whole	LEG : PANTS
Group/Example	BIRD : EAGLE
Example/Group	BASEBALL : SPORT
Type of Person/ Essential Quality	PHILANTHROPIST : KIND
Essential Quality/ Type of Person	STAMINA : ATHLETE
Creature or Thing/ Associated Quality	MOUSE : QUIET
Associated Quality/ Creature or Thing	SPEED : GAZELLE
Sequence	FIRST : SECOND
Person or Thing/ Function or Action	ARTIST : CREATES
Object/Action	HAMMER : BANGS
Profession/Tool	LUMBERJACK : AX

You should also be aware that in certain cases there is no relationship between the original pair of words. Whenever this is the case, you should choose a pair of words where each word is a synonym of the corresponding word in the original pair. For example, if the original pair is INTELLIGENT : SHOWY, the correct answer might be *smart : flashy.*

Tips for Answering Analogy Questions

1. First, determine the relationship in the given pair of words.

2. Parts of speech may be a clue. Generally, the correct answer will consist of a pair of words that are the same parts of speech as the original pair.

3. Make sure that your choice reflects or parallels the structure of the given word pair. If the relationship of the given pair is greater to lesser, the relationship of the words in the pair you choose must also be greater to lesser, not lesser to greater.

4. Because a number of the pairs of words may express relationships *somewhat* similar to that of the original pair, make sure that the relationship of the pair you choose is the *most* similar to that of the original pair.

Sentence Completions

Sentence completion items require you to choose a word that correctly completes the meaning of a sentence. Before you begin a group of sentence completions, you will encounter directions similar to the following. Read these directions thoroughly now and study the example.

Directions: Each of the following sentences has a blank space, indicating that a word has been omitted. Beneath the sentence are five lettered words. Choose the word that best completes the meaning of the sentence as a whole. Blacken the letter of your answer on the answer sheet.

Example:

Although she was usually _____ her own convenience, my grandmother insisted that night on having the nicest room at the hotel.

(A) supportive of
(B) open to
(C) indifferent to
(D) appreciative of
(E) enchanted by

Indifferent to is the correct answer. You would have filled the circle marked C on your answer sheet.

Answering Sentence Completion Items

The best way to approach answering a sentence completion question is by first reading only the sentence and supplying your own word or words for any gap. You will usually have a distinct feeling for what type of meaning is required. With that in mind, look at the answer choices and cross out those that make no sense. If that leaves you with more than one answer choice, pick the one that seems most logical and convincing.

The sentences given frequently have two or more clauses, and one of them contains a verbal clue to what is expected. If one clause is introduced by *therefore, for, since, because, furthermore, moreover, similarly,* or *in addition,* you know that what follows will either substantiate, explain, or elaborate what is said in the other clause or clauses. On the other hand, any clause that is introduced by *but, however, although, though, despite, conversely, nevertheless,* or *nonetheless* should express something opposed to what is said in the other clause or clauses.

Review the example that appeared beneath the directions. Note that the first clause begins with the word *although*, indicating that the information in the first clause expresses something opposed to what is said in the second clause. With this in mind, you should look at the second clause and think about what the grandmother is demanding. Clearly, the second clause would not oppose the first if the grandmother were *supportive of, open to, appreciative of,* or *enchanted by* her convenience. Therefore, the only logical response is *indifferent*, which fits into the sentence perfectly.

Tackling the Two-Blank Sentence

When dealing with a sentence with two blanks, you must select the best pair of words in the answer choices. The first word of the answer pair goes into the first blank, and its companion goes into the second blank. Both words have to make good sense in the sentence. Therefore, as soon as you find that one word does not fit, you must eliminate the entire pair. Read the following two-blank sentence and try to determine the best answer.

After the _____ ball game Jim was so _____ that he went right to sleep.

The impression we get from reading the uncompleted sentence is that Jim's game was very tiring. The adjective that fits into the first blank should help to explain why Jim's game was so draining. If we look at the first word in each pair, we will see that choices B and C can be eliminated because both *relaxing* and *restful* contradict the impression conveyed in the rest of the sentence. However, the three other choices must remain under consideration because the words *difficult, challenging,* and *strenuous* all help to explain why Jim's game was tiring.

The word that fits into the second blank should describe Jim's condition. Since two choices have already been eliminated, only A, D, and E remain under consideration. When we look at the second word in each of these pairs, the correct answer becomes obvious. Neither *nervous* nor *bored* fit into the sentence. Yet the word *fatigued* fits perfectly. Therefore, the answer is D.

Tips for Answering Sentence Completions

1. Use context clues to help you unlock the meaning of the sentence.

2. Look for signal words, such as *because, therefore, but, however,* or *although,* that indicate a structural relationship in the incomplete sentence.

3. When completing a sentence with two blanks, remember that both words in the correct pair have to fit logically into the sentence.

4. If you are unfamiliar with one of the word choices, try fitting each of the remaining choices into the sentence. If one of them fits perfectly into the sentence, select it as your answer. On the other hand, if the remaining four choices all seem unsuitable, the unknown word is probably the right one.

5. If you are unfamiliar with one of the word choices following a two-blank sentence, test the unknown word's companion in its proper blank. If it does not fit, you can eliminate the entire pair. If it does fit, proceed with the other answer choices. If none of them seem good, the choice with the unknown word is probably the right one. However, if one of the other word pairs fits perfectly, choose that one as your answer and forget the rest.

Acknowledgment

Certain SAT directions and answer sheet segments were selected from the verbal part of the SAT examination. However, the test questions are produced entirely by the publisher. Reprinted by permission of Educational Testing Service, the copyright owner.

Permission to reprint the SAT material does not constitute review or endorsement by the Educational Testing Service or the College Board of this publication as a whole or of any other testing information it may contain.

Test 1

Antonyms

Directions: Each of the following questions consists of a word in capital letters, followed by five lettered words or phrases. Choose the word or phrase that is most nearly *opposite* in meaning to the word in capital letters. Mark the letter of your answer on your answer sheet. Since some of the choices require you to distinguish fine shades of meaning, consider all the choices before deciding which is best.

Example:

COMPLICATED:

(A) fair
(B) reasonable
(C) simple
(D) preoccupied
(E) indifferent

Simple is the correct answer. You would have filled in the circle marked C on your answer sheet.

---

1. CONVOLUTED:

   (A) imaginative
   (B) real
   (C) surreal
   (D) circuitous
   (E) straightforward

2. DEFTNESS:

   (A) clumsiness
   (B) crudeness
   (C) swiftness
   (D) rapidity
   (E) cruelty

3. IMPERCEPTIBLY:

   (A) fairly
   (B) justly
   (C) conspicuously
   (D) irregularly
   (E) barely

4. REVELING:

   (A) advising
   (B) interrogating
   (C) chastising
   (D) cursing
   (E) lamenting

5. INTERMINABLE:

   (A) everlasting
   (B) suave
   (C) gross
   (D) hasty
   (E) proud

6. DOUGHTY:

   (A) bold
   (B) clandestine
   (C) resilient
   (D) fearful
   (E) useless

7. CREDULITY:
    (A) skepticism
    (B) incredible
    (C) creed
    (D) folly
    (E) loyalty

8. PROSAIC:
    (A) mosaic
    (B) ripe
    (C) ordinary
    (D) fanciful
    (E) plain

9. AVARICIOUS:
    (A) stingy
    (B) generous
    (C) recalcitrant
    (D) odious
    (E) inflexible

10. BIBULOUS:
    (A) sober
    (B) sickly
    (C) colorful
    (D) disheveled
    (E) infamous

11. VENTURE:
    (A) routine
    (B) risk
    (C) chance
    (D) debate
    (E) ambiguity

12. PEONS:
    (A) snakes
    (B) birds
    (C) aristocrats
    (D) laborers
    (E) wanderers

13. FLOUT:
    (A) revere
    (B) disrespect
    (C) disregard
    (D) dissuade
    (E) dismember

14. SOBRIETY:
    (A) dislocation
    (B) safety
    (C) myopia
    (D) levity
    (E) inebriation

15. AWRY:
    (A) crooked
    (B) twisted
    (C) clear
    (D) emulous
    (E) straight

16. LITERALLY:
    (A) figuratively
    (B) unimaginative
    (C) pedantically
    (D) avuncularly
    (E) plainly

17. LONGEVITY:
    (A) faithlessness
    (B) ambiguity
    (C) fervor
    (D) brevity
    (E) ennui

18. IMPERATIVE:
    (A) unnecessary
    (B) conclusive
    (C) significant
    (D) corrupt
    (E) empirical

19. GRIMACE:
    (A) smile
    (B) swift
    (C) titanic
    (D) ambitious
    (E) cheap

Verbal Analogies

Directions: Each of the following questions contains a related pair of words in capital letters, followed by five lettered pairs of words. Choose the pair that best expresses the relationship most similar to that expressed in the original pair. Mark the letter of your answer on your answer sheet.

Example:

BRAVE : COWARD ::

(A) dumb : stupid
(B) loud : abrasive
(C) fearful : hero
(D) strange : pleasant
(E) cursed : funny

Fearful : hero is the correct answer. You would have filled in the circle marked C on your answer sheet.

---

20. INDULGENCE : FORGIVENESS ::

(A) charity : kindness
(B) ennui : excellence
(C) anger : protest
(D) apathy : antipathy
(E) brutality : ignorance

21. GRIMACING : PAIN : :

(A) groveling : happiness
(B) smelling : hunting
(C) smiling : pleasure
(D) sitting : standing
(E) blessing : renovating

22. LACQUERED : EXPOSED ::

(A) coated : devoured
(B) dipped : dripped
(C) deified : reified
(D) envied : enlightened
(E) shielded : revealed

23. FLICKER : BIRD ::

(A) estuary : lake
(B) light : sun
(C) bovine : mammal
(D) waver : fly
(E) cremate : bury

24. MESAS : MOUNTAINTOPS ::

(A) ponds : lakes
(B) debris : explosion
(C) catastrophe : upset
(D) sojourn : voyage
(E) cascade : surreptitious

25. INDOLENCE : HOBO ::

(A) veracity : stupidity
(B) desolation : despair
(C) creativity : artist
(D) edelweiss : botany
(E) countenance : physiognomy

26. DEFERENCE : CONSIDERATION ::

(A) ignominy : prejudice
(B) insensitivity : avarice
(C) akimbo : malign
(D) respect : politeness
(E) ennui : enigma

27. SURMISED : DETECTIVE ::

(A) submerged : pilot
(B) aloft : spelunker
(C) evaporate : runner
(D) inferred : sleuth
(E) deferred : Svengali

---

28. SURREPTITIOUS : SPY ::

 (A) dishonest : club
 (B) honest : cloud
 (C) courageous : dome
 (D) tricky : magician
 (E) stealthy : cow

29. BEVELING : CARPENTER ::

 (A) milking : manufacturer
 (B) slicing : golfer
 (C) mapping : cartographer
 (D) testing : confidant
 (E) releasing : polluter

30. REBUKE : CONDEMNATION ::

 (A) chagrin : chastisement
 (B) disclaimer : harangue
 (C) pommel : plummet
 (D) patriotism : chauvinism
 (E) criticism : denunciation

31. DESOLATION : WAR ::

 (A) artistry : poets
 (B) disruption : recess
 (C) progress : cooperation
 (D) idiocy : generals
 (E) fascism : army

32. EXTENUATING : ALIBIS ::

 (A) excusing : justification
 (B) disqualified : unimpeded
 (C) avuncular : cheap
 (D) beveled : departed
 (E) billeted : buffered

33. EDELWEISS : MOUNTAIN ::

 (A) dune grass : beach
 (B) seaweed : river
 (C) moss : cliff
 (D) magnolia : savannah
 (E) alp : ocean

34. CHAMOIS : ANTELOPE ::

 (A) bone : dog
 (B) tusk : whale
 (C) tail : unicorn
 (D) ivory : elephant
 (E) skin : snake

35. ZENITH : BASE ::

 (A) peak : foundation
 (B) top : side
 (C) circle : square
 (D) equator : middle
 (E) point : bottom

36. COUNTENANCE : MOOD ::

 (A) soul : ice
 (B) word : lip
 (C) indolence : disobedience
 (D) generosity : slavishness
 (E) expression : feeling

37. VERACITY : DISHONESTY ::

 (A) repute : dispute
 (B) honesty : rivalry
 (C) truthfulness : deceit
 (D) guile : bile
 (E) integrity : serendipity

Test 2

Sentence Completions

Directions: Each of the following sentences contains one or two blank spaces to be filled in by one of the five lettered choices below. Select the word or group of words that best completes the meaning of the sentence. Mark the letter of your answer on your answer sheet.

Example:

Because they were _____, the boys were punished by their coach.

(A) fair
(B) studious
(C) conscientious
(D) disobedient
(E) punctual

Disobedient is the correct answer. You would have filled in the circle marked D on your answer sheet.

---

1. Our teachers demonstrated great _____ during the emergency at our school.

   (A) poise
   (B) suave
   (C) libations
   (D) jurisdiction
   (E) sagacity

2. His innocence was supported by the _____ of an eyewitness who supplied an alibi.

   (A) taciturn
   (B) jostling
   (C) avowal
   (D) inert
   (E) claque

3. The embargo _____ the citizens to rely on their own energy supplies.

   (A) dilapidated
   (B) stipulated
   (C) forded
   (D) rebuked
   (E) constrained

4. His good cheer, as sincere as it was _____, helped everyone enjoy the cruise.

   (A) poised
   (B) impassive
   (C) assimilating
   (D) inert
   (E) infectious

5. Her _____ manner and strict upbringing made Sheila seem unfriendly.

   (A) taciturn
   (B) ford
   (C) ecstatic
   (D) suave
   (E) inert

6. Despite his _____ appearance and legendary philosophic detachment, the Roman orator Cicero was in fact a man capable of deep feeling and passion.

   (A) dilapidated
   (B) impassive
   (C) avowal
   (D) constrained
   (E) incredulous

7. The visitors from the countryside were upset when they were _____ by the pedestrians on the crowded streets of the city.

(A) forded
(B) sacrificed
(C) stipulated
(D) jostled
(E) insinuated

8. Although she seemed _____ in her initial interview, Mrs. Foster failed to impress our company's vice-president during her audition.

(A) dilapidated
(B) infectious
(C) suave
(D) marzipan
(E) inert

9. After the _____, the ancient Greeks completed the ceremony with a procession around the altar.

(A) libation
(B) ford
(C) sagacity
(D) sovereigns
(E) jostling

10. The victim of the accident was _____ when the ambulance arrived.

(A) suave
(B) inert
(C) impassive
(D) incredulous
(E) marzipan

11. Although they have not won the championship in several years, the players on that ball club speak _____ about how easy it will be for them to win this year's race.

(A) ford
(B) ecstatically
(C) evocatively
(D) arrogantly
(E) taciturn

12. At the end of Dr. Restaino's address, the audience enthusiastically applauded those sections of her speech that were _____ of President Kennedy's remarks about social justice.

(A) assimilating
(B) ford
(C) evocative
(D) claque
(E) surreptitious

13. The summit failed to bring leaders to agreement on the demands _____ by those who wished to disrupt the balance of power in the area.

(A) jostled
(B) assimilated
(C) discouraged
(D) eradicated
(E) stipulated

14. The revolt attempted to _____ all social evils from the society.

(A) stipulate
(B) jostle
(C) eradicate
(D) rebuke
(E) jerk

15. The orchestra was led that evening by Leonard Bernstein, a conductor noted for his _____ moving performances.

(A) incredulous
(B) imperiously
(C) prosaically
(D) ecstatically
(E) arrogantly

Antonyms

Directions: Each of the following questions consists of a word in capital letters, followed by five lettered words or phrases. Choose the word or phrase that is most nearly *opposite* in meaning to the word in capital letters. Mark the letter of your answer on your answer sheet. Since some of the choices require you to distinguish fine shades of meaning, consider all the choices before deciding which is best.

Example:
GENEROUS:

(A) cowardly
(B) mean
(C) stingy
(D) recalcitrant
(E) odd

Stingy is the correct answer. You would have filled in the circle marked C on your answer sheet.

16. WARRENS:

(A) curves
(B) mazes
(C) straightaways
(D) hills
(E) okapis

17. TITANIC:

(A) tremendous
(B) powerful
(C) catastrophic
(D) minuscule
(E) relaxing

18. PARANOIA:

(A) sanity
(B) desperateness
(C) silliness
(D) transmission
(E) delusions

19. CAVORTING:

(A) rolling around
(B) standing still
(C) twisting
(D) speaking
(E) preaching loudly

20. TREMULOUS:

(A) quivering
(B) boasting
(C) convulsing
(D) steady
(E) uneasy

21. PSYCHOPATHIC:

(A) restless
(B) disturbed
(C) normal
(D) enigmatic
(E) peculiar

22. OFFICIOUS:

(A) jealous
(B) lazy
(C) dumb
(D) unobtrusive
(E) ridiculous

23. MOTTLED:

(A) uniforms
(B) inconsistent
(C) extreme
(D) pleasant
(E) transparent

24. AUDACIOUSLY:

    (A) fearfully
    (B) magnanimously
    (C) generously
    (D) irrelevantly
    (E) irreligiously

25. IMPERIOUSLY:

    (A) slowly
    (B) quickly
    (C) quietly
    (D) loudly
    (E) humbly

26. PURIFIED:

    (A) disregarded
    (B) encumbered
    (C) soiled
    (D) dallied
    (E) ensconced

27. CONTRITION:

    (A) pride
    (B) confession
    (C) contradiction
    (D) innocence
    (E) ennui

28. PROMONTORIES:

    (A) mesas
    (B) buttes
    (C) hills
    (D) valleys
    (E) boroughs

29. LUMINOUS:

    (A) brilliant
    (B) copied
    (C) genuine
    (D) irregular
    (E) opaque

30. SUPPLICATION:

    (A) demand
    (B) request
    (C) curse
    (D) prayer
    (E) proposal

31. CONVULSIVE:

    (A) unusual
    (B) usual
    (C) predictable
    (D) controlled
    (E) urgent

32. BOASTED:

    (A) underestimated
    (B) dilapidated
    (C) cavorted
    (D) exaggerated
    (E) evaluated

33. PLAUSIBILITY:

    (A) verity
    (B) improbability
    (C) naivete
    (D) purity
    (E) warrens

Test 3

Verbal Analogies

Directions: Each of the following questions contains a related pair of words in capital letters, followed by five lettered pairs of words. Choose the pair that best expresses a relationship most similar to that expressed in the original pair. Mark the letter of your answer on your answer sheet.

Example:

WEALTHY : POOR ::

(A) rich : impoverished
(B) smart : artistic
(C) obedient : intelligent
(D) odd : sinful
(E) loud : weird

Rich : impoverished is the correct answer. You would have filled in the circle marked A on your answer sheet.

1. ABALONE : SEA ::

   (A) land : earth
   (B) sky : ceiling
   (C) dry : wet
   (D) bird : sky
   (E) fish : tree

2. NURSERY : TREES ::

   (A) prison : jail
   (B) hospital : welfare
   (C) gardens : flowers
   (D) railroad : caboose
   (E) skyscraper : glass

3. LUSTER : BRILLIANCE ::

   (A) dead : grave
   (B) spirit : sky
   (C) glow : shine
   (D) arm : leg
   (E) manipulation : wrestling

4. HUES : PAINTING ::

   (A) notes : song
   (B) legends : television
   (C) myths : aborigines
   (D) waves : sailors
   (E) handcuffs : officers

5. AKIN : ALIEN ::

   (A) related : strange
   (B) hostile : terrifying
   (C) relaxing : initiating
   (D) musical : artistic
   (E) affluent : servile

6. MASQUE : PERFORMANCE ::

   (A) seashell : mermaid
   (B) convention : party
   (C) play : show
   (D) convent : rectory
   (E) monk : robe

7. AUGUST : HAUGHTY ::

   (A) conspicuous : imminent
   (B) erratic : stuffy
   (C) grisly : untamed
   (D) lonely : enlarged
   (E) reverent : sanctimonious

8. CANDELABRUM : CANDLE ::

   (A) geese : flock
   (B) ducks : birds
   (C) flagstaff : flag
   (D) delusion : dream
   (E) disease : death

9. ARABESQUE : PLAIN ::

   (A) fixed : doleful
   (B) erratic : moribund
   (C) faint : sorrowful
   (D) comic : depressing
   (E) elaborate : simple

10. DISAPPROBATION : ACCEPTANCE ::

   (A) willing : unwilling
   (B) painfulness : ennui
   (C) censure : endorsement
   (D) morose : fatigue
   (E) salvation : sanctification

11. PHANTASM : GHOST ::

   (A) illusion : dream
   (B) delusion : despair
   (C) curtail : appearance
   (D) simulation : sanctity
   (E) spirit : elaboration

12. HABILIMENTS : TAILOR ::

   (A) clouds : farmers
   (B) horses : ranchers
   (C) architect : yacht
   (D) owner : store
   (E) tables : carpenter

13. MUMMER : PANTOMINE ::

   (A) singer : stage
   (B) ball : game
   (C) doctor : nurse
   (D) teacher : student
   (E) actor : play

14. APPURTENANCES : ESSENTIALS ::

   (A) items : people
   (B) manners : morals
   (C) accessories : requirements
   (D) brandishments : illusions
   (E) demons : pariahs

15. CONSPICUOUS : LOUD ::

   (A) dismal : lonely
   (B) pronounced : intentional
   (C) moribund : august
   (D) piquancy : noteworthy
   (E) noticeable : bright

16. LACQUERING : STRIPPING ::

   (A) covering : disclosing
   (B) discovering : showing
   (C) polishing : smoothing
   (D) opening : closing
   (E) revealing : exorcising

Antonyms

Directions: Each of the following questions consists of a word in capital letters, followed by five lettered words or phrases. Choose the word or phrase that is most nearly *opposite* in meaning to the word in capital letters. Mark the letter of your answer on your answer sheet. Since some of the choices require you to distinguish fine shades of meaning, consider all the choices before deciding which is best.

Example:

LIGHT:

(A) night
(B) bright
(C) dark
(D) dim
(E) faded

Dark is the correct answer. You would have filled in the circle marked C on your answer sheet.

17. DELUSION:

(A) reality
(B) deception
(C) assumption
(D) mistake
(E) error

18. IMMINENT:

(A) remotely possible
(B) rarely happening
(C) frequently occurring
(D) sporadically appearing
(E) unannounced

19. PARIAH:

(A) hero
(B) hunter
(C) priest
(D) rabbi
(E) outcast

20. ERRATIC:

(A) random
(B) mackintosh
(C) arabesque
(D) predictable
(E) oracular

21. GRISLY:

(A) engaged
(B) pleasant
(C) divorced
(D) abandoned
(E) endangered

22. IMPERTURBABLE:

(A) demanding
(B) resourceful
(C) circumstantial
(D) excitable
(E) eligible

23. SURCEASE:

(A) commencement
(B) graduation
(C) recess
(D) renovation
(E) devaluation

24. SUBSIDIARY:

(A) essential
(B) common
(C) disproportionate
(D) bogus
(E) primary

25. CIRCUMVENT:

(A) disclaim
(B) propose
(C) cause
(D) prevent
(E) depict

26. STALWART:

(A) egocentric
(B) unabashed
(C) deceptive
(D) underhanded
(E) faint-hearted

27. HEIRLOOMS:

(A) baubles
(B) doldrums
(C) dolmens
(D) fagots
(E) quinces

28. SMITTEN:

(A) clothed
(B) naked
(C) measured
(D) promoted
(E) unmoved

29. EMACIATED:

(A) enamored
(B) broken
(C) billowed
(D) obese
(E) malevolent

Sentence Completions

Directions: Each of the following sentences contains one or two blank spaces to be filled in by one of the five lettered choices below. Select the word or group of words that best completes the meaning of the sentence. Mark the letter of your answer on your answer sheet.

Example:

The soldier received a _____ wound when he was riddled with gunshots.

(A) superficial
(B) mortal
(C) elegiac
(D) surface
(E) stalwart

Mortal is the correct answer. You would have filled in the circle marked B on your answer sheet.

30. The poet mentioned _____ and _____ in his epic in order to give local color to the poem.

(A) akin-pathos
(B) certitude—covert
(C) damsons—wattles
(D) quinces—enigmas
(E) svelte—paddocks

31. The _____ were studied by botanists for signs of disease.

(A) quinces
(B) paddocks
(C) fagots
(D) railleries
(E) sylvans

32. The _____ of the Irish estate contained charming displays of flowers and trees.

    (A) paddocks
    (B) eulogy
    (C) luster
    (D) disdain
    (E) billowing

33. The priest's _____ praised the dead hero whose funeral was well attended.

    (A) delusion
    (B) eulogy
    (C) ingrate
    (D) pariah
    (E) oracle

34. The _____ gusts of wind filled and emptied the sails of our sailboat in a fickle manner all day long.

    (A) pathos
    (B) temporal
    (C) billowing
    (D) exquisite
    (E) imperious

35. His _____ remarks were often quoted by the newspapers that wished to give as brief an account as possible.

    (A) superfluous
    (B) terse
    (C) ingrate
    (D) covert
    (E) amenable

36. Playwrights avoid trying to create feelings of _____ for the villains that they fashion for their plays.

    (A) pathos
    (B) delusion
    (C) oracle
    (D) damsels
    (E) eulogy

37. Although the evil character in the novel possessed a definite _____, she was frequently depicted making kind and generous gestures.

    (A) edifice
    (B) pathos
    (C) malevolence
    (D) eulogy
    (E) disdain

38. Mrs. Lhun _____ the apples and oranges before making her purchases at the market.

    (A) scrutinized
    (B) lacquered
    (C) emaciated
    (D) billowed
    (E) converted

39. While rejecting the new student at their school, the prejudiced students showed their _____ for outsiders.

    (A) edifice
    (B) railleries
    (C) disdain
    (D) malevolence
    (E) gamboling

40. We were convinced of the _____ of the doctor's judgment even though we hoped his answer would be different from what it was.

    (A) edifice
    (B) habiliments
    (C) sylvan
    (D) syringa
    (E) certitude

41. Her _____ interruptions and pointed sense of humor made Mrs. Willey the most unpopular and avoided person on our cruise ship.

    (A) gamboling
    (B) covert
    (C) imperturbable
    (D) grisly
    (E) superfluous

42. The _____ honking of car horns in the street outside interrupted the meeting we were trying to have.

    (A) incessant
    (B) solicitous
    (C) disreputable
    (D) august
    (E) sardonic

43. At the turn of the last century, art critics began to criticize _____ works while urging artists to return to the more classical models that provide a logical and wholesome example.

    (A) exquisite
    (B) conspicuous
    (C) sylvan
    (D) decadent
    (E) imperturbable

44. The rustic beauty of the area prompted the newly-weds to choose this _____ location for their wedding pictures.

    (A) syringa
    (B) ingrate
    (C) phosphorescent
    (D) sylvan
    (E) erratic

Test 4

Sentence Completions

Directions: Each of the following sentences contains one or two blank spaces to be filled in by one of the five lettered choices below. Select the word or group of words that best completes the meaning of the sentence. Mark the letter of your answer on your answer sheet.

Example:

The teacher questioned all those _____ of stealing the class mascot.

(A) suspected
(B) deserving
(C) capable
(D) worthy
(E) incapable

Suspected is the correct answer. You would have filled in the circle marked A on your answer sheet.

1. The philosopher _____ the speaker's remarks for _____ that might prove to be untrue if examined in the light of logic.

    (A) spared—weakness
    (B) viled—non-sequitur
    (C) transcended—philosophy
    (D) scrutinized—subtleties
    (E) mettled—sophistry

2. Part of the bride's _____ included silverware that was handed down in her mother's family for generations.

    (A) dowry
    (B) paraphernalia
    (C) philosophy
    (D) ensign
    (E) emulation

3. A _____ is often contained in hymns that treat the theme of _____ nature.

    (A) chastisement—corrupt
    (B) covert—human
    (C) tempest—animal
    (D) lamentation—mortal
    (E) piety—supernatural

4. Many pastoral paintings depict the _____ atmosphere of farm life with a feeling of _____ and effortlessness.

    (A) surly—ease
    (B) mettle—chagrin
    (C) sultry—excitement
    (D) serene—complacence
    (E) destitute—chorister

5. The crime of _____ is one that _____ many other offenses of a less serious nature.

    (A) mutiny—transcends
    (B) envy—exploits
    (C) discourse—establishes
    (D) emulation—imitates
    (E) blasphemy—mimics

6. The _____ of the _____ included explosives, revolutionary literature, and copies of sworn oaths that promised to sacrifice everything for the cause of social justice.

   (A) blasphemy—rebels
   (B) mettle—villains
   (C) vile—outlaws
   (D) paraphernalia—anarchists
   (E) resolution—associates

7. Our president's _____ contained both promise and _____ while outlining his plans for programs designed to improve conditions of the cities.

   (A) oration—suit
   (B) oration—replication
   (C) discourse—resolution
   (D) mutiny—lamentation
   (E) suit—conjecture

8. Detective Brown's _____ was so thorough and precise that his friends gave him the nickname "Encyclopedia."

   (A) exploit
   (B) emulation
   (C) malice
   (D) conjecture
   (E) ensign

9. The _____ at the window prompted us to guess that more than two people were in the room when the murder took place.

   (A) pieties
   (B) sultries
   (C) anarchists
   (D) subtleties
   (E) silhouettes

10. The _____ birds circled over the injured camel in the desert.

    (A) slanderous
    (B) serene
    (C) carrion
    (D) imminent
    (E) sated

11. All the guests were _____ by the abundance of food and quality of service at the banquet.

    (A) sated
    (B) entreated
    (C) conjectured
    (D) repealed
    (E) exploited

12. Some Greek philosophers are noted for their _____ worded aphorisms.

    (A) surly
    (B) portentously
    (C) sententiously
    (D) sultry
    (E) mortally

13. _____ weather provided us with a good day at the beach.

    (A) Serene
    (B) Carrion
    (C) Augmented
    (D) Entreated
    (E) Sultry

14. The boy's _____ to his father was a signal of weakness instead of respect.

    (A) discourse
    (B) oration
    (C) deference
    (D) blasphemy
    (E) replication

15. Audiences generally dislike characters in plays who are both _____ and _____.

    (A) sated—contemptuous
    (B) surly—vile
    (C) covert—clandestine
    (D) dowry—mortal
    (E) confounded—scorned

16. _____ is a quality that reflects rever-
ence, while _____ is a word used to label disrespect for religious matters.

    (A) Chorister—replication
    (B) Piety—blasphemy
    (C) Resolution—ensign
    (D) Spurn—reject
    (E) Emulation—akimbo

17. A single_____ is sometimes called upon
to deliver a closing speech in Greek
tragedy.

    (A) chorister
    (B) legacy
    (C) tempest
    (D) mettle
    (E) conspiracy

18. Alice's _____ of the sounds she heard
on the night of the murder were frightening and believable.

    (A) complacence
    (B) deference
    (C) replication
    (D) ensign
    (E) lamentation

19. A medieval knight's _____ was judged
on his fidelity to the code of chivalry.

    (A) mettle
    (B) deference
    (C) piety
    (D) tempest
    (E) conspiracy

20. A _____ physique is often thought of as
a sign of a healthy person.

    (A) spare
    (B) imminent
    (C) repealing
    (D) confounded
    (E) slanderous

21. Jason's emotional difficulty was caused
by a(n) _____ that doctors were never able to identify accurately.

    (A) envy
    (B) chastisement
    (C) legacy
    (D) infirmity
    (E) replication

22. The _____ forced our ship to seek shelter in the nearest harbor.

    (A) complacence
    (B) deference
    (C) anarchy
    (D) subversion
    (E) tempest

23. Her cautionary remarks on Friday
evening seemed _____ after so many
things went wrong with our trip on Saturday and Sunday.

    (A) surly
    (B) dowry
    (C) portentous
    (D) entreated
    (E) spare

24. My town's Fourth of July fireworks display ended with a _____ finale that
could be heard five miles away.

    (A) dowry
    (B) mortal
    (C) scrutinized
    (D) prodigious
    (E) augmented

25. Generals always try to _____ their
forces prior to engaging in combat.

    (A) augment
    (B) serene
    (C) carrion
    (D) malice
    (E) entreat

26. Demonstrators _____ the authorities to change the law that seemed wrong to them.
    (A) augmented
    (B) entreated
    (C) scrutinized
    (D) spared
    (E) envied

27. The _____ of those who launched the _____ was as apparent as it was fanatical.
    (A) malice—conspiracy
    (B) complacence—coup
    (C) silhouettes—uprising
    (D) philosophy—treaty
    (E) ensign—mutiny

28. Readers of gossip columns enjoy learning about the _____ of famous stars even when there is reason to think that what is written might be _____.
    (A) vile—unsubstantiated
    (B) exploits—slanderous
    (C) discourse—true
    (D) replication—exaggerated
    (E) lamentation—silly

29. Younger students may not understand the differences between a dissertation and a(n) _____.
    (A) legacy
    (B) oration
    (C) dowry
    (D) carrion
    (E) deference

30. When the sinking of the ocean liner seemed _____, the captain ordered all passengers to abandon ship.
    (A) sultry
    (B) scrutinized
    (C) imminent
    (D) confounded
    (E) slanderous

31. The political dissident was _____ when she received news of the order recalling her to the capital.
    (A) repealed
    (B) confounded
    (C) transcended
    (D) sultry
    (E) carrion

32. The chairperson issued a stern _____ to the committee member for her _____ remarks about other participants.
    (A) chastisement—vile
    (B) subtlety—mortal
    (C) philosophy—covert
    (D) oration—spurn
    (E) conjecture—sententious

33. The dictator's avowed _____ contained the _____ seeds of racism.
    (A) ensign—outward
    (B) paraphernalia—conspicuous
    (C) worldview—imminent
    (D) philosophy—covert
    (E) tempest—hidden

34. The _____ was assigned to a battleship that was sailing to the Pacific Ocean.
    (A) ensign
    (B) emulation
    (C) chorister
    (D) anarchist
    (E) dowry

Test 5

Antonyms

Directions: Each of the following questions consists of a word in capital letters, followed by five lettered words or phrases. Choose the word or phrase that is most nearly *opposite* in meaning to the word in capital letters. Mark the letter of your answer on your answer sheet. Since some of the choices require you to distinguish fine shades of meaning, consider all the choices before deciding which is best.

Example:

DIRTY:

(A) immaculate
(B) suspicious
(C) learned
(D) careful
(E) remorseful

Immaculate is the correct answer. You would have filled in the circle marked A on your answer sheet.

---

1. PROPRIETY:

   (A) remorse
   (B) discretion
   (C) impropriety
   (D) forgiveness
   (E) guilt

2. PUNCTILIOUS:

   (A) forgetful
   (B) careless
   (C) kind
   (D) demanding
   (E) unforgiving

3. ABATED:

   (A) increased
   (B) torn
   (C) damaged
   (D) scrupulous
   (E) apathetic

4. MALIGNANT:

   (A) absent
   (B) incoherent
   (C) delirious
   (D) benign
   (E) serpentine

5. CRYPTIC:

   (A) heavy
   (B) concentrated
   (C) informed
   (D) straightforward
   (E) forceful

6. STAUNCH:

   (A) inconsistent
   (B) regular
   (C) stoic
   (D) stolid
   (E) solid

7. BUNDLING:
   (A) launching
   (B) readying
   (C) delivering
   (D) dawdling
   (E) celebrating

8. BRITTLE:
   (A) complimentary
   (B) flattering
   (C) recalcitrant
   (D) disobedient
   (E) pliant

9. TROD:
   (A) tripped
   (B) fell
   (C) dropped
   (D) flew
   (E) slithered

10. FORLORN:
    (A) egocentric
    (B) popular
    (C) cheery
    (D) cautious
    (E) dynamic

11. INAUGURATING:
    (A) concluding
    (B) ranking
    (C) coping
    (D) washing
    (E) endorsing

12. EXHILARATES:
    (A) watches
    (B) waits
    (C) depresses
    (D) lifts
    (E) cooperates

13. DILAPIDATED:
    (A) quartered
    (B) sliced
    (C) spliced
    (D) broken
    (E) renovated

14. PROSAIC:
    (A) poetic
    (B) artistic
    (C) musical
    (D) uninformed
    (E) preposterous

15. CHASTISING:
    (A) rebuking
    (B) confronting
    (C) opening
    (D) complimenting
    (E) departing

Sentence Completions

Directions: Each of the following sentences contains one or two blank spaces to be filled in by one of the five lettered choices below. Select the word or group of words that best completes the meaning of the sentence. Mark the letter of your answer on your answer sheet.

Example:

The warden told the guards to _____ everywhere for the missing prisoners.

(A) search
(B) articulate
(C) research
(D) dispel
(E) dispose

Search is the correct answer. You would have filled in the circle marked A on your answer sheet.

16. _____ was a popular sport in the Middle Ages.

(A) Falconry
(B) Exertion
(C) Disdain
(D) Opacity
(E) Fluke

17. The _____ boy was thought to lack ambition.

(A) cryptic
(B) docile
(C) wallowed
(D) priming
(E) repulsive

18. The _____ scenes of the novel that depicted violence unnecessarily were criticized by many reviewers.

(A) perverse
(B) averted
(C) obligatory
(D) idyllic
(E) lethargic

19. Those _____ on the survey made the marketing analyst question the accuracy of the data.

(A) arias
(B) aberrations
(C) fragilities
(D) literalisms
(E) sensibilities

20. The snake _____ after being struck by the stick.

(A) pillaged
(B) engendered
(C) writhed
(D) dissected
(E) averted

21. The _____ condition of the survivors prompted journalists to think that they were mistreated in captivity.

(A) terse
(B) infirm
(C) tenuous
(D) opaque
(E) rural

22. Acts of _____ are forbidden by international codes of conduct dealing with the behavior of soldiers in war.

    (A) literalism
    (B) lather
    (C) pillage
    (D) evasiveness
    (E) windfalls

23. Her sarcastic remarks did not _____ much allegiance among the members of her staff.

    (A) engender
    (B) disdain
    (C) infirm
    (D) writhe
    (E) abate

24. The _____ of the animals made it difficult for the explorers to locate them.

    (A) throes
    (B) wariness
    (C) relief
    (D) ribald
    (E) propriety

25. The rebellious forces _____ the power of the empire.

    (A) averted
    (B) lathered
    (C) negotiated
    (D) usurped
    (E) engendered

26. _____forces seemed to work against the project in ways that ruined our chances of success.

    (A) Obligatory
    (B) Tenuous
    (C) Malevolent
    (D) Lethargic
    (E) Rural

27. Doctors speculated that the ulcer was caused by _____ emotions.

    (A) priming
    (B) repressed
    (C) sensible
    (D) repulsive
    (E) rigorous

28. The weather that day provided a charming and _____ circumstance for the wedding.

    (A) transcendental
    (B) idyllic
    (C) staunch
    (D) opaque
    (E) docile

29. Cramped cages will sometimes make captive animals seem _____.

    (A) terse
    (B) lethargic
    (C) mauled
    (D) predator
    (E) logistic

30. The general's _____ made him seem indifferent to the suffering of his soldiers.

    (A) predilection
    (B) exertion
    (C) aloofness
    (D) aberration
    (E) opacity

31. Doctors suspect _____ when their patients report certain types of unusual discomfort.

    (A) perverse
    (B) melancholy
    (C) aloofness
    (D) ribald
    (E) relief

32. After they _____ a new contract, the leaders of management and labor celebrated their mutual victory.

(A) throes
(B) deployed
(C) repressed
(D) negotiated
(E) usurped

33. The sailors felt an almost _____ danger in the night air that surrounded the forbidden island.

(A) palpable
(B) ribald
(C) negotiated
(D) pillaged
(E) prosaic

34. Her _____ remarks offended the pirncipal of our school.

(A) idyllic
(B) ribald
(C) mauled
(D) dissected
(E) rigorous

35. The _____ of his answers made the police certain that Mr. Smith was guilty of some part of the crime.

(A) exertion
(B) literalism
(C) throes
(D) evasiveness
(E) fragility

Verbal Analogies

Directions: Each of the following questions contains a related pair of words in capital letters, followed by five lettered pairs of words. Choose the pair that best expresses the relationship most similar to that expressed in the original pair. Mark the letter of your answer on your answer sheet.

Example:

RICH : AFFLUENT ::

(A) good : bad
(B) ice : heat
(C) summer : winter
(D) burden : poor
(E) rocky : stony

Rocky : stony is the correct answer. You would have filled in the circle marked E on your answer sheet.

36. DEPLOYING : USING ::

(A) coercing : forcing
(B) insisting : having
(C) squabbling : demoting
(D) fighting : making up
(E) enhancing : enchanting

37. AMBIGUITY : RIDDLE ::

(A) giggle : tear
(B) confession : stopping
(C) revelation : character
(D) enigma : puzzle
(E) charity : forgiveness

38. UNETHICAL : SWINDLER ::

(A) copy : photocopy
(B) praiseworthy : hero
(C) monstrosity : helper
(D) dementia : insanity
(E) devilish : grasp

39. DISOWN : COVET ::

(A) disobey : inflame
(B) discuss : disobey
(C) forfeit : cherish
(D) depart : relay
(E) assert : transfer

40. CLICHES : PHRASES ::

(A) jargon : words
(B) sarcasm : suggestion
(C) drivel : deal
(D) compact : languages
(E) cliffs : descriptions

41. PARSIMONIOUS : MONEY ::

(A) barter : store up
(B) zealous : enthusiasm
(C) overprice : deplete
(D) escape : riddle
(E) divulge : restore

42. SUBVERSION : SPY ::

(A) allowance : trickster
(B) cash : crook
(C) allegiance : cook
(D) ball : batter
(E) devastation : polluter

43. MINISTRATION : REVERENTLY ::

(A) education : wisely
(B) piracy : dumbly
(C) eating : financially
(D) politics : wildly
(E) medicine : selfishly

44. CRITERION : JUDGE ::

(A) call : umpire
(B) ballgame : player
(C) banner : flag
(D) standard : critic
(E) royalty : pain

45. COHERENT : ARGUMENT ::

(A) judgment : jury
(B) cogent : explanation
(C) logical : divestiture
(D) clean : booke
(E) alien : being

Test 6

Antonyms

Directions: Each of the following questions consists of a word in capital letters, followed by five lettered words or phrases. Choose the word or phrase that is most nearly *opposite* in meaning to the word in capital letters. Mark the letter of your answer on your answer sheet. Since some of the choices require you to distinguish fine shades of meaning, consider all the choices before deciding which is best.

Example:

WISE:

(A) smart
(B) foolish
(C) quick
(D) expensive
(E) bookish

Foolish is the correct answer. You would have filled in the circle marked B on your answer sheet.

---

1. LAMENTING:

   (A) disputing
   (B) disagreeing
   (C) edifying
   (D) rejoicing
   (E) parting

2. WHIMPERS:

   (A) purrs
   (B) announces
   (C) caresses
   (D) mauls
   (E) evokes

3. COQUETTISH:

   (A) bizarre
   (B) reserved
   (C) delinquent
   (D) cozy
   (E) manipulative

4. IMPUDENT:

   (A) respectful
   (B) distinguished
   (C) maniacal
   (D) destined
   (E) equitable

5. LANGUOROUS:

   (A) old
   (B) lazy
   (C) enthusiastic
   (D) inefficient
   (E) competent

6. DESOLATE:

   (A) cheerful
   (B) unbelievable
   (C) guilty
   (D) suspicious
   (E) paranoid

7. CARESS:

 (A) touch
 (B) smash
 (C) list
 (D) lift
 (E) enlist

8. TREMULOUS:

 (A) nervous
 (B) calm
 (C) spooky
 (D) inane
 (E) tough

9. FLURRIEDLY:

 (A) wildly
 (B) chaotically
 (C) patiently
 (D) humorously
 (E) crudely

10. DIFFUSE:

 (A) concentrated
 (B) expensive
 (C) inexpensive
 (D) peculiar
 (E) overworked

11. RIGOROUS:

 (A) soft spoken
 (B) unaccommodating
 (C) undemanding
 (D) unclean
 (E) immaculate

12. MUTED:

 (A) loud
 (B) annoying
 (C) particular
 (D) general
 (E) weird

13. TAUTLY:

 (A) dumbly
 (B) intelligently
 (C) quickly
 (D) mightily
 (E) loosely

14. ERRANT:

 (A) conformed
 (B) expelled
 (C) bewitched
 (D) likeable
 (E) disinclined

15. VENERABLE:

 (A) easy
 (B) quick witted
 (C) disreputable
 (D) tragic
 (E) explosive

16. ARRANT:

 (A) moderate
 (B) revolutionary
 (C) unguarded
 (D) disallowed
 (E) expelled

17. TEMPERATE:

 (A) livid
 (B) unattractive
 (C) debilitating
 (D) moderate
 (E) extreme

18. BANAL:

 (A) original
 (B) unoriginal
 (C) busy
 (D) exemplary
 (E) condemned

19. EXPEDIENT:
    (A) nostalgic
    (B) eternal
    (C) hectic
    (D) inconvenient
    (E) lonesome

20. ABANDONMENT:
    (A) acceptance
    (B) disapproval
    (C) divorce
    (D) provocation
    (E) exiting

Verbal Analogies

Directions: Each of the following questions contains a related pair of words in capital letters, followed by five lettered pairs of words. Choose the pair that best expresses the relationship most similar to that expressed in the original pair. Mark the letter of your answer on your answer sheet.

Example:

SMART : DUMB ::

(A) lazy : stupid
(B) mental : intellectual
(C) physical : verbal
(D) hard : soft
(E) cool : cold

Hard : soft is the correct answer. You would have filled in the circle marked D on your answer sheet.

21. THRALL : SLAVERY ::
    (A) exile : expulsion
    (B) captive : punishment
    (C) desire : urge
    (D) passion : compassion
    (E) pity : scorn

22. HULKING : HIPPOPOTAMUS ::
    (A) meanness : eagle
    (B) beauty : fish
    (C) svelte : gazelle
    (D) brave : worm
    (E) protected : shark

23. SCHOONER : SAIL ::
    (A) plane : explode
    (B) boat : sink
    (C) kite : fly
    (D) volcano : swim
    (E) anger : mind

24. SPAR : SAIL ::
    (A) gloves : hands
    (B) pants : zipper
    (C) shirt : button
    (D) flagstaff : flag
    (E) hat : armband

25. SHROUD : MAST ::
    (A) tombstones : undertakers
    (B) kites : birds
    (C) nickels : dimes
    (D) guns : roses
    (E) rope : tent

26. WHEELING : BRONCO ::
    (A) jumping : bear
    (B) slithering : snake
    (C) spitting : eagle
    (D) hunting : tiger
    (E) squealing : crow

27. INITIATING : CONCLUDING ::

   (A) bumping : jostling
   (B) concentrating : walking
   (C) beginning : ending
   (D) starting : delaying
   (E) losing : trying

28. STRIPLING : PUPPY ::

   (A) truant : tyrant
   (B) teacher : principal
   (C) clown : acrobat
   (D) veteran : imp
   (E) novice : kitten

29. FLAILING : SOOTHING ::

   (A) fixing : reaping
   (B) appearing : image
   (C) whipping : petting
   (D) lifting : moving
   (E) laughing : scolding

30. SCYTHES : REAPERS ::

   (A) shovels : gravediggers
   (B) towels : lifeguards
   (C) plows : astronauts
   (D) hoes : teachers
   (E) computers : athletes

31. HONES : CUTLERY ::

   (A) cages : hunting
   (B) pipes : plumbing
   (C) rulers : countries
   (D) motors : automobiles
   (E) gasoline : engine

32. SUMMITS : MOUNTAINS ::

   (A) tops : bottoms
   (B) sandwiches : lunch
   (C) cellars : basements
   (D) roofs : houses
   (E) boats : basins

33. OCCULT : FORBIDDEN ::

   (A) cathedral : peak
   (B) desert : sand
   (C) divine : blessed
   (D) glass : furniture
   (E) athletic : crutches

34. TEPID : BOILING ::

   (A) cut : bleeding
   (B) joke : laughing
   (C) cold : sweltering
   (D) nice : mean
   (E) cool : freezing

35. GLENS : VALLEYS ::

   (A) hills : mountains
   (B) rivers : oceans
   (C) lakes : rivers
   (D) peaks : flatlands
   (E) ranges : plates

Sentence Completions

Directions: Each of the following sentences contains one or two blank spaces to be filled in by one of the five lettered choices below. Select the word or group of words that best completes the meaning of the sentence. Mark the letter of your answer on your answer sheet.

Example:

Acts of _____ are hard to forgive.

(A) hospitality
(B) hostility
(C) hospitalization
(D) disaster
(E) concern

Hostility is the correct answer. You would have filled in the circle marked B on your answer sheet.

---

36. The _____ grew along the banks of the rivers throughout Wales.

    (A) caress
    (B) sedge
    (C) monotones
    (D) drones
    (E) amulets

37. The withered _____ must have been exposed to the sun for too long.

    (A) floweret
    (B) impudent
    (C) quickstep
    (D) whimpers
    (E) shrouds

38. The superstitious woman believed her _____ would ward off evil spirits.

    (A) thrall
    (B) schooner
    (C) spar
    (D) amulet
    (E) abandonment

39. The ambassador was _____ with a rare case of the disease almost unknown in Africa.

    (A) muted
    (B) trekked
    (C) stricken
    (D) diffused
    (E) flailed

40. The judge asked for a medical evaluation of the defendant's condition because of her _____ behavior.

    (A) lamenting
    (B) deranged
    (C) desolate
    (D) stricken
    (E) tremulous

41. The immense _____ of the wind toppled the entire bridge.

    (A) vermin
    (B) pith
    (C) hones
    (D) sumac
    (E) vermillion

42. Most people are disgusted by the sight of _____.

    (A) vermin
    (B) glens
    (C) summits
    (D) scythes
    (E) sumac

43. Soviet rescue workers _____ across the frozen reaches of Siberia searching for the missing plane.

    (A) flailed
    (B) droned
    (C) lamented
    (D) trekked
    (E) muted

44. The farmer carried the _____ of corn to the market at the end of September.

    (A) sheaves
    (B) spews
    (C) sinews
    (D) assurances
    (E) monotones

45. An artist will sometimes _____ for days before starting a new project.

    (A) azure
    (B) muse
    (C) diffuse
    (D) derange
    (E) countenance

Test 7

Antonyms

Directions: Each of the following questions consists of a word in capital letters, followed by five lettered words or phrases. Choose the word or phrase that is most nearly *opposite* in meaning to the word in capital letters. Mark the letter of your answer on your answer sheet. Since some of the choices require you to distinguish fine shades of meaning, consider all the choices before deciding which is best.

Example:

HAPPINESS:

(A) boredom
(B) ennui
(C) excitement
(D) loneliness
(E) sadness

Sadness is the correct answer. You would have filled in the circle marked E on your answer sheet.

---

1. DEMATERIALIZE:

   (A) recognize
   (B) image
   (C) evaporate
   (D) form
   (E) dissolve

2. SUMPTUOUS:

   (A) gaudy
   (B) shabby
   (C) sacrilegious
   (D) bumptious
   (E) officious

3. PROWESS:

   (A) power
   (B) effortlessness
   (C) agility
   (D) sensitivity
   (E) weakness

4. HOMAGE:

   (A) disrespect
   (B) goal
   (C) plenitude
   (D) humor
   (E) youth

5. PROFFERED:

   (A) spent
   (B) given
   (C) retracted
   (D) loaned
   (E) lost

6. STATELY:

   (A) new
   (B) undignified
   (C) official
   (D) officious
   (E) original

7. TACIT:
   (A) quiet
   (B) noisy
   (C) explicit
   (D) whispered
   (E) cursory

8. VIBRANTLY:
   (A) greedily
   (B) apathetically
   (C) religiously
   (D) fervently
   (E) lethargically

9. CAPACIOUS:
   (A) filthy
   (B) cramped
   (C) soiled
   (D) empty
   (E) delightful

10. CONTENTIOUS:
    (A) evocative
    (B) provocative
    (C) disagreeable
    (D) cooperative
    (E) sycophantic

11. PRODIGIOUS:
    (A) minuscule
    (B) myopic
    (C) restive
    (D) festive
    (E) superficial

12. VULNERABLE:
    (A) dumb
    (B) unenlightened
    (C) invincible
    (D) uninspired
    (E) embryonic

13. DETONATE:
    (A) ignite
    (B) release
    (C) erupt
    (D) defuse
    (E) contend

14. DELIRIOUS:
    (A) unrelieved
    (B) lucid
    (C) symbiotic
    (D) delicious
    (E) wavering

15. LUDICROUS:
    (A) silly
    (B) offensive
    (C) necessary
    (D) sensible
    (E) informed

16. ERRATIC:
    (A) erroneous
    (B) disrespectful
    (C) silly
    (D) consistent
    (E) uninformed

17. CONTEMPT:
    (A) ruination
    (B) downfall
    (C) reverence
    (D) disrespect
    (E) fair

18. DISCERN:
    (A) blow
    (B) overlook
    (C) scorn
    (D) dispatch
    (E) explicate

19. CULMINATE:
    (A) bottom out
    (B) taper off
    (C) tear around
    (D) raise up
    (E) reconvene

20. QUERULOUS:
    (A) unreflective
    (B) bovine
    (C) agreeable
    (D) cursory
    (E) inquisitive

21. SURMISE:
    (A) copy
    (B) know
    (C) prove
    (D) imagine
    (E) surprise

22. GUILEFUL:
    (A) dishonest
    (B) straightforward
    (C) decrepit
    (D) disconnect
    (E) inebriated

23. PARODY:
    (A) flattering imitation
    (B) strong opposition
    (C) weak defense
    (D) essential elements
    (E) rare disease

24. ASSIMILATE:
    (A) move
    (B) remove
    (C) expel
    (D) declare
    (E) embrace

25. LAMENTATION:
    (A) feast
    (B) prayer
    (C) hymn
    (D) celebration
    (E) dissolution

Verbal Analogies

Directions: Each of the following questions contains a related pair of words in capital letters, followed by five lettered pairs of words. Choose the pair that best expresses the relationship most similar to that expressed in the original pair. Mark the letter of your answer on your answer sheet.

Example: WET : DRY ::
    (A) heavy : cold
    (B) warm : hot
    (C) hot : cold
    (D) open : crack
    (E) plentiful : complete

Hot : cold is the correct answer. You would have filled in the circle marked C on your answer sheet.

26. STICKLER : ATTENTIVENESS ::

   (A) doctor : precaution
   (B) alcoholic : intoxication
   (C) ecologist : science
   (D) brother : forgiveness
   (E) spelunker : skydiver

27. POMMEL : SWORD ::

   (A) heel : arrow
   (B) belt : button
   (C) knob : door
   (D) lamp : light
   (E) operation : scapel

28. IMPREGNABLE : WEAKENING ::

   (A) vulnerable : strong
   (B) diaseased : hospitalized
   (C) invincible : fading
   (D) pregnant : delivering
   (E) preventable : avoiding

29. WORTHY : DESERVING ::

   (A) cheap : expensive
   (B) relaxed : asleep
   (C) myopic : farsighted
   (D) esteemed : important
   (E) contrary : stubborn

30. VOID : VACUUM ::

   (A) emptiness : hollow
   (B) nature : storm
   (C) hole : blackness
   (D) space : heaven
   (E) lost:discount

31. TREASON : ANARCHIST ::

   (A) rob : soldier
   (B) reading:singer
   (C) disobedience : superintendent
   (D) rebellion : insurgent
   (E) surgery : pediatrician

32. FORFEITURE : ACQUISITION ::

   (A) release : entrapment
   (B) straying : evaporation
   (C) conquest : invasion
   (D) journey : voyage
   (E) ruin : plantation

33. FORD : MARSH ::

   (A) branch : tree
   (B) cloud : rain
   (C) path : forest
   (D) street : avenue
   (E) rocket : cosmos

34. BUFFET : HAND ::

   (A) hair : head
   (B) strike : match
   (C) stomp : face
   (D) food : foot
   (E) whistle : lip

35. ENCHANTMENT : FOREST ::

   (A) symbol : stigma
   (B) learning : school
   (C) humor : television
   (D) loudness : library
   (E) desolation : livery

36. REPAST : CHEF ::

   (A) prescription : doctor
   (B) discern : bucket
   (C) laugh : tragedian
   (D) relief : comedian
   (E) antiquity : historian

37. WITHERED : BLOSSOMED ::

   (A) destroyed : defeated
   (B) culminated : ended
   (C) discouraged : prevented
   (D) destroyed : enlivened
   (E) convened : confined

38. REDEEMED : SAVIOR ::

   (A) brandished : guardian
   (B) villain : protector
   (C) rescued : helper
   (D) created : composer
   (E) condemned : executioner

39. OUTSTRIP : FOLLOW ::

   (A) empty : refill
   (B) close : reopen
   (C) stretch : pull
   (D) counterfeit : mail
   (E) lead : imitate

40. BOWER : CONCEAL ::

   (A) showcase : reveal
   (B) television : examine
   (C) school : punish
   (D) factory : strike
   (E) automobile : seated

41. RHETORICALLY : RESPONSE ::

   (A) theatricaly : filibuster
   (B) stoically : emotion
   (C) gracefully : answer
   (D) patriotically : forfeit
   (E) devilishly : declaration

42. SOLACE : MOTHER ::

   (A) understanding : friend
   (B) ennui : neighbor
   (C) energy : boss
   (D) apathy : slave
   (E) entertainer : enthusiasm

43. AESTHETE : COLOR ::

   (A) worker : machine
   (B) mechanic : water
   (C) sentence : word
   (D) singer : melody
   (E) general : mistake

44. INCONGRUITY : LOGIC ::

   (A) beauty : beast
   (B) ugliness : aesthetics
   (C) sublimity : philosophy
   (D) horror : occult
   (E) tension : stress

45. DECREPIT : FETAL ::

   (A) askew : old
   (B) ancient : valuable
   (C) dilapidated : embryonic
   (D) broken : unrelated
   (E) circuitous : circumstantial

Sentence Completions

Directions: Each of the following sentences contains one or two blank spaces to be filled in by one of the five lettered choices below. Select the word or group of words that best completes the meaning of the sentence. Mark the letter of your answer on your answer sheet.

Example:

A terrific batter, Ted Williams was frequently able to _____ fans with his hitting accomplishments.

   (A) disappoint
   (B) frustrate
   (C) entertain
   (D) befuddle
   (E) convince

Entertain is the correct answer. You would have filled in the circle marked C on your answer sheet.

46. Queen Mabila was thrown violently from her_____ at the end of the chase.

    (A) manor
    (B) wroth
    (C) sundry
    (D) palfrey
    (E) pommel

47. Our opponent's obvious agility and _____ made us unsure whether we could successfully compete against so impressive a foe.

    (A) grace
    (B) damsel
    (C) chagrin
    (D) homage
    (E) treason

48. The_____of the new teacher made students uncomfortable.

    (A) parody
    (B) incongruity
    (C) surmise
    (D) contempt
    (E) vagaries

49. Lou Abbot was famous for his _____ sense of humor.

    (A) worthy
    (B) impregnable
    (C) sumptuous
    (D) droll
    (E) proffered

50. Medieval knights were expected to behave honorably in all their dealings with _____.

    (A) sticklers
    (B) damsels
    (C) aesthetics
    (D) bowers
    (E) furrows

51. The basketball team has a disappointing record this year because of _____reasons.

    (A) void
    (B) raftered
    (C) sundry
    (D) pinnacled
    (E) delirious

52. The prince's irrational behavior made him seem _____ to all the subjects of the land.

    (A) ford
    (B) palfrey
    (C) giddy
    (D) querulous
    (E) impervious

53. They_____their weapons in order to frighten away the intruders.

    (A) surmised
    (B) bowered
    (C) brandished
    (D) voided
    (E) proffered

54. There were few complaints issued by the serfs who lived on the _____overseen by Sir Laurence.

    (A) surmise
    (B) discern
    (C) solace
    (D) manor
    (E) ford

55. Pirates frequently had_____complexions because of their constant exposure to the sunlight on various voyages.

    (A) redeemed
    (B) swarthy
    (C) stately
    (D) withered
    (E) ludicrous

56. Inside sections of the huge hall were
    _____ in order to accommodate the
    tremendous weight of the roof.

    (A) assimilated
    (B) guileful
    (C) culminated
    (D) buffeted
    (E) raftered

57. _____ discovered in Ireland have
    caused archaeologists to speculate
    about the comparable patterns found in
    structures located in Spain.

    (A) Barrows
    (B) Furrows
    (C) Aesthetics
    (D) Drolls
    (E) Fords

58. Because they are _____ as few domes are,
    the tops of buildings in certain sections
    of southeast Asia are regarded as pecu-
    liar.

    (A) pinnacled
    (B) domed
    (C) unadorned
    (D) checkered
    (E) platooned

59. Elaborate and unexplained _____ ap-
    peared in the cornfields throughout the
    area, and a worldwide debate about
    their meaning filled the media for the
    next two years.

    (A) bowers
    (B) giddies
    (C) furrows
    (D) homages
    (E) buffets

60. The _____ of the students frightened
    the school officials and prompted them
    to call for military assistance during the
    uprising.

    (A) surmise
    (B) anarchy
    (C) lamentation
    (D) homage
    (E) lethargy

Name _____ Date _____

Test Number _____

ANSWER SHEET

Using pencil, completely blacken the answer space of your choice. Mark only one answer for each questions. Erase stray marks.

1. Ⓐ Ⓑ Ⓒ Ⓓ Ⓔ   16. Ⓐ Ⓑ Ⓒ Ⓓ Ⓔ   31. Ⓐ Ⓑ Ⓒ Ⓓ Ⓔ   46. Ⓐ Ⓑ Ⓒ Ⓓ Ⓔ

2. Ⓐ Ⓑ Ⓒ Ⓓ Ⓔ   17. Ⓐ Ⓑ Ⓒ Ⓓ Ⓔ   32. Ⓐ Ⓑ Ⓒ Ⓓ Ⓔ   47. Ⓐ Ⓑ Ⓒ Ⓓ Ⓔ

3. Ⓐ Ⓑ Ⓒ Ⓓ Ⓔ   18. Ⓐ Ⓑ Ⓒ Ⓓ Ⓔ   33. Ⓐ Ⓑ Ⓒ Ⓓ Ⓔ   48. Ⓐ Ⓑ Ⓒ Ⓓ Ⓔ

4. Ⓐ Ⓑ Ⓒ Ⓓ Ⓔ   19. Ⓐ Ⓑ Ⓒ Ⓓ Ⓔ   34. Ⓐ Ⓑ Ⓒ Ⓓ Ⓔ   49. Ⓐ Ⓑ Ⓒ Ⓓ Ⓔ

5. Ⓐ Ⓑ Ⓒ Ⓓ Ⓔ   20. Ⓐ Ⓑ Ⓒ Ⓓ Ⓔ   35. Ⓐ Ⓑ Ⓒ Ⓓ Ⓔ   50. Ⓐ Ⓑ Ⓒ Ⓓ Ⓔ

6. Ⓐ Ⓑ Ⓒ Ⓓ Ⓔ   21. Ⓐ Ⓑ Ⓒ Ⓓ Ⓔ   36. Ⓐ Ⓑ Ⓒ Ⓓ Ⓔ   51. Ⓐ Ⓑ Ⓒ Ⓓ Ⓔ

7. Ⓐ Ⓑ Ⓒ Ⓓ Ⓔ   22. Ⓐ Ⓑ Ⓒ Ⓓ Ⓔ   37. Ⓐ Ⓑ Ⓒ Ⓓ Ⓔ   52. Ⓐ Ⓑ Ⓒ Ⓓ Ⓔ

8. Ⓐ Ⓑ Ⓒ Ⓓ Ⓔ   23. Ⓐ Ⓑ Ⓒ Ⓓ Ⓔ   38. Ⓐ Ⓑ Ⓒ Ⓓ Ⓔ   53. Ⓐ Ⓑ Ⓒ Ⓓ Ⓔ

9. Ⓐ Ⓑ Ⓒ Ⓓ Ⓔ   24. Ⓐ Ⓑ Ⓒ Ⓓ Ⓔ   39. Ⓐ Ⓑ Ⓒ Ⓓ Ⓔ   54. Ⓐ Ⓑ Ⓒ Ⓓ Ⓔ

10. Ⓐ Ⓑ Ⓒ Ⓓ Ⓔ   25. Ⓐ Ⓑ Ⓒ Ⓓ Ⓔ   40. Ⓐ Ⓑ Ⓒ Ⓓ Ⓔ   55. Ⓐ Ⓑ Ⓒ Ⓓ Ⓔ

11. Ⓐ Ⓑ Ⓒ Ⓓ Ⓔ   26. Ⓐ Ⓑ Ⓒ Ⓓ Ⓔ   41. Ⓐ Ⓑ Ⓒ Ⓓ Ⓔ   56. Ⓐ Ⓑ Ⓒ Ⓓ Ⓔ

12. Ⓐ Ⓑ Ⓒ Ⓓ Ⓔ   27. Ⓐ Ⓑ Ⓒ Ⓓ Ⓔ   42. Ⓐ Ⓑ Ⓒ Ⓓ Ⓔ   57. Ⓐ Ⓑ Ⓒ Ⓓ Ⓔ

13. Ⓐ Ⓑ Ⓒ Ⓓ Ⓔ   28. Ⓐ Ⓑ Ⓒ Ⓓ Ⓔ   43. Ⓐ Ⓑ Ⓒ Ⓓ Ⓔ   58. Ⓐ Ⓑ Ⓒ Ⓓ Ⓔ

14. Ⓐ Ⓑ Ⓒ Ⓓ Ⓔ   29. Ⓐ Ⓑ Ⓒ Ⓓ Ⓔ   44. Ⓐ Ⓑ Ⓒ Ⓓ Ⓔ   59. Ⓐ Ⓑ Ⓒ Ⓓ Ⓔ

15. Ⓐ Ⓑ Ⓒ Ⓓ Ⓔ   30. Ⓐ Ⓑ Ⓒ Ⓓ Ⓔ   45. Ⓐ Ⓑ Ⓒ Ⓓ Ⓔ   60. Ⓐ Ⓑ Ⓒ Ⓓ Ⓔ

Answer Key

Test 1

1. E	14. E	26. D
2. A	15. E	27. D
3. C	16. A	28. D
4. E	17. D	29. C
5. D	18. A	30. E
6. D	19. A	31. C
7. A	20. A	32. A
8. D	21. C	33. A
9. B	22. E	34. D
10. A	23. C	35. A
11. A	24. A	36. E
12. C	25. C	37. C
13. A		

Test 2

1. A	12. C	23. A
2. C	13. E	24. A
3. E	14. C	25. E
4. E	15. D	26. C
5. A	16. D	27. A
6. B	17. C	28. D
7. D	18. D	29. E
8. C	19. B	30. A
9. A	20. D	31. D
10. B	21. C	32. A
11. D	22. D	33. B

Test 3

1. D	16. A	31. A
2. C	17. A	32. A
3. C	18. A	33. B
4. A	19. A	34. C
5. A	20. D	35. B
6. C	21. B	36. A
7. E	22. D	37. C
8. C	23. A	38. A
9. E	24. E	39. C
10. C	25. C	40. E
11. A	26. E	41. E
12. E	27. A	42. A
13. E	28. E	43. D
14. C	29. D	44. D
15. E	30. C	

Test 4

1. D	13. E	24. D
2. A	14. C	25. A
3. D	15. B	26. B
4. D	16. B	27. A
5. A	17. A	28. B
6. D	18. C	29. B
7. C	19. A	30. C
8. D	20. A	31. B
9. E	21. D	32. A
10. C	22. E	33. D
11. A	23. C	34. A
12. C		

Test 5

1. C	16. A	31. B
2. B	17. B	32. D
3. A	18. A	33. A
4. D	19. B	34. B
5. D	20. C	35. D
6. A	21. B	36. A
7. D	22. C	37. D
8. E	23. A	38. B
9. D	24. B	39. C
10. C	25. D	40. A
11. A	26. C	41. B
12. C	27. B	42. E
13. E	28. B	43. A
14. A	29. B	44. D
15. D	30. C	45. B

Test 6

1. D	16. A	31. B
2. A	17. E	32. D
3. B	18. A	33. C
4. A	19. D	34. E
5. C	20. A	35. A
6. A	21. A	36. B
7. B	22. C	37. A
8. B	23. C	38. D
9. C	24. D	39. C
10. A	25. E	40. B
11. C	26. B	41. B
12. A	27. C	42. A
13. E	28. E	43. D
14. A	29. C	44. A
15. C	30. A	45. B

Test 7

1.	D	21.	C	41.	B
2.	B	22.	B	42.	A
3.	E	23.	A	43.	D
4.	A	24.	C	44.	B
5.	C	25.	D	45.	C
6.	B	26.	A	46.	D
7.	C	27.	C	47.	A
8.	E	28.	C	48.	E
9.	B	29.	D	49.	D
10.	D	30.	A	50.	B
11.	A	31.	D	51.	C
12.	C	32.	A	52.	C
13.	D	33.	C	53.	C
14.	B	34.	E	54.	D
15.	D	35.	B	55.	B
16.	D	36.	A	56.	E
17.	C	37.	D	57.	A
18.	B	38.	C	58.	A
19.	B	39.	E	59.	C
20.	E	40.	A	60.	B